WESTERN EUROPE

WAYNE C. THOMPSON

THE WORLD TODAY SERIES®

2019–2020

38TH EDITION

Graphic Materials Acknowledgments

For their generosity in providing certain visual material for use in this book, and in order of their appearance, special thanks to the following:

European Community Information Services
Delegation of the European Union in Washington
North Atlantic Treaty Organization
The Swiss National Tourist Office
The Government of Liechtenstein
The Government of Andorra
French Cultural Services, New York
The Royal Netherlands Embassy
The Embassy of Belgium
The Embassy of Ireland
The British Embassy
The Embassy of Italy
The Embassy of Malta
The Sovereign Military Order of Malta
The Government of Monaco
The Embassy of Spain
The Embassy of Portugal

First appearing as *Western Europe 1982*, this annually revised book is published by:

Stryker–Post Publications
An imprint of The Rowman & Littlefield Publishing Group, Inc.
4501 Forbes Blvd., Suite 200, Lanham, MD 20706
www.rowman.com

Library of Congress Control Number Available

ISBN 978-1-4758-5202-8 (pbk. : alk. paper)
ISBN 978-1-4758-5203-5 (electronic)

Cover design by Sarah Marizan

Cartographer: William L. Nelson

Typography by Barton Matheson Willse & Worthington
Baltimore, MD 21244

DEDICATION

To the memory of my mother and father

ACKNOWLEDGMENTS

I am especially grateful to the Alexander von Humboldt Foundation, a farsighted German organization which, since 1869, has persistently nurtured the spirit of intellectual discovery and has sought to tighten the links between Europe and the rest of the world, for having granted me a two-year research fellowship at the University of Freiburg in Germany. Without its aid, I would have been unable to complete the first edition of this book.

No author could possibly write a book with the breadth of this one without the assistance of numerous persons and organizations. Mark H. Mullin, a Harvard graduate who earned an MA as a Marshall Scholar, Oxford University, wrote the first drafts of all but the political and economic sections of the chapters on the United Kingdom and the Republic of Ireland. I have updated them over the years. I thank my fellow author, Malcolm B. Russell, whose chapter on Cyprus we have moved to this volume after its accession to EU membership in 2004. We have also moved Greece to this book from our Nordic, central and southeastern Europe volume in order to group Mediterranean Europe together.

I wish also to thank my colleagues and acquaintances throughout western Europe and the US who took the time to read or to comment upon various chapters dealing with their own countries or specialties. They include Peter Strohm, David M. Keithly, Richard Laurijssen, Jacky Paris, Philippe Vidal, and Maureen and Peter Ward. I am grateful to my students at the College of Europe who critiqued the chapters on their native countries. They are Andres Arnaldos Montaner (Spain), Ritienne Bonavia (Malta), Nuno Borges (Portugal), Diego Calatayud (Spain), Núria Carrasco Comes (Spain), Isabelle Costa (Monaco), Laurence Deglain (France), Yannis Couniniotis (Greece), Francisco Bossa Dionisio (Portugal), Elena Donnari (Italy), Sylvain Dufeu (France), Javier Fernandez Gonzalez (Spain), Maaike Göbel (Netherlands), Gregory Gosp (France), James Hughes (UK), Vincent Imperiali (Belgium), Eelco Keij (Netherlands), José Maria Lanzarote (Spain), Koen Lenssen (Netherlands), Antoine Kopp, Jean Micallef Grimaud (Malta), Bérénice Orban de Xivry (Belgium), Nuno Queirós (Portugal), Laura Requejo (Spain), Alejandro Ribo Labastida (Spain), Emmanuel Lenaerts (Belgium), Panagiotis Papadopoulos (Greece), Chryso Ritsou (Greece), Hélène Stergiou (Netherlands), Sabine Tomordy (Liechtenstein), Tim Van Broeckhoven (Belgium), Edwin Van Os (Netherlands), Stijn Van Wesemael (Belgium), and Giuseppe Zaffuto (Italy). Renée Maeyaert and Anne Heber-Suffrin, librarians at the College of Europe, Bruges, consistently gave me important assistance in obtaining European newspapers and visuals for this book. Sonja Fernandez (France) kindly collected for me French newspapers reporting on the 2008 US election. Jean-Michel Cassiers and Monika Sapilak provided me in Brussels with information and materials on Belgium's language laws and practices. Michael Nix did a wonderful job in 2006 of reading every word of this book and making copious editorial changes based on his decades of experience as a Canadian government editor. I am deeply grateful for the generous gift of his time and talent. The late Catherine L. Lowe thoroughly read the entire manuscript in order to comb out style, spelling, and typographical errors. My wife, Susan L. Thompson, took some of the photographs and carefully proofread some of the manuscript. My daughter, Juliet Bunch, also provided photos for this book.

I am grateful to Pro Helvetia, which arranged and financed a week-long study tour of Switzerland, as well as to numerous embassy and foreign ministry officials who provided information and arranged visits to western European capitals to speak with representatives of parties, parliaments, universities, research institutes, and news media about this book. A Fulbright Teaching Fellowship to Estonia in 1995–1996 enabled me to become more familiar with Nordic Europe. A second Fulbright professorship in the spring semester of 2001 at the College of Europe in Bruges provided me with intellectual stimulation by top graduate students from all over Europe, in addition to an in-depth look at the BENELUX countries and EU and NATO institutions. My dear friend, the late Philip F. Stryker, was without doubt one of the most competent, encouraging, and congenial publishers with whom an author could work. Finally I would like to thank David T. Wilt, who supports my work in countless ways.

W.C.T.

Lexington, Virginia, June 2019

Wayne C. Thompson . . .

Professor Thompson taught politics at Washington and Lee University in Lexington, Virginia. He is also an emeritus professor at the Virginia Military Institute in Lexington. He attended Ohio State University (BA in government) and Claremont Graduate University (MA and PhD, with distinction). He did further graduate study at the Universities of Göttingen, Paris/Sorbonne, and Freiburg im Breisgau, where he was subsequently a guest professor. He studied and researched many years in Germany as a Woodrow Wilson, Fulbright, Deutscher Akademischer Austauschdienst (DAAD), Earhart, and Alexander von Humboldt Fellow. He served as scholar-in-residence at the Bundestag and as a Fulbright professor in Estonia. During the 1999–2000 academic year, he was a visiting professor at the Air War College in Montgomery, Alabama. In the spring semester of 2001, he had a second Fulbright professorship at the College of Europe in Bruges and continued for seven years to teach at the Bruges and Warsaw campuses of that graduate institution. In the fall semester of 2003, he was a visiting professor of politics at the American University of Bulgaria. He is the author of *In the Eye of the Storm: Kurt Riezler and the Crises of Modern Germany* (Iowa City: University of Iowa Press, 1980), *The Political Odyssey of Herbert Wehner* (Boulder, CO: Westview Press, 1993), and *Historical Dictionary of Germany* (Metuchen, NJ: Scarecrow, 1994) and coauthor of *Redefining Transatlantic Security Relations: The Challenge of Change* (Manchester University Press, 2004). He has written two other books in the World Today Series: *Canada*, as well as *Nordic, Central, and Southeastern Europe*. He also coedited *Perspectives on Strategic Defense and Space: National Programs and International Cooperation* and *Margaret Thatcher: Prime Minister Indomitable* (Boulder, CO: Westview Press, 1987, 1989, 1994). He has written many articles on European politics, philosophy, and history which have appeared in such periodicals as *The American Political Science Review, Western Political Quarterly, East European Quarterly, Journal of Politics, Central European History, The American Review of Canadian Studies, German Studies Review, Das Parlament, Current History, The Yearbook on International Communist Affairs, The History Teacher, Armed Forces and Society, Freedom at Issue, Communist and Post-Communist Studies, Contemporary French Civilization, Europe-Asia Studies*, and *Virginia Social Science Journal*. He is currently working on a book about George C. Marshall as secretary of defense.

CONTENTS

Badische

eserservice 0800 - 22 24 22 0
'rivate Kleinanzeigen 0800 - 22 24 22 1
entrale 07 61 - 496 - 0
nternet www.badische-zeitung.de

Freiburg im Breisgau · Donnerstag,

A new president and First Lady meet the queen.

IRELAND
UNITED KINGDOM
NETHERLANDS
BELGIUM
LUXEMBOURG
LIECHTENSTEIN
SWITZERLAND
FRANCE
MONACO
SAN MARINO
ITALY
ANDORRA
VATICAN
PORTUGAL
SPAIN
GREECE
MALTA
CYPRUS

Western Europe Today

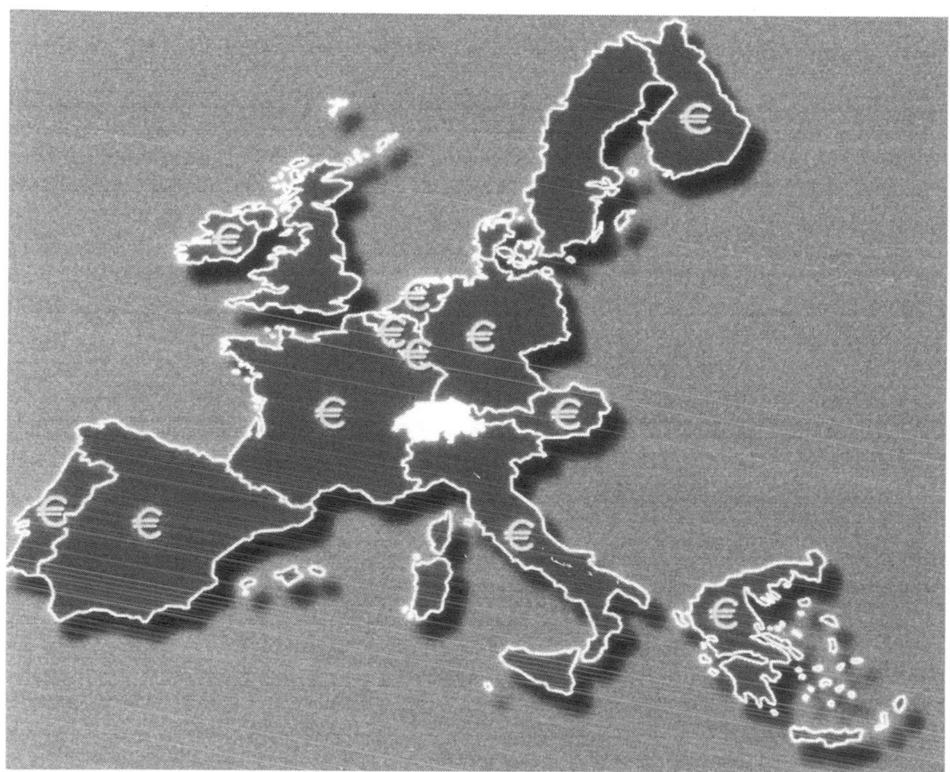
First countries to adopt the euro

"McDonald's? Me? Always!!!"

In 1945 much of Europe lay in ruins, its peoples destitute and demoralized following a war on its own soil more destructive than any conflict in history. Two world wars in the 20th century (World War I from 1914 until 1918 and World War II from 1939 until 1945) had brought Europe's dominance over world affairs to an end and had led to a rise of the United States of America and the Soviet Union as the world's most powerful nations. These wars also ended Europe's colonial hold on much of the world, a hold which, despite some negative effects, had spread European civilization to the Western Hemisphere, Africa, the Middle East, and the Far East.

Western Europe is a region rich in diversity, with a population of 262 million persons (382 million if one adds Germany, Austria, and the Nordic countries and over 500 million if one considers the entire European Union). This compares to over 311 million in the US.

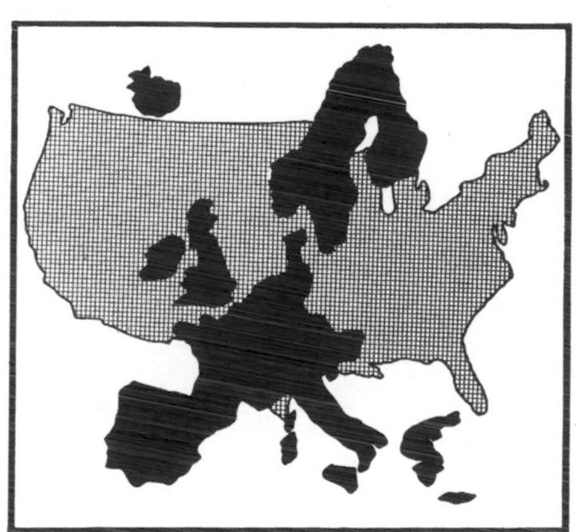

Geographically, western Europe is much smaller than the US. The entire region is scarcely more than twice the size of Alaska and would easily fit into the continental US west of the Mississippi with much room to spare. Like the US, western Europe offers a very rich diversity of climates and landscapes, from the permafrost and midnight sun of northern Norway to the hot, dry, sunny Mediterranean; from the fog and rain of northern Germany to the warm blue skies of the Azores and to the snows and arctic winds of Iceland; and from the Alpine peaks of Austria and Switzerland to the flat and sub-sea level terrain of the Netherlands.

With the collapse of communism in Europe, the unification of Germany, and the dissolution of the Soviet Union, Europeans are faced with the most significant alteration of their continent's political map since World War II. Because two hostile Europes no longer face each other, Europe has doubled its size. From Moscow to Lisbon and Dublin to Budapest, democracies exist in which free elections provide the only legitimate claim to power and which are basically committed to freedom, individual rights, and some variant of capitalism.

Looking eastward, western Europeans see more than a dozen newly independent nations and a few more emerging, all in difficult economic circumstances and some with ethnic scores to settle and millions of discontented and frightened citizens who may decide to seek a better future in the west. Most are clamoring for admission to the plentiful western European table and a place under the Atlantic alliance's security umbrella. The December 1991 collapse of the former Soviet Union temporarily destroyed central authority and dispersed power among its various republics.

Western Europe still has many cultures and many lands and regions with characters and appearances of their own. However, there are many things which make much of modern western Europe and the US look similar: large shopping centers, fast-food restaurants, freeways, modern cities with skyscrapers and much concrete, many automobiles, and everywhere signs of prosperity.

Americans and western Europeans face many of the same problems and have many of the same concerns, though in differing degrees: the role and rights of women in modern society, illegal immigration, the integration of racial and religious minorities, a steady stream of political refugees, urban violence, the protection of the environment and the quality of life, the defense of their homeland and values in an age of terrorism and weapons of mass destruction, the provision of adequate supplies of energy and raw materials, and the maintenance of prosperity and generous social security programs in an age of globalization.

The reader will confront numerous abbreviations and acronyms, and one must understand not only what the letters signify but also what function the indicated institutions serve. Therefore, in the following pages, these acronyms will be presented in the context of a more general discussion of some of the more important European bodies and organizations.

Today, western Europe is a region that is, on the whole, highly prosperous, though it is relatively poor in natural resources. It has a large industrial base, much capi-

Western Europe Today

tal and know-how and a highly educated and skilled workforce. It is also secure militarily. Such prosperity and security are partly due to the countries' high degree of voluntary cooperation, formalized in numerous international organizations. All major western European countries are full members of the United Nations (UN), and all participate in the many organizations linked to the UN, such as the UN Educational, Scientific, and Cultural Organization (UNESCO); the UN Conference on Trade and Development (UNCTAD); the World Court, which sits in the stately Peace Palace built with funds contributed by Andrew Carnegie in The Hague, Netherlands; the International Labor Organization (ILO); the UN Industrial Development Organization (UNIDO); the World Health Organization (WHO); the Food and Agriculture Organization (FAO); and a number of others.

NATO headquarters, Brussels, Belgium, commemorating 9-11 victims

Defense

Most western European countries would be unable to defend themselves alone. Therefore, the majority has chosen to join the North Atlantic Treaty Organization (NATO), also known as the Atlantic Alliance. It is housed outside of Brussels in a steel and glass structure that symbolizes the transparent modern NATO. In 2016 it moved into a new headquarters nearby. Created in 1949, NATO links the power of the United States and Canada and the geographic position of Iceland (which has no military) with the military resources of Belgium-Netherlands-Luxembourg (BENELUX), Great Britain, Norway, Denmark, the Federal Republic of Germany (FRG or Germany), Italy, Portugal, Turkey, Greece, France, and Spain and, since 1999, Poland, Hungary, and the Czech Republic. At its 2002 Prague summit, NATO invited seven more countries to join in April 2004: the three Baltic states (Estonia, Latvia, and Lithuania), Slovakia, Slovenia, Romania, and Bulgaria. At its April 2008 summit in Bucharest, NATO leaders invited Albania and Croatia to join, which they did the following April. The alliance has 29 members. The only major western or Nordic European countries that remain neutral or nonaligned are Ireland, Switzerland, Austria, Sweden, and Finland.

When the question arose concerning the organization of a European military combination, France, Italy, and West Germany initiated in 1952 a treaty creating a European Defense Community (EDC). It was intended to bring into being an integrated European army under a unified command structure, which would ultimately include troops from West Germany and the BENELUX countries. However, in 1954 the French National Assembly rejected this plan, fearing the possible loss of its sovereignty if it relinquished command over its army.

As a compromise, Great Britain proposed a Western European Union (WEU), composed of the BENELUX countries, France, Italy, Germany, Great Britain, Greece, Spain, and Portugal, with headquarters in Brussels. Turkey, Norway, and Iceland became associate members. It conducted contingency planning, organized and controlled small all-European military operations (with the possibility of using NATO units and equipment), and attempted to coordinate the defense policies and armaments programs of its members.

At the 1991 EU summit meeting in Maastricht, it was agreed that the WEU would be Europe's own defense system, albeit "linked to" NATO. It largely ceased to exist, the end of 2000, and most of its staff and activities were folded into the EU. At its Helsinki summit in 1999, the EU decided to create a 60,000-strong rapid-reaction corps, officially operational in 2003, to act in crises when the US and NATO choose not to get involved.

It also began the creation of about a dozen "battle groups" of 1,500 soldiers for rapid deployment anywhere in the world. In July 2003 the French formed such a group, which included Swedish troops for the first time, to carry out a limited peace-keeping mission in the Democratic Republic of Congo. This was the EU's first solo military mission outside of Europe. In July 2006 the Germans commanded a similar battle group to the Congo to oversee elections, and in the spring of 2008, the French organized a battle group to deal with violence in Chad. By 2013 the EU had active military missions in Bosnia, Mali, and Somalia. However, there is no European army.

In 2003 the EU adopted its first security doctrine, entitled "A Secure Europe in a Better World." It emphasizes that the union is a global actor and that the alliance with

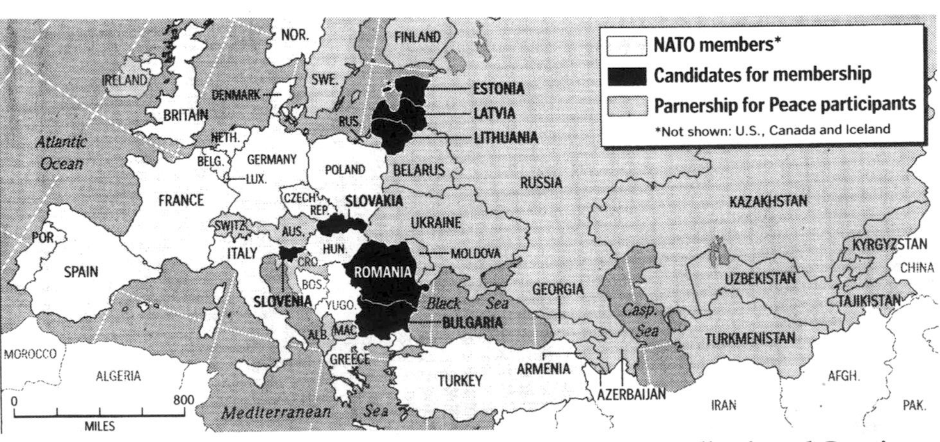

The candidates become members, April 2004, joined in 2009 by Albania and Croatia.

Source: *The Washington Post*

Jens Stoltenberg

the United States is indispensable. An informal organization within NATO known as the "Eurogroup," composed of all European members of NATO except France, Portugal, and Iceland, serves as a forum for some European states within NATO to discuss their special defense needs.

NATO itself has both political and military components. The highest political organ and decision-making body is the North Atlantic Council (NAC). It selects the secretary-general of NATO, who chairs all meetings and seeks consensus among members. By tradition he is always a European. In 2014, former Norwegion prime minister Jens Stoltenberg replaced Denmark's ex–prime minister Anders Fogh Rasmussen. Each member country sends a permanent ambassador to the NATO headquarters in Brussels, and these ambassadors meet once a week. Less frequently, the member countries' heads of government or foreign, defense, or finance ministers meet to iron out higher-level political problems. All decisions are reached by consensus, not by majority vote. In other words, each member has an actual veto power, although such vetoes are seldom cast.

The ambassadors or ministers of all but those nations that do not participate in the integrated defense system (France and Iceland) also take part in the Defense Planning Committee (DPC), which is assisted by a variety of committees and working groups. A staff of about 1,000, divided into divisions of political affairs, defense planning and policy, defense support, and scientific affairs, are in Brussels to assist in the NATO effort.

The highest NATO military authority is the Military Committee, made up of the chiefs of defense from all states participating in the NATO military command, plus France (since 1995). By tradition it is chaired by a European officer, but in 2006 a Canadian general, Ray Henault, occupied the post. Although the chiefs-of-defense meet infrequently, their permanent representatives meet regularly in their absence. The Military Committee's primary role is to advise the DPC.

NATO has an integrated system of commands. The Supreme Allied Commander Europe (SACEUR), who by tradition is always an American, heads the Allied Command Europe (ACE). He also commands all US forces in Europe, and his European command encompasses Russia and all of Africa except the Horn. General Philip M. Breedlove was SACEUR. He was replaced in 2016 by General Curtis M. Scaparrotti. The position of deputy SACEUR alternates between a British and German officer.

ACE is based outside Mons, Belgium, at the Supreme Headquarters Allied Powers Europe (SHAPE). In case of war, ACE is responsible for military operations in the entire European area and wherever in the world NATO forces are deployed. Since the 2002 Prague summit, this strategic command for operations, which remains in Belgium, was made leaner, more efficient, more effective, and more deployable. A British or a German general alternate in commanding one of its two top regional subcommands in Europe, the Regional Command North, in Brunssum, Netherlands. The Regional Command South in Naples, Italy, is always entrusted to an American admiral. The US Sixth Fleet provides the most potent naval forces in the Mediterranean area.

Before the 2002 Prague summit, the other major NATO strategic command was the Allied Command Atlantic (ACLANT), commanded by an American admiral or general and headquartered in Norfolk, Virginia. A strategic command is based in Norfolk, Virginia, with a presence in Europe. It is responsible for continuing transformation of military capabilities and interoperability of allied forces. After reentering NATO's integrated command structure in 2009, France provides the commander for this transformation effort, as well as the top commander of NATO's regional headquarters in Lisbon, Portugal, which organizes the alliance's rapid-reaction force.

Only the US engages in negotiations with Russia aimed at limiting nuclear forces in Europe. But western European members are consulted about any American negotiating positions which might affect European interests. Europeans have developed bodies, such as the NATO Nuclear Planning Group (NPG) and the less formal Special Consultative Group, which serve as channels to inform the US of its allies' views and to keep the latter informed of US objectives.

In 1989 the Conventional Forces in Europe (CFE) negotiations in Vienna replaced the moribund Mutual Balanced Force Reduction (MBFR) talks. This culminated in an agreement between NATO and the now-defunct Warsaw Pact in 1990 to thin out their military equipment in the center of Europe. It did not apply to troops. Several years after the Warsaw Pact collapsed, the terms of the CFE Treaty began to be reexamined, at Russia's insistence, to take account of the fact that Moscow no longer has allies and has potentially serious internal instability.

In 1991 President George H. W. Bush announced unilateral nuclear cuts that went far beyond the Strategic Arms Reductions Talks (START) Agreement reached

SONNTAG AKTUELL

Heute Schausonntag im stilwerk Stuttgart

stilwerk

DIE SIEBTE AUSGABE IHRER ZEITUNG — 5. April 2009

President Obama and Secretary of State Clinton at a NATO summit

Western Europe Today

The European Council and European Commission, Brussels
Courtesy: Central Audiovisual Library, European Commision

in July. European allies and Soviet president Mikhail Gorbachev gave Bush's plan unanimous backing. The greatest impact was on Europe, where the only targets for NATO's tactical nuclear weapons were in areas that are no longer enemies, such as Poland and eastern Germany. Officially endorsed by NATO, the cuts did not make Europe nuclear-free: NATO still has some atomic bombs on dual-capacity aircraft to provide a measure of nuclear deterrence against unknown threats. NATO declared in May 2010 that it would retain its tactical nuclear weapons to protect its total population of 900 million "as long as nuclear weapons exist." Also, Britain and France retain some of their nuclear systems. But European defense has become almost entirely nonnuclear.

The sweeping American disarmament proposals, following the disappearance of a clearly identifiable foe, prompted Europeans to develop a distinct European Security and Defence Policy (ESDP), now called Common Security and Defence Policy (CSDP). A consensus exists that such a European identity is necessary, while preserving NATO in one form or the other.

In 1999 the EU created a new post of "high representative" to breathe life into its Common Foreign and Security Policy (CFSP) and named Javier Solana Madariaga to occupy it. In 2010 he handed the reins to Lady Catherine Ashton of the UK, who in 2014 was succeeded by Federica Mogherini of Italy. To give CFSP a military arm, the EU created ESDP with a rapid-reaction force. This enabled the EU to take command of the small peacekeeping force in North Macedonia in 2003 and in Bosnia in December 2004. By 2008 the EU was running more than a dozen foreign operations, and there were nearly 200 admirals and generals based in EU institutions in Brussels. They are increasingly engaged in planning, an activity always dominated by NATO. By 2010 there was a "Director General of the European Union Military Staff."

No European country wants the total withdrawal of American troops, which had already been drawn down from 320,000 to under barely 30,000 (plus 14,000 in the Sixth Fleet) by 2013. Americans have called on Europeans to bear a greater responsibility for their own defense and but not in competition with NATO, which remains the major pillar for American influence in Europe. One American diplomat said, "Sure, we want the Europeans to do more, but we're always going to be wary of anything that looks like it could push the U.S. out of Europe."

In order to facilitate greater European security independence, NATO in 1998 reduced the number of its command headquarters from 65 to 20, emphasized a multinational approach to the manning of these headquarters, and arranged them in a way that they can support both regular NATO tasks as well as combined joint task forces (CJTF), authorized in 1994. If certain members, such as the US, do not wish to participate in a certain military operation, a coalition of those that do can use NATO units and assets under EU leadership. This is called "Berlin Plus." Non-NATO countries can also be included in such combined joint task forces.

International military groupings have proliferated in Europe since the end of the Cold War. Within NATO, a Dutch-German corps under alternate command has been formed; its troops use English. British, German, Dutch, and Belgian troops constitute a multinational division with an airmobile brigade. It is part of the ACE rapid-reaction force. The Dutch navy has merged its naval headquarters with those of Belgium. A corps has been created with headquarters in Szczecin, Poland, that comprises Polish, German, and Danish troops and is commanded by a Polish officer.

This unit was modeled on the French-German Eurocorps in Strasbourg, France, created in 1992. The Eurocorps now includes BENELUX and Spanish troops and uses English as its common language. In the summer of 2000, this Eurocorps took temporary charge of the NATO-led peacekeeping operation in Kosovo (KFOR); in 2003–2004 it fielded peacekeeping forces in Afghanistan. In 2009 it was announced that German troops would be stationed permanently on French soil for the first time since the Second World War; a battalion is located in Alsace-Lorraine.

A US combat division serves in a German-led corps, while a German division is part of a US-led corps. Outside NATO, Italy, Austria, and Slovenia created a joint land-based force, and the Spanish, French, Portuguese, and Italians formed a rapid operational force called EUROFOR based in Florence. Many NATO troops served alongside other European and non-European soldiers in the Stabilization Force (SFOR) to guard the peace in Bosnia and Herzegovina, as well as in KFOR.

In 1991 NATO was transformed into a more political organization seeking to reach out to its former enemies. It created a North Atlantic Cooperation Council (NACC, renamed in 1997 the Euro-Atlantic Partnership Council—EAPC) comprising 44 countries at century's end to provide for regular consultations between NATO and the former Soviet republics and eastern European nations on such subjects as security issues, arms control, and the conversion of defense industries. In 1994 NATO initiated the Partnership for Peace (PfP), which links a dozen and a half nonmember countries, including Russia, in bilateral treaties with NATO. The purpose is to expand and intensify political and military cooperation and to strengthen stability and peace, primarily through training

EU members

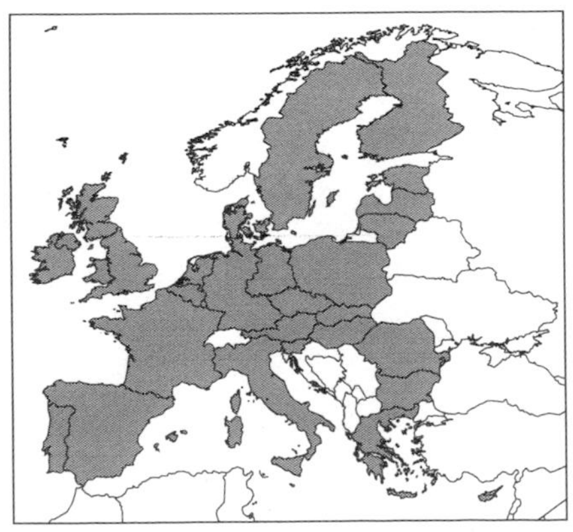

forces for peacekeeping operations. A special NATO-Ukraine Commission was established to deepen cooperation with that important country.

These nations are also linked in the 55-member Organization for Security and Cooperation in Europe (OSCE, known until 1994 as the CSCE), to which all European states, former Soviet republics, and the United States and Canada belong. It meets irregularly to consider how to defuse threats to peace through mediation, crisis management, and the dispatch of observers during elections.

Many countries regard PfP as a steppingstone to full NATO membership. In principle, the alliance is prepared gradually to accept new members on the condition that they have solid democratic credentials, including a firm civilian grip on the armed forces, and can make a genuine military contribution to the common defense. The door remains open to European democracies.

Russia opposes such enlargement, especially insofar as former Soviet republics, such as the Baltics, are concerned. To assuage Moscow's fears, the Atlantic allies signed with Moscow in 1997 a NATO-Russia Founding Act. This is not a legally binding treaty, but it states that NATO has no need, intentions, or plans to create additional capabilities or permanently station troops or nuclear weapons in the new member states. Agreements in 2006 permit such stationing of small numbers of American forces in Romania, Bulgaria, the Baltics, and Poland. NATO gets around objections about permanent stationing of troops there by rotating them. NATO also created a Permanent Joint Council (PJC) at its headquarters, in which Russian officials could discuss, though not veto, NATO policies and decisions.

In the wake of close Russian-US cooperation in the war against terrorism after the September 11 terrorist attacks in New York and Washington, the PJC was upgraded and renamed in 2002 the NATO-Russia Council. The spirit of cooperation was severely damaged by Russia's 2008 invasion of Georgia and its February 2014 military takeover of the Crimea, which is a part of Ukraine. NATO cooperation with Russia was temporarily suspended. The NATO-Russia Council did not convene for two years.

NATO's outdated doctrine of containing Soviet power through "forward defense" and "flexible response" was replaced by one that gives NATO a reason to exist in the changed European environment. Smaller, highly mobile, conventional, and multilateral forces are being created which can be deployed on short notice anywhere in the world and which can help manage unpredictable crises and instability in eastern Europe, the Balkans, the Mediterranean area, and beyond. To remain relevant, NATO must provide security beyond just Europe. The allies benefited from the experience of fighting together for more than a dozen years in Afghanistan, temporarily ending in late 2014. It improved its multinational rapid deployment capability by creating a NATO Response Force (NRF), with a headquarters and 13,000 highly ready and technologically advanced troops on a rotating basis by members. It can be used against enemies in or out of Europe and is intended to be "the tip of the spear" for future alliance deployments.

European Integration

No region in the world has been so successful in creating voluntary economic unions of sovereign states as western Europe. In 1922 the Belgium and Luxembourg Economic Union (BLEU) was created, which made the two countries a single unit for importing and exporting purposes and established a unified currency. In 1944 the Netherlands joined to form BENELUX, which was later extended to include even noncustoms matters.

In order to help the devastated countries of Europe recover economically, the United States offered Marshall Plan aid in 1947 but insisted that all countries receiving such aid sit down together and decide as a group how the money should be spent. Thus, the US provided an important initial impetus for a unified Europe. In response, the Europeans created in 1948 the Organization for European Economic Cooperation (OEEC) for making the decisions and the European Payments Union (EPU) for administering US funds.

In 1960, the US and Canada joined the OEEC, which was renamed the Organization for Economic Cooperation and Development (OECD), with headquarters in Paris. Later other western industrialized nations and Japan, Australia, and New Zealand joined OECD, making a total of 30 members by 2007. It does economic analysis and forecasting for industrialized countries, including estimates of future growth, inflation, unemployment, and gross domestic product (GDP, a measurement of an economy's total production of goods and services. A related and less used term, gross national product—GNP—adds to this value citizens' foreign earnings and subtracts foreigners' income within the country). The OECD also attempts to coordinate members' economic and development aid, and it provided a forum for member states to hammer out an antibribery convention in international commerce. All western European countries belong. Wanting closer contact with the world's industrial leaders, the Czech Republic, Hungary, Poland, and Slovakia joined, and Russia decided to enter. With only 16% of the world's population, its 30 members produce two-thirds of the world's economic output.

The Council of Europe was created in Strasbourg in 1949. Its 40 members include all western European countries and most newly independent countries in eastern Europe. Its assemblies of parliamentarians from the member states serve as a forum for discussing political, economic, social, and cultural issues of interest to all European countries. Perhaps its main contribution has been its various conventions, especially its Convention for the Protection of Human Rights and Fundamental Freedoms (known as the European Convention on Human Rights—ECHR), adopted in 1950. Acceptance of all the convention's principles is a precondition for EU membership. Since 1991 it has been particularly

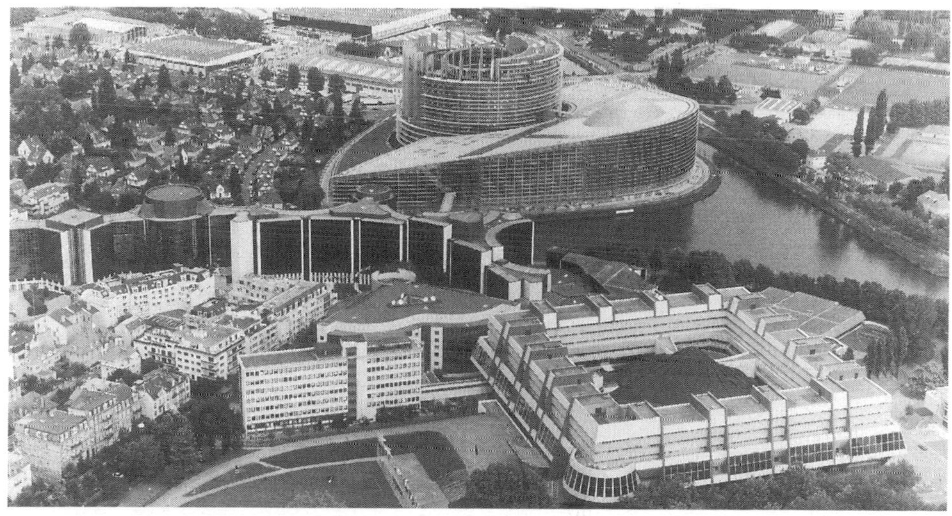

European Parliament building, Strasbourg, France

Courtesy: Central Audiovisual Library, European Commision

active in trying to strengthen democracy and human rights in eastern Europe. The United States requested and was granted observer status in 1996 in order to be able to promote democracy more effectively in eastern Europe.

The BENELUX countries, together with France, West Germany, and Italy, made in 1951 the first significant move toward transferring a portion of their national sovereignty to a supranational organization by creating the European Coal and Steel Community (ECSC). Many persons could scarcely believe at the time that six countries that had been locked only six years earlier in a bloody struggle would be willing to transfer sovereignty over questions relating to these commodities, which are so crucial for heavy industry. Not only was it bold and farsighted to share these important goods rather than to fight wars over them, but also the ECSC gave these nations the practice in economic cooperation needed to convince the six that a move to create a unified Europe could succeed.

The same six nations signed the Treaties of Rome in 1957, which created both the European Economic Community (EEC, frequently called the "Common Market") and EURATOM, which seeks to coordinate the six countries' atomic research and policy. Both came into existence the following year and merged with the ECSC under the same overall organization. This union provided for the elimination of tariffs and customs among themselves, common tariff and customs barriers toward nonmembers, the free movement of labor and capital within the union and equal

10 giugno.
Elezioni per il Parlamento Europeo.
Il tuo voto per la tua Europa.

Italian election poster for the European Parliament: "Your vote for your Europe"

agricultural price levels through the establishment of the Common Agricultural Program (CAP). To avoid giving the impression that the three communities were only *economic* in nature and to express the fact that they are managed by common institutions, they were referred to in the singular as the European Community (EC). On January 1, 2002, when its 50-year mandate came to an end, the ECSC was fully absorbed into the EU.

The 28 member states (with over 500 million citizens, almost two-thirds more than the US) now include the BENELUX countries, France, Germany, Italy, Great Britain, the Republic of Ireland, Denmark, Greece, Spain, and Portugal. In 1995 Austria, Finland, and Sweden joined. In 2002, 10 more countries were invited: Estonia, Latvia, Lithuania, Poland, Hungary, the Czech Republic, Slovakia, Slovenia, Malta, and Cyprus (the Greek section); they entered on May 1, 2004. Romania and Bulgaria joined on January 1, 2007, with Croatia following on July 1, 2013. In 2016 the UK voted to leave the EU, and negotiations for a "Brexit" commenced in March 2017. This raises the question about the role of English as the dominant language, as English would be the primary tongue spoken only in tiny Ireland and Malta!

Because of its questionable human rights record, constitutional grant of political power to the military, continued Greek wariness, and fear by some western European countries that a flood of Turkish immigrants would arrive at their doorstep, Turkish consideration for entry was postponed until 2006. The Turkish part of Cyprus must also await unification of the island before becoming part of the EU. The irresistible logic of European unity has affected countries all over the continent. Norway was offered membership in 1972 and 1994, but its voters rejected it both times.

The issue of immigrants and refugees is a very sensitive one. Some western Europeans fear that they bring in crime and terrorism and overburden their generous welfare states at a difficult time when their economies are suffering under the challenges of the global economy.

Controlling the movement of outsiders who have entered the EU area has been made more difficult by the Schengen Agreements of 1985 and 1990 that eliminated many of Europe's internal border controls. The idea is that one need only go through border formalities when entering one of the membership states; then one can pass freely into the others, submitting only to occasional spot checks. All of the earlier 15 EU members except the UK and Ireland have joined. Since the Nordic countries long since abolished internal border controls among themselves, Norway and Iceland are automatically included. In 2005 Swiss voters chose to take part starting 2007. On December 21, 2007, nine more countries joined the Schengen Zone: Estonia, Latvia, Lithuania, Poland, the Czech Republic, Slovakia, Hungary, Slovenia, and Malta.

Jean-Claude Juncker, the president of European commission

On November 1, 1993, the Maastricht Treaty came into force, bringing with it terminological confusion. It created a European Union (EU), which added common foreign and security policy and cooperation in justice and police matters to the EC. But unlike the EC, the EU has neither a single decision-making process nor a legal persona; it cannot conclude international agreements. Although the EC and EU are technically not exactly the same entities, most scholars and journalists now employ the term EU instead of EC. The term "EU" is used throughout this book.

It is this political element that had prevented some other European states, such as Switzerland, from joining the EU. But the EU has successfully dealt with this problem by granting associate membership (which generally excludes agricultural aspects only) to most non-full-member states in western Europe. Regular contacts are also maintained with 70 African, Caribbean, and Pacific (ACP) countries linked to the EU through the Lomé Convention of 1975. Since 2002 the EU has a European Neighborhood Policy (ENP) to facilitate ties with former Soviet Republics in Europe and with Middle Eastern countries from Morocco to Turkey. In 2009 another multilateral grouping of nations not in the EU was formed: the Eastern Partnership Initiative, which links Armenia, Azerbaijan, Belarus, Georgia, Moldova, and Ukraine to the EU.

Most of the success the EU can claim has been in the economic field. The record is most impressive. With only 7% of the world's population, the EU accounts for 22% of the world's economic output, making it the world's top commercial power. It provides almost half (47%) of the development aid.

Together, the US and the EU states account for over half of the world's GDP and a third of global trade. They exchange $2.6 billion in goods and services each day. Their annual commercial relationship, including investments, amounted in 2005 to $2.5 trillion, the equivalent of 20%–25% of each side's GDP. They are working on an ambitious transatlantic free-trade deal called the Transatlantic Trade and Investment Partnership (TTIP). EU officials speak of creating "something approaching a transatlantic single market in goods." Big business wants this, and labor unions and Greens no longer oppose it. Tariffs are low (below 3%), but the hard part is the numerous nontariff barriers and reaching "regulatory convergence" (common rules).

In terms of foreign direct investment (FDI), they are each other's favorite targets. Two-thirds of America's FDI flow to Europe, while three-fourths of Europe's are directed to the United States, with Texas as the favorite state. America's preferred investment site is the UK, where total US investment is roughly equivalent to that in Asia, Latin America, Africa, and the Middle East combined. It invests 10 times more in the Netherlands (and 2.5 times more in Ireland) than in China. No wonder many observers claim that economics is the stabilizer of the European-American relationship.

Having cornered a fourth of global trade, the EU is the world's largest trading power. Politically, western Europe is and will probably remain a region of sovereign states, which ultimately make their own decisions about the vital matters that affect them. For example, in May and June 2005, French and Dutch voters decisively rejected an EU constitution that would have strengthened Europe's political union. About 90% of lengthy document's contents were salvaged two and a half years later in the EU treaty signed in Lisbon.

European Union

The EU has a well-developed institutional apparatus. It has a dual executive: The European Council is the major decision-making body and is composed of the heads of state or government; it is called the Council of Ministers when member state ministers with responsibilities for finance, agriculture, etc., depending upon the specific matter which is pending, meet.

The second part of the executive that directs the day-to-day business of the EU is the European Commission, which meets in Brussels. The commission is composed of 28 members, 1 from each member state. The 2000 Nice Treaty stipulates that there be fewer by 2009. The Lisbon Treaty, which went into effect in 2010, calls ultimately for each member to lose the right to send a commissioner. The total number will instead be capped at a rotating two-thirds of the number of member states. In the meantime, up to three members are proposed by the gov-

Le Monde

Albert Camus au Panthéon ?

Page 13, entretien avec Olivier Todd page 26

Notre magazine France métropolitaine, Belgique et Luxembourg uniquement

► En Tchétchénie avec Jonathan Littell

► Rencontre avec le chanteur Renaud

Samedi 21 novembre 2009 - 65e année - N°20163 - www.lemonde.fr - Fondateur : Hubert Beuve-Méry - Directeur : Eric Fottorino

2,50 € ou 9,45 € avec le double CD-livret (en France métropolitaine uniquement). Ne peut être vendu sans « Le Monde Magazine ».

AZF : le parquet fait appel, après la relaxe générale

Justice Trente et un morts, des milliers de victimes, mais pas de coupables. Dans le procès AZF, le tribunal correctionnel de Toulouse a prononcé une relaxe générale au bénéfice du doute, mais un autre procès aura lieu après l'appel du parquet. **P. 12**

OGM : le grand découragement des chercheurs français

Sciences La récente destruction d'une vigne transgénique en Alsace va-t-elle sonner le glas de la recherche en France sur les OGM ? Dépités, la plupart des chercheurs qui travaillent sur le sujet mènent leurs expériences à l'étranger. **P. 4**

Climat : comment éviter un échec à Copenhague ?

Débats Avant la conférence sur le réchauffement climatique,

Les nouveaux représentants de l'Europe vont devoir s'imposer

■ Le Belge Van Rompuy est nommé président du Conseil, la Britannique Catherine Ashton aux affaires étrangères

■ Un entretien avec Valéry Giscard d'Estaing : « Les Européens n'ont pas fait le choix d'un George Washington »

Deux inconnus à la tête de l'Europe. Après une dizaine d'années de réflexion pour rendre l'Union européenne (UE) plus efficace et plus influente dans le monde, après être laborieusement venu à bout de la ratification du traité de Lisbonne qui dote l'Union élargie de nouvelles institutions, les vingt-sept chefs d'Etat et de gouvernement, réunis jeudi 19 novembre à Bruxelles, ont choisi deux leaders sortis de l'ombre.

Au poste de président du Conseil européen, le peu visible et néanmoins estimé premier ministre belge, Herman Van Rompuy, 62 ans ; à celui de haut représentant pour les affaires étrangères, la commissaire britannique Catherine Ashton, 53 ans, jamais élue, jamais ministre, peu expérimentée en matière diplomatique. Britannique, femme et de centre gauche, elle rassemblait trois critères nécessaires au délicat équilibre requis entre les postes de responsabilité européens.

On avait fait miroiter un président flamboyant. Felipe Gonzales, brillant président du gouvernement espagnol pendant douze ans et proeuropéen convaincu. Le contesté Tony Blair, l'inventeur du New Labour, trois fois élu à la tête du Royaume-Uni, déconsidéré par sa croisade en Irak auprès de George Bush. Le plus discret Jean-Claude Juncker, visage de l'Europe depuis toujours.

Le président du Conseil européen et la haute représentante pour les affaires étrangères. DIRK WAEM/EPA

EU president Herman Van Rompuy and High Representative Catherine Ashton (until autumn 2014)

Western Europe Today

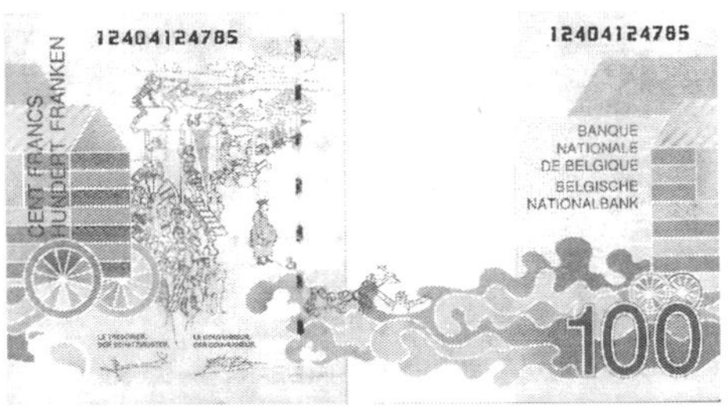

Old currencies go . . .

ernment of his or her country for five-year renewable terms. The EC president selects one and assigns that commissioner a specific portfolio. After joining the College of Commissioners, each commissioner is expected to make decisions based not upon the interests of his or her home country but upon the interests of the EU as a whole. The commissioners decide issues by a simple majority vote; none has the power of veto.

The Lisbon Treaty created a confusing structure, with lines of responsibility blurred. It partially fixed the problem of the rotating six-month presidency of the all-powerful European Council (which is composed of the chiefs of government) by creating a standing president elected by the council for a two-and-a-half-year term, renewable once. The idea is to give the EU political prominence in the world that matches its economic weight.

Taking office in January 2010 as the first EU president was Herman Van Rompuy (ROM-pow). He is a multilingual economist and was Belgium's prime minister for almost a year. He is a skilled negotiator who reduced the influence of the European Commission. His term ended in 2014, and he was replaced by former Polish prime minister Donald Tusk. He was reelected in 2017. The six-month rotating presidency still exists, but the country's leaders do not chair meetings of the European Council (done by the EU president) or gatherings of foreign ministers (done by the high representative).

The council gained a simplified voting system relying more on majority voting as long as 55% of the states containing 65% of the total EU population say yes to a measure. Vetoes are more difficult to cast. Members try to make as many decisions as possible by consensus.

The high representative is like a foreign minister in all but name, combining the former posts of commissioner for external affairs and foreign policy spokesman for the council. The first to be elected by the council was Lady Catherine Ashton, a former Labour leader in the UK House of Lords and EU trade commissioner. She had almost no foreign policy experience. However, she proved to be effective in sealing a peace agreement between Serbia and Kosovo, in chairing the six powers negotiating with Iran over its nuclear program, and in dealing with the chaos in Ukraine in 2014. She was succeded by Federica Mogherini of Italy.

One of her main tasks was to create a European External Action Service (EEAS), a future 6,000-strong diplomatic corps that one day would coordinate and supplement but not replace the national diplomats and foreign offices. Former French ambassador to the US, Pierre Vimont, was named head of this diplomatic organization. The EU has its own intelligence analysis unit, Intcen.

A total of 34,000 persons work in the EU institutions. Two-thirds of them are at the commission, and most are in Brussels, with a minority working in Luxembourg and Strasbourg. This amounts to fewer civil servants (dubbed "Eurocrats") than work in medium-sized city governments in Europe.

The highest EU official is the European Commission president, selected by member countries and confirmed by the European Parliament for a five-year renewable term. In 2004 President José Manuel Barroso, former Portuguese prime minister, became president. He was reelected in 2009 by a secret ballot in the European Parliament and served until 2014. An example of unclear authority stemming from the Lisbon Treaty was Barroso's appointment in 2010 of his former chief of staff and countryman Joao Vale de Almeida as the new EU ambassador in Washington. He was criticized for not consulting the member states, the EU president, or the high representative.

The 751-seat European Parliament is the world's only directly elected international legislature. The formula for seats is based roughly on the population size of the member states, but larger states are underrepresented and smaller ones overrepresented. It meets seven to eight times a year for one-week sessions. Formerly, the parliament met in both Strasbourg and Luxembourg. However, in 1981 the parliament voted to hold all its sessions in Strasbourg, leaving only the administrative headquarters in Luxembourg. Parliamentary committees meet in Brussels. Since most of the real bargaining and revising takes place in the committees and since "additional" plenaries can be held in Brussels, most members of the European Parliament (MEPs) do all of their work in Brussels. In a 2011 poll, 91% of MEPs and their staffs preferred to stay full time in Brussels.

Since 1979 its members, who work in 24 languages, have been elected directly in their home countries according to each country's own preferred method of election. Its members do not sit in national delegations but in party groupings, such as the Communists and Allies, Socialist European People's Party (Christian Democratic), European Progressive Democratic, and Liberal and Democratic Groups. There are a few unaffiliated members.

The Lisbon Treaty requires that the European Council "proposes" a candidate who is then "elected" by parliament. But it

THE EURO BANKNOTE DESIGNS
LES MAQUETTES DES BILLETS EN EURO
DIE ENTWÜRFE DER EURO-BANKNOTEN

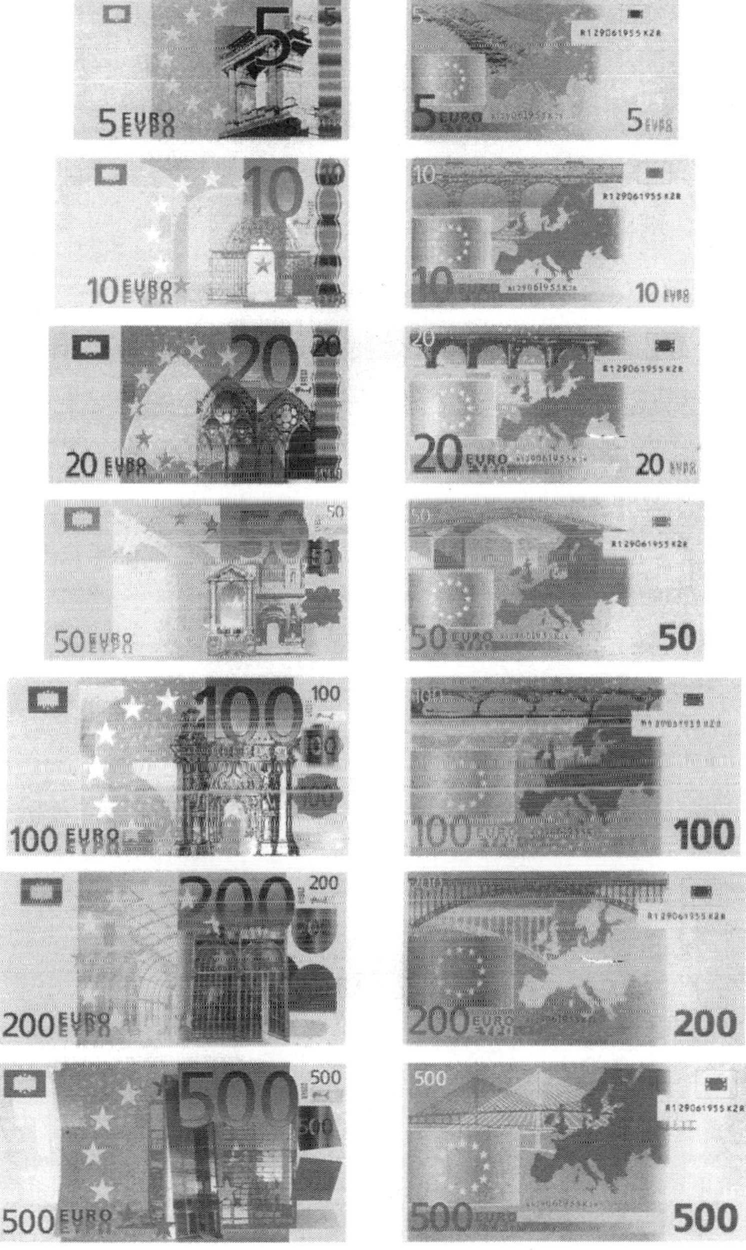

EUROPEAN MONETARY INSTITUTE

. . . and a new one arrives. Courtesy: Central Audiovisual Library, European Commision

also stipulates that EU leaders must "take into account" the EP election results when selecting the EC president. Nobody knows exactly what that means. In a departure from past practice, these parties entered the May 2014 EP elections with "top candidates" selected to lead them. Their expectation is that the leader of the party that does best would be the EC president, not a politician chosen by the member governments.

The European Parliament is officially entitled to oversee the work of the European Commission and to approve or reject the EU's budget. Since the SEA was introduced in 1987, the parliament's power and influence have grown, and it got another boost from the Lisbon Treaty. It has a say over almost 90% of all legislation, but it does not have a veto over most of it. Some legislation, most importantly that covering measures to bring into effect a unified European market, can be altered or amended by the parliament. It must approve the budget. It can veto the accession of new member states to the EU, as well as new trade agreements with non-EU countries. It can launch investigations. Finally, it oversees the commission, a power that was dramatically demonstrated in 1999 and 2004.

For years it had been asking questions about waste and mismanagement, but the commission responded with arrogance and indifference. In January 1999 the parliament threatened a vote of censure; a two-thirds majority could have removed all the commissioners. This threat was averted when a panel of five independent experts was appointed to investigate financial impropriety. In March the panel published a devastating report accusing the well-paid commissioners ($200,000 salary and expenses in 1999) of tolerating widespread fraud, corruption, nepotism, favoritism, and mismanagement. All commissioners felt compelled to resign.

The consequence of this scandal was not only more democratic accountability but also a dramatic alteration of the political balance of power in favor of the elected European Parliament. It showed its muscle again in 2004, when it questioned the competence of five of the proposed commissioners. This forced EC president Barroso to reshuffle his lineup of commissioners in order to win parliamentary approval. This was the first time this had ever happened.

Finally, there is a European Court of Justice, with its seat in Luxembourg and composed of 28 justices, each chosen by member states for six-year renewable terms; they are assisted by eight advocates general. The court judges violations of three major documents, the ECSC and the EU and Euratom Treaties, as well as all subsequent EU treaties that are collectively called the Treaty of the European Union (TEU). This includes the Nice Treaty of 2000. It redistributed national votes, restricted vetoes, revamped certain institutions, limited the number of commissioners, and granted the European Parliament more power and seats. The court rules on whether national laws are in accordance with European laws in those fields within the EU's competence (jurisdiction). It is the final arbiter of the Lisbon Treaty, which gave the Charter of Fundamental Rights legal force.

The Single European Act (SEA) amends the European treaties by spelling out certain EU objectives: completion of the European internal market, creation of a great area without frontiers, technological development, progress toward economic and monetary union, improvement of the

Western Europe Today

environment and working conditions, creation of more effective and democratic institutions, and institutionalization of cooperation among member states in the field of foreign policy. The target year of 1992 was chosen for its symbolic importance: 500 years after the discovery of the New World.

From 1979 the European Monetary System (EMS) attempted, not always successfully, to coordinate the monetary affairs of certain western European countries by trying to link their currencies. At their 1991 Maastricht summit, EU leaders agreed to create a single European currency (called the "euro") and a European Central Bank (ECB) located in Frankfurt. The criteria for joining this Economic and Monetary Union (EMU)—a budget deficit of not more than 3% of GDP and a total national debt not in excess of 60% of GDP—placed political strains on member governments. The inevitable austerity policies were resented by many of their voters. Many Europeans thought that the price to be paid for the euro was not worth it. However, the euro crisis that emanated from Greece in 2010 showed that many eurozone members had disregarded the criteria.

In 1998 the governments of 11 members (known unofficially as the "eurozone") decided to adopt the euro as of January 1, 1999, with Britain, Sweden, Denmark, and Greece waiting until later to join. Danish voters rejected the euro again in a September 2000 referendum. Greece enthusiastically entered on January 1, 2001. Despite the fervent support by their government, Swedish voters rejected the new currency in 2003. Slovenia joined on January 1, 2007, and Malta and Cyprus joined a year later, making 15 EU member states in the eurozone. Slovakia joined in 2009, and Estonia was admitted in January 2011.

In order not to hurt national feelings, the new euro bills bear generic European designs: Gothic arches, bridges, windows, and a map of Europe. No scene from a particular country is recognizable. The only national concession for paper money was made to Greece, which does not use Roman letters. The word for the currency appears both as "EURO" and "EYPO." Bulgaria became the first EU member to use the Cyrillic alphabet, and that may be added, as well. The coins are uniform on one side, but each participating country made its own design for the reverse side. Thus 17 different coins circulate but are legal tender throughout the eurozone.

The new EU members were expected to join the eurozone within four to five years after entering the EU in 2004 and 2007, but most had to postpone adoption. The euro is a qualified success: By 2007 there were more of them in circulation around the globe than US dollars, although the dollar remained the favorite reserve currency for central banks. However, the 2010 euro crisis and the need for an emergency EU and IMF standby rescue fund raised doubts in the world's first currency that is not backed by a sovereign state.

A few countries that are not full members of the EU belong to the European Free Trade Association (EFTA), which was created in 1959 and whose headquarters are located in Geneva. Whereas the EU has a huge bureaucracy and budget, EFTA is a shoestring operation, with about 60 full-time staff. English is the working language, even though no member nation uses it as its mother tongue. EFTA has no political objectives, and its members have not relinquished a shred of sovereignty.

EFTA eliminated tariffs and customs on all industrial products bought or sold from all member nations, but it does not include agricultural or fishing products. All EFTA members have separate free-trade agreements with the EU. EFTA's economic importance declined after Great Britain, Ireland, and Denmark left to join the EU in 1972, and Finland, Sweden, and Austria, in 1995. To restore EFTA's significance, its members—Switzerland, Liechtenstein, Norway, and Iceland—concluded cooperation agreements with Egypt, Morocco, and Tunisia.

In 1991 the EU and EFTA countries agreed to form a European Economic Area (EEA), which creates a market of 500 million customers extending from the Mediterranean to the Arctic and accounting for over 40% of world trade. Within the

EEA, EFTA members enjoy the EU's "four freedoms"—of goods, services, capital, and people—but EEA does not include agriculture, fish, energy, coal, and steel. EFTA members live under many EU rules, although they have no voice in their writing; this lack of representation gives them added incentive to join the EU as full members.

All Scandinavian countries are in the Nordic Council, which meets regularly to discuss nonmilitary problems that they have in common. Eleven nations belong to the European Space Agency (ESA) which, with American assistance, launched the first European Spacelab into orbit at the end of 1983. Onboard this Spacelab was the first European astronaut to travel into space with Americans—Dr. Ulf Merbold, a German physicist. In 1988 ESA also joined with the US and Japan to begin construction of the Space Station Freedom.

Western European countries are active in such international economic treaties or organizations as the General Agreement on Trade and Tariffs (GATT); the World Trade Organization (WTO), which since 1995 attempts to resolve disputes relating to the GATT Treaty; the International Monetary Fund (IMF), which provides funds for countries with balance-of-payments problems; the International Bank for Reconstruction and Development (World Bank); and the European Bank for Reconstruction and Development (EBRD). Headquartered in London, the EBRD was created after the collapse of communism to help central and eastern European countries make successful transitions to free-market economics.

The International Energy Agency (IEA) exists to ensure that all industrialized nations have minimally sufficient energy supplies in times of crisis. No European country belongs to the Organization of Petroleum Exporting Countries (OPEC), whose headquarters is in Vienna. Nevertheless, those western European countries which export large quantities of oil, such as Great Britain and Norway (from the North Sea), note what is charged by the OPEC countries before setting their own prices.

Interpol, headquartered in Paris, provides some coordination in fighting international crime. Europol, based in The Hague, shares information among national police forces and cooperates in a limited way with the US. SitCen exists for intelligence sharing among EU countries. Eurojust coordinates the EU countries' prosecuting authorities. Following the September 11 attacks in the US, EU governments rapidly accepted a single European arrest warrant to facilitate the struggle against terrorism.

This high degree of cooperation and organization explains in great measure the tremendous growth of the economy of western Europe. In a sense it may be likened to the United States, which, after discarding the Articles of Confederation and creating the present Constitution two centuries ago, abolished tariffs on goods shipped between the states and laid the groundwork for ever-closer cooperation among formerly sovereign entities. Through the many organizations they have formed and joined, western European nations are better equipped and prepared to face the complicated problems of today.

September 11, 2001

For the United States, the world changed dramatically on September 11, 2001, when fanatical Islamic al-Qaeda terrorists, trained and financed by Osama Bin Laden and sheltered in Taliban-ruled Afghanistan, hijacked four American commercial airliners and crashed three of them into the Twin Towers of the World Trade Center in New York and the Pentagon in Washington, killing more than 3,000 persons from 81 different countries. More British and French citizens perished that day than in any previous terrorist attack.

Americans' feeling of invulnerability from outside threats went up with the noxious smoke from the buildings' rubble. Any temptations to pursue an isolationist, North America–focused policy disappeared, at least temporarily. A shaken America looked for help from its friends, and the most steadfast of them were Europeans and Canadians. They responded with emotion and resolve. Within 36 hours of the attack, NATO offered to invoke the mutual-defense clause, article 5, for the first time in its half-century history.

Former EC president Romano Prodi called an emergency session the next morning. After a moment of silence for the victims of the attacks, he decided to send "the strongest possible signal of European solidarity with the American people" and to "call for a common European approach to all aspects of this tragedy." In moving language he announced, "this barbaric attack was directed against the free world and our common values. It is a watershed event, and life will never be quite the same again. . . . In the darkest hours of European history, the Americans stood by us. We stand by them now."

In a poll taken a week after the attack, Europeans showed a strong willingness to support a US military assault: 80% in Denmark, 79% in Britain, 73% in France, 58% in Norway and Spain, and half in Germany. The EU called for a three-minute silence on September 14, and from Finland to Italy and Berlin to Paris, businesses and stock exchanges, buses and shoppers stopped to honor the dead and reflect upon their world that had changed so suddenly.

The Complexity of US-European Cooperation

The transatlantic relationship is intense, multilayered, exceedingly complex, increasingly interdependent, and fraught with fluctuations and frictions. It takes place within several interrelated channels. The United States and all European states conduct bilateral relations with each other. In times of crisis, Washington tends to prefer these bilateral contacts because they bring action and cooperation more quickly than does a complicated evolving structure like the EU. The same applies to European governments. The German daily *Die Welt* called the antiterrorist crisis "the moment of the nation-states, the time in which individual European governments turn to the American partner after consulting among themselves."

The allies interact closely within NATO. The highest political leader within the alliance, the secretary-general, is always a European. But American military leadership is institutionalized through the permanent appointment of an American general as the SACEUR. Decisions are reached on the basis of consensus. However, not all European countries belong to this organization, and not all members participate in the integrated command structure, such as France and Iceland, although they have a part in NATO's political structure. The partners collaborate in a wide variety of international fora, such as the OSCE, the G8 (which includes Japan, Canada, and Russia), the G20 (which includes the G-8 and major developing countries, especially China, India, and Brazil), and most importantly the United Nations. Finally and of ever-increasing importance, the US has had to adapt to and work intensively with an evolving EU. This was symbolized in February 2005 by the first visit by an American president to the EU institutions in Brussels.

The transatlantic partnership involves the meshing of many different systems of government—the US central government and individual American states; the EU; its member states; and, in some federations such as Germany, states or "*Länder*." Thus political authority is dispersed, and there are many points where one or more of the numerous players can veto policies. On both sides of the Atlantic, domestic politics is of vital importance. Negotiators often need to make domestic tradeoffs that adversely affect the foreign policies they are trying to pursue. Since all the states involved in this thick network of links are democracies, electoral cycles strongly affect the effort to reach agreements. On the American side, it is often pointed out that presidents and Congress find it especially harrowing to make bold, potentially unpopular moves within a year of reelection. It is no different in the EU.

The American political system divides power both geographically (between the central government and the states) and within the governing institutions inside Washington and the 50 state capitals. This can create diplomatic nightmares for both American and European leaders. For instance, American states have become more and more assertive in global politics and conduct their own foreign policies, particularly in economic and trade matters. Ignoring Washington, the Massachusetts legislature passed a "Burma Law" in 1996 forbidding the state and its agencies from buying anything from companies or individuals that invest in or trade with Myanmar (Burma), which is under military rule. The same can happen in Europe. Germany's *Länder* have supremacy over certain aspects of immigration policy. Thus they can impede both the policy of the German central government in Berlin and that of the EU itself.

Europeans must deal with America's large, highly decentralized institutions, which wield power of their own and often seem to be hostile to each other. Separation of powers is particularly troublesome for foreign policy: It is often impossible for a president to produce what he promises to foreign leaders. An American president occupies a central position in the making of effective foreign policy. If he is not personally involved or committed to achieving important foreign policy goals, little gets done. The political system enables persons who are largely unknown in Europe to rise to the highest national political office through a painfully long and complicated electoral system. The unique American selection procedure permits a person to arrive in the White House who had pursued a nonpolitical career as a soldier (Eisenhower), farmer (Carter), actor (Reagan), or governor of a state (Carter, Reagan, Clinton, George W. Bush). It almost always brings to the White House a neophyte in foreign policy; Eisenhower and the first George Bush were the exceptions. Most presidents learn diplomacy as on-the-job training, learning by doing.

When that president seems to overlook the multilateral dimension of America's dealings with the outside world and the need to engage former adversaries, Europeans react negatively. Although many of the red-letter issues—such as the Comprehensive Test Ban Treaty, the Kyoto Protocol, and the International Criminal Court—had gained prominence during the Clinton administration, Bush's predecessor was able to give the appearance in public that he supported these issues and to put the blame on the Republican Congress for not ratifying them.

A newly elected president may have little or no experience in foreign affairs and yet have the power to select a multitude of foreign policy advisers, secretaries, and agency chiefs, many with little or no foreign or defense policy background themselves. Such a presidential "team" appears often to operate in an uncoordinated way, frequently sending off widely differing signals. This inevitably creates and fuels doubts about American leadership capabilities and the continuity of US foreign policy. The complicated and extensive interagency bargaining in Washington confuses many people, European and American alike.

The powerful US Congress can also be frustrating. In the last two decades of the 20th century, Congress underwent significant changes: The seniority system in committees had weakened, and the number of committees and subcommittees proliferated. Also, the workload became so demanding that congressmen and senators are retiring earlier. Therefore, an increasingly high percentage of the legislators are new in Congress. For example, by the mid-1990s, half the members of the House of Representatives had entered the chamber after the fall of the Berlin Wall. What these changes did was to take much of the power that used to be concentrated in a few key figures and dispersed it within Congress. In this more decentralized (or, more positively, "democratized") Congress, legislative work has become much more complicated. For instance, more than 40 congressional committees and subcommittees deal with the defense budget alone.

In the absence of the kind of strong party discipline that exists in most European parliaments, American congressmen and senators are more protective of their constituents' interests and can safely vote against their party leaders or the president if an issue of great interest in their districts or states is at stake. Thus there is no stable coalition on foreign policy matters. Nevertheless, the Congress is not as obstructionist and isolationist as it might sometimes seem from across the Atlantic. For example, in the 1990s and the first half-decade of the 21st century, it supported the United States' entry into the North America Free Trade Association (NAFTA), the World Trade Organization (WTO), and two enlargements of NATO. Its unflagging and vigorous support of President Bush's antiterrorist measures after September 11 revealed yet again that presidential-congressional unity is the norm in times of crisis.

President George W. Bush took more straightforward opposition to policies he thought would damage American interests, and he suffered for it in European public opinion. Most Europeans were convinced that he knew less about Europe than did his predecessor, even though Clinton's opinions did not substantially differ from Bush's on many key issues. The sole Bush policy favored by Europeans was his decision not to withdraw American troops from Bosnia and Kosovo. Bush's gestures to patch up the transatlantic relationship after his reelection in 2004 were unprecedented, but they had only limited effect.

The election of Barack Obama as president of the United States in November 2008 satisfied a European longing for the return of an America that could again be a source of hope, not of fear. He made a triumphant tour of Europe, attending G20, NATO, and EU summits in April 2009. European leaders vied to be photographed at his side, and his charismatic wife, Michelle, helped underscore what a dramatic historic change had occurred in America. French commentator Dominique Moïse wrote, "America, thanks to Mr. Obama, has returned to be the emotional center of gravity of the world." Many Europeans believed that President Obama, who grew up in the Pacific, no longer focused as much on Europe as did his predecessors. Most Europeans have a negative opinion of his successor, Donald Trump.

Complexity on the European Side of the Atlantic

One exasperated American official during the Nixon administration described the European Community to be "as mystifying as the Tibetan theocracy." William Wallace was more subdued, calling the EU institutional structure "complex and opaque." Desmond Dinan attributes this to the "incremental, often untidy nature of European integration." The European Union is in the process of steady evolution; it is a polity in the making. The American ambassador to the EU, Richard Morningstar, put it this way: "If we look 20 years into the future, we know what the U.S. will look like. But Europe? It is hard to predict what the relationship will be when we do not know what one part will be."

Those who deal with Europe must constantly adapt to its changing institutions. It is therefore not simple for Europeans and Americans alike to know precisely who has the authority to make decisions on what, what exactly is the division of labor among many bodies of the community, or where the line is between EU competence and that of the member states. The Lisbon Treaty merely added to this confusion. This is one reason the United States still prefers to utilize its bilateral ties with European allies in times of emergency.

European countries all have variations of parliamentary systems, which simplify the conduct of foreign policy. Responsibility is clearer than one finds either in the EU or the US, and once policy is established by the central government, there are fewer obstacles to its implementation. Given party discipline and the fact that a prime minister or chancellor is in office precisely because his party or coalition has a parliamentary majority, it is not easy for its foreign policy to be thwarted by legislative action. Nor does a European government need to worry as much about ratification after having negotiated a treaty as does an American president.

One of the difficulties of EU foreign policy is created by the presidency of the European Council. Until the Lisbon Treaty became operative in 2010, it revolved every six months. The member states still rotate, but they now do this alongside an elected EU president. Each brings its own perspectives and priorities to its presidency. For instance, the Spanish presidency brought a redirection of attention to Latin America, something in which Finland would have only mild interest. But the Finnish presidency heralded the "Northern Dimension," with which Spain would not share a strong affinity.

The member states have differing opinions on how the community's relations with the US should be, and this can affect the transatlantic relationship. A country can assume the presidency with a firm agenda but find it hijacked by international events. The presidency is so important for setting the EU agenda that the US and other nonmembers cannot ignore it. But such a short presidency inevitably create discontinuity and could disrupt or complicate ongoing negotiations. It is the job of the newly elected EU president to provide stability, continuity, and predictability; it is unknown if he will succeed.

In determining who really makes decisions in EU external policy, the outsider must decide now among a variety of powerful figures: the EU president, the EC president, the European Council's high representative, the trade commissioner or the prime minister or foreign minister of the current presidency country. A prestigious German daily wrote what many people already know: "Neither the European public nor Europe's partners understand the distribution of competencies (if there is one)." All travel around the world speaking in the name of Europe. It continues, "The same applies to operative politics. The EU has countless commissioners and representatives for special regions or issues, but outside the EU apparatus, nobody knows what powers they have and in whose name they speak."

Despite the many headed EU leadership that still exists, this stable of influential EU leaders represents considerable progress toward enhancing the community's ability to conduct foreign policy. Former secretary of state Henry Kissinger was mistakenly reported to have asked what number he should dial when he wanted to call Europe. He denied ever having said that. But former senior director for European affairs on the US National Security Council Antony J. Blinken argued that there is now a number to call at the EU, depending on the problem. "It is true, however, that while each has the receiver in one ear, he also has 15 [now 28] European ministers whispering in the other. As a result, Brussels' executive decision-making authority is circumscribed." In an interview with the German weekly *Die Zeit*, ex–commissioner for external affairs Chris Patten admitted: "I don't claim for a minute that there will be one single telephone number in the near future, which a Secretary of State Kissinger could dial.

LE FIGARO

4€

« Sans la liberté de blâmer, il n'est point d'éloge flatteur » Beaumarchais

Vins

Le projet de réforme des AOC en France. Exclusivité

Page 19

Aujourd'hui, Le Figaro et ses magazines avec le DVD "Ridicule" 7€

L'ESSENTIEL

ÉDITORIAL

Nouvelles Europes

Par Jean de Belot, page 13

Le témoignage de Bush

Le président américain et le vice-président ont déposé devant la commission sur le 11 septembre.

International Page 5

Irak : il y a un an, la « fin de la guerre »

Le 1er mai 2003, Bush proclamait le terme de l'offensive, mais les combats n'ont jamais cessé depuis.

International Page 5

1er mai : Raffarin optimiste

Les observateurs gouvernementaux n'ont relevé aucun indice d'une forte mobilisation syndicale.

Politique Page 8

Imam de Vénissieux : vide juridique

Alors qu'un recensement des prêcheurs est en cours, le Conseil français du culte musulman est divisé.

Société Page 9

Le gouvernement prêt à améliorer le Pacs

Raffarin estime que le pacte civil de solidarité ne donne pas entièrement satisfaction et promet de le revoir.

Société Page 10

Découverte du plus ancien foyer de l'humanité

Les chefs d'Etat et de gouvernement seront demain à Dublin pour célébrer l'élargissement de l'Union

Les défis de l'Europe à 25

L'Europe est à la veille de son « Big Bang ». Demain, l'union accueillera dix nouveaux partenaires issus pour la plupart de l'ancienne Europe communiste. Cet élargissement est le plus important jamais réalisé depuis les débuts de la construction européenne dans les années cinquante. L'Union européenne sera alors le troisième plus vaste ensemble de population au monde derrière la Chine et l'Inde.

La « réunification » du Vieux Continent se fera en fête à Dublin, actuel siège de la présidence tournante. Les 25 chefs d'Etat et de gouvernement de la future Europe élargie y sont attendus demain. Le centre de la capitale irlandaise sera transformé en grande foire européenne, où les 25 pays, ainsi que la Roumanie, la Bulgarie et la Turquie seront représentés. Une réunion placée sous haute surveillance par crainte de violences terroristes ou de débordements. Pas moins de 5 000 policiers et 2 500 soldats sont mobilisés pour sécuriser la ville. Chaque pays a par ailleurs prévu de marquer l'événement à sa manière. A Paris, un « marathon musical » de la création européenne est notamment annoncé.

Par avance, les Etats-Unis ont salué « chaleureusement » l'élargissement en récusant l'idée que les nouveaux membres aient à faire le choix entre Bruxelles et Washington. Mais cette nouvelle Europe suscite aussi des craintes. A l'étranger, comme en Inde et dans les pays arabes où l'on redoute une plus forte concurrence commerciale, mais également parmi les pays de l'Union. Hier, Jacques Chirac s'est efforcé de dissiper les doutes des Français en affirmant que l'Europe était un espace de pro-

The United Kingdom of Great Britain and Northern Ireland

Political power's most coveted address: 10 Downing Street, residence of the prime minister

Area: 89,038 sq. mi. (230,609 sq. km., slightly smaller than Oregon).

Population: 62.4 million.

Capital City: London (pop. 8.1 million, including the city's sprawling suburbs).

Climate: Mild and temperate, rarely above 86°F (30°C) or below 41°F (5°C).

Neighboring Countries: Ireland (a short distance across the Irish Sea to the west); France, Belgium, and the Netherlands (a short distance across the English Channel or North Sea to the east).

Official Language: English.

Other Principal Tongues: About a fourth of the population of Wales speaks Welsh, and about 60,000 Scottish speak a form of Gaelic. Both are Celtic dialects.

Ethnic Background: Angle, Saxon, Celtic, and Nordic.

Principal Religions: Christian 90%. In England, Church of England (Anglican) 49%; Roman Catholic 7%; in Scotland, Church of Scotland (Presbyterian) 19%; in Wales, Church of Wales; Muslim 3%; Sikh and Hindu 2%; Jewish 1%; other 4%.

Main Exports: Finished and semifinished manufactured products, oil and gas, foodstuffs, chemicals, motor vehicles.

Main Imports: Manufactured goods, foodstuffs, fuels.

Major Trading Partners: EU (50.5% of exports and 48.6% of imports), Germany (10.6% of exports and 12.5% of imports), US (9.6% of exports and 5.8% of imports), Netherlands (7.6% of exports and 7% of imports), France (7.1% of exports and 5.7% of imports), Ireland (5.8% of exports), China (8.2% of imports).

Currency: Pound sterling.

National Holiday: Celebration of the birthday of the queen is in June, although she was actually born on April 21.

Head of State: Her Majesty Queen Elizabeth II, b. 1926. Married Lieutenant Philip Mountbatten (Prince of Greece and Denmark) on November 20, 1947; he had been created Duke of Edinburgh on the preceding day and (in 1957) Prince of Great Britain. Queen Elizabeth II succeeded to the throne on the death of her father, George VI, on February 6, 1952; her coronation took place on June 2, 1953.

Heir Apparent: His Royal Highness Prince Charles (b. November 14, 1948), Prince of Wales. His son, Prince William of Wales (b. June 21, 1982), is second in succession to the throne.

Head of Government: Boris Johnson (since July 2019).

National Flag: The Union Flag—a dark blue charged with the white cross of St. Andrew (for Scotland), the red cross of St. Patrick (for Ireland), surmounted by the red cross of St. George (for England) bordered in white. Sometimes called the Union Jack.

No country in the world has closer ties with the United States in language, history, shared assumptions, and emotion than does the United Kingdom. In the capital of each country, there stands a prominent statue of one of the greatest leaders of the other. Abraham Lincoln gazes at the Houses of Parliament in London, and in a prominent section of Washington, Winston Churchill (himself half American) stands giving his famous "V" for victory salute. Although the Brit-

The United Kingdom

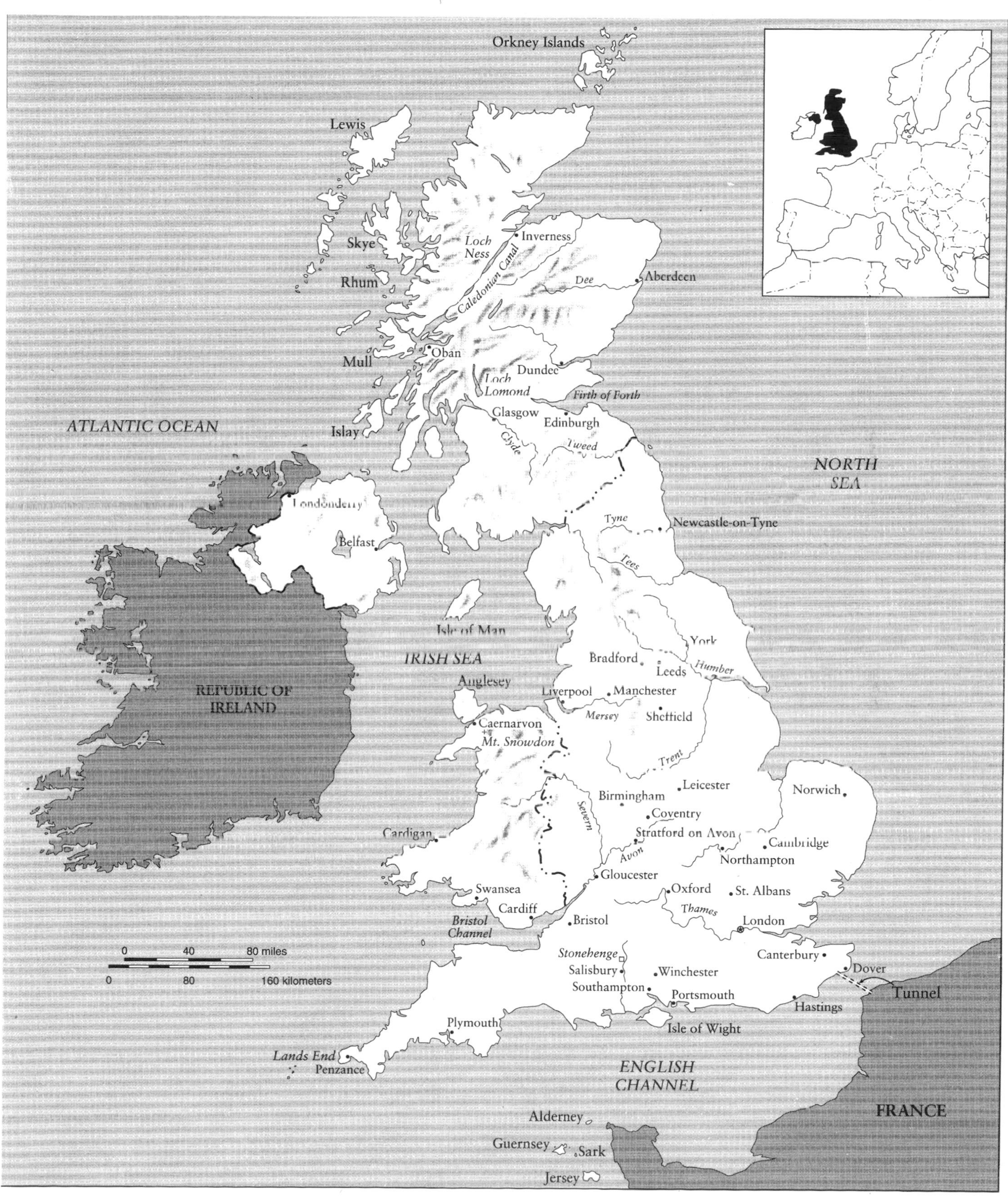

The United Kingdom

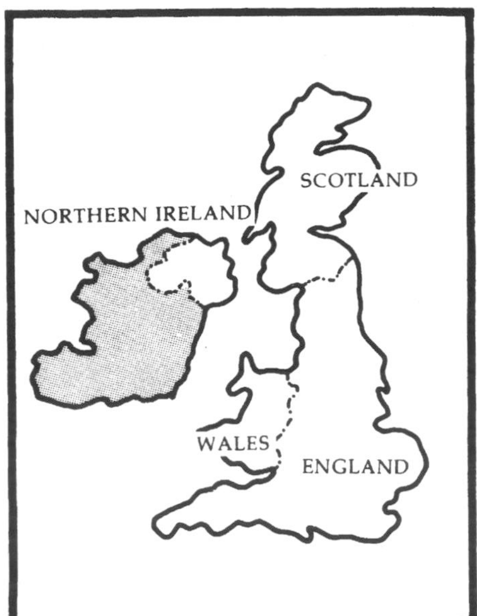

ish influence on the United States is not surprising, what is remarkable is the influence that the United Kingdom has had on the rest of the world. It is striking that a moderate-sized island off the coast of Europe should achieve first a pivotal role in European affairs and then domination of much of the entire globe.

Britain is blessed with a moderate climate, despite its northerly location, due to the warmth of the Gulf Stream, which after originating in the Caribbean Sea crosses the Atlantic. Its waters provide a warmer, albeit moister, climate than would otherwise be the case. Rain is frequent but not overabundant. The sun shines in most parts for one out of four to eight daylight hours during the winter. The mountains of the west modify this pattern, condensing the clouds into rainfall, which is more abundant there.

The climate is not suited to plant life needing heat, but it is ideal for water-seeking crops, particularly grasses. With a population density of about 640 persons per square mile, much of Britain is urbanized. In spite of the fertile soil, it is an importer of foodstuffs. The Industrial Revolution, for which Britain is renowned, resulted in a particularly dense type of city building construction. Wales is a mixture of industry, agriculture, and herding. Virtually all sheep and cattle are consumed within the country; the sheep support production of fine woolens, few of which are exported. Scotland, about one-quarter the size of England and Wales, consists of a small area of lowlands and the larger highlands, which actually reach a maximum height of only 4,400 feet. The cities of Glasgow on the Clyde River and Edinburgh on the Firth (Bay) of Forth are seats of heavy industry and are highly urbanized. The mountains are widely interspersed with valleys, where intensive sheep raising supports the production of world-famous Scotch tweeds and plaids, treasured by tailors throughout the world.

While Roman remains can be found in various parts of England today, the most important architectural work is virtually invisible. London, located at the spot closest to the sea where the Thames could most easily be bridged, was walled and became a Roman center, even though the Celtic name was retained. It became the hub from which spokes of roads headed out to other parts of the island. This pattern still shapes the roads and rails of Britain. The city today extends far beyond the boundaries of the original wall.

Natural resources that were important in the early Industrial Revolution in the late 18th and 19th centuries have been a second blessing. Its island location has protected it from invasion for more than 900 years and encouraged it to use the sea for commercial and political gain. But its greatest blessing has been a relatively stable history that developed quite early in a tradition of freedom and representative government. Americans are sometimes confused by the various names applied to Britain. Its official name is the United Kingdom of Great Britain and Northern Ireland. Four areas combine to make up the country: England, Wales, Scotland, and Northern Ireland. The word "Britain" encompasses the first three. The last is composed of the six northern Irish counties. Because England is the site of the capital and over the centuries came to control the other areas, the term "England" or "the English" is sometimes (but inaccurately) used to describe the whole country. Residents of Wales, Scotland, and Northern Ireland prefer to use the term "Great Britain" or "British."

The growth toward world leadership and representative democracy in Britain has not been smooth or steady, but the history of Britain has been a stage on which royal pageantry has combined with remarkable commercial, industrial, and political success of more humble citizens.

HISTORY

The Early Period

It must have been quite a shock for the Roman legionnaires who left the brilliant sunshine of Italy, marched across Gaul, and then made the short but perilous crossing of the English Channel. They arrived in a land of soft greens, frequent rains, and fearsome warriors who painted themselves blue and drove chariots armed with sharp blades at the axles. These Celts had come to the island during the Iron Age and spoke a dialect known as Brythonic, and thus their land was known as Britain.

Julius Caesar led two expeditions to Britain in 55 and 54 BC, but it was not until 43 AD that the Roman emperor Claudius began to establish settlements. The campaign to stamp out Celtic Druid beliefs, with all of their mysticism, that have faded into the mists of time, produced the first of the great British queens, Boadicea, who managed to kill several thousand Romanizing Britons before finally being captured and committing suicide. While the popular image has always seen the British as chauvinists in their men's clubs, the fact that in the 1980s both the throne and the office of prime minister were occupied by women is less surprising when one remembers that the first resistance leader and the monarchs with two of the greatest reigns

The prehistoric ruins of Stonehenge on the Salisbury Plain, which scholars date from 1800 to 1400 BC

in English history, Elizabeth I (1558–1603) and Victoria (1837–1901), were women, however different they were. The first was an astute monarch, who is reported to have utilized amorous affairs to advance the affairs of state. The latter was conservative, conventional, prudish, and astute, devoted only to her husband, Albert. Indeed, rightfully or wrongfully, an entire age is known by the name of each in the English-speaking world.

Celtic tribalism continued in the mountains of Wales and Scotland. Hadrian's Wall ran for miles to seal off the northern borders of the Roman area, since the people in the mountains there were beyond conquest. No attempt was made to invade Ireland.

A castle in Wales

The Early Christian Era

Roman soldiers and merchants brought Christianity with them to the island. Their persecution by Emperor Diocletian produced the first Christian martyr of the island, St. Alban. But after Emperor Constantine legalized Christianity in the empire, the church began to flourish in Britain.

The Romans occupied England for about 400 years, but as the empire collapsed inward, barbarian pressure on England increased. Angles, Saxons, and Jutes, Teutonic tribes from what is now northern Germany and Denmark, filled the vacuum left by the Romans. Now it was the Celts leading their tribal lives in Wales, Scotland, Ireland, and Cornwall, who kept alive the light of western civilization and Christian culture.

King Arthur may be more legendary than historical, but his story represents the urge to restore Christian order during the dark period that lasted for two centuries. In 597 the monk Augustine (named for the more famous St. Augustine of Hippo) was sent from Rome to convert the English. He established Canterbury as his see and became its first archbishop. As Roman Christianity spread, it came into contact and then into conflict with Celtic Christianity. The synod of Whitby, meeting in 664, decided that Roman Christianity would prevail. This proved to be a most significant decision, for England was thus brought once more under the influence of Rome; its culture, politics, and religion would be shaped by events on the Continent. Nearly 900 years later, when England turned away from Roman Christianity, the effects would be even more important. During the 8th century, English culture flourished. The first English historian, Venerable (later Saint) Bede, wrote his *Ecclesiastical History of the English People*; the great Anglo-Saxon epic *Beowulf* was written; and the Saxon monk Alcuin of York was a leading intellectual of Charlemagne's court.

Viking Invasion and Expulsion

By the 9th century, Vikings (Norsemen, Northmen, Normans) from Norway and Denmark attacked and then conquered much of the British isle. In response, the only English king to be known as "the Great," Alfred of Wessex, whose capital was at Winchester, organized an army, developed a navy, founded schools, and stopped the growth of Norse Danish power. It is ironic that the Norsemen then invaded France, where their region became known as Normandy. Almost two centuries later, one of their leaders would head the last successful conquest of England. Although Alfred died in 899, his son Edward the Elder conquered the remaining Danish-controlled areas and thus became the first king of a united England.

For the next 100 years, Anglo-Saxons and Norsemen merged during a golden age of relative peace. As the English historian Trevelyan said, "Had it not been for the Scandinavian blood infused into our race by the catastrophes of the 9th century, less would have been heard in days to come of British maritime and commercial enterprise." Again ironically, at about the same time, the Scandinavians were invited to Russia to establish order among the belligerent, disorganized Slav warlords.

By the start of the 11th century, a weak king, Ethelred the Unready, allowed his kingdom to fall into confusion. The Danish king Canute invaded the island in 1016, and England became part of an empire that included Denmark and Norway. Canute was followed by his two sons, each of whom died shortly after ascending the throne. Ethelred's son Edward the Confessor, who was half Norman and had lived in Normandy during the reign of Canute and his sons, was placed on the throne. He made two decisions with far-reaching consequences. He founded Westminster Abbey outside of London, starting the separation of the government from the city. Because he was childless, he promised his cousin, William Duke of Normandy, that the throne would one day be his.

The Final Conquest and the First Plantagenets

The year 1066 is to the English school children what 1492 is to Americans. In that year, Edward the Confessor died. The Witan (national council) elected his brother-in-law Harold as his successor. A Norwegian invasion in Yorkshire called Harold to the north. Seizing the opportunity, William landed a Norman force in the south of England. Harold raced south to meet his death—at the Battle of Hastings, he was killed by a sword blow, and William established himself and his Norman lords as rulers of England.

William chose to rule by a rigorous system of feudalism. He established Normans loyal to himself as lords of all the great manors. But they were tenants on the land; ownership was the king's right. The most important lords made up the Great Council, the forerunner of parliament. William also placed Normans in the most important positions in the church hierarchy and ruled that clergy would be tried in ecclesiastical rather than secular courts.

All over England, Norman buildings characterized by massive rectangular towers showed that the conquerors had come to stay. The most notable were the Tower of London and Westminster Hall. Scores of parish churches, castles, and monasteries dotted the landscape. William dispatched Norman legal scholars to go among the people and inquire by what laws (including customs which were virtually laws) they lived. These were organized into the Common Law—the law of the people, which were to be used in secular courts. Whenever William's judges determined the law, that would be uniform law for the entire realm. This greatly pacified the conquered people, since they corresponded with what had prevailed before the Norman conquest. Writs were established which were an intriguing combination of Latin, Anglo-Saxon, and French—*Assumpsit*, *Trespass Quare Clausum Fregit*, *Indebitatus*, etc.

William's great-grandson Henry II (the first of the Plantagenets) came to the throne in 1154. He asserted the power of the king at the expense of the barons by tearing down unlicensed castles and creating a militia instead of depending upon the nobility for armed troops and created traveling judges. The decisions of these judges were based on the Common Law, which operated by establishing written precedents rather than a codified law. Henry II also invaded Ireland and, with the permission of the pope, established himself as king of England's western neighbor. No one could possibly foresee what enormous consequences this would have for England in the years to come—consequences that affect Britain to this day.

Henry might have foreseen the consequences for which he is most remembered. He got into a dispute with his archbishop Thomas Becket over the issue of whether the clergy should be tried in church courts or civil courts. Whether Henry ordered that Becket be killed or merely hinted that it would please him will never be known. But Becket's murder turned him into a martyr and Canterbury into a shrine. Henry's two sons, Richard and John, were low points in the history of the English monarchy. Richard (who came to be known as the Lion-Hearted) spent most of his reign out of the country as a crusader, trying to wrest Jerusalem and Israel from the Arabs. His absence did England little good, but it did provide that great scene in stories and movies where, when he returns to England, he reveals himself to Robin Hood.

Mark H. and Mrs. Martha Mullin chat with Prince Charles.

John was not only ineffective but also very unpopular. He lost English possessions on the Continent, including Normandy, and ran up such a debt that the barons were able to force him to sign the Magna Carta in 1215. This document was not the forward-looking cornerstone of freedom that it is sometimes portrayed to be, but rather it guaranteed the rights that the nobility and the church expected. At the same time, it established the principle that there are limits on the powers of the monarch, and thus it was a first step toward the largely unwritten constitutional monarchy of today.

The 13th century was a time of intellectual growth. Groups of scholars gathered at Oxford, and a splinter group later moved to Cambridge. Roger Bacon was a leading teacher stressing scientific experimentation. The King's Council was expanded to include representatives of shires and boroughs; thus the way was prepared for a representative House of Commons. At the end of the century, Edward I epitomized the medieval monarch. Physically imposing, he aided the growing spirit of nationalism by checking the power of the barons and the church and by increasing English power in Wales and Ireland. However, unsuccessful attempts to invade Scotland led Edward into financial difficulties, and in 1297 he was forced to sign a confirmation of the Magna Carta. He agreed that the king could not impose taxes without the consent of the newborn parliament.

Edward's grandson Edward III attempted to reassert English power on the Continent. In 1337 the Hundred Years, War began. At first, success came to the English, and the war strengthened the nation. However, in 1348 the Black Death (Bubonic Plague) swept the country, and nearly half the population died. The country sank into economic depression, and by the time the king died in 1377, all the lands he had conquered in France had been lost, except for a small area around Calais.

The period produced the first great work of literature in primitive English, Chaucer's *Canterbury Tales*. For centuries, Latin had been spoken by the church and French by the nobility, but now the nation was uniting with the use of the English language.

The War of the Roses and the House of Tudor

Among Edward's sons were John of Gaunt, Duke of Lancaster, and Edmund, Duke of York. During the first half of the 15th century, the Lancaster branch held the throne, but in 1455 the Wars of the Roses, symbolized by the red rose of Lancaster and the white rose of York, subjected the country to a brutal civil war. Shakespeare puts the words "Uneasy lies the head that wears a crown" in the mouth of Henry IV, the first of the Lancastrian kings.

The instability of a monarch's life continued throughout the 15th century. Perhaps the best example was Richard III of the House of York, who usurped the throne by allegedly having two of his nephews, young princes, murdered in the Tower of London. He was brutally assassinated at age 32 in the aftermath of the Battle of Bosworth Field against Henry Tudor of the House of Lancaster in 1485.

The most reviled of English monarchs, Richard III was hastily buried by friars. More than five centuries later, in 2012, he burst into the public eye again when his unmarked skeleton was discovered beneath a city parking lot in Leicester. DNA evidence confirmed the authenticity. In March 2015 he was given a quasi-state funeral. His coffin was marched to Bosworth and back, escorted by people in period dress and suits of armor and greeted by "Long live the king!" He was interred in Leicester Cathedral.

Despite the battles for the throne, the 15th century was one of growing prosperity for England, especially in wool and foreign trade. To this day, the lord chancellor's seat in the House of Lords is a woolsack.

With the arrival of the Tudors, the medieval world drew to a close. During the first Tudor reign (Henry VII), Columbus sailed for the New World. The wealth that Spain acquired there provided constant problems for the Tudors, and it was not until their successors, the Stuarts, that English colonies were firmly established. Soon the winds of the Reformation would bring even greater changes to England.

King Henry VIII

Anne Boleyn

Henry arranged for his eldest son, Arthur, to marry Catherine of Aragon, daughter of the king of Spain. This was a particularly important match for diplomatic reasons, because Spain controlled the Netherlands through which much of English trade entered the Continent.

Arthur died in 1502 before his father. Despite both scriptural and canon law injunctions against marrying one's brother's widow, the pope granted a dispensation allowing Arthur's brother Henry to marry the young widow. Henry's sister Margaret married the king of Scotland, thus providing England with marital allies on several sides. When Henry VIII assumed the throne after his father's death, he realized the importance of a male heir. But his union with Catherine only produced a daughter, Mary. It is important to note that Henry was initially loyal to Roman Catholicism, and because of a work he authored attacking the doctrines of Martin Luther, the pope granted him the title "Defender of the Faith." It is ironic that his non–Roman Catholic descendants still carry that title.

Because Henry realized that Catherine would not produce a son, and because he was lusting after the attractive, dark-haired Anne Boleyn, he asked the pope to grant him an annulment of his marriage to Catherine, claiming that it had been illegal in the first place. Unfortunately for Henry, Catherine's uncle Charles V of the Holy Roman Empire had his troops in Rome at the time. When the pope refused to grant Henry's request, in an unprecedented move, Henry had himself declared head of the church in England. His marriage to Anne Boleyn, however, produced only a daughter, Elizabeth, and Henry then proceeded through four more wives, making six in all, only one of whom produced a son, Edward. Pupils learn to keep track of Henry's wives by the saying "Divorced, beheaded, died, divorced, beheaded, survived."

Edward VI followed his father to the throne in 1547 at 11 years of age. His guardians moved the country rapidly in the direction of Protestantism. But the sickness-prone boy died six years later (he was possibly murdered), and the first of Henry's daughters, Mary Tudor, assumed the throne. Had Mary wanted to move England back to the religious position of her father, she probably would have lasted. But she felt a calling to return the nation to full Roman Catholicism and further alienated her subjects by taking Philip of Spain as her husband.

Although the number of resisting Protestants who were burned at the stake was actually quite small, there were enough prominent bishops ignited to earn the queen the historical title of "Bloody Mary." The words of one of these bishops—"Be of good cheer, Master Ridley, we shall today light such a candle as will by God's grace never be extinguished in England"—proved to be prophetic. On Mary's death after only five years on the throne, her half-sister, Elizabeth I, became queen, and with her, one of the great ages in English history began.

The Elizabethan Period

Since the Catholic Church considered Elizabeth illegitimate, she moved the country back toward Protestantism. It was a moderate protestant position, with the old forms of worship retained in English and no vigorous attempt to be overly scrupulous in matters of doctrine. As Elizabeth put it, "We shall make no window into any man's soul." Elizabeth's cousin Mary Stuart abdicated the throne of Scotland in favor of her son James and fled to England. For years, Roman Catholic attempts to oust Elizabeth flurried around Mary, who was Catholic. Despite "that divinity that doth hedge a king" (or queen), Elizabeth finally yielded to the advice of her court and had Mary beheaded in 1587.

That same year, Sir Francis Drake, having already stolen Spanish gold from the New World, raided the port of Cadiz. In reprisal, the next year Spain sent a Great Armada to invade and conquer England. But a "Protestant wind" and English naval tactics carried the day; less than half of the armada managed to limp back to Spain. England had established itself as a ruler of the seas, a position it would continue to enjoy for almost 400 years.

The Elizabethan Age was a flowering of English culture, and the brightest blooms were uses of the language that still affect our thought and speech. Although William Shakespeare was the most magnificent of the blossoms, others, such as Spenser, Drayton, Donne, and Marlowe, bloomed in the sunshine.

The United Kingdom

Thomas Cranmer produced a *Book of Common Prayer* in 1549 whose magnificent collects shaped the way the English-speaking world addressed God and whose words start the most important ceremony in most people's lives: "Dearly beloved, we are gathered here together in the sight of God and in the face of this company to join together this man and this woman in holy matrimony: which is an honorable estate instituted of God, signifying unto us the mystical union that is betwixt Christ and His church." The musical liturgy of the book was done with assistance from Lutherans, who had retained Catholic plainsong chant traditions in German; they were adapted to English. Further, harmonized Anglican chant was first produced. All of this is preserved with little change in many churches to this day.

In the last part of Elizabeth's reign, William Shakespeare began to write his plays. Their plots shape our view of history, or romance, and humor, and his phrases fill our speaking and our reading, even when we do not know the source of the words. Finally, shortly after Elizabeth's death, the language of the *Book of Common Prayer* and the language of Shakespeare came together in the most influential of all English books, the King James Bible. Until recently, it was read by more people than any other book in the English language, and for many Americans on the frontier, it was their only book in the English language. It has been only in the past five decades that serious attention was paid to any of the "modern" English translations.

The Tudor monarchs were able to dominate England by their political skill and by the force of their personality. All except Edward and Mary enjoyed considerable popularity, and if those who followed them had enjoyed similar success, the Parliament might have melted out of British life. But the Stuarts, of whom it could be said, "They learned nothing and forgot nothing," tried to push the doctrine of the divine right of kings farther than the English wished to have it carried. When Elizabeth died unmarried in 1603, James Stuart, king of Scotland, became James I of England, and the whole island was united under one monarch.

The Stuarts' Brief Tenure

The second of the Stuarts, Charles I, came to the throne in 1625. He soon began to have trouble with Parliament over taxation, and his inflexibility and demands for royal absolutism only angered the democratic movement within the country. Moreover, Charles was a "high" churchman, with Roman Catholic leanings, and most members of Parliament were Puritan Protestant in inclination (i.e., a full, chanted Eucharistic service with all ceremonial acts, including incense, holy water, etc., versus three hymns, a psalm, lessons, and sermon). For 11 years Charles managed to rule without Parliament, and his persecution of Puritans led to the founding of the colonies in New England. In order to raise revenues, Charles reconvened Parliament in 1640, and soon civil war broke out in England. Catholics, high churchmen, the nobility, and the rural people of the north and west supported the king; Puritans, people of trade and commerce, and most important, Londoners, supported Parliament.

Religious and Civil Turmoil

Unlike the Wars of the Roses, the civil war of the 17th century was not simply a fight over who should occupy the throne but also an ideological struggle to determine the very nature of English society. Oliver Cromwell emerged as leader of the parliamentary forces after Charles had been captured. Cromwell purged Parliament of all but his loyal supporters, abolished the House of Lords, and in 1649 had Charles beheaded. He was the only English monarch to die for religious reasons and the last to be killed for political reasons. Whether Charles was a martyr for the causes of royal stability and the Anglican Church or whether he justly died for opposing the representatives of the people depends on one's viewpoint—and perhaps both views are true.

The Commonwealth Period and Return of Monarchy

Cromwell had hoped to rule in a liberal and democratic way, but continued factionalism and the threatening anarchy in English society caused him to assume absolute power as Lord Protector. This

Queen Mary I

Queen Elizabeth I

period was known as the Commonwealth. When Cromwell died in 1658 and the monarchy was restored in 1660, Charles II, the son of the dead king, returned from the Continent, to which he had escaped, and was greeted by a joyful people.

During Charles' reign, English culture extricated itself from the heavy burden of Puritanism and flourished again; Bunyan, Milton, and Pepys were the most famous writers. The Great Fire of 1666 destroyed much of London but allowed such master architects as Christopher Wren to rebuild a new and even more glorious city. On another continent, the Dutch were driven out of North America, and New Amsterdam became New York.

James II followed his brother to the throne but did not renounce his faith in Roman Catholicism. The English then turned to William of Orange, a grandson of Charles I, who came to England and later defeated James in the July 1690 Battle of the Boyne in Ireland. From then on, the fact that England was Anglican (not Roman Catholic or Puritan) was settled. But both William of Orange and his wife were childless. The most logical successor was Queen Anne, daughter of James II, but she died childless in 1714. What was the answer for a people accustomed to a monarchy?

The House of Hanover (Later Windsor) and Parliament Power

Britain turned to George of Hanover (a great-grandson of James I and a Protestant) to become king. The fact that he could speak no English (only German) was of immense importance. It meant that the king had to leave many of his powers in the hands of the chairmanship of his council, and that person was the leader of the Whig Party, with a majority in the House of Commons. Thus, England developed the tradition of having a prime minister preside over a cabinet that grew out of Parliament.

During the middle part of the 18th century, the first British Empire took shape. English forces defeated the French for control of much of India, and the defeat of the French forces at Quebec in 1759 meant that Canada and the area west of the 13 colonies were brought under British rule. In 1760, George III succeeded to the throne. Since he believed a king should rule the country, he suspended the cabinet government, intending that the king and the "king's friends" would rule.

As the British Empire expanded with Captain Cook's discovery of Australia, relations with the 13 American colonies deteriorated. By 1782 they had been victorious in their revolution, and the period of the First British Empire was largely over. With the disaster in North America came the return of the cabinet system to England, as William Pitt the Younger became the new prime minister. For the next 50 years, the Tories would lead the country and maintain a steady and conservative posture while the French Revolution and then the armies of Napoleon forced Britain once again to demonstrate its mastery of the seas.

George III (1738–1820)

19th-Century Change

At the turn of the century, the Act of Union dissolved the Irish parliament and incorporated Catholic Ireland into the United Kingdom. Tragically, religious persecution of the Catholics kept the Irish from full integration into British society, and thus, the union was doomed from the start.

But change was occurring in England. The Industrial Revolution, gradual at first, gathered momentum. Early machines made of wood were replaced by stronger and more efficient ones of iron. James Watt's inventions harnessed the power of steam. Reforms in agriculture improved food production but caused many farmers to leave the land. Thus, as industry and commerce were growing, along with the wealth and power of those who controlled them, so, too, there was a growing urban class kept in degrading poverty. As populations shifted, Parliament became less representative.

In so-called rotten boroughs, a few voters could control who was elected to Parliament. In one district in Cornwall, a single voter could elect two members! It is coincidental but symbolic that in 1830 the Reforming Whigs Party obtained a majority in Parliament and the first railroad line on which the Rocket whizzed along at 35 miles an hour was opened.

The Whigs were able to get their Reform Bill through Parliament in 1832. This most important piece of legislation abolished many "rotten" boroughs, gave representation to the new towns, and significantly lowered the property qualifications necessary to be a voter. Many observers think that this Reform Bill saved the country from revolution, which had become so popular in the rest of Europe. Certainly, it gave new power to the middle classes and was an important step toward mass democracy.

The United Kingdom

John Constable's *Hay Wain* (1821) National Gallery, London

Victoria

In 1837 the 18-year-old Victoria began the longest reign in British history. As the last half of the 17th century had belonged to Elizabeth, so the 19th century belonged to Victoria. During Victoria's reign, reform acts gradually increased the number of people enfranchised and gave protection to the lower classes. The repeal of the "Corn Laws" and free trade not only stimulated industry but also reduced the cost of living for the poor. Thus, under the leadership of such greats as Palmerston, Gladstone, and Disraeli, Parliament found a course that kept England moving toward democracy without being caught up in the excesses that racked so much of the Continent. By 1846 Canada had been made self-governing, and within a few years, Australia and New Zealand were given internal self-rule. Thus, the concept of the empire of free countries bound to the mother country by loyalty to the queen was born.

Two great events marked the reign of Victoria. The Great Exhibition of 1851 demonstrated British industrial might and middle-class prosperity, whereas the Golden Jubilee of the queen in 1887 marked the high point of the empire. The claim that the sun never set on the British Empire was indeed true. Its members included Canada in North America, British Guiana in South America; the United Kingdom in Europe; South Africa, Kenya, and Somaliland in Africa; India and Ceylon in Asia; and Australia and New Zealand in the Pacific. The greatest problem, however, was closest to home, and various attempts to solve the Irish problem through home rule were unsuccessful.

Until 1900 the roar of the British lion could be heard throughout the world. Britain controlled over one-fifth of the earth's land surface and ruled a quarter of the world's population. Its flag flew on every continent, and the largest and most powerful navy in the world protected its magnificent empire. At the same time, Britain was invulnerable to foreign invasion. This meant that, unlike many other nations with frontiers instead of shorelines, it could leisurely develop a democratic form of government. Nations under the constant threat of attack often could not afford the luxury of a relatively inefficient and cumbersome governmental order that involved parliamentary meetings, long debates, votes, press coverage, and criticism. As a nation equally invulnerable, the Americans shared this advantage with their English forebears.

Also, Britain did not need to maintain a large standing army. As the history of many countries indicates, ambitious soldiers led by prestigious officers close to the political heart of the country sometimes cannot resist meddling in the political affairs of a nation. The British never had difficulty in maintaining control over their military; a military putsch is unthinkable in the British context. Fortunately, the tradition of civilian supremacy over the military was passed on to many (though not all) of its former colonies, including the United States.

Political Power Struggles and Social Change

A watershed year in the growth of power of the House of Commons was 1911. The Liberal Party government had proposed a land tax, and although tradition had it that only Commons controlled finances, the House of Lords rejected the bill. The Parliament bill of 1911 deprived the Lords of any control of finance and limited their power over other bills to a two-year delay. In a move to make the Commons more responsive to the popular will, the maximum life of a Parliament was reduced from seven to five years. When it appeared that the Lords would veto this bill, George V threatened to increase the number of Lords and pack the Upper House with those favorable to the bill. The Lords yielded to the threat, and thereafter the House of Commons gained virtual total control of legislation. In the same year, members of the House of Commons began to receive pay, and thus, those without independent incomes could be in Parliament.

World War I, known then as the "Great War," devastated a generation of Englishmen. In 2009 the last survivor among the millions of British soldiers who fought in the trenches, Harry Patch, died at age 111. But the bloody conflict helped to produce changes in society. As recognition for their part in the war effort, women received the vote in 1918. Because they involved so much of the population, both world wars did much to further popular democracy and reduce the differences between social classes. Shortly after World

THE BRITISH NAVY guards the freedom of us all

War I, the southern part of Ireland left the United Kingdom and achieved dominion status as the Irish Free State. Protestants living in the north clung tenaciously to their membership in the United Kingdom and their loyalty to the Crown, but their conflict with Catholics living alongside them has not been solved to this day.

Following World War I, trade unions grew in power and were able to call a general strike in 1926. But the Great Depression of the 1930s significantly reduced the power of the Labour government, and the conservatives led the country in the years before World War II. The last crisis to affect the monarchy occurred in 1936. Edward VIII ascended the throne, but within months he abdicated so that he could marry the divorced Wallis Simpson, an American.

The Hitler Threat and World War II

As Hitler began to threaten more and more of Europe, Prime Minister Neville Chamberlain practiced a policy of appeasement. This only whetted the German appetite; after an attack on Poland in September 1939, Britain joined France as allies in World War II. In May of the next year, Winston Churchill became prime minister. His courage and his words epitomized the best of the British spirit. They inspired the nation to rescue 340,000 British and French soldiers from the beaches of Dunkirk and to withstand withering aerial attacks from bombers and rockets in the Battle of Britain, launched in 1940. Germany's Operation Sealion was the first invasion of England since 1066. With tremendous but belated assistance from the US, Britain and its allies were victorious. But the United Kingdom was prostrated and devastated by the end of the conflict in 1945.

The Postwar 1940s and 1950s

Two world wars in the 20th century brought enormous changes. These included revolutions in many European countries; the rise of the United States and the Soviet Union as the most powerful countries in the world; and the relative decline of the traditional global powers, including the United Kingdom, in terms of political and military significance. As a victorious ally, Britain gained a veto right in the United Nations Security Council, but it had to liquidate most of its foreign investments to finance its own recovery; these foreign investments had once paid for a third of British imports. The merchant marine was depleted, and factories and equipment were either destroyed or obsolete.

The negative economic consequences of the wars reduced Britain's ability to be a global power and stimulated in many British colonies the desire for independence. By proclaiming the Truman Doctrine, the US assumed from Britain the burden of economic and military aid to Greece and Turkey and relieved the UK of its responsibility for supporting the struggle against communist forces in the Greek civil war. The British also found themselves in the crossfire between Jews and Arabs in Palestine and Hindus and Muslims in India and were forced in 1947 to abandon both important regions. In 1952 it lost control of Egypt. When Egypt seized the Suez Canal in 1956, Britain, supported by France and Israel, attempted to reconquer that important waterway. However, stiff joint United Nations, US and Soviet opposition to this move, which seemed like the last gasp of colonialism, forced the British, French, and Israelis to back down.

In 1959 Britain still ruled over 53 countries with a population of 81 million, and 86,000 British troops were deployed around the world outside of Europe. But the floodgates opened, and by the 1960s a tidal wave of separations swept through Africa, the Middle East, and Asia. Having lost most of its Asian empire in the late 1940s, the British recognized the inevitability of African independence. Fortunately, Britain had trained many Africans as capable administrators and had established there a relatively efficient system of local administration. Therefore, when they gradually relinquished their hold, well-trained Africans were usually able to take their places. An exception was Rhodesia, whose tiny white minority took power in 1965 and held it for years before finally handing the reins of power to the new black-ruled state of Zimbabwe.

Britain spearheaded the international UN boycott of Rhodesia. But the UK was in the throes of such economic distress that it was not only unable to steer events in Africa but it was also forced in 1971 to terminate most of its military and political responsibilities "east of Suez." This withdrawal was unfortunate for the US, which was trapped at the time in the quagmire of Vietnam. The US felt compelled to assume Britain's prior responsibility for maintaining "stability" in the Middle East. It thereby became embroiled in one of the world's least stable regions. This untimely responsibility prompted American administrations in the 1970s to help build up the shah's power. The hope was that a modernized and well-armed Iran could maintain order in the oil-rich Persian Gulf region and keep the Soviet Union's power and influence out of the area. The Americans paid heavily in the 1980s for this gamble.

Elizabeth II succeeded her father, George VI, on the British throne in 1952. Thirty generations separated her from her ancestor William the Conqueror, and she began her reign in a nation struggling to find a new role in the modern world. The empire became a commonwealth of independent nations, bound together by language, democratic principles, and a residue of loyalty to the person (but not the power) of the British monarch. Decolonization had a serious negative economic impact on Britain by depriving it of many protected markets, sources of raw materials at low prices, and cheap food. The resulting economic difficulties harassed the United Kingdom for a quarter century following the Second World War.

Domestic Politics before Thatcher

On July 5, 1945, voters delivered a dramatic blow to the Tories by electing the first Labour prime minister with a clear majority of 145 seats in the House of Commons, Clement Attlee. Although the British deeply admired Churchill as a great wartime leader, they associated his Conservative Party with the soup lines and unemployment of the prewar Depression. Labour had ably guided the home ministries in the national government during the war. It had impressed the British as being the best team for creating full employment, housing, and better social security and health care for a people who had just sacrificed so much in the war effort.

Although ideologically divided, as always, between more pragmatic and radical wings, the Labour Party moved boldly to make many sweeping economic changes, including the nationalization of the Bank of England, hospitals, railways, aviation, and public transport and the gas, electrical, coal, and steel industries. Unlike France and Italy, though, the newly nationalized industries were placed under the direction of autonomous corporations (subsidized from the state treasury) rather

Horse guardsmen leaving their barracks for duty at Buckingham Palace

than government agencies and ministries. In 1946 the National Insurance Act and National Health Service Act were the prime examples of popular social welfare legislation which strengthened or created old-age pensions, unemployment compensation, education, social insurance, and free health service. No sooner were these innovations in place, though, than the Labour government began losing popularity. It was badly divided, British influence abroad was noticeably eroding, the pound was losing its value, and economic recovery was painfully slow.

At age 77 Winston Churchill was returned to power in 1951, and his Tories ruled until 1964, the longest period of continuous party government in modern British history until Margaret Thatcher and John Major ruled 18 years from 1979 to 1997. His government returned the iron and steel industries and road transport to private ownership, although Labour renationalized iron and steel in 1967. However, accurately sensing the sentiments of the British nation, the Tories did not make a radical U-turn. It accepted the national welfare and health services, as well as the commitment to full employment.

Following a stroke, Churchill was finally persuaded to step down in 1955. His successor was his longtime foreign minister Anthony Eden. After only a year, Eden had to resign in the aftermath of the Suez crisis of 1956. He was followed by Harold Macmillan, who, like Churchill, had an American mother. He optimistically predicted a turnaround in Britain's economic fortunes (for which reason he was dubbed "Supermac"). There was a short-lived economic boom in the late 1950s, and the living standards of some British rose. But inequalities of wealth remained which the government could not alleviate because of a rising imbalance of payments and a serious sterling crisis. Britain was obviously not keeping up with its international trade competitors,

Winston S. Churchill, surrounded by the royal family

and management and trade unions were not inclined to introduce more efficient and modern methods of production. In an attempt to protect the value of the pound, the government had to introduce an unpopular wage freeze and raise the bank rate. Macmillan sought to halt the growing economic malaise and increase British industry's competitiveness by leading Britain into the EU, but French president Charles de Gaulle vetoed its entry in 1963.

Following this humiliation came the coup de grace for the Macmillan government: a lurid sex scandal involving Secretary of War John Profumo. He was alleged to be involved with a call girl who had been asked by the Soviet naval attaché to gather information from him on the UK's nuclear weapons. No government could possibly benefit from such a spicy and embarrassing affair. But what forced Macmillan to demand Profumo's resignation was not so much the illicit activity itself as the fact that he had insulted Parliament by lying to it about his involvement. He thereby dragged both himself and the prime minister down.

The colorless Sir Alec Douglas-Home replaced Macmillan in the fall of 1963. Home (pronounced Hume) was a rare example of a prime minister being drawn from the House of Lords, even though he scrambled to win a by-election seat to the Commons. He had sat in the Commons earlier, but when his father died, he was obligated to become a Lord. Parliament passed a law permitting Lords to renounce their title. Home could not quiet the growing desire for a change, and with only a razor-thin majority, he could not prevent Harold Wilson's Labour Party from winning power in October 1964.

A former Oxford University economics don (lecturer), Wilson was from the more conservative, reformist wing of the Labour Party. Faced with daunting economic problems, he not only pared down the UK's military commitments abroad, but he also applied the traditional conservative policies of increasing taxes and reducing government spending. These unpopular economic policies widened ideological divisions within his own party, sparked industrial unrest and strikes and brought Wilson into a head-on collision with the trade unions. Widening trade imbalances, another devaluation of the pound, and a renewal of strife between Catholics and Protestants in Northern Ireland all spelled disaster for Wilson in the June 1970 elections, when the Tories, led by Edward Heath, returned to power.

Heath's government knew little happiness, aside from Britain's entry into the EU in 1973. His bitter confrontations with the assertive coal miners brought serious economic disruptions and forced the prime minister to declare states of emergency five times. The crippling coal strike in the winter of 1973–1974 destroyed what credibility remained for the cabinet. Voters brought Wilson's Labour Party back to power in February 1974 on the assumption that they would have better relations with the powerful unions.

Wilson had only a miniscule majority, which he widened in a snap election in October 1974. He expended precious energy and patience fending off an ambitious radical left wing within his own party which sniped at him constantly and openly advocated such unpopular policies as a "socialist transformation" of British society, massive nationalizations of large companies, the abolition of such elite institutions as the House of Lords and private schools, withdrawal from NATO and the EU, and unilateral disarmament. These leftist antics ultimately drove some moderates out of the party and led to the formation in 1981 of the now-defunct Social Democratic Party (SDP).

It is hardly surprising that Wilson was unable to improve the economic situation. The skyrocketing price of oil resulting from the 1973 OPEC embargo hit the struggling British economy hard, despite the discovery of oil in Britain's own sectors of the North Sea. Inflation rose to a dizzying level, and for the first time since the war, unemployment reared its ugly head. These problems made hopes for harmonious labor relations a pipe dream, as the spate of disruptive strikes indicated. In 1976 an exasperated and tired Harold Wilson turned the keys to Number 10 Downing Street over to his foreign minister, James Callaghan. The new prime minister was no more successful than Wilson had been in controlling the unions, improving the overall economy, and coping with rising violence in Northern Ireland and growing separatist movements in Scotland and Wales.

It has been said that the world stands aside for a man who knows where he is going. By the spring of 1979, the British voters were prepared to do just that, with one historical twist: They brought to power the first woman prime minister in British politics, Margaret Thatcher. She acted with such determination and decisiveness that, by January 3, 1988, she had become the longest continuously serving British prime minister in the 20th century. Ruling over a country with the highest economic growth of any major economy, low inflation, declining unemployment, a rising pound, and tamed unions, she had every reason to believe that she would remain at the helm into the 21st century and perhaps even overtake the record of Sir Robert Walpole, whose 21 consecutive years of service as prime minister began in 1721.

Attitude and Political Change

Terrorism related to the unsolved problem of Northern Ireland, along with rising crime in Britain, helped shift British voters' view of the world in an important way. It helped many of them shape a tough-minded attitude and become more receptive to political appeals based on "law and order," replacing the compromise politics of the 1960s.

The parliamentary elections of 1979 and 1983 took many foreign observers by surprise because they revealed that the political landscape in Britain had dramatically changed. Upon closer scrutiny, it can be seen that these changes are the consequence of important changes in Britain's economy and society in the course of the 1970s. Those changes broke down much of the class structure of Britain, which traditionally had shaped British politics to such a large extent.

Public opinion polls and election analyses continually confirm that fewer and fewer British spontaneously identify with a particular class and that class-consciousness has and is declining markedly. Class itself has become only one of many factors shaping individual attitudes and preferences. It has become harder to classify Britons by class, which has increasingly become more a matter of taste and culture rather than of income and occupation. With less than a quarter of workers in manufacturing jobs, fewer than two workers in five belong to a labor union. Two-thirds of all British own or are buying their homes; even one of three unskilled manual laborers is a homeowner. Also, leisure is no longer the privilege of a few; instead, almost all full-time workers receive four weeks of leave. In short, more workers have become middle class. Young people from all economic strata mingle more easily and are more likely to intermarry than they used to. Since Britons have become more individualistic, their social attitudes and political behavior have become less predictable. These changes are bound to have a negative effect on political parties whose appeals have traditionally been heavily class-based, especially the Labour Party.

Since 1979, Britain's population has barely grown, but the size of the electorate increased from 39.3 million in 1970 to 42.2 million in 1983. The voting age was dropped to 18 in 1970, but the number of pensioners has grown, so the average voter today is actually older than in 1970. He or she is also more highly educated; more likely to be divorced and live alone or in small households; own his own home; and, despite high unemployment, have a higher standard of living than in the 1970s. Disenchantment with unions and changes in social patterns (see "Culture") that were occurring in the 1970s set the stage for dramatic political shifts in Britain. After 1979 these effectively altered much of the conventional wisdom about British politics and realigned the structure.

Although the diminishing numbers of unionized workers in the mines and factories retained their traditional loyalty to the Labour Party and the managers remained steadfast to the Conservative Party, their diminishing numbers hoisted the flag of change on the pole in the 1970s. Soaring inflation and rising unemployment, accompanied by increasingly strident union demands, alienated the people. Their revulsion at the excessive "unelected power" which union bosses wielded boiled to the surface in "the winter of discontent," 1978–1979, when coal and transportation strikes threatened to paralyze the entire nation.

These changes led to conditions whereby a party leader would advocate a policy based on the notions that the best help was self-help; that initiative deserved rewards; that an economic pie must be baked before it is divided; that welfare could not produce prosperity; that private business is better than nationalized industries; that the problem of inflation is more important than the problem of unemployment; and, finally, that the government cannot control the economy. In other words, traditional Keynesian economics was no cure for British problems but was part of the disease. That leader was Margaret Thatcher, leader of the Conservative Party (Tory) since 1975, who was elected prime minister in 1979. Leading a changed party, she captured the mood of an altered society and spoke for the new social realities.

Return to the Conservative Party

When she moved into the prime minister's office, she promised "three years of unparalleled austerity," and for three years the pain of Thatcherism was far more evident than the benefits. Unemployment rose, and economic conditions worsened. She was unable to cut government spending significantly because of greater numbers on welfare and pay raises for government workers to bring them into equity with the private sector. Nevertheless, the "Iron Lady," as she began to be called, held firm to her monetarist policies (restricting the money supply) and vowed, "I will not stagger from expedient to expedient." By 1982 her party was well behind the Labour Party in the polls, and she seemed to be heading for sure defeat in the next elections, when the unexpected occurred.

The Falklands War

Argentine troops invaded and captured a small group of offshore islands that had long been settled and ruled by the British. Mrs. Thatcher galvanized the nation with her firmness and resolution in organizing the recapture of the Falklands Islands. The British basked again briefly in imperial glory, and an overwhelming majority of them applauded their leader for her ability to deal with a crisis, winning back control of the islands, albeit at a tremendous financial cost. The Falklands War boosted her party's popularity, and the economy fortuitously began to revive at the same time, with inflation shrinking to the lowest level in 15 years. The electorate became convinced that her economic medicine had been a harsh necessity and that she was a true leader. Sensing the political winds blowing briskly at her back, she took advantage of the prime minister's privilege to set an election whenever it suits his or her party. It was called for June 1983 and demonstrated beyond doubt that the party landscape had greatly changed and that a new Conservative Party had become the dominant force in British politics by the mid-1980s.

Her astonishing electoral triumph in June 1983, which made her the first Conservative prime minister in the 20th century to be reelected to a second term, revealed both her leadership image, established in the Falklands War, and the extent to which most social and economic groups in Britain accepted her diagnosis of the nation's problems. Most voters did not even blame her for the country's most pressing problem: continuing unemployment, which shot up from 5.4% to 13.3% during her four years of rule. They clearly patted her on the back for bringing inflation down.

"The Iron Lady"

She was a fundamentally cautious politician, whose bark was often more powerful than her bite. She did take modest steps to return some of the nationalized industries to private hands, but she did not precipitously withdraw the public from the economy; in 1988 government spending amounted to 42% of GNP, about the same as in 1979. Nor did she dramatically reduce public employment, welfare assistance, or taxes; she disliked spending what she did not have. Therefore, most voters did not see in her a fanatic ideologue who wished to turn the clock backward.

She never enjoyed "popularity," as her many nicknames reveal: "Leaderene," "Attila the Hen," "Rhoda the Rhino," and "Nanny," to mention only a few of the "kinder" ones. Many saw her as uncaring, cold, and obsessed. But she had authority and respect because of what she accomplished and what she represents. She strode firmly forward to remake her country in her own self-image: brisk, hardworking, frugal, and self-sufficient. She combined some of the best 19th-century values with 20th-century energy. She was a strong leader who entered office with a sense of mission: to make Britain great again. Of course, she benefited from an opposition that was in disarray.

Part of Thatcher's appeal was that she represented a new kind of Conservative Party that had emerged. The image of the party as the preserve of the landed gentry, bankers, or high-level civil servants, which could display charity when needed toward the lower classes and which assembled in prayer in the Church of England, has changed.

The attitude of most citizens, an overwhelming majority of whom are baptized Protestant, is now indifference toward religion—its traditional role in politics has all but vanished. Tory leaders cannot count on the support of the Church of England, containing many clergy bitterly opposed to its policies.

Thatcher was an example of the "new" kind of Tory, who worked her way up in the world. The daughter of a dressmaker and grocer from Grantham, Lincolnshire, she lived with her family in an apartment above the shop and worked all her childhood in her father's store. She studied

Mr. Denis Thatcher and former prime minister Thatcher

Hyde Park Corner, London

chemistry at Oxford, where she led the Conservative student organization and held off-campus jobs. She later acquired a law degree after marrying a successful businessman, Denis Thatcher, who served as the nation's "First Gentleman," staying a discreet half-pace behind the prime minister. She was never an insider in "the establishment," and she harbored a bias against the party elite. She served only four years in the early 1970s as education secretary before gaining the party leadership in 1975.

Having emerged from the middle class herself, she was well able to forge an alliance between skilled workers and the middle class in a society which is becoming more and more middle class. She capitalized on the dream of owning one's home by giving residents of government-built houses the opportunity to buy them at bargain prices. About a half-million gratefully did so. This was the greatest transfer of wealth to the British working class in history. By the time her Tory Party was voted out of power in 1997, 68% of all housing units were owner-occupied, a higher percentage than in the United States or elsewhere in Europe.

She benefited from a transformation within the party, which extends from the grassroots all the way up to Parliament. Its seats are no longer occupied primarily by traditional local notables but increasingly by insurance agents, housewives, teachers, salesmen, and self-made middle-management types. Perhaps as good an example of the new kind of Tory as Thatcher herself was a speaker of the House, Bruce Bernard Weatherill, a former tailor who always carried in his pocket a thimble to remind himself of his humble background. It is said that, when he entered Parliament, one aristocratic Conservative MP was overheard saying to another, "I don't know what this place is coming to, Tom: they've got my tailor in here now!" The point is that the tailor to whom they were referring was a Tory.

In April 2013 Lady Thatcher died of a stroke in a suite in London's Ritz Hotel. There was an outpouring of sympathy, reverence, and respect. She was hailed as Britain's greatest peacetime prime minister and "the great transformer." A special session of Parliament debated for seven hours her importance for Britain. The queen granted her a funeral with military honors in St. Paul's Cathedral costing £10 million ($16 million). She agreed to attend, the first time since Winston Churchill's death in 1965 that she was present at a former prime minister's funeral. However, there were many reminders of how divisive and hated she had been. "Death parties" were held in major cities with banners reading "Rejoice, Rejoice!" The song, "Ding Dong: The Witch Is Dead," shot up to number 1 in the pop music charts. A coal miners' unionist proclaimed, "It's a great day. She did more damage to us than Hitler did." Another unemployed coal miner added, "Mrs. Thatcher? She should rot in hell for what she did to us."

GOVERNMENT

Simplicity and Flexibility

Speaking of his country, the great Victorian prime minister Benjamin Disraeli stated, "In a progressive country, change is constant, and the great question is not whether you should resist change which is inevitable, but whether that change should be carried out in deference to the manners, the customs, the laws and the traditions of the people." Americans often imagine the British as a conservative nation. In fact, Britain has skillfully adjusted to change for centuries, and today it confronts fundamental shifts in its society, economy, political system, and place in the world. The British genius is to combine astonishing continuity with necessary change; they excel in pouring "new wine into old bottles."

Great Britain remains a monarchy with a noble class that still enjoys certain privileges. However, Britain is the birthplace for the most durable democratic model of government in the world. Unlike the complicated American democratic system, which has almost never been successfully adapted to other societies, the "Westminster model" not only fits the British people and circumstances, but it can quite easily be made to fit other nations, as well. Its secret lies in its simplicity and its flexibility. It can be modified and tailored to other peoples' needs and circumstances without losing its essentially democratic character.

British politics operates according to an unwritten constitution that prescribes the "rules of the game" and places limits on the rulers. In the UK voters elect 650 members of the House of Commons, the lower house of Parliament. The leader of the party that wins a majority of the seats (or has more seats than any other party) becomes the prime minister, the most powerful political figure in the land. The monarch is the head of state, but her role is largely symbolic; she makes no important political decisions. The prime minister selects other ministers, who are also parliamentary leaders in the party, to sit in the cabinet.

Contrasts with the US

Unlike the United States, where both houses of Congress are equally powerful, the British upper house, the House of Lords, has far less power than the House of Commons. Also, unlike in the United States, there is neither "separation of power" among the executive, legislative, or judicial branches nor a distribution of political powers among the national government and many state governments. Executive and legislative powers are fused, and the prime minister is both the chief executive and the chief legislator. Through party discipline the prime minister controls the House of Commons. Further, political power is concentrated in the central government. Britain is a *unitary*, not a *federal*, state, so he/she does not have to contend with separate states that wield constitutionally granted powers of their own. No court in the country can judge a law unconstitutional. Parliamentary supremacy is the fundamental principle of British government.

This setup is the basic model for most democracies in the world. Even the founders of the American government, whose political views had been shaped by British political ideas but who had consciously sought to depart from that model, adopted more from the British system than many Americans care to remember. After all, what the founders had deemed to be so unjust and tyrannical was the fact that Americans had been "denied their rights as Englishmen." Even the arguments and wording of the Declaration of Independence bear striking resemblance to the work by the 17th-century English philosopher John Locke, entitled *The Second Treatise of Government*, an important blueprint and philosophical foundation for British government.

The American Founding Fathers were certainly aware of their debt to Westminster when they included in the American Constitution such provisions as the necessity of senatorial confirmation of cabinet ministers, congressional election of the president in the event that no candidate wins a majority in the electoral college, and the possibility for the national legislature to impeach and remove a president. It is indeed fitting that the statue on the top of the Capitol faces toward London, symbolic of the extent to which the American government, the political habits, and the thinking of its people have been shaped by Great Britain.

The Unwritten Constitution

As the British political system is more closely examined, perhaps the first striking aspect is the fact that the country's constitution is *unwritten*; that is, there is no single document, as in the United States. One must refer to one or all of five sources to know what is constitutional: First are particularly important documents, such as the Magna Charta (1215); the Habeas Corpus Act (1679); the Bill of Rights (1689), which, unlike the American Bill of Rights, defines rights of Parliament, not rights of individual citizens; the Parliament Act of 1911; and the Statute of Westminster (1931). Then there are interpretations of courts of law and principles of common law (which has itself been in a constant state of change). For example, basic individual liberties, such as the freedom of assembly, speech, and religion, are all derived from common law. There is the Law and Custom of Parliament, which deals with the special privileges which Parliament and each member of Parliament (known as MP) enjoy.

Finally there are wholly unwritten elements, known as conventions. These include such practices as: Parliament must meet at least once a year, the government must resign if it loses a vote of confidence, and the monarch cannot attend cabinet meetings or enter Parliament without permission. On the occasion of her Diamond Jubilee on December 18, 2012, the cabinet invited her attend one of its meetings. This was the first time in more than a century that this honor had been extended. On the same day, a large expanse of Britain's Antarctic territory was christened Queen Elizabeth Land.

The monarch always opens Parliament with a speech from the throne in the House of Lords. She is there in all her finery, displaying the majesty and royal tradition that stretch back continuously over so many centuries. Yet, she is surrounded by members of Parliament, freely elected by the people and operating within the context of an effective multiparty system. Her speech does not contain her own ideas but puts forward the program of the prime minister and the government which holds a majority in the lower house of Parliament. Members of the opposition party, often called the "Loyal Opposition," listen to it. Because the monarch delivers the speech, tradition requires that even critics refer to it as "the gracious speech." For example, opposition leader John Major responded to Prime Minister Tony Blair's text read by the queen in May 1997 as follows: "The road to hell is paved with good intentions, and this gracious speech is very full of good intentions."

Perhaps no other idea has been a more important gift of the British to the growth of free government than the concept of the "Loyal Opposition." That someone may be opposed to the present government's policies and yet still be loyal to the country and not subject to political punishment is incomprehensible in totalitarian or one-party states.

No politician could violate these conventions without touching off a serious political crisis. The well-informed and respected *Economist* described Britain's constitution as a "contraption, stuck together from old laws, bits of precedent, scraps of custom and practice and blind faith in the steering ability of its driver, the prime minister of the day. The machine is notoriously short on brakes: the checks and balances which are a feature of written constitutions." A Constitutional reform advocate Peter Facey said in 2010 that it is "like a wet bar of soap. You try and catch it and it slips out of your hands." A favorite joke is that, "if you got rid of three or four elderly commentators on our constitution, there would be no one around to tell us what it is."

Why does a nation of 61.9 million persons have no written constitution? One reason is that Britain is one of the few democracies in the world to enter the democratic age without a revolution. After successful revolutions, winners are far more inclined to put in writing the kind of guarantees and rights that had been denied them by the former rulers. The outlines of the British regime were established before the Industrial Revolution in the 19th century. Therefore, the economic and social conflicts which that revolution sparked could ultimately be reconciled within the system. Also, the British aristocracy had the foresight to make concessions to the middle and working classes, prompting the latter to realize that they could achieve change and satisfaction through reform rather than rebellion. This is one reason Marxism was never as potent a political force in Britain as it was on the European continent. Further, Britain is not a federal state, so there is no need for a careful delineation of jurisdictions between various governments, as in the US.

Most important, however, is the kind of political culture one finds in Britain. There is widespread agreement on basic political values, and the population broadly supports the leading institutions. This consensus has meant that disagreements over policies have (except under Cromwell) never led to fundamental challenges to the regime and constitution. The British have changed their political system only gradually. Important changes usually only occur after much dialogue and after the major parties have reached general agreement on them. The British also are a law-abiding people, a fact that makes it especially shocking to read about bombings or racial riots in that country. They tend to be moderate and pragmatic and are remarkable for their unwillingness to mount the barricades over abstract or idealistic principles.

They are inclined to boil political disputes down to conflicting interests rather than to conflicting morals or ideas, and this makes compromise much easier. Finally, there is a widespread acceptance of democracy and pluralism. Any foreigner who needs a reminder of the fact that there are many different groups or viewpoints which have a right to exist and be heard in Britain can go to Hyde Park on any Sunday morning to hear the soapbox speeches of dozens of advocates.

The Monarchy

Britain is a monarchy, and in theory the queen or king has sweeping powers. She theoretically appoints the prime minister, assembles or dissolves Parliament, approves of all laws, makes foreign policy, commands the "Armed Forces of the Crown," and appoints officers who hold their rank by "Royal Commission." The trappings of political power would seem to confirm this. The "Queen's government" contains "Ministers of the Crown," who propose laws which always begin with the following words: "Be it enacted by the Queen's Most Excellent Majesty, by and with the consent of the Lords Spiritual and Temporal and Commons in this present Parliament assembled." She is the

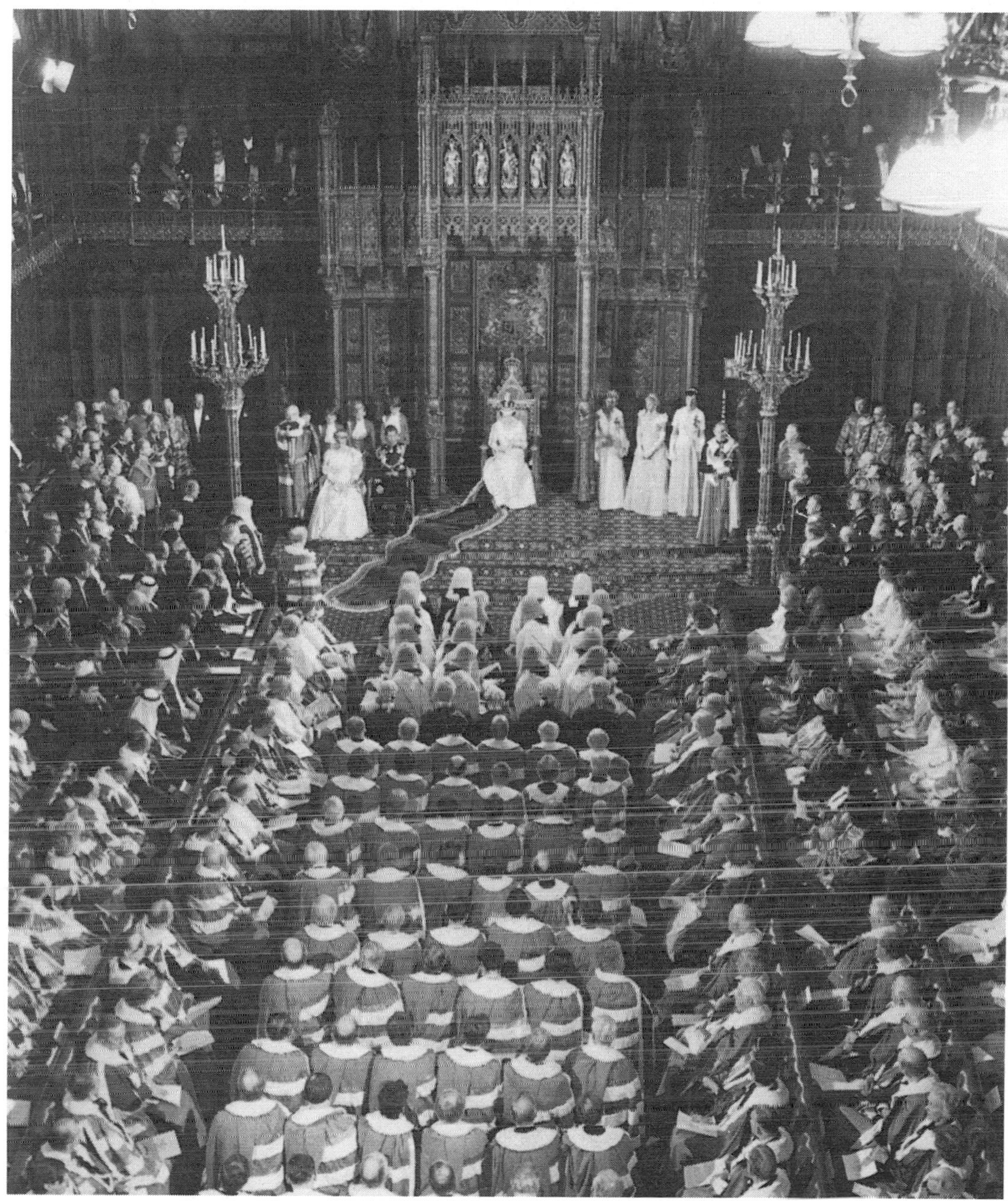

Her Majesty Queen Elizabeth II opens Parliament in the House of Lords.

temporal head of the Church of England, the country's official religion, and she appoints the leading priests. Also, in theory, sovereignty resides not in the people but in the "Crown," which is not the person of the monarch but rather the symbol of supreme executive power.

Actually, she no longer exercises any of the above powers. She "reigns but does not rule." The "Glorious Revolution" in 1688 established parliamentary supremacy and spelled the end of any monarchical pretense to rule absolutely. The last exercise of royal veto power was in 1707. Walter Bagehot wrote in 1867, "the greatest wisdom of a constitutional king would show itself in well-considered inaction," and Queen Elizabeth II has obeyed this dictum.

By the 21st century, the real reason "the Queen can do no wrong" is that the government never permits her to make any important decisions. In the case of Elizabeth, she does not even express her opinions publicly. In 2012 it was considered to be a shocking breach of etiquette when a BBC correspondent declared in a radio interview that the queen had once told him she was "pretty upset" about a radical Islamic cleric in North London. Prince Charles is more willing to express his opinions on such things as the environment, architecture, farmers' burdens, Britain's military, helicopters, or the aspects of Russian foreign policy that resemble Hitler's.

This does not mean that the monarch does not perform any important functions whatsoever. She retains the right "to be informed, to advise and to warn." This right confers no power, but it does provide influence. As constitutional expert Ivor Jennings notes, "she can be as helpful or as obstreperous as she pleases: and she is the only member of the Cabinet who cannot

The United Kingdom

The Order of Succession to the Throne

The heir apparent, eldest son of the queen:

1. His Royal Highness the **Prince CHARLES Philip Arthur George**, Prince of Wales and Earl of Chester, Duke of Cornwall and Rothesay, Earl of Carrick, Baron of Renfrew, Lord of the Isles and Great Steward of Scotland, b. November 14, 1948. Married Lady Diana Frances Spencer (third daughter of the Eighth Earl Spencer) July 29, 1981. Divorced August 28, 1996. Married Camilla Parker Bowles April 9, 2005. Parker Bowles was granted the title Duchess of Cornwall.

The first son of Prince Charles:

2. His Royal Highness **Prince WILLIAM Arthur Philip Louis of Wales**, b. June 21, 1982. Married Catherine (Kate) Middleton April 29, 2011, and were granted the titles Duke and Duchess of Cambridge. In addition, William also became the Earl of Strathearn and Baron Carrickfergus. Thus, Middleton became the Countess of Strathearn and Baroness Carrickfergus.

The children of the union:

3. His Royal Highness **Prince GEORGE Alexander Louis**, b. July 22, 2013. Known as Prince George of Cambridge, he will one day become King George VII.
4. Her Royal Highness **Princess CHARLOTTE Elizabeth Diana**, b. May 2, 2015. Known as Princess Charlotte of Cambridge.
5. His Royal Highness **Prince LOUIS Arthur Charles**, b. April 23, 2018. Known as Prince Louis of Cambridge.

The second son of Prince Charles:

6. His Royal Highness **Prince HENRY Charles Albert David of Wales,** b. September 15, 1984. Known as Prince Harry, Duke of Sussex. Married Meghan Markle May 19, 2018, and were granted the titles Duke and Duchess of Sussex. In addition, Harry also became the Earl of Dumbarton and Baron Kilkeel. Thus, Markle became the Countess of Dumbarton and Baroness Kilkeel.

The son of the union:

7. **ARCHIE Harrison Mountbatten-Windsor**, b. May 6, 2019.

The second son of the queen:

8. His Royal Highness the **Prince ANDREW Albert Christian Edward**, Duke of York, b. February 19, 1960. Married Sarah Margaret Ferguson July 23, 1986. They separated in 1992 and were divorced in 1996.

The daughters of that union:

9. Her Royal Highness **Princess BEATRICE Elizabeth Mary of York**, b. August 8, 1988.
10. Her Royal Highness **Princess EUGENIE Victoria Helena of York**, b. March 23, 1990. Married Jack Brooksbank October 12, 2018.

The third son of the queen:

11. His Royal Highness the **Prince EDWARD Antony Richard Louis**, Earl of Wessex, b. March 10, 1964. Earl of Wessex. Married Miss Sophie Rhys-Jones June 19, 1999.

The son and daughter of that union:

12. **JAMES Alexander Philip Theo Mountbatten-Windsor**, Viscount Severn, b. December 17, 2007.
13. **Lady LOUISE Alice Elizabeth Mary Mountbatten-Windsor**, b. November 8, 2003.

Her Majesty Queen Elizabeth II with her successors Charles (left) and William (right)

The daughter of the queen:

14. Her Royal Highness the **Princess ANNE Elizabeth Alice Louise**, Princess Royal, b. August 15, 1950. Married Captain Mark Anthony Peter Phillips, November 14, 1973. The marriage was dissolved April 23, 1992. Married Commander Timothy James Hamilton Laurence, RN, December 12, 1992.

The son of the first union of Princess Anne:

15. **PETER Mark Andrew Phillips**, b. November 15, 1977. Married Autumn Kelly May 17, 2008.

The daughters of that union:

16. **SAVANNAH Anne Kathleen Phillips**, b. December 29, 2010.
17. **ISLA Elizabeth Phillips**, b. March 29, 2012.

The daughter of the first union of Princess Anne:

18. **ZARA Anne Elizabeth Tindall** (née Phillips), b. May 15, 1981. Married Michael James Tindall July 30, 2011.

The daughters of that union:

19. **MIA Grace Tindall**, b. January 17, 2014.
20. **LENA Elizabeth Tindall**, b. June 18, 2018.

The sister of the queen:

Princess MARGARET Rose, Countess of Snowdon, b. August 21, 1930. Married Anthony Armstrong-Jones, First Earl of Snowdon, May 6, 1960. They divorced July 11, 1978. She died February 9, 2002.

The son of Princess Margaret:

21. **DAVID Albert Charles Armstrong-Jones**, Second Earl of Snowdon, Viscount Linley, b. November 3, 1961. Married Hon. Serena Alleyne Stanhope (only daughter of Viscount Petersham, son and heir of the 11th Earl of Harrington) October 8, 1993.

Buckingham Palace

The son and daughter of that union:

22. **CHARLES Patrick Inigo Armstrong-Jones**, Viscount Linley, b. July 1, 1999.
23. **Lady MARGARITA Elizabeth Rose Alleyne Armstrong-Jones**, b. May 14, 2002.

The daughter of Princess Margaret:

24. **Lady SARAH Frances Elizabeth Chatto** (née Armstrong-Jones), b. May 1, 1964. Married Daniel Chatto July 14, 1994.

The sons of that union:

25. **SAMUEL David Benedict Chatto**, b. July 28, 1996.
26. **ARTHUR Robert Nathaniel Chatto**, b. February 5, 1999.

The first cousin of the queen, the son of the Prince Henry, Duke of Gloucester:

27. His Royal Highness **Prince RICHARD Alexander Walter George**, Duke of Gloucester, b. August 26, 1944. Married Birgitte Eva Van Deurs (of Denmark) July 8, 1972.

The son of Prince Richard:

28. **ALEXANDER Patrick Gregers Richard Windsor**, Earl of Ulster, b. October 24, 1974. Married Claire Alexandra Booth June 22, 2002.

The son and daughter of that union:

29. **XAN Richard Anders Windsor**, Lord Culloden, b. March 12, 2007.
30. **Lady COSIMA Rose Alexandra Windsor**, b. May 20, 2010.

The eldest daughter of Prince Richard:

31. **Lady DAVINA Elizabeth Alice Benedikte Windsor**, b. November 19, 1977. Married Gary Christie Lewis July 31, 2004. They divorced in 2018.

The daughter and son of that union:

32. **SENNA Kowhai Lewis**, b. June 22, 2010.
33. **TĀNE Mahuta Lewis**, b. May 25, 2012.

The youngest daughter of Prince Richard:

34. **Lady ROSE Victoria Birgitte Louise Gilman** (née Windsor), b. March 1, 1980. Married George Gilman July 19, 2008.

The daughter and son of that union:

35. **LYLA Gilman**, b. 2010.
36. **RUFUS Gilman**, b. 2012.

The first cousin of the queen, the first son of the Prince George, Duke of Kent:

37. His Royal Highness **Prince EDWARD George Nicholas Paul Patrick**, Duke of Kent, b. October 9, 1935. Married Katharine Lucy Mary Worsley, June 8, 1961.

The first son of Prince Edward:

38. **GEORGE Philip Nicholas Windsor**, Earl of St. Andrews, b. June 26, 1962, was excluded from the line of succession upon his marriage to Sylvana Palma Tomaselli, a Roman Catholic, January 9, 1988. He was restored to the line of succession March 26, 2015, with the Succession to the Crown Act 2013.

The son and daughters of that union:

EDWARD Edmund Maximilian George Windsor, Baron Downpatrick, b. December 2, 1988. He became Roman Catholic in 2003, excluding himself from the line of succession.

Lady MARINA Charlotte Alexandra Katharine Helen Windsor, b. September 30, 1992. She became Roman Catholic in 2008, excluding herself from the line of succession.

39. **Lady AMELIA Sophia Theodora Mary Margaret Windsor**, b. August 24, 1995.

The second son of Prince Edward:

Lord NICHOLAS Charles Edward Jonathan Windsor, b. July 25, 1970. He became Roman Catholic in 2001, excluding himself from the line of succession. Married Paola Doimi de Lupis Frankopan Šubić Zrinski November 4, 2006.

The sons of that union:

40. **ALBERT Louis Philip Edward Windsor**, b. September 22, 2007.
41. **LEOPOLD Ernest Augustus Guelph Windsor**, b. September 8, 2009.
42. **LOUIS Arthur Nicholas Felix Windsor**, b. May 27, 2014.

The daughter of the Prince Edward:

43. **Lady HELEN Marina Lucy Taylor** (née Windsor), b. April 28, 1964. Married Timothy Verner Taylor July 18, 1992.

The sons of that union:

44. **COLUMBUS George Donald Taylor**, b. August 6, 1994.
45. **CASSIUS Edward Taylor**, b. December 26, 1996.
46. **ELOISE Olivia Katherine Taylor**, b. March 2, 2003.
47. **ESTELLA Olga Elizabeth Taylor**, b. December 21, 2004.

The first cousin of the queen, the second son of the Prince George, Duke of Kent:

48. His Royal Highness **Prince MICHAEL George Charles Franklin of Kent**, b. July 4, 1942, was excluded from the line of succession upon his marriage to Baroness Marie Christine von Reibnitz, a Roman Catholic, June 30, 1978. He was restored to the line of succession March 26, 2015, with the Succession to the Crown Act 2013.

The son of Prince Michael:

49. **Lord FREDERICK Michael George David Louis Windsor**, b. April 6, 1979. Married Sophie Winkleman September 12, 2009.

The daughters of that union:

50. **MAUD Elizabeth Daphne Marina Windsor**, b. August 15, 2013.
51. **ISABELLA Alexandra May Windsor**, b. January 16, 2016.

The daughter of Prince Michael:

52. **Lady GABRIELLA Marina Alexandra Ophelia Kingston** (née Windsor), b. April 21, 1981. Known as Lady Ella. Married Thomas Henry Robin Kingston May 18, 2019.

The first cousin of the queen, the daughter of the Prince George, Duke of Kent:

53. Her Royal Highness **Princess ALEXANDRA Helen Elizabeth Olga Christabel**, the Honourable Lady Ogilvy, b. December 25, 1936. Married the Honourable Sir Angus James Bruce Ogilvy (second son of the 12th Earl of Airlie) April 24, 1963.

The son of Princess Alexandra:

54. **JAMES Robert Bruce Ogilvy**, b. February 29, 1964. Married Julia Caroline Rawlinson July 30, 1988.

The son and daughter of that union:

55. **ALEXANDER Charles Ogilvy**, b. November 12, 1996.
56. **FLORA Alexandra Ogilvy**, b. December 15, 1994.

The daughter of Princess Alexandra:

57. **MARINA Victoria Alexandra Ogilvy**, b. July 31, 1966. Married Paul Julian Mowatt February 2, 1990. They divorced October 15, 1997.

The son and daughter of that union:

58. **CHRISTIAN Alexander Mowatt**, b. June 4, 1993.
59. **ZENOUSKA May Mowatt**, b. May 26, 1990.

Charles, Prince of Wales, and Camilla, Duchess of Cornwall

be informed that her resignation would assist the speedy dispatch of business."

In unusual circumstances or in times of crisis, the monarch could actually exercise considerable influence. If a prime minister dies or resigns and a successor has to be appointed from the same party, or if an election yields no majority, the queen could wield authority, so long as she would not act according to personal preference. For instance, in 1963 Queen Elizabeth named a member of the House of Lords, Sir Alec Douglas Home, as prime minister, an exercise of her theoretical powers about which many Britons were unhappy. Home survived in office for one year when his party was defeated in elections.

The monarch holds other significant "prerogative powers," such as dissolving Parliament or rejecting requests for dissolution. The ultimate guarantee that the monarch will not overstep her bounds is the British people, who are sovereign in reality, if not in theory. Prince Charles, who turned 71 in November 2019 and is the oldest heir to the throne in history, admitted this fact frankly, saying, "something as curious as the monarchy won't survive unless you take account of people's attitudes. I think it can be a kind of elective institution. After all, if people don't want it, they won't have it."

Much more importantly, she symbolizes the unity of the nation and the continuous thread through a millennium of English history. She is thus the focus of national pride. Politics touches not only the mind but also the heart, and she helps to provide her subjects with an emotional attachment to their country. She is therefore an important cornerstone for the kind of low-keyed but deep-rooted patriotism most Englishmen share. Finally, because of her dual position as head of state and defender of the faith, she helps to link governmental with religious authority in the minds of many Englishmen.

In his brilliant book published in 1867, *The English Constitution*, Walter Bagehot distinguished between the "dignified" and "efficient" parts of government. The "dignified" parts, especially the glittering monarch and nobility, were useful in securing authority and loyalty for the state from the citizenry, while the "efficient" parts actually used the power and resources of the state to rule. In his book *The Body Politic*, Sir Ian Gilmour argued that "legitimacy, the acceptance by the governed of the political system, is far better aided by an ancient monarchy set above the political battle than by a transient president, who has gained his position through that battle. . . . Modern societies still need myth and ritual. A monarch and his family supply it; there is no magic about a mud-stained politician."

Bagehot had written, "we must not let daylight in upon magic." But in an age of nondeferential journalists and citizens in Britain, royal indiscretions have completely exposed that "magic." In the wake of lurid reports in the tabloid press about marital breakdowns and infidelity within the royal family, which over the years have included Elizabeth and especially Philip themselves, the succession to the throne and the very future of the monarchy in Britain are being questioned. The concept of a family monarchy, a Victorian-era notion that granted a symbolic and public role to royal offspring and consorts, as well as to the king or queen, has been severely shaken.

Three of Queen Elizabeth II's four children were unable to sustain a stable first marriage. The year 1992 saw the formal separation of Prince Charles from Diana, a superstar princess who overshadowed the estranged crown prince until her tragic death in Paris in 1997. In 1999 he began appearing in public with his longtime love, Camilla Parker Bowles. On April 9, 2005, he became the first heir to the throne to marry a divorcée. They were betrothed in a civil ceremony that the queen and her husband, Prince Philip, refused to attend. However, his parents were present at the church service that followed.

Polls indicated that most Britons either approved of or were indifferent to the wedding. However, a sizable majority did not want to see Camilla become queen. To assuage that sentiment, Charles emphasized that Camilla wants only to be called "princess consort" and will have the lower title of "Duchess of Cornwall," not "Princess of Wales," as Diana was called. Nevertheless, the Department for Constitutional Affairs confirmed that the marriage would not be "morganatic," meaning one in which the spouse of inferior status has no claim to the status of the other. Unless Parliament passes a law barring Camilla from becoming queen, she will assume that title the moment Charles becomes king. She has come a long way from the time the tabloids cast her as Britain's most hated woman. Thanks to her discretion and to her embracing Charles' two sons, polls reveal a sharply reduced level of animosity toward her.

Prince Andrew is divorced from Sarah Ferguson, whose nonregal antics embarrassed the royal family more than once. In 2010 she was videotaped by the tab-

Prince William

loid *The News of the World*, which folded in July 2011, promising to introduce a fake "rich businessman" to her former husband for a price of about $717,000. She took $40,000 in cash on the spot. Until 2011 Prince Andrew served successive governments as an envoy to promote British exports. His royal status enabled him to entertain customers by sponsoring splendid business lunches and receptions at Buckingham Palace.

In 1992 Princess Anne, who divorced her first husband, Mark Phillips, became the first top-ranking British royal since King Henry VIII to divorce and remarry. She wed a divorced naval commander, Timothy Laurence. The ceremony had to be held in Scotland because the Church of England does not condone second marriages. In 2002 she suffered the indignity of becoming the first member of the royal family to be convicted of a criminal offense since Charles I was beheaded for treason in 1649.

Edward announced his engagement to Sophie Rhys-Jones in 1999. They married and had their first child in 2003.

Personal revelations about the royals are dangerously corrosive because an unelected institution in a democracy depends on the popular will for its legitimacy. Despite the bad publicity, a MORI poll in 1996 confirmed that the royals still enjoy considerable trust: When voters were offered a choice among 13 candidates for an elected president, the clear favorite was Princess Anne. A 1997 poll taken September 7, the day after Diana's moving funeral and an outpouring of grief that saw 60 million bouquets placed around the royal palaces, revealed that the mood toward the monarchy had changed: 73% of respondents (82% if Diana's eldest son, William, were to be the next monarch) favored its retention (down from 85%–90% a decade earlier); fewer than half thought it would survive the next 50 years; and 39% thought less of the royal family. In 2012, 80% favored continuing the monarchy; only 13% preferred a republic. This was the strongest support for the monarchy in two decades.

A hostile mood was shown in the reaction to a fire that caused $90 million worth of damage to Windsor Castle in 1992. The royal family had invented its name Windsor after this favorite castle in 1917 in order to shed its German name (Saxe-Coburg-Gotha) during the war against Germany. Popular outrage greeted the government's decision to pay the costs of the repair, which were completed beautifully in 1998.

The flames reignited the debate over whether the monarch should pay taxes and whether the state should provide annual incomes to the members and staffs of a very wealthy royal family. To quiet the fury, Queen Elizabeth announced that she would pay income taxes amounting to about $4 million annually and about $1.9 million to most members of her family out of her own fortune, estimated by *Forbes* in 2010 to be worth £300 million ($500 million). She noted in 1997 that the cost of operating the monarchy had fallen by 39% since the beginning of the decade and that the royal yacht *Britannia*, had been decommissioned for financial reasons. It is understandable that, on the 40th anniversary of her coronation she publicly described 1992 as an annus horribilis.

In 2010 the Conservative government announced as a part of its austerity program a change in the financing of the Crown. Her income would fall 14% until the new system began in 2013. It would end the arrangement struck with George III in 1760 transferring income from the Crown lands to the government in return for the "Civil List," an annual payment voted for and scrutinized by Parliament. Instead the monarch will take an annual share of revenues from the Crown Estate, a sprawling £6.6 billion ($11 billion) property and land empire, whose assets range from Regent Street to 265,000 acres of agricultural land and to the British seabed extending to the 12-nautical-mile limit. This income is estimated to amount to £30 million ($48 million) per year from 2013 on. This freed the Crown from having to go to Parliament every time it needs more funding.

Prince Charles receives his own independent income from the Duchy of Cornwall, and that has been profitable. The family remains exempt from inheritance tax and from the more than £50 million ($80 million) price tag for police protection. The need for this was seen in December 2010, when an anarchic mob of young people purporting to be protesting a rise in university tuition fees attacked the car carrying Prince Charles and Camilla, broke windows, and appeared to threaten the frightened royal couple.

Princess Diana's death in 1997 was one of the few times the queen was ever personally criticized by the media; she felt obliged to share her grief publicly and to lower the flag at Buckingham Palace to half-mast. She made a rare gesture of humility by bowing her head when the princess's casket passed Buckingham Palace on the way to the funeral. Her predicament and the role played by the newly elected prime minister Tony Blair in helping point Elizabeth in the right direction were portrayed with insight and sympathy in the British film *The Queen*. Helen Mirren, herself an opponent of the monarchy until she immersed herself in the role of Elizabeth II, won an Oscar as best actress.

After Diana died the royals made a real effort to be more accessible and open. They hired pollsters to help them come closer to the people and to read the public's message. Elizabeth II admitted, "Read it we must." It appears to be working. In 1996 only 41% of Britons thought that Charles would make a good king; by 1998 that had risen to more than 60%.

The year 2002 was the jubilee to celebrate Queen Elizabeth II's half-century on the

House of Commons, view of the chamber showing the speaker's chair and seating for clerk of the House and assistants.

throne. But it was also a year of death. On February 10 Princess Margaret died, and she was followed on March 30 by the most popular royal, the 101-year-old Queen Mother. The splendor of her burial showed that the British public still likes monarchical dignity and theater. But the funeral could not stifle the noisy national debate about the role of an inherited monarchy in a nation that champions democracy and meritocracy. One caller to the BBC said, "The Queen Mum had 40 people waiting on her, and we taxpayers had to cough up 600,000 quid [over $1 million] to support it. What did she do to deserve it, except marry the right bloke 80 years ago?"

On April 21, 2006, Elizabeth II celebrated her 80th birthday as a remarkably popular monarch after 54 years on the throne. By the end of 2007, she had become both the first reigning British monarch to celebrate a diamond (60 years) wedding anniversary and the oldest-ever monarch at 243 days after her 81st birthday. Her husband, Philip, who turned 90 in June 2011 and who is known for uttering rude, off-the-cuff remarks for which he never apologizes, is the longest-serving consort in British history. In 2019, at age 97, he was driving without his seatbelt fastened and crashed into another car, slightly injuring its passengers. He voluntarily surrendered his driver's license.

At age 86 in June 2012, Elizabeth celebrated a rare event: a Diamond Jubilee marking 60 years on the throne. Not since 1897 had such a celebration taken place. In September 2015 Elizabeth surpassed Queen Victoria's length of reign (63 years). She now elicits almost no criticism from politicians or press. Polls show there are only 15 million republicans in a kingdom of about 63 million. There is a steady rise in Britons who think the monarchy will exist 10 years into the future, even though only 10% of those between the ages of 16 and 24 think the monarchy is important to their lives.

On April 29, 2011, more than a third of the Earth's population watched the televised wedding of Prince William, the second in the line of succession, with commoner Catherine (Kate) Middleton. They met at St. Andrews University eight years earlier. She became the first royal bride with a university degree, and William would be the first monarch with a university diploma. They were also the first royals to live together before marriage. He was a Royal Air Force search-and-rescue helicopter pilot in northern Wales. He deployed to the Falkland Islands in 2012, his first overseas military tour. He was involved in the rescue of 149 people. After seven years of service, he retired from the military in 2013 to focus on his charitable and conservation work. Her parents are self-made wealthy people who provided their three children with a stable family environment and an excellent modern education.

The funeral cortege of Diana, Princess of Wales, proceeds through Hyde Park toward Westminster Abbey.

Photo: Edward Jones

The Windsors desperately needed a marriage that works in order to have the stability and glamor necessary to save the monarchy in the long run. Kate is very attractive, and she is liked by the press and the public. Her middle-class origins and her maturity (age 28 at her marriage) are pluses.

In expectation of the royal couple's first child on July 22, 2013 (a boy, George Alexander Louis, Prince George of Cambridge), followed on May 2, 2015, by a sister, Princess Charlotte Elizabeth Diana, the government moved to change the law of succession in Britain and in all 16 of the queen's realms, such as Canada, New Zealand, and Australia. In a historic agreement at the Commonwealth heads-of-government meeting on October 28, 2011, it was agreed without dissent that the prince's children would succeed in order of seniority, regardless of sex. They also agreed to scrap an ancient law, rooted in earlier religious wars, forbidding the monarch's spouse from being a Roman Catholic. However, the monarch himself or herself still cannot be Catholic. All 16 sovereign governments had to pass the necessary legislation and then backdate it to the October 2011 agreement. In 2018 Prince Harry married American actress Meghan Markle. A divorced biracial American, her marriage reflects the extent to which British society has changed.

Parliamentary Government

The seat of power was once the House of Commons, which elected and controlled the prime minister and the cabinet. It debated the great issues of the day and shaped the laws of the land. It was supreme, and no political institution in the entire kingdom can block its will. A century later this was no longer true. The rise of powerful catchall parties firmly controlled by party leaders had largely converted the majority in the House of Commons into the tail wagged by the dog in Number 10 Downing Street, the residence of the prime minister. Observers gradually stopped speaking about parliamentary government and began talking first of cabinet government, then prime ministerial government.

The prime minister is not all-powerful. He must face a powerful civil service (collectively called Whitehall), sometimes count his votes carefully in the Commons, and deal with a multitude of quasi-governmental and interest groups. In theory, the British political process is simple; in practice, it is surprisingly haphazard. British governments do at least as much "muddling through" as they command. The need to persuade, coax, beg, threaten, or compromise with so many groups and institutions, all with independent standing of some sort, changes the traditional picture of British government, which is centered on the prime minister and cabinet, who can do anything they want. In truth, British government has never been exactly as it appears to be on the surface. While clothed in basically the same institutional garb, the reality of British politics is always changing.

The House of Commons

Since 2010 the House of Commons has 650 members of Parliament (MPs, 646 in 2005 and 639 in 2007) elected at either general elections, which must be held at least every five years, or at by-elections, held when a seat falls vacant because of the death or resignation of a member. From the Great Reform Bill of 1832 until the electoral reform of 1970, the suffrage was gradually expanded until all men and women 18 years and older can vote. Also, all citizens of the Republic of Ireland who reside in the United Kingdom are allowed to vote. Compared with American elections, British campaigns are very short.

Usually only about four weeks elapse between the time the prime minister sets the date for new elections and the polling day. Many voters complained that the six-week campaign in 1997, the longest in 70 years, was much too long. The threat of sending MPs out on the hustings with very little notice is a powerful tool of persuasion in the hands of the prime minister. The MP does have certain advantages over the US congressman at election time: The parties pay the bulk of the campaign expenses. Also, since the MP's constituency has only one-seventh as many inhabitants as an American congressional district, he or she is able to canvass the voters at their doorstep and get the full blast of public opinion face to face.

MPs are elected by a system that is very simple and controversial: the single-member simple plurality. The candidate with the most votes in each of the 650 constituencies is elected, even if he or she won fewer than 50% of the votes. This electoral system has the advantage of preventing many parties from gaining seats in Parliament. By bolstering the two-party system, proponents say it enhances political stability. Since one or the other of the large parties usually has a majority in the House of Commons, there had never been the need for a formal coalition to rule. That changed in May 2010, when no party won a majority.

Opponents say that it is undemocratic and unfair because it favors the larger parties by enabling them to win a far higher proportion of parliamentary seats than the percentage of votes they won nationally. For example, in the May 2015 elections, the Conservative Party climbed to 36.9% of the votes, among the lowest shares for a winner since the Reform Act of 1832. But it captured 331 seats or 51% of the total. The Labour Party won 30.4% of the total vote. Nevertheless, it received 232 seats, or 36% of the total.

The SNP won only 4.7% of the national vote, but got 56 seats, 8.6% of the total. In stark contrast, the Liberal Democrats, with 7.9% of the total vote, captured only 8 seats or a mere 1.2% of the total. No wonder they demanded a reform of the electoral system as the price for its entry into the governing coalition with the Conservatives. They have long been in favor of a proportional representation (PR) system, which would award seats in proportion to the total votes won. In two postwar elections (1951 and February 1974), the party with the largest number of votes only received the second-largest number of seats. In three others (1950, 1964 and October 1974), the winner's shaky parliamentary majority was in the single figures.

The questions are: Does the current system really produce more decisive majorities? Exactly how could elections be made fairer? Would the two large parties go along? It is increasingly common for MPs to be elected with the support of fewer than half the voters; in the House of Commons elected in 1997, 312 of 659 were in this situation. A Liberal Democrat, Sir Russell Johnston, won his Inverness constituency in 1992 with only 26% of the votes.

Virtually every other European democracy has some form of PR. But the British political system has needed an electoral method that offers voters a clear choice between the governing party or coalition, whose performance can be judged, and an opposition party, whose promises can be weighed and considered. This facilitates a change of government within an hour and a half after the votes have been counted, including visits to the queen. There is no 10-week transition period like a newly elected American president has before taking office. In some European democracies, it can take months to hammer together a coalition government. In May 2010 the Conservatives and Liberal Democrats did it in five high-drama days. In the past, the clear distinction between the two sides discouraged third parties from developing. It prevented the formation of coalition governments since 1940–1945, when Winston Churchill led a wartime coalition government of all three major parties.

In 1998 then–prime minister Blair appointed a commission under Lord Jenkins to examine the electoral system but with two stipulations: that the need for "stable government" should be kept in mind and that the link between MPs and their constituencies should be preserved. The conclusion was that a "lack of democracy" would have to be accepted at the national level in the interest of retaining a stable, one-party government, while proportional representation could be practiced at the regional and local level. That is exactly what is done in regional elections in Scotland, Wales, and Northern Ireland, as well as in elections to the European Parliament.

Desperately needing the Liberal Democrats as coalition partners, Prime Minister David Cameron agreed to a referendum May 5, 2011. on a new way of voting that is not proportional representation; it is called the alternative-vote (AV) system. This would change the "first-past-the-post" method. (Whoever gets the most votes wins the seat, whether he wins a majority or not.) AV would allow voters to rank candidates on the ballot in order of preference instead of merely marking the one preferred candidate. If no candidate in the constituency receives 50% of the first-preference votes, then the second choices of those who voted for the last-placing candidate are redistributed until one candidate gets an absolute majority (50%). If this system had been used in the May 2010 elections, the Lib Dems would have won 22 more seats, all from the Conservative Party. It was defeated by 68% to 32%. Voters liked the old system because it is simple, and it usually produces a governing majority. They agree with Benjamin Disraeli, who once said, "England does not love coalitions."

The very organization and physical structure of the House of Commons de-

Queen Elizabeth II and six former prime ministers celebrate the 250th anniversary of 10 Downing Street as the official residence of the prime minister.

pends upon a government and an opposition, without a wide spectrum of opinion. The House of Commons is arranged in rows of benches facing each other rather than in seats facing the podium. This arrangement encourages debate and questions because members of the opposing parties sit facing each other across an aisle. By ancient custom, and for good reason, the aisle is two sword-lengths wide so an MP may not reach across it with a sword and skewer his opponent during debate. The government sits on the front row to the right of the speaker's throne, and the leaders of the opposition (known also as the "shadow cabinet") sit on the first row to the speaker's left. MPs on the lower end of the pecking order in their respective parties sit higher up on the back rows and are therefore called "backbenchers."

The speaker from 2000 to 2009 was Michael Martin, a former sheet-metal worker; the speaker directs the debate. By tradition the speakership alternates between the two main parties, and the new speaker resigns from his party. But like his predecessor, Betty Boothroyd, Martin was a Labour MP. A former shop steward and son of a stoker, he grew up in poverty in Glasgow. He observed the tradition of feigning reluctance to assume the post and having to be tugged to the speaker's chair, a throwback to the days when speakers were occasionally beheaded because of their uncomfortable position between the Commons and the monarch. When he strides into the chamber, his aides call for the long-standing ritual of respect: "Hats off, strangers!" The speaker has little control of the Commons' business. The Leader of the House, who belongs to the cabinet, organizes this.

A skillful speaker can protect the prerogatives of the House against the government and the people, but Martin was not able to do this. In 2009 *The Daily Telegraph* published the names of more than 200 MPs who had padded their expense accounts at a time when the nation was being battered by economic recession. Citizens were furious, and he became the first speaker since 1695 to be ejected from office. He was replaced in June 2009 by Conservative MP John Bercow, who was reelected after the 2010 general election. His influence expanded in Parliament, passionately divided on the question of leaving the EU.

Unlike in the United States, the opposition party in Britain has an alternative cabinet that is preselected and ready to assume office at a moment's notice. Indeed, a major strength of British parliamentary democracy is that talented leaders in a government which loses an election still retain their front-row seats in Parliament and are therefore kept in reserve until a later date when the electorate's moods change and their services are again desired. This shadow government leads what is known in Britain as "Her Majesty's loyal opposition," a concept grounded in the notion that two persons of goodwill can disagree agreeably on an important issue. In contrast to the US, though, the "loyal opposition" has no means of delaying governmental action through filibuster in Parliament.

In theory, Parliament checks and controls the executive (the prime minister and the cabinet). In practice, it is normally the other way around. Parliament lacks the facilities to watch over the government competently, and MPs are underpaid, understaffed, and underinformed. Despite some recent pay increases, MPs still earn far less than their American counterparts. In 2014 their base salary was £66,396 ($106,234), plus more than $72,000 for secretarial and research assistance. MPs do receive expenses for travel, phoning, postage, and housing allowances (if they must maintain two homes). After the 2001 elections, the salary for a cabinet minister was raised to the equivalent of about $155,000 and that of the prime minister in 2010 to £197,000, or the equivalent of $315,000.

Two-thirds continue working at their normal jobs. For centuries until 2002 the hours of the parliamentary sessions had been set from 2:30 p.m. to 10:30 p.m. in order to accommodate that need. Now parliamentary business starts at 11:30 and must normally be concluded no later than 7:30 p.m. in order for MPs to have a more "family-friendly" schedule. Exceptions are sometimes approved. One-third even work for private lobbying firms and other businesses with interest in legislation, something forbidden for US congressmen. They have inadequate office space and receive only a modest sum for secretarial and research assistance, while the average American congressman has 16 aides, and the average senator, 36. With such minuscule staffs, ordinary MPs have great difficulty acquiring sufficient information to challenge the government, which has the entire civil service to provide it with facts.

Unlike the US Congress, the House of Commons does not have a well-developed committee system to do the detailed work which cannot be done on the floor of the House. The ad hoc "standing committees" have too little expertise and are too large to be truly effective. The smaller "select committees" have a relatively permanent membership, are often chaired by an opposition MP, and do play a more important role. In 1980, new committees were set up to oversee the work of specific ministries and to deal specifically with Scottish and Welsh affairs. There is considerable discussion of reforms to improve the committee structure in the House, but in the absence of successful reforms, it is likely to remain more a forum to debate the important issues of the day than a powerful lawmaking body. In 1988 the Commons voted to allow television to record its often-rowdy deliberations.

It remains the government's job to determine what will be the law of the land. All important legislation, including the budget, is drafted by the government and Whitehall. Since the government determines the order of parliamentary business, its proposals always take priority over those of private members or the opposition. Parliament can make amendments and must give its approval, but the government has numerous ways to ensure that its policies will be accepted. First, all MPs are almost always party members (after 2001 there were three independents, one of whom had been elected as such), and they can jeopardize their careers if they defy their party leaders. Renegades are seldom reelected. Second, as many as 110 MPs are actually members of the government, and all are expected to vote with the government.

Finally, since the very survival of the government depends upon maintaining a majority, MPs are under far greater pressure from the cabinet to support the government than is the case in the US. Rigid party discipline on most bills has always been essential in order to make the political system work. MPs are permitted to "vote their conscience" on moral issues, such as abortion and gun control (Britain has a near total ban on handguns.). In 2005–2006 it applied to votes to outlaw smoking in public places by 2007, to permit pubs to remain open after 11 p.m., and in 2013 to allow same-sex partnerships in England and Wales. The latter grants the same property and inheritance rights as married heterosexual couples and gives partners the same pension, immigration, and tax benefits. Among the first takers was pop singer Sir Elton John, who formalized his relationship with David Furnish.

Control by the government is much less effective than it once was. From 1945 to 1970, no government lost a vote of the full House of Commons. The 1970s brought a significant change. The Conservative government of Edward Heath suffered defeat in Parliament six times. Before 1970 it would have been unthinkable for a government so defeated to remain in office, but he returned to the 19th-century practice of resigning only upon losing a declared vote of no confidence. The Labour government that ruled from 1974 until 1979 suffered 23 such defeats, and Thatcher was defeated twice. MPs can now often vote against the government without bringing it down. This encourages backbenchers to revolt without severely endangering their careers.

The days are over when the backbenchers automatically vote as their leaders order.

The Blair government changed the raucous "prime minister's question time" in the House of Commons by converting it into a more serious, once-a-week, half-hour session every Wednesday in which more questions from opposition backbenchers are allowed. The leadership confrontations with the opposition leader remain the most entertaining and sometimes most embarrassing interchanges for the prime minister. In order to be able to prepare better for these weekly duels, Blair switched the day for his weekly half-hour audience with the queen in 2004 from Tuesdays to Wednesdays after question hour. It was switched back to Tuesdays.

Such audiences date back to 1739 and are a valuable opportunity for the head of government to tap the vast reservoir of knowledge Queen Elizabeth has accumulated in her more than half-century on the throne. David Cameron is her 12th prime minister since Churchill, and Barack Obama is the 11th president with whom she has dealt. By tradition, the opinions expressed at such audiences are strictly confidential. Even the prime minister's closest aides are kept in the dark.

Harold Wilson (1964–1970) regarded the queen as the only person with whom he could confide without thinking a knife was being sharpened behind his back. John Major (1990–1997) said no notes were taken, and the sanctity of the event was preserved by the "total block" on the discussions. He remembered that he could talk to the monarch in a way he did to no one else. Tony Blair (1997–2007) initially viewed the meetings as "ancient etiquette." But he soon found them to be a great opportunity to talk to a very wise person in the knowledge that it would go no further. Only Margaret Thatcher (1979–1990) is reported to have had an uncomfortable relationship with Elizabeth.

The House of Lords

Great Britain is a monarchy, and it should therefore not be surprising that its aristocracy continues to enjoy certain political privileges. These are institutionalized in the upper house of Parliament, the House of Lords. Before 1999, of the 1,164 members (known as the "peers"), 650 had hereditary titles. This meant that all the offspring of these peers who inherited the titles would automatically be entitled to a seat in the House of Lords. These titles, in order of precedence, are duke, marquess, earl, viscount, and baron, all except Dukes being commonly addressed as "lord." Some peerages have ancient origins, such as the Marquis of Salisbury or the Duke of Norfolk, but half the hereditary peerages were created in the 20th century "for services to the nation." No new hereditary peerages were created after 1964 until Prime Minister Thatcher ennobled senior minister William Whitelaw and retiring speaker of the Commons George Thomas.

A law of 1958 creating "life peers" set an irreversible trend. Such peers are appointed for their learning or their distinguished public service. However, after they die, their heirs cannot claim their seats. Among the life peers named in 1997 was composer (now baron) Andrew Lloyd Webber. Sir Paul McCartney (now a knight) and *Dynasty* star Joan Collins (now an officer of the Order of the British Empire) were not awarded peerages.

By 2014 there were only 781 active peers remaining in the reformed House of Lords, although that number can go up if the prime minister so decides. There are 92 are hereditary peers, whose tenure remains uncertain. Their heirs can assume their titles, but they no longer have the right to sit in Parliament. There are 23 Church of England lord bishops and archbishops. The rest are life peers, half of whom entered the House of Lords since Labour came to power in 1997; Tony Blair appointed 374, and David Cameron packed the chamber. Approximately 67 are peeresses, such as the late Margaret Thatcher. By 2006 the largest party was Labour (206 seats), followed by Tories (205) and Liberal Democrats (74). In 2012, 30.3% of the seats were Labour, 27.7% Tory, 8.8% Liberal Democrat, 23.6% cross-bench (independent), and 6.9% other. In this new House of Lords, most peers attend regularly and are less inclined than earlier to do what the governments tells them. A 2006 poll revealed that 68% of respondents think it is all right for the lords to vote against government bills.

As the democratic wave caused a steady expansion of the franchise in the 19th and 20th centuries, the powers of the House of Lords came under increasing attack. In the Parliament Acts of 1911 and 1949, its veto right was taken away; now the only kind of bill it can veto is one to prolong the life of Parliament beyond five years. Also, its power to delay legislation was reduced; it can now hold up bills for 13 months at the most (only 30 days for a financial bill). Until the Thatcher era, it seldom exercised its power out of fear that, if it fully used its powers, it would ultimately lose them.

The Labour Party has long sought "to abolish the undemocratic House of Lords as quickly as possible." One of Labour's most influential leftists even renounced his title of Viscount Stansgate, giving up his right to sit in the House of Lords. He also shortened his name from Anthony Neil Wedgewood Benn III to the more proletarian Tony Benn. He married an American. His 2014 obituary called him a "dazzling orator" and "scion of a political family." His son, Hilary Benn, shared his father's aristocratic appearance and mannerisms. A state secretary for international development in Tony Blair's government and later shadow foreign minister, he emphasized that he is "a Benn, not a Bennite."

In normal times, opposition to the prime minister's policies is exercised in the House of Commons. But Thatcher so dominated that body until 1990 that another institution performed that function: the House of Lords. One Labour lord said in 1988, "It hurts to admit it, but on many issues we are the government's only real opposition." A Liberal baroness added, "As an unelected body, it would obviously be quite improper for us to try to kill a bill outright. But there is nothing to stop us from being an utter nuisance to the government. We call it playing Ping-Pong—holding up a bill for so long that the government is compelled to accept our amendments just to get the thing passed." In fact, by 1988 Thatcher had suffered 107 defeats in the House of Lords, compared with only 2 in the House of Commons. Between 1999 and 2007, the lords defeated more than 350 government bills.

Why is such a privileged house, to which no one is elected, retained in a democratic country? In fact, debates in the House of Lords are at least as well informed and much less partisan than in the lower house. In order to demonstrate this fact, debates in the upper house began to be televised in 1985. The lords' main job is to examine and to revise bills that have proceeded too hastily through the House of Commons. With such experienced peers, the most active of whom had already distinguished themselves in all walks of life outside Parliament, the lords perform an important function in improving legislation by applying their expertise. Also, the fact that the most active lords are persons of great prestige and influence in British society means that no government systematically ignores the House of Lords.

Supported two to one in a 1997 MORI poll, Tony Blair's Labour government moved swiftly to enact its campaign promise to remove "the absurdity of the hereditary element." He appointed a royal commission that produced a white paper in 1999. It recommended that the hereditary peers' right to sit and vote be removed, that the nomination of life peers be accomplished through an independent appointments committee (not the prime minister), that some be indirectly elected by such bodies as the new regional assemblies, and that longer-term reform be considered.

To move this reform through the legislative process, Blair agreed to a temporary compromise with the Tory leader in the House of Lords: 92 hereditary peers were permitted to stay until a final second-stage reform of the house could be undertaken; over 600 life peers retained their seats. Two Labour peers were suspended in 2009 for offering to amend laws in exchange for cash payments. This was the first time any member had been removed from the House of Lords since 1642. In 2011 a lord was found guilty of falsely claiming more than £11,000 ($18,000) in travel expenses. He became the first member of the upper house to be convicted in a jury trial. Peers receive no salary, but they get £300 ($465) a day tax free for attending. They get a desk in Parliament and lifetime access to its parking lot, restaurants and bars.

After facing further opposition, in the upper house, the Blair government proposed additional constitutional reforms. It abolished the ancient and powerful position of lord chancellor, who was speaker of the lords, a cabinet minister, head of the country's judiciary, and titular member of the highest court, the now-abolished Law Lords. The position was broken into three posts. Since 2005 a speaker of the House of Lords presides over the upper house. In 2006 a Labour Party baroness, Helene Hayman, became the first elected lord speaker. The lord chancellor's other roles were assumed by a Department for Constitutional Affairs. In October 2009 the reform replaced the 12 Law Lords with a Supreme Court, which is the highest court in England and Wales.

The House of Lords had been doing a good job scrutinizing laws, producing quality reports, and challenging Commons; that is why the pressure to reshape the lords comes from politicians, not the voters. In 2007 a majority in the House of Commons voted in favor of an all-elected House of Lords. This was a nonbinding vote, but it will influence the government's future choices.

It is unclear what will ultimately happen to the lords; its reform is a work in progress. The Tory-Liberal Democrat government that took power in May 2010 vowed to produce a wholly or partly elected House of Lords. It unveiled a set of proposals in May 2011 calling for the abolition of the present House of Lords. After a transition period, the 781 current members would be replaced by a semi-elected house that could be called a senate with as few as 300 members. Eighty percent of the members would be elected for a single 15-year term by a form of proportional representation to help smaller parties get seats. The remaining 20% would be appointed. The 92 hereditary peers would be removed, as would be half or more of the 23 Anglican lord bishops and archbishops who now have seats. It is too early to tell if these recommendations will be enacted, watered down, or dropped.

View of London across the Thames, with "Big Ben" (right)

Although the House of Commons approved the bill, many Tory MPs block progress because they fear that an elected upper house would challenge the primacy of the lower house.

Prime Ministerial Government

The nerve center of British politics is "the government," a collective term to describe the prime minister; the 16 to 23 cabinet ministers; and the parliamentary secretaries or junior ministers, a team which may total from 70 to 110 members.

In theory, the prime minister is the "first among equals" within the governing team. But as a senior Whitehall official noted at the end of the 20th century, "The idea that the prime minister is primus inter pares is wrong. The prime minister is not pares. He's way above that. Like Caesar he bestrides the world like a colossus." The prime minister is the leader of the party that has a majority (or at least a plurality) in the House of Commons. Thus, the holder of this highest office is an MP who has worked his or her way upward through the legislative system. In earlier times, the average prime minister had served a quarter-century in the House of Commons and had occupied several cabinet posts. That is no longer the case. The prime ministry was Tony Blair's and David Cameron's first post, and the latter had been in Parliament only eight years before become prime minister. Nevertheless, it is unlikely that a stranger to the national capital, such as Jimmy Carter, Ronald Reagan, Bill Clinton, or George W. Bush, could become prime minister. The powers of the post are so great that the description "first among equals" is misleading.

The prime minister's powers, which are almost nowhere clearly spelled out in statute, strike the American as sweeping. As the nation's chief executive, chief legislator, and chief administrator, he is the primary focus of political attention. After the election, he is rather free to appoint and dismiss cabinet members, thereby largely determining the broad political direction the government will take. The convention of "collective responsibility" prevents his ministers from criticizing him in public, and the tradition of secrecy shields many of his decisions and actions from the public eye.

He decides on the agenda for cabinet meetings and appoints the cabinet committees, which prepare government policies or deal with crises and carry out most ministerial business. For example, in 1982 Thatcher formed a "war cabinet" to manage the Falklands crisis; she also had influential committees for economic, foreign and defense, domestic, and legislative policy. Such grand committees have subcommittees. There are no votes taken in cabinet meetings, and the prime minister interprets the sense of the cabinet. Cabinet minutes are sparse in detail and taken in long hand to keep them that way.

Given the tradition of cabinet secrecy, the Brown government was shocked in February 2008, when Britain's information commissioner, citing the "gravity and controversial nature" of the decision to go to war in Iraq in 2003, ordered the government to release the minutes of two cabinet meetings discussing the legality of the invasion. The government appealed the order, arguing that it set a "dangerous precedent" for releasing cabinet papers, which cannot normally be published for 30 years.

Regardless of how the debate in the secret cabinet meetings might have gone, he can always announce the meaning in a way which conforms to his own views. As ex-Labour cabinet member Richard Crossman revealed, any prime minister who is subordinate to the cabinet is "consciously refusing to make use of the powers which now constitutionally belong to the office." In practice, most issues are decided either in Whitehall or in cabinet committees and are not even discussed in full cabinet meetings, which are normally held twice a week, including each Thursday morning. The modern cabinet is increasingly a reporting and reviewing body and less and less an executive one. Crossman was correct. Collective decision making has been replaced by a system in which ministers have been reduced to agents of their leader, forced to deal with him bilaterally rather than as part of a collectively responsible group. The prime minister directs the nation's sizable civil service.

He determines the country's foreign and defense policies and at one time could commit Britain to a policy that the cabinet and Commons could do little to alter. Prime Minister Cameron suffered a spectacular defeat in August 2013, when a narrow parliamentary majority rejected his bid to use military force in Syria. The opponents included 30 members of his own Tory Party and 9 Liberal Democrats in his coalition. This was the first time since 1782 that a prime minister had been defeated in Parliament on a matter of war and peace. The vote reflected public opinion: Only 22% of the population favored such use of force.

He can enter treaties with foreign nations that need not be approved by Parliament; foreign policy was a "royal prerogative" which was never passed to Parliament, although a prime minister does customarily discuss with it treaties and declarations of war. The 2003 war in Iraq demonstrated that even a strong and activist prime minister like Tony Blair must be very attentive to both British law and popular and parliamentary sentiment when using the prime minister's war powers.

Finally, as leader and chief strategist for the national party, he alone can decide the date of the general election and thus determine when the entire government and Commons must face the voters. That power was clipped by the Fixed-Term Parliaments Act, which requires two-thirds disapproval by MPs to dissolve Parliament immediately. He is burdened neither by separation of powers nor by a federal structure. No American president wields such power.

Limitations on the Prime Minister

A closer look at the contemporary British political system reveals that the prime minister's power is more restricted that initially meets the eye. Although he appoints and dismisses the cabinet members, he can hardly lord over them. Unlike most American cabinet members, the British ones are often experienced and influential members of Parliament with whom the prime minister has worked for some years. He cannot scout the country for talented individuals whose main responsibility is to carry out the chief executive's policy; he can only choose from his colleagues in Parliament who have political bases of their own in the party and in the nation. He thus does not normally deal with minions but with somewhat-powerful political office holders who would be less afraid to stand up to him in private.

He must retain the confidence of the most important factions within the parliamentary majority party. He must inevitably take into the cabinet some persons who disagree with him on some fundamental issues. This has tended to weaken the convention of cabinet solidarity. Thatcher had to cope with scarcely concealed criticism from those within her own cabinet, whom she dubbed "wets." John Major lost the 1997 elections in part because he never succeeded in silencing Tory colleagues who opposed his policy toward Europe. Finally, since 1999 the prime minister must deal with regionally elected parliaments in Scotland, Wales, Northern Ireland, and since 2000 a Greater London Assembly.

It is often argued that the prime minister enjoys the advantage of not having to direct huge ministries, as cabinet members do. Therefore, he is freer to deal with larger political questions. To some extent, this is true, but the other side of the coin is that he lacks manageable administrative backing. He has no department to provide him with independent analyses and advice. His "private office" at his residence, Number 10 Downing Street, is too small. More valuable to him is the "cabinet office," headed by a top civil servant, which organizes the agenda for cabinet discussions. Thatcher established a "policy unit" at Number 10 composed of some expert advisers. Yet these specialists were no match for the massed expertise available to departmental ministers. Thus, the quality of the prime minister's information is not generally better than that of his cabinet members.

He must deal with a complicated network of ministries and departments with diverse views and a good deal of autonomy in their own areas of responsibility. By American standards, there is virtually no "spoils system" in British politics. The prime minister is able to send to each ministry only one minister and one to three parliamentary secretaries. But when they arrive, often with little or no detailed experience in the particular areas of responsibilities and with no staffs of their own, they are faced with a permanent secretary, the senior civil servant of his department with several decades of experience. He and his subordinate civil servants have the facts at their fingertips and brief the minister.

Although it is his job merely to give technical advice and let the minister set the political direction, it is but a short step from persuasively "giving the facts" to actually determining departmental policy. Usually continuity, not change, wins out. New policies must be negotiated with these bodies, not simply imposed upon them. Nevertheless, if the minister comes to clear, firm decisions, then his officials will almost always carry them out.

Bureaucracy and the Civil Service

As in all advanced countries, much of the work which used to be done by leading politicians has now been delegated to the civil service, which numbers about 640,000 bureaucrats. Most do not actually work in Whitehall, that small area in London where the chief administrative buildings are located. Britain is fortunate to have civil servants who generally work efficiently, who are almost entirely uncor-

Author's daughters feeding the pigeons, Trafalgar Square, London

rupted, and whose decisions usually arise not from personal or political reasons but from good administrative ones.

Personnel are frequently criticized because they, the top people, come from too narrow a social background and because they operate under a blanket of secrecy. It remains essentially true that the top 3,500 administrators are drawn heavily from the "Oxbridge" (Oxford and Cambridge) Universities after having received a generalist's education, despite the fact that the three-class hierarchy was replaced in 1971 by a single, open structure. The recruitment system remains largely unchanged.

Not only the cabinet but also the top 3,500 or so civil servants must take oaths of secrecy. Among cabinet ministers, this convention is breaking down somewhat, as they leak information to the press or write revealing memoirs. The civil servants' oath makes it a crime to disclose any official information, whether it is classified or not; he is bound to remain silent for life.

A vigorous campaign was launched by a variety of groups to punch some holes in this screen of secrecy by adopting a law similar to the US Freedom of Information Act. One hole appeared in 1991, when for the first time the newly appointed chief of the MI5 Security Service (counterespionage) Stella Rimington (the first woman ever to occupy the post) was identified by name; now the chief speaks publicly. MI5 is the first British intelligence organization to advertise for recruits. Its head is known as "M."

Secret Intelligence Service (SIS, still widely referred to as MI6), deals with foreign intelligence. It provides intelligence on "requirements" from the field and is primarily a collection agency that relies heavily on human sources, agents who operate under cover and in dangerous situations. Its existence was only publicly admitted in 1994. In 2010 for the first time in MI6's 100-year history, the head, Sir John Sawers, made a public speech. This was a step toward greater transparency and improved public confidence. Like his predecessors, he is referred to as "C", after the service's first chief, Mansfield Cumming, and he signs his letters with green ink, as tradition dictates. Sir John noted that more than a third of MI6's resources were directed toward counterterrorism. He emphasized the importance of sharing intelligence with the US, "an especially powerful contributor to UK security." The communications intelligence service, GCHO, was completely unknown to the media. In November 2013 the three heads made history when they appeared live on TV before Parliament's Intelligence and Security Committee.

All three of these agencies have long inspired the imagination of thriller writers. When disgruntled former MI6 agent, Richard Tomlinson, put the names of more than 100 British secret agents on the World Wide Web in 1999, British security officials conceded that the Internet is so far-flung that no government can control the flow of information on it.

Despite the Official Secrets Act and tradition, the British news media have always been an important check on governmental power. Britain has more newspapers per capita than any other country. Nevertheless, the Blair government introduced in 2005 a Freedom of Information Act, a reform with the backing of three-fourths of the population. Unlike its equivalent in the US, where Americans have to take their government to court to force it to share its secrets, a British information commissioner does this job for Britons.

Acts of Parliament usually merely establish the basic principles of law, and the civil service fills in the details. Bureaucratic regulations now vastly outnumber actual laws, as is the case in the United States. Traditionally, the treasury, led by the chancellor of the exchequer (treasury minister), has been the main coordinator of the many departments and ministries. Since it was responsible for the budgets of the various departments, it gained the right to comment on any policy proposal from any department. There is some skepticism about the treasury's ability to oversee and review all policy effectively. But if anybody is master of Whitehall, it is the treasury and not the cabinet as a whole.

In addition to the huge bureaucracy, the prime minister must deal with a maze of so-called quasi-autonomous nongovernmental organizations, mercifully shortened to "quangos." Depending on how wide the net is thrown, these organizations number up to 5,521 and include such bodies as the Arts Council, the University Grants Committee, the Commission for Racial Equality, the BBC, Trustees of National Museums, and the nationalized industries. Many are purely advisory, but some dispense large sums of money. All consider themselves to be more or less autonomous, but most are financed, and most members are named by the central government, usually by a department of Whitehall. The government can sometimes force these "quangos" to comply with overall policies by giving or withholding grants, but it frequently faces stiff opposition and must often modify its policies in order to win compliance. They have taken over many services formerly performed by local authorities. The budget-conscious Cameron government announced in 2010 that 481 of these would be merged, reformed, or abolished in order to cut spending.

Alongside the "quangos" are especially important interest groups that have semiofficial status with the government or with various ministries. They include the Church of England, the universities, and the umbrella organizations for the unions and industry—the Trades Union Congress (TUC, which has 6.2 million in 58 unions) and the Confederation of British Industry (CBI). The latter is the largest employers' association in the world, with a highly professional bureaucracy.

The Judiciary

Another limitation on the government's power, which has long been one of the chief cornerstones of British liberty, has been an independent judiciary. Political leaders are forbidden to obstruct the judicial process, even though judges make decisions that significantly influence politics. As with most other aspects of the British public life, the legal structure is fragmented and complicated. There are different court systems: one for England and Wales; one for Northern Ireland, and one for Scotland, which has always retained its own separate, Roman-based legal system. There are different layers of courts. At the pinnacle were the 10 to 12 Lords of Appeal (known as the "Law Lords"), who sat in the House of Lords and who, constituted as the Judicial Committee of the Privy Council, could even hear appeals from some parts of the British Commonwealth.

Usually the Law Lords' hearings were dry and poorly attended; they involved less pomp and ritual than does the US Supreme Court. But the eyes of the world were on them in 1998–1999, when former Chilean leader General Augusto Pinochet went to Britain for medical treatment. While there, Spain and other European countries demanded his extradition because of his alleged international human rights violations. He claimed immunity as a former head of state and current member of the Chilean senate, so the Law Lords were asked for a ruling.

Normally the top British jurists do not have reputations for their political leanings, as do American Supreme Court justices, but their politics became an issue in the long legal battle. In the end, they rendered seven judgments that revealed differing interpretations on points of law. Nevertheless, they ruled that Pinochet could be extradited to Spain to face charges of torture but only for those acts committed after December 1988, when Britain implemented the 1984 Torture Convention.

They made another landmark decision in December 2004, when, sitting for only the second time since the Second World War in a panel of nine justices instead of the usual five, they struck down the government's practice of detaining terrorist

Siambr y Tŷ

Dyluniwyd Siambr bresennol Tŷ'r Cyffredin gan y diweddar Syr Giles Gilbert Scott ac fe'i hagorwyd ym 1950. Cymerodd le'r Siambr a ddyluniwyd gan Syr Charles Barry, a ddefnyddiwyd gyntaf gan Dŷ'r Cyffredin ym 1852, ac a ddinistriwyd gan fomio'r Almaenwyr ym 1941. Cafodd aelodau Tŷ'r Cyffredin eu cartref parhaol cyntaf ym 1547, pan neilltuwyd Capel San Steffan ar eu cyfer. Fe'i defnyddiwyd gan y Tŷ tan 1834, pan gafodd ei ddinistrio gan y tân a ddifaodd Balas San Steffan bron yn llwyr. Gorosoedd rhan isaf capel San Steffan y tân, ac fe'i hadnabyddir bellach fel 'Capel y Crypt'. Ar yr union safle hwn y lleolir Neuadd San Steffan, y bydd ymwelwyr yn cael mynediad trwyddi i'r Cyntedd Canolog, ac mae hi'r un maint â'r hen Siambr.

O ran ei ffurf a'i maintioli mae'r Siambr bresennol bron yn atgynhyrchiad o Siambr Barry, er bod ei haddurniadau'n llai cywrain, a bod orielau mwy wedi'u darparu ar gyfer ymwelwyr. Ehangiad yw trefniadau eistedd cyffredinol y Tŷ mewn gwirionedd ar y trefniadau eistedd a ddefnyddid bedwar can mlynedd a rhagor yn ôl yng Nghapel San Steffan, pan fyddai'r Aelodau'n eistedd yn eisteddleoedd y côr a phan safai Cadair y Llefarydd ar risiau'r allor. Mae 650 o Aelodau Seneddol; ond ceir eisteddleoedd (gan gynnwys yr orielau ochr) ar gyfer 437 yn unig. Mae'r cyfyngiad hwn yn fwriadol; nid fforwm ar gyfer areithiau gosod mo'r Tŷ; i raddau helaeth mae'r trafodaethau'n ymddiddanol yn eu hanfod; ac ar gyfer llawer ohonynt – rhai arbenigol dros ben o ran themâu, neu o natur rigolaidd – ychydig o Aelodau a fydd yn bresennol, a llawer o'r lleill yn brysur â dyletswyddau Seneddol eraill ym Mhalas San Steffan. Gan hynny mae Siambr fach ac agos atoch yn fwy cyfleus. I'r gwrthwyneb, ar achlysuron o bwys, pan fydd y Tŷ yn llawn a phan fydd rhaid i'r Aelodau eistedd yn y rhodfeydd neu ymgasglu o amgylch Cadair y Llefarydd, ger y Bar ac yn yr orielau ochr, cryfheir drama'r Senedd ac yng ngeiriau Syr Winston Churchill, ceir 'ymdeimlad o dorf ac o frys'.

Ymgorfforwyd mwyaduron yn y gwaith coed yng nghefn pob mainc. O bwyso yn ôl ychydig yn hytrach na phwyso ymlaen gall ymwelwyr glywed yn well.

Arddangosir gwybodaeth am yr hyn sy'n digwydd yn y Tŷ ar setiau monitor teledu yn ymyl y ffenestri yn yr Orielau ochr.

Gellir cael ffurflen archebu ar gyfer prynu Adroddiad Swyddogol (Hansard) eisteddiad y dydd drwy'r post oddi wrth y Porthorion neu o'r Swyddfa Archebion Mynediad.

Os oes arnoch angen rhagor o wybodaeth ynglŷn â'ch ymweliad, neu am waith y Tŷ'n gyffredinol, ffoniwch y Swyddfa Hysbysrwydd (01-219 4273).

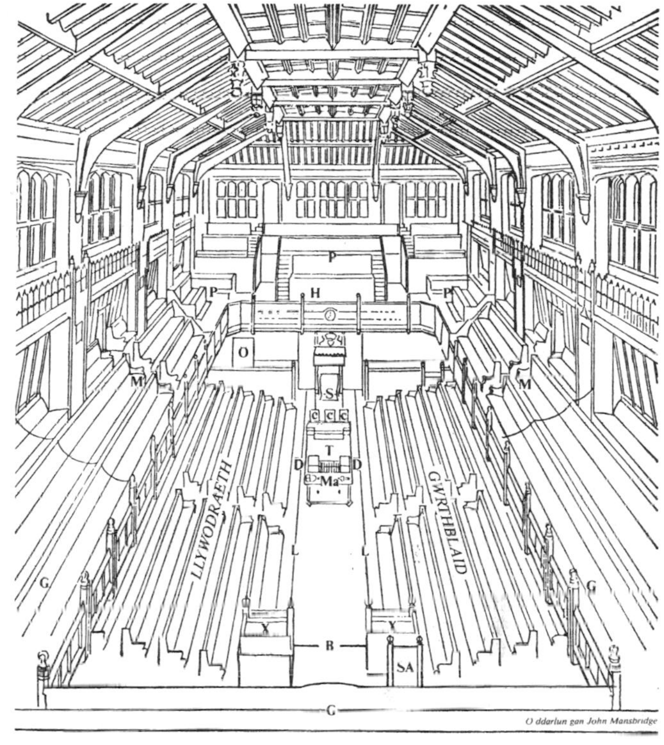

- S — Mr Llefarydd
- P — Orielau'r Wasg
- H — Gohebwyr *Hansard*
- O — Blwch Swyddogion y Llywodraeth (ymgynghorwyr y Gweinidogion)
- C — Clercod y Tŷ*
- T — Bwrdd y Tŷ
- D — Blychau Gohebiaeth
- Ma — Brysgyll †
- L — Llinellau ‡
- B — Bar y Tŷ
- X — Meinciau Traws
- SA — Rhingyll Arfau
- M — Orielau'r Aelodau
- G — Orielau'r Ymwelwyr

*Pan fydd y Tŷ'n Pwyllgora, bydd y Llefarydd yn ymadael â'r Gadair a'r Cadeirydd yn eistedd yng nghadair Clerc y Tŷ, sef yr un ar y chwith. † Pan fydd y Tŷ'n Pwyllgora, rhoddir y Brysgyll "islaw'r Bwrdd" ar fracedi. ‡ Llinellau nad oes hawl gan Aelodau gamu drostynt tra byddant yn siarad o'r meinciau blaen.

Welsh description of House of Commons

suspects indefinitely without trial. They ruled in December 2005 that evidence obtained through torture in other countries could not be used in British courts. Four months later they struck down a key provision in the government's antiterrorism law allowing house arrest for suspects. In 2005 the House of Lords voted down the Blair government's antiterrorist package four times until the prime minister offered an acceptable concession: to allow Parliament to review it within a year.

In October 2009 the Law Lords gave way to a new Supreme Court of 12 judges appointed by the government. Parliament is not involved in the selection process. Its president, Lord Phillips, said this new court was "the last step in divorcing the law lords from any connection with the legislative business of the House of Lords." This enhances the court's image of independence. It cannot strike down statutes as unconstitutional since Parliament itself is supreme. But it can return to Parliament or refer to the European Court of Justice laws it deems to contravene the European Convention on Human Rights, incorporated into British law in 1998.

It has the same powers of the former Law Lords except that it can rule on devolution issues. It must be established to what extent Scotland, which possesses its own legal system, will defer to it. The Supreme Court shares its members and the Middlesex Guildhall in Parliament Square with the Judicial Committee of the Privy Council. The latter hears appeals from some smaller Commonwealth countries and from private jurisdictions, such as professional or academic bodies. Among the Supreme Court's first decisions were that Jewish schools cannot favor applicants based on whether one's mother is Jewish and that LGBTQ asylum seekers cannot be deported if they face persecution in their home countries.

Much of criminal law and most civil law in Britain do not come from acts of Parliament but instead from "common law." Unlike "civil law," which most European democracies have, "common law" is based on tradition, a slow development of rules based on previous cases ("precedents") which are reported in writing, indexed, and published in an elaborate system for reference. It is law made by judge and jury. In order to make legal language more comprehensible for litigants, civil courts eliminated Latin legal terms from proceedings in 1999, replacing them with plain English.

Britain's tradition of parliamentary supremacy excludes the possibility of "judicial review," such as exists in the United States. This would permit the courts to overturn acts of Parliament on the ground that they were unconstitutional. This was theoretically impossible since nobody could be superior to Parliament. That ended in 2000. A kind of individual bill of rights went into effect by incorporating into British law the European Convention for the Protection of Human Rights and Fundamental Freedoms (often referred to as the European Human Rights Charter or EHRC). This convention includes such protections as rights for criminal defendants and freedom of speech, religion, and assembly. These are rights that have been recognized for centuries under common law. To these freedoms is now added a defendable right of privacy.

A half-century earlier, British jurists had played a leading part in drafting the charter, and it has applied to British citizens since the UK entered the EU in 1973. But it was not enforceable in British courts. That has changed. Parliament should not make laws that violate the EHRC. Judges still do not have the right of judicial review, that is, the right to strike down legislation.

However, they can now make a "declaration of incompatibility" when British laws conflict with the EHRC. Parliament or the government must determine whether the "incompatible" statute can remain. The government can bypass Parliament by amending the law by statutory instrument. Although the legislative and executive branches have the last say, political pressure is very strong to bring any law in line with the European charter.

Only a small part of the governing of Britain is carried out by parliamentary acts. Ministers, civil servants, local government authorities, and "quangos" must use discretion in applying general laws to concrete situations, and it is precisely this discretion that can be checked by the courts. In the 1970s a group of parents took the minister responsible for education to court on the charge that the way in which he had applied the school reform was illegal, and the court ruled in their favor. In order to deal with concrete cases, judges must decide what the laws mean. It is in such interpretation that judges have most of their power; the whole thrust of a law can be changed or bent by judges. When judges have this kind of power, one might ask, Who needs judicial review?

As in the United States, there is much controversy over the question of whether the courts have too much power and whether they are, in fact, political. There can be no question that judges' ability to assess the propriety of ministerial actions opens up another course of action to persons who oppose the government's policy. Of course, if Parliament does not like what the courts are doing, it could make new laws that are clearer and more specific, but Parliament has taken that step only once since 1945. It is far too busy to monitor the judges' use of their discretionary power. Whether one likes it or not, the impact of judicial interpretations will remain political and will continue to place limits on governmental power. However, judicial restraint still prevails in Britain to a greater degree than in the United States.

Local Government

Largely because of historical circumstances, the United Kingdom is a unitary, not a federal, state. That is, it is not a collection of "united states." Unlike the United States of America, the UK was not consciously created by sovereign states that carefully retained important powers. The English conquered Wales militarily in the 12th century; it was politically integrated with England in 1536. The thrones of England and Scotland were united in 1603, and the process of union was completed in 1707. The question of succession to the throne led to Anglo-Scottish conflicts in 1715 and 1745, which culminated in the occupation of Scotland by English armies. Ireland was simply taken by force, and the 6 northern counties remained in the United Kingdom in 1922, when the southern 26 counties became independent.

Therefore, the British government is, in theory, freed from the problems of getting its policies accepted by powerful states or provinces. This centralization would seem to fit well with the land and its people—it is a small country, no bigger than the state of Oregon, with a population of almost 60 million. It is highly urbanized, with 40% of the population living in only seven urban centers that account for less than 4% of the total land area.

London, with a population of 8 million (over 15% of the United Kingdom's total), is seven times larger than the second-largest city, Birmingham. Only four other cities have more than a half-million inhabitants: Liverpool, Manchester, Sheffield, and Leeds. A massive migration into London is taking place. Only two-thirds of Londoners were born there. Unlike Washington, New York, Ottawa, or many national capitals, London is simultaneously the center of government, finance, the mass media, and the arts. Nearly three-quarters of the people who earned a place in Who's Who live within a 65-mile radius of London. Half the MPs never resided in their constituencies before their election, and many of them are from London. Further, most ambitious civil servants climb the career ladder in London.

Nevertheless, unitary government does not mean that orders from Number 10 Downing Street, Westminster, or Whitehall are automatically carried out in all corners of the UK. There are many institutions that give much scope for local resistance to central authority. Let us look first at local government.

It is not a surprise that, like most other British political and legal institutions, the structure of local government is diverse and highly complicated. In 1974 a reorganized structure of local government came into effect in an attempt to produce a fairly uniform pattern throughout the entire kingdom. This reform scarcely made the structure of local government easier for the foreigner to understand. To begin with, local government still differs in England, Wales, Scotland, and Northern Ireland. In the first three, there are two tiers of administration, each with elected councils, taxing authority, and its own powers. The top tier (composed generally in England of metropolitan or county councils and in Scotland of nine regional councils) and the lower tier (composed of borough, or district, councils) together provide schools; local roads; government-owned housing (known as "council housing"); and an array of services, such as buses, garbage pickup, libraries, swimming pools, and (except in London) police protection.

These two tiers often clash with each other, especially in metropolitan areas. To muddle things even more, there is usually even a third tier composed of parish or community councils with powers of their own. In all, there are more than 14,000 local governments in Britain. These local units account for a quarter of all government spending. Most is handed out by the central government rather than raised locally, but they do provide for close to half of their own expenses through local property taxes (known as "rates") and fees for services. They employ almost 3 million people (over 12% of the total workforce), far more than the central government.

Former prime ,inister Thatcher locked horns with local authorities. In 1988 she sought to abolish the existing system of local taxes based on the size and value of personal property and to replace it with a flat-rate levy, or community charge, which would spread the tax burden to residents of all incomes. Opponents said this was regressive and unfair, while she said that, by spreading taxes evenly, the new tax would bring pressure to bear on local councils, many of which are dominated by Labour politicians, to reduce their budgets. Thus, a motive to modernize the tax system was mingled with one to reduce the opposition's power even further. So unpopular was this flat-rate levy that it helped lead to her downfall in 1990.

She also moved to abolish the metropolitan councils, at least in part because some of them had become centers of leftist power. These included the Greater London Council (GLC) and what was sometimes derisively referred to in Tory circles as the "Socialist Republic of Yorkshire." While eliminating the GLC in her 1986 reform, the elected councils in London's 32 administrative areas, such as Kensington and Chelsea, Westminster, and Lambeth and Hackney, continued to exist. Within days of assuming office in May 1997, Prime Minister Blair proposed a referendum for Londoners to create an elected government and mayor.

In 1998, 72% voted in favor of a directly elected mayor, and in May 2000 self-proclaimed socialist Ken Livingstone, running as an independent, was elected London's mayor. He was known as "Red Ken" because of his outspoken opposition to Thatcher and his earlier policies as GLC head of declaring the capital a nuclear-free zone, making common cause with IRA supporters, and backing LGBTQ rights. He vowed to rid Trafalgar Square of pigeons, which he described as "rats with feathers."

In 2003 he launched a revolutionary program to diminish central London's traffic congestion, among the world's worst. Every private automobile and truck driving into an eight-square-mile area in the heart of the city on weekdays between 7 a.m. and 6:30 p.m. must pay the equivalent of $14 per day for the privilege. The proceeds are spent on public transport projects. When in 2006 the US embassy and other foreign embassies called this a tax (from which they should be exempt) and refused to pay it, Livingstone called the US ambassador "a chiseling little crook" and a "car salesman." The forthright mayor was also suspended from office for four weeks in 2006 for saying a Jewish reporter was "just like a concentration camp guard."

Even Blair had called him and his colleagues a "ragbag of Trotskyists" and threw him out of the Labour Party. In May 2008 Livingstone was voted out of power when the Conservatives won 44% of the popular votes in the London local elections. The flamboyant, eccentric ex-journalist and TV personality Boris Johnson became mayor. He was reelected in May 2012, narrowly defeating his predecessor, Ken Livingston.

Sometimes strong-armed measures toward local governments do work, depending largely on the skill and determination of the prime minister. Nevertheless, it would be more accurate to describe the overall relationship in terms of bargaining between interdependent levels of government.

Island Governments

The United Kingdom includes certain island groups, such as the Outer Hebrides, Orkney, and Shetland, which have more local authority than county, district, or metropolitan county councils on the mainland. For instance, Shetland controls oil developments in its own territory and has launched a strong movement toward total internal autonomy. The Isle of Man in the Irish Sea and the partly French-speaking bailiwicks of Guernsey and Jersey off the French coast already have autonomous legal status; Norman-based legal systems; their own parliaments; and governments which control domestic, fiscal, and economic policy. They are quaint anomalies in that they are not part of the UK but are Crown dependencies. They are also not in the European Union, so their citizens do not enjoy the freedom to move and work in its member states.

The Channel Islands had been occupied by 30,000 Germans during World War II. In 1993 embarrassing evidence was released that islanders had collaborated with, profited from, or slept with the German masters. In one notorious incident in 1942, local authorities helped the Germans identify 2,100 Jews and English-born residents to be deported to camps in Germany. These revelations reopened old wounds and prompted Britons to think about how they might have reacted if Hitler's forces had overrun the entire country.

Wales, Scotland, and Northern Ireland

The three large regions on the outer fringe of the United Kingdom comprise about a fifth of the UK's total population: Wales (2.9 million), Scotland (5.6 million), and Northern Ireland (1.9 million). These populations compare with 48.7 million in England. By 2004, however, the usual migration had been reversed, and Scotland and northern England were gaining people. Until 1999 all were, in varying degrees, Celtic in background and relatively poor economically. All three were ruled by departments of the central government: the Wales Office, the Scottish Office, and the Northern Ireland Office, each with a mini Whitehall at its disposal. The prime minister appointed a secretary of state for each, and these politicians, who never come from the areas they control, sat in the cabinet.

Although these regions' relations with London have rarely been smooth, regionalism was seldom a major factor in British politics. The differences were masked by a common language, the facade of unitary government, and economic prosperity. This changed dramatically in the 1970s. Strapped with a disproportionate number of dying industries and unhappy with the remoteness of central government, nationalist parties in Wales and Scotland grew. At the end of the century, Westminster transferred important powers to these regions. "Devolution," which resulted in all three having their own elected parliaments in 1999, represents a historic shift in the way Britain is governed.

Wales

Wales is technically a principality whose titular ruler is the Prince of Wales, who is always the heir apparent to the English throne. It lost all traces of political identity through the Act of Union with England in 1535. However, its social integration with England proceeded much more slowly. English was the language of the government after 1535, but until the 19th century, the Welsh language, which is a Celtic dialect related to Irish, Scottish, and Breton, was spoken by a majority of the people. It is the strongest surviving Celtic language. Now only one-fifth of the Welsh population speaks it, mainly in rural areas and small towns in North Wales, but one-third claim to have "some understanding" of the language. Welsh speakers form a majority in outlying areas in the west, inhabited by only 10% of the population. All public-sector bodies give Welsh equal status with English.

Unlike Scotland, it was the preservation of the language more than independence from England which fired the Welsh nationalist movement in the 1970s. Lacking its own aristocracy, the Welsh always tended to be somewhat more egalitarian in their outlook. The coal mining and basic industry, especially in the more populous South Wales, have always made it a Labour Party stronghold. In 1978 London offered both Wales and Scotland regional assemblies whose powers would have fallen short of American state legislatures. But in a 1979 referendum, Welshmen rejected such an assembly by a margin of four to one, largely because of the revulsion English-speaking Welshmen felt toward the pretensions of the Welsh-speaking minority.

To help satisfy Welsh nationalist urges, Welsh-language schools were established. By 2006 they numbered 448 primary and 54 secondary schools that teach mostly or entirely in Welsh. Since they tend to be good schools, parents, even newcomers from nearby England, want their children to attend them. The result is that a new generation of articulate nationalists is graduating from Welsh-language schools. Welsh is a compulsory subject until age 16 in English-language schools. For the first time since reliable statistics have been taken, the proportion who claim to speak Welsh is rising: Between 1991 and 2001, the proportion grew from 19% to 21% (and from 5.8% two decades ago to 10.9% in the capital, Cardiff). Teenagers are more likely to speak than their parents. Since 1993, public agencies are obliged to provide service in both languages, and court cases can be heard in Welsh if the plaintiff or defendant wishes. Welsh speakers are favored in the job market and earn 6%–8% more than English-only rivals.

Second, a separate Welsh-language television channel was established (Sianel Pedwar Cymru—channel 4—S4C), which, due to the small viewing audience, is one of the most expensive television channels in the world. BBC Wales has a Welsh-language station, Radio Cymru. Whereas Scots have their own newspapers, most Welsh read the English press. Finally, the Welsh Language Act of 1993, which declared that Welsh and English were to be considered "on a basis of equality," enabled Welsh speakers to be more insistent that Welsh be spoken more. Language disputes are mild compared with Belgium or Quebec.

A colony of a few thousand Welsh speakers was found in Patagonia. Having emigrated to Argentina in the 19th century, they are being actively recruited to return to Wales to help keep the language alive, despite their noticeable Spanish accents. In 2004 one such Patagonian lady became the first person to take her naturalization oath in the Welsh language.

Holyrood, Scottish Parliament

Welsh nationalism is alive though not robust. A nationalist party, Plaid Cymru (pronounced "Plide Cumry"), founded in the 1920s amid anti-English feeling, no longer talks much about an independent Wales with a seat in the United Nations, since most citizens do not want that. A pressure group, the Independent Wales Movement, was organized in 2000 outside Plaid's ranks. It is more exuberantly nationalist, forcing Plaid leader Ieuan Wyn Jones to speak of "full national status" for Wales. He explained that this meant the same standing as Ireland has within the EU.

It settled for the referendum leading to an elected Welsh Assembly. In 1997 a razor-thin majority in Wales, with only half the eligible voters participating, voted in favor of its first elected parliament in nearly 600 years. This National Assembly has 60 members (AMs). Its powers are more limited than those of the new Scottish Parliament. It can amend certain acts of Westminster, but it cannot pass its own laws or raise taxes. It can decide how to spend the budget formerly administered by the Welsh Office, including for health, housing, and education, and scrutinize and alter the administration of Wales.

In 1999 the first elections were won by Labour. A new electoral system modeled on that of Germany was used: Each voter has two votes, one for his preferred representative (called member of the Welsh Parliament—MWP) in the 40 constituencies and one for the party of his choice. Thus it is a combination of Britain's "first-past-the-post" system and proportional representation. Secretary of State for Welsh Affairs Alun Michael of the Labour Party handed over his powers to himself in his new capacity as first secretary of the Welsh Assembly. In 2000 Labour's popular Rhodri Morgan was elected as first minister.

A 2007 survey revealed that a majority of Welsh believe devolution has improved the way Wales is governed and favor more powers to their own assembly, which will come. Though not as desirous of independence as are Scots, three-fifths of them prefer to call themselves "Welsh" rather than "British." That Welsh identity is more cultural than political. In the May 2010 British elections, Labour remained the largest party, winning 26 of Wales's 40 seats. The Conservatives snatched four of Labour's seats, climbing from three to eight. Only three went to Plaid Cymru. Labour performed strongly in the May 2011 local and regional elections, narrowly failing to win an overall majority in the devolved parliament. Two months earlier, voters overwhelmingly supported proposals in a referendum for more devolution. From May 2011, the Welsh Assembly can initiate laws in 20 areas, including education. It is growing more independent from Westminster.

Scotland

Scotland, which is still a kingdom in its own right, joined England by agreement in 1707. Although the Scottish Parliament voted itself out of existence at that time, other institutions remained intact, such as the legal system, based on Roman law; a distinctive educational system; and a Presbyterian Church of Scotland. By long-standing custom, the queen worships as a Presbyterian in Scotland and as an Episcopalian in England. One should therefore not wonder at the fact that the Scots have a secure sense of separate national identity that has survived union with England.

Scottish nationalist feeling has simmered for two and a half centuries, but the intensity and strength surged furiously in the 1970s, when oil was discovered in the North Sea off Scotland's coasts. The Scottish Nationalist Party (SNP), founded in 1928, argued that "It's Scotland's Oil!" and that it would make this relatively poor region in the UK wealthy and capable of independence. In the 1974 parliamentary elections, its vote surged to 30%. In the face of such rising nationalism in their traditional party stronghold, the ruling Labour government offered to create a popularly elected Scottish assembly if such a move were approved by a majority in a referendum.

Such an instrument of "direct democracy" means that, between parliamentary elections, the people, not Parliament, decide. Because of the tradition of parliamentary supremacy, there were no referendums in Britain until the 1970s. Parliament did stipulate that at least 40% of the eligible Scottish voters had to approve the transfer of powers to the region (a process known as "devolution"). The referendum was held in March 1979, and 51.6% of the voters approved of the assembly; however, only 33% of the eligible voters participated, so Parliament repealed the devolution act for Scotland. The Labour Party, which had always won most of the Scottish seats, reasserted itself in Scottish affairs and picked up the torch of devolution.

The 1990s witnessed a resurgence of Scottish nationalism and the SNP. Polls in 1992 indicated that 80% of Scots wanted either a Scottish parliament or outright independence. One native son, actor Sean Connery, compared Scotland to the independent Baltic states. This was quite a role reversal for "James Bond," who onscreen risked everything to serve the British Crown. He said he would permanently move from his adopted home in the Bahamas back to Scotland if it were ever to win its independence. The hit movie *Braveheart* in the mid-1990s also boosted the movement for greater Scottish independence. Even more Scotsmen began saying, "We're not free. We need a William Wallace."

This feeling helped fuel an upsurge of interest in learning Scotland's Gaelic language, which had declined to only 60,000 speakers, or about 3%–4% of Scotsmen, who may use it in the assembly if they choose. Still there is no language motive to Scottish nationalism, as in Wales. Nor are there religious ones, as in Northern Ireland, or ethnic motives, as in eastern Europe. Nor is cultural nationalism as strong as it is in Wales. SNP leader Alex

Salmond remarked, "we are a mongrel nation."

In the 1997 elections the SNP, which captured six seats, for the first time in Scotland's history drove the Tories out completely. Scottish MPs in Westminster enjoy the privilege, known as the "West Lothian question," that they can vote on all matters that concern the entire UK, whereas English, Welsh, and Northern Irish MPs cannot vote on matters devolved to Scotland. This quirk helps stimulate "English nationalism." Some polls have shown that two-thirds of the English support an English-only Parliament, and the proportion who define themselves as "English, not British," had by 2005 risen to 40%.

While Labour dominated Westminster until May 2010, devolution of powers to Scotland and Wales came back on the agenda. A referendum in Scotland in 1997 paved the way to a democratically elected assembly in 1999. Voters overwhelmingly approved a 129-seat parliament, Scotland's first in 300 years, with wide powers over such local matters as health, education, municipal government, economic development, housing, criminal and civil law, fisheries and forestry. They also voted for the right to raise or lower income taxes by up to 3% and to levy charges, such as road tolls. Each Scot continues to receive about 1,000 pounds ($1,500) in subsidies from London.

The polling set the stage for the most important constitutional change in British government in modern times. It also signaled the peaceful rebirth of a nation in an extraordinary way: no guerrilla army, separatist terrorists, civil disobedience, or even mass demonstrations. Edinburgh has become Britain's second diplomatic capital, with 16 foreign missions established there by 2005. A couple of dozen Scotsmen work in "external relations," a term carefully selected so as not to irritate British diplomats in the "foreign office." Half of those diplomats work in Brussels, Washington and Beijing.

On May 6, 1999, voters elected their first Members of the Scottish Parliament (MSP). Using the same mixed single-member constituency/PR electoral system as the Welsh, they favored Labour. This was a setback for the SNP's independence cause. In 2000, Labour's leader Donald Dewar slipped on his front porch and quickly died of a brain hemorrhage. This was a blow to those who advocated autonomy rather than separation from Britain.

The SNP, under John Swinney, had clearly failed to persuade voters in May 2003 that it would be a plausible government and that full independence would be a good thing. The party was divided between those who wanted to return to being a protest party and those who believed that a gradual accumulation of power by the Scottish Parliament is the best route to go.

Scottish first minister
Nicola Sturgeon

Gerry Adams,
president, Sinn Fein

SNP leader Alex Salmond, a former economist with the Royal Bank of Scotland, concluded that an election victory in Scotland would no longer be a sufficient mandate for independence. It would need to be followed by a referendum before an SNP government could enter negotiations to remove Scotland from Britain. Scots appeared to want to see how devolution worked before leaping into independence. Indeed it seemed that devolution, not independence, was still the preferred direction, even among some SNP voters. Although three-quarters of Scots prefer to be called "Scottish" than "British," only about a third favor independence, according to polls. But "independence" can mean different things to different people. When they went to the polls in May 2007—the 300th anniversary of the Treaty of Union with England—to elect a Scottish Parliament, two-thirds voted for parties that favor union with Britain.

Although there was no mandate for independence in 2007, the results were still a sensation: For the first time since 1959, Labour came out in second place, winning only 46 to the SNP's 47 seats in the 129-seat assembly. The Tories got 17, and the Liberal Democrats, 16. This ended a half-century of Labour dominance of Scottish politics. It presents a real problem for Labour: It cannot win Britain without winning Scotland. An elated Salmond declared that "never again will the Labour Party think it has a divine right to govern." He became first minister in a minority government. With the SNP in power, the English can no longer be blamed for everything that goes wrong in Scotland.

By the standards of separatist movements around the world, Scottish nationalism has been a peaceful success story. The May 5, 2011, Scottish elections were nothing short of historic: The SNP gained 23 seats to win a majority of 69 out of 129 seats in the Scottish Parliament. Labour lost 8 seats to capture 37, and the Tories slipped from 20 to 15. This spectacular outcome does not mean that most voters would support independence in a referendum. More voters like the SNP and its leader, Nicola Sturgeon, more than they like the idea of severing from the UK. The SNP must define precisely what independence means in the modern age.

In October 2012 Salmond and Prime Minister Cameron signed a referendum deal to stage a Scottish vote on September 18, 2014. The ballot question was a simple in-or-out one: "Should Scotland be an independent country?" Sixteen- and seventeen-year-olds were permitted to vote. All three major parties in Parliament opposed it.

Salmond confirmed that he would seek a currency union with the UK, but all three main parties flatly rejected this. EC president Barrosa stated that it would be almost impossible for Scotland to join the EU. Salmond promised to issue Scottish passports, create a separate defense force, and expel British nuclear submarines from Scottish bases. Scotland would remain in NATO, retain the monarchy, and claim 90% of the North Sea oil and gas revenues. Britain would lose 8% of its economy and population, along with a third (32%) of its territory. The "no" vote won by 55% to 45% in 2014. However, in the May 2015 parliamentary elections, the SNP scored a dramatic victory, capturing 56 of 59 Scottish seats, wiping out the previously dominant Labour Party. Nicola Sturgeon, a charismatic SNP member since age 16, triumphantly announced that "the political firmament, the tectonic plates of Scottish politics [have] shifted." Independence is back on the agenda. However, its citizens overwhelmingly favor remaining in the EU.

In 2004 the queen officially opened the new ultramodern Scottish Parliament, Holyrood, right across the street from her official Scottish residence. Housing 129 lawmakers, it was three years late and, at £431 million ($650 million), 10 times over budget. Sitting in its beautiful interior, MSPs can look out over the rugged hills that symbolize their land.

Northern Ireland

The UK's most serious regional problem by far was Northern Ireland. The Irish island can be said to be England's oldest colony, having been invaded by the English in the 12th century and ruled as a colony until 1800, when it received its own parliament. Ireland remained legally a part of the United Kingdom until 1922, when the 26 predominantly Catholic southern counties formed what is now the Republic of Ireland. The Protestant majority in the six northern counties rejected "home rule" (independence from Britain). The British at the time pledged that no change in the link between Northern Ireland and the United Kingdom would occur without the consent of the majority of the people. Every subsequent British government held firmly to this commitment.

The largely Presbyterian and Church of Ireland Protestants are descendants of Scottish immigrants who began arriving in the 17th century. Their loyalty to the English Crown is based upon the monarch's historical status set forth in the 1689 Bill of Rights as "the glorious instrument of delivering this kingdom from Popery and arbitrary power." It is not surprising that this historical attitude, along with the Protestants' rejecting unification of the two parts of Ireland, has always antagonized the Catholic minority in Northern Ireland (who comprise 42% of the population of 1.6 million). Although Northern Ireland is officially a secular (i.e., nonreligious) state, in actual practice the friction between Catholics and Protestants dominates politics there.

Northern Ireland was in turmoil since 1968, when a Catholic civil rights movement organized internationally publicized street demonstrations to object Protestant discrimination in housing, jobs, and electoral representation. British governmental pressure on the Northern Irish parliament (which has existed since 1921 and is known as Stormont because it met in Stormont Castle) to meet many of the Catholic demands created a Protestant backlash. Peaceful street demonstrations in 1969 gave way to open violence, and British troops were sent to reestablish order.

The Irish Republican Army (IRA) sprang to life again and launched a modern terrorist campaign to remove the British from the territory and to reunify the entire island. It received money and arms from overseas sources ranging from Gadhafi in Libya to the Irish Northern Aid Committee—NORAID—in the United States. Due to bad publicity, IRA fundraising in the US became more difficult. It found a lucrative substitute: extortion and racketeering in Northern Ireland itself. Because it also seeks the overthrow of the Dublin government, it has been banned in the south since 1936.

In retaliation, some Protestants in the north organized illegal forces. The best-known illegal Protestant paramilitary group, known for its violence, is the Ulster Volunteer Force (UVF). This illegal unit should not be confused with the Ulster Defence Regiment (UDR—the British army in Northern Ireland), the Royal Ulster Constabulary (RUC—the mainly Protestant police force), or the Ulster Defence Association (UDA—a moderate and legal Protestant paramilitary group). In 1993 Protestant gunmen murdered more people than did the IRA.

The British disbanded Stormont in 1972 and resorted to the unpleasant task of ruling the region directly, through a secretary of state for Northern Ireland. Successive British governments sought earnestly for ways to devolve governmental power to the Northern Irish themselves. The problem was always how to protect the Catholic minority's interests against a perpetual Protestant majority. This difficulty revealed a major weakness of the English model of parliamentary democracy, which presents great power to any political group that commands an electoral majority: The model does not work well in societies which are divided religiously, ethnically, or racially because minorities can be voted down so easily.

Realizing this, the British government had to reject in 1975 a proposal by the leaders of the Protestants that a constitution be drawn up for Northern Ireland that would copy British parliamentary practice. Instead, British governments sought some form of "power-sharing" arrangement that would guarantee the minority Catholic parties a place in any Northern Irish executive. This idea infuriated the two Protestant political parties, the Ulster Unionists and the Democratic Unionists.

The IRA, which became a dedicated and ruthless band of 400 to 500 paramilitaries operating in small cells called "active service units," was divided into two groups: The "official" IRA was formerly Marxist, but now it seeks power through elections; the "provisional" IRA (Provos) was strictly nationalist, but it shifted to armed struggle to convert Ireland into a Marxist state. This shift was one reason Irish Americans became less generous toward the IRA. Both these wings face some competition from the smaller but more radical Irish National Liberation Army (INLA, the paramilitary wing of the Marxist Irish Republican Worker's Party).

From 1976 to 1982, the IRA campaigned for special treatment as "political prisoners." After the failure of such tactics as refusing to wear prison garb and smearing the walls of the cells with their own excrement, they resorted to hunger strikes. The deaths of 10 IRA hunger strikers in Maze Prison in 1981 sparked renewed militant Catholic nationalism. Shortly before his death, one of the hunger strikers, Bobby Sands, even managed to win a seat in the House of Commons while he was still in prison.

In response, the British government tried again to restore a measure of devolved government by means of the 1982 Northern Ireland Act. Elections for a 78-seat Northern Ireland Assembly and an executive branch were held in 1982. This new body was to have the power to make proposals to the British government on how to return to self-government. It failed. Neither the mainly Catholic, moderate, and law-abiding Social Democratic and Labour Party nor the militant Sinn Fein (the political arm of the IRA, pronounced "Shin Fane," receiving only 10% of the total votes) took their seats in it. The Ulster Unionist Party also walked out and vowed that it would not return until security had been restored in Northern Ireland.

That is exactly what the British tried to do. In 1975 it ended the detention of both Catholic and Protestant terrorist suspects without trial, and it refused to declare martial law in the violence-torn area. Because of the risk of intimidation against jurors, nonjury courts (known as "Diplock Courts") were created for those accused of terrorist-related offenses. The British have always contended that the fundamental principles of British justice—a fair trial, the onus on the prosecution to prove guilt, the right to be represented by a lawyer, the right of appeal if convicted—are maintained for all.

The most effective antiterrorist measure undertaken by the government in 1983 was the granting of pardon or lenience to onetime terrorists if they would tip off the police (in Northern Irish slang, "to grass") on the whereabouts of active terrorists. The testimony of such "supergrasses" led to a dramatic number of arrests in both the IRA and Protestant Ulster Volunteer Force. These organizations were so paralyzed that terrorist deaths in Northern Ireland dropped by half in one year, from 97 in 1982 to about 50 in 1983. IRA terrorists did give British Christmas shoppers a grisly indication they were alive in 1983, however, when they exploded a bomb outside of the bustling Harrods Department Store in London, claiming still more innocent lives (including an American teenager, a fact that hurt IRA fund-raising in the US) in their ruthless struggle.

The Brighton bombing of 1984 was another grim reminder of the IRA's intent to wreak as much havoc as possible, this time by assailing the highest levels of British government itself. Having organized into "cells," the IRA became more difficult for police to combat. The violence prompted the Irish Republic to ratify the European convention on terrorism, which requires the extradition of terrorists.

By 2003 the toll stood at over 3,600 since 1969. In doing its bloody work, the IRA had the tactical advantage over the 30,000 security forces, which were kept on the defensive by the IRA's meticulous planning and constant shifting of tactics. To minimize its own losses, it increasingly struck at "soft targets," such as bands, military hospitals, off-duty RUC officers, and civilian firms that supply goods and services to the security forces. It also acquires state-of-the-art equipment; for example, it has surface-to-air missiles to use against army helicopters.

Democracy still existed at the local level in Northern Ireland, and voters send 27 MPs to the House of Commons in London. Protestants win a majority of these seats. Catholics would take more if the competing SDLP and Sinn Fein would unify in constituencies with predominantly Catholic populations. In the 1997 elections, the two Catholic parties captured an unprecedented 40.2% of the votes.

The Protestant unionist parties also have trouble working together, with Ian Paisley's hard-line Democratic Unionists taking five seats and David Trimble's larger Ulster Unionist Party winning six. Sinn Fein traditionally refused to take any seat in the British Parliament, whose authority it does not recognize and which would require them to swear allegiance to the queen. In 2002 Adams and three other party members took a historic step by going to the House of Commons and signing up to use all of the facilities except actually occupying a seat. Adams emphasized, "There will never ever be Sinn Fein MPs sitting in the British houses of Parliament." In 2005 the party's parliamentary expenses of £400,000 ($6,400) were withheld to punish the party for IRA crimes.

In 1997 Sinn Fein won an all-time high of 16% of the votes in Northern Ireland. Two of its candidates, Gerry Adams and Martin McGuinness (an IRA leader who has served jail sentences), won seats, which remained vacant. Sinn Fein does occupy seats in local councils on both sides of the Irish border and in the Northern Ireland Assembly. In 2002 it decided to run for seats in the Irish Republic's elections, and it won five; there was general relief when it lost one of those seats in May 2007. In June 2002 Sinn Fein won control of Belfast, and Alec Maskey became lord mayor.

There was progress in addressing the problem of social and economic discrimination. For members of the growing Catholic middle class, life has never been better. They are upwardly mobile and increasingly move into middle-class Protestant neighborhoods, where they are tolerated. Catholics now outnumber Protestants at universities by four to three. The unemployment gap is shrinking. Three out of 10 persons are employed in the public sector, and hiring policies are scrupulously equal and fair. They have begun to intermarry; one-tenth of marriages are mixed. Tourists are returning to the province, which has the lowest rate of violent crime in the UK. Investment is entering from the Irish Republic, which has become Europe's third-richest country. Businesses on both sides of the border are working together. There would be even more cooperation if corporate taxes (30% in Northern Ireland and 12.5% in the Republic) were more equal. However, there is still mistrust. A quarter of respondents said in a 2004 poll that a close relative had died in the Troubles. That figure is probably higher in working-class areas.

In 1985 former Irish taoiseach (prime minister) Garrett FitzGerald and British prime minister Thatcher signed an Anglo-Irish agreement on Northern Ireland. This marked the first time the British government formally permitted the Irish Republic involvement in Northern Ireland's affairs, a concession many Northern Irish Protestants could not accept. It is regrettable but perhaps not surprising that all groups in Northern Ireland condemned this landmark act, despite the fact that its first article stated that no change in the province's status would come about without the consent of a majority of its people.

Peace Talks in Northern Ireland

In 1993 optimism was ignited by a joint declaration by the British and Irish prime ministers offering Sinn Fein a seat at the bargaining table to discuss Northern Ireland's future if the IRA renounced violence. Former prime minister John Major, who admitted that his government had conducted secret contacts with the IRA, promised that Britain would not stand in the way of a united Ireland if a majority of Northern Ireland residents supported such a step. His Irish counterpart pledged that there would be no change in the six counties' status without majority consent.

The following year President Bill Clinton, betting that the IRA wants peace in Northern Ireland, made a risky decision to grant a visa to Sinn Fein leader Gerry Adams to come to the US. Although the British government criticized him for this, it triggered a series of historic events. On August 31, 1994, the IRA declared a cease-fire, which prompted the Irish government to begin meeting with Sinn Fein leaders. Six weeks later Protestant loyalists also declared a truce. While paramilitaries on both sides continued to terrorize their own communities, intersectarian violence and IRA attacks on British forces stopped. As a result, the British government relaxed its security measures in Northern Ireland and began drawing down its 18,000 troops. In December London opened direct talks with Sinn Fein and, later, with the Protestant paramilitaries. In February 1995 the British and Irish governments issued a "Framework for Agreement," outlining their proposals for Northern Ireland's future.

The US government did its part to keep the momentum going by permitting Sinn Fein to open an office near Dupont Circle in Washington in 1995 and to raise money legally in the US Much to London's displeasure, Clinton invited Gerry Adams to a St. Patrick's Day party in the White House honoring Ireland's taoiseach. In May the US also organized a Northern Ireland Investment Conference in Washington that brought together more people from more different Northern Irish parties under one roof than ever before. It was also attended by top government officials from the UK and Ireland and was the venue for the first meeting between Gerry Adams and Britain's ex–secretary of state for Northern Ireland Patrick Mayhew. This was the highest-level meeting between British and IRA leaders in 75 years and a giant step toward Adams's goal of receiving the same recognition and treatment accorded to Northern Ireland's other political leaders.

Clinton gave another powerful boost to the peace process in November 1995 by paying the first visit to Belfast ever made by an American president. It was a triumph. The very approach of his historic visit helped dissolve a stalemate in the talks and revitalized cooperation. Hours before his arrival the Irish and British prime ministers met and agreed to a breakthrough: preliminary all-party talks, led by former US senator George

Mitchell, would be held, while an international "decommissioning commission," led by former Canadian chief-of-staff and ambassador to Washington General John De Chastelain, sought a way around the weapons impasse.

John Major admitted that Clinton's coming helped "concentrate the mind." Greeted everywhere in Belfast by cheering crowds waving American flags, Clinton addressed over 100,000 people, the largest throng in memory to gather in the square of Belfast City Hall. He appealed to everyone to put aside "old habits and hard grudges" and to seek peace. One witness said, "I've never seen anything like this before. Everybody's come together." His American optimism reportedly made a deep impression. He met with all major leaders in the conflict and invited them to a reception at Queen's University; most came, which would have been unthinkable earlier. It was a very different Belfast that he saw: Gone are the soldiers on the hunt, the countless roadblocks, and the barbed wire. Although the ugly wall topped with razor wire separating Protestants and Catholics, inaptly called the "peace line," still stands, most of the blockaded streets have been reopened in Belfast.

There is little support in Northern Ireland or elsewhere for immediate reunification of Ireland. But not since 1969 had there been so many grounds for optimism that "the Troubles" can end and that the Northern Irish can discuss their future peacefully. As a symbol of returning normalcy with Britain in 1995, Prince Charles became the first member of the royal family to make an official visit to the Irish Republic since 1922. Also in 1995, David Trimble, leader of the Ulster Unionist Party, the main Protestant group, traveled to Dublin and met with the Irish taoiseach. This was the first time since 1922 a Unionist leader was received in Dublin. In 1996 the IRA ended an 18-month cease-fire and launched a bombing campaign in Britain and Northern Ireland. Negotiations resumed in June 1997.

Since the Labour government is not dependent upon Unionist MPs from Northern Ireland to win important votes in Parliament, as John Major was, it had more political flexibility on Northern Irish issues. A couple weeks after becoming prime minister, Blair lifted the ban on official contacts with Sinn Fein in order to explain London's position and to assess whether the IRA was really prepared to renounce violence. Gerry Adams accepted the offer. Blair dropped London's insistence that terrorists disarm before joining peace talks. He visited Northern Ireland on May 16, 1997, in order to demonstrate that he is willing to take risks for peace in the six counties.

To continue the negotiation process, he invited Gerry Adams to a meeting in Downing Street in December. This was the first visit by an Irish Republican leader to the prime minister's private residence in 76 years. It was a richly symbolic encounter, with the meeting over tea held in the cabinet room, the target of an IRA mortar attack only six years earlier. A month later, in January 1998, Adams returned to Downing Street to hear from the prime minister that the peace process is an "absolute priority" and that "the status quo is not an option." To balance his gesture to Sinn Fein, Blair told Protestants that "none of us . . . , even the youngest, is likely to see Northern Ireland as anything but a part of the United Kingdom."

Talks involving eight Northern Ireland parties and the British and Irish governments continued, despite the outbreak of renewed violence following the assassination of a Protestant terrorist, Billy Wright, in Maze Prison just after Christmas. American George Mitchell emphasized the importance of the negotiations: "We're talking about, literally, people's lives, the possibility of the resumption of the terrible conflict that enveloped this society with fear and anxiety. So, frustrating and tedious as it seems—and it is—you have to be patient and recognize how tough it is for them to move."

Good Friday Agreement

In the early-morning hours of Good Friday 1998, after a series of marathon sessions, all parties at the table reached a historic agreement: A new 108-member Northern Ireland Assembly would be elected using the Irish Republic's system of proportional representation with the transferable vote. To protect Catholics from being permanently outvoted on sensitive "cross-community" issues and to necessitate consensus, a majority of both Catholic and Protestant blocs or an overall "weighted majority" of 60% would be required for decisions. The cabinet would consist of 10 seats distributed proportionally to the 4 largest parties.

The assembly would share power with a new North-South Ministerial Council, composed of ministers from the republic and Northern Ireland. This gives the Irish Republic its first formal role in Northern Ireland's affairs. In return, Ireland's leaders agreed to give up the republic's claim to the north. All parties pledged to use their influence to persuade armed groups to turn in their weapons within two years, and imprisoned members of those armed groups would be released within two years, as well.

On May 22, 1998, referenda were held on both sides of the border, and 71% of Northern Irish and 94.4% in the republic approved of the Good Friday settlement. The following month, the first elections to the new assembly were held, and David Trimble's UUP came out on top with 28 seats. John Hume's SDLP (later led by Seamus Mallon) was second, with 24 seats. For their indispensable role in the entire peace process, Trimble and Hume shared the 1998 Nobel Prize for Peace. Hume had declared that "we finally decided that agreement for the whole community is more important than victory for one side." Other seats went to the DUP (20), Sinn Fein (18), the Alliance (6), the UKUP (5), Independent Unionists (3), and the Women's Coalition and PUP (2 each). The great number of parties winning seats demonstrated the effect of the proportional representation electoral system. Trimble became first minister, and the body met for the first time in the traditional Stormont building on July 4.

This being Ireland, an island with so much history and so many memories, things were not destined to go smoothly. In August 1998 a fringe Catholic organization calling itself the "Real IRA" exploded a car bomb in the Northern Irish city of Omagh, killing 29 people. The public was so repelled by this grisly act that the "Real IRA" apologized and announced a permanent cease-fire on September 12. This was soon broken, and the IRA was forbidden from raising money in the United States.

After the BBC named four men it said were involved in the attack, three were arrested in 2000. In 2002 the first was convicted and sentenced to 14 years in jail. Colm Murphy, a wealthy pub owner and building contractor, was found guilty by a three-judge panel in a special criminal court in Dublin. To the chagrin of the victims' families, Murphy's conviction was overturned by a Dublin appeals court. He faced retrial and was acquitted again in February 2010 for lack of sufficient evidence. Another suspect, Sean Gerard Hoey, was charged in 2005 for participating in the bombing. But all convictions were subsequently overturned, including that of Hoey in December 2007. Nevertheless, the tragedy ultimately strengthened support for the peace process. In June 2009 the victims' relatives won a civil case against the "Real IRA" splinter group. They were awarded $2.6 million in damages.

The "Real IRA" was also the prime suspect in the September 2000 rocket attack against the London headquarters of MI6, Britain's foreign intelligence service. To maintain his credibility in the Protestant community, Trimble called for a beginning of "decommissioning" (turning in) of weapons even before the creation of a Northern Ireland cabinet. Noting that this precondition had not been in the agreement, Sinn Fein balked at completing the peace process.

Endless haggling over paramilitary groups laying down their arms threatened the peace deal. However, both sides began taking cautious steps to implement the agreement. On December 1, 1999, a new coalition government in Ulster was formed that shared power devolved from Westminster in London. It included both the party of hard-line Protestant Reverend Ian Paisley and former IRA commander, Martin McGuinnes as minister of education. However, this government was suspended in February 2000 after the IRA failed to meet the Unionists' deadline for starting turning in its arms.

Power sharing was reestablished in May 2000, when the Unionists accepted an IRA pledge to put its arsenal "beyond use" and to allow limited inspections by international observers to verify that that the promise is being kept. Such visits were conducted in June and October 2000, and the arms dumps were reported to have a substantial amount of military material that was safely stored. For a year and a half, the IRA dragged its heels. As a result David Trimble, leader of Northern Ireland's power-sharing government, quit in 2001, and things came to a standstill.

In November 2001 the IRA finally began destroying some of its weapons under international supervision. In quick response to this breakthrough, Britain began demolishing military installations, including army watchtowers overlooking regions with high IRA support. Trimble led his Ulster Unionist Party back into the assembly and was narrowly reelected first minister with the help of the Alliance Party, which had steered a middle road between unionists and republicans. Peace was back on track.

Genuine struggles remain on such emotional symbolic issues as flying flags over official buildings and reforming and renaming the Royal Ulster Constabulary (RUC), which is 93% Protestant. A top American law enforcement official, Tom Constantine, former head of the Drug Enforcement Administration (DEA), was appointed as "oversight commissioner" to scrutinize changes in the RUC. But progress is undeniable. The bloodletting has subsided, although armed dissidents abound. Maze Prison, just outside of Belfast, was emptied and closed in September 2000. Ex-prisoners had played a role in the peace process; they were crucial in the maintenance of their various organizations' cease-fires. The British closed 6 bases along the Irish border and looked forward to reducing the number of bases from 64 to no more than 20 and of troops from 13,500 to 10,500 in 2005 and ultimately to only 5,000.

In July 2002 the IRA stunned everybody with an expression of "sincere apologies and condolences" for all the persons it had killed in the Northern Irish sectarian violence. The "Troubles" appeared to be close to an end when a spy scandal at the heart of the Northern Irish government broke in October 2002. After raiding Sinn Fein homes and offices at the Northern Ireland Assembly, British authorities charged three members of gathering intelligence from Britain's Northern Ireland Office that could be used for terrorist operations. Police found sensitive political material, including minutes of conversations between Blair and his Northern Ireland secretary of state, and names, home addresses, and license plate numbers of many provincial police officers and British security personnel. It was feared that some of the information could be used for assassinations.

Sinn Fein leaders denied the allegations and claimed the police had orchestrated a frame-up. The British suspended the assembly, and Protestant leaders vowed that they would not resume participation unless the IRA renounces violence unmistakably. The IRA then broke off all contact with the independent panel established to oversee disarmament, which had already supervised the destruction of two caches of IRA weapons. One Sinn Fein leader, Martin McGuinness, announced that he had abandoned his fight with Britain and was committing himself to preventing the deaths of any more people: "My war is over." Nevertheless, the peace process had suffered its most serious blow since the Good Friday Agreement five years earlier.

In April 2003 President George W. Bush visited Blair and Irish prime minister Bertie Ahern in Belfast to lend his endorsement to the peace plan. The president had aroused the ire of the British government when Gerry Adams was invited to a White House St. Patrick's Day party in March, this when IRA operatives had been arrested while traveling undercover in the US. Although Blair sensed that breaking the stalemate was "frustratingly close," all his efforts to get the IRA to make a crystal-clear statement that it had given up paramilitary activities like gathering intelligence, threatening and attacking adversaries, and acquiring weapons failed. Adams's statement that there would be "no activities which will undermine in any way the peace process or the Good Friday Agreement" was not enough.

The atmosphere became even more strained when the head of London's Metropolitan Police released evidence in 2012 that agents working for the British army had worked with death squads in Northern Ireland. This included the 1989 murder of Belfast lawyer Patrick Finuncane, who had represented IRA terrorists. Two gunmen from the outlawed Ulster Defence Association broke into his home and shot him 14 times at point-blank range before the very eyes of his wife and three children. One of the gunmen left prison in 2006 under the terms of the 1998 peace accord. Nearly a quarter-century later, an official report detailed how British intelligence was implicated in the murder. Prime Minister Cameron immediately went to Parliament. There he condemned the murder as "an appalling crime" and apologized to the family.

Despite unprecedented direct talks in the fall of 2003 between David Trimble and Gerry Adams, the results of those elections, which were finally held in November 2003, brought a cruel surprise: The confrontational parties outpolled the conciliatory ones, which were the architects and supporters of the peace process. Ian Paisley's Democratic Unionists (DUP) won 30 seats in a 108-seat assembly that does not function, and David Trimble's Ulster Unionist Party (UUP) captured only 27. On the nationalist side, Sinn Fein got 24 seats, while the more moderate Social Democratic and Labour Party (SDLP) fell from 24 to 18. The nonsectarian Alliance Party held on to its six seats, and independents got three.

The same thing happened in the May 2005 British parliamentary elections, which delivered convincing victories to the hard-line parties and moved Northern Ireland closer toward a two-party system. David Trimble resigned his leadership of the Ulster Unionist Party after losing the seat he had held for 15 years. This capped a decade of steadily declining influence for the party. In June 2006 he was granted a life peerage in the House of Lords. Ian Paisley's Democratic Unionists captured half of the 18 seats allotted to Northern Ireland. Sinn Fein took five, and Gerry Adams won easy reelection. The SDLP held on to its three seats. Blair noted in 2003 that "it is more than a little frustrating." Paisley's DUP must be included in any talks to restore devolved government. But Paisley's position as of May 2005 was that the Good Friday Agreement is "finished completely" and "only paper."

A hoped-for settlement ended in December 2004, when the IRA refused to permit photographic verification of its disarmament. Then the IRA was accused of masterminding a spectacular £26.5 million ($40 million) bank robbery in Belfast. A month later, a Catholic father of two, Robert McCartney, was beaten and stabbed to death by a dozen IRA thugs outside a Belfast pub. Seventy-two witnesses in the pub were intimidated in the usual IRA way from testifying. But the man's wife and five sisters decided to depart from the

The Daily Telegraph

WHY WE LOVE THE QUEEN

HOW ROYAL CHARM HAS CAPTIVATED REPUBLICAN AMERICA BACK SECTION PAGE B9

Wednesday, May 9, 2007 | No 47,253 | PRINTED IN BRUSSELS | BRITAIN'S BEST-SELLING QUALITY DAILY

'Green' tax to hit buy-to-let property owners

Laughter returns to Ulster

Brown's credits overpaid to tune of £6bn

STYLE Jefferson Hack Our new style guru B11

FEATURES Gabby Logan Interview B10

ARTS

Former first minister Ian Paisley and Deputy First Minister Martin McGuinness enjoy their historical moment.

traditional code of silence and bring the matter to international attention.

With increasing publicity on both sides of the Atlantic, Sinn Fein found itself in the limelight as the incident galvanized public opinion against the IRA. It made one of its most extraordinary blunders ever: it offered to shoot all the IRA members involved in the killing, an offer McCartney's family rejected out of hand. Four of the sisters were invited to Sinn Fein's annual conference in 2005 and were seated in the front row to hear Gerry Adams call on the killers to turn themselves in and to confess. However, since Sinn Fein/IRA rejects police authority, it advised witnesses to offer statements to lawyers, a policy widely criticized in Northern Ireland.

An even greater invitation was extended to the six women from the American president, who met with them on St. Patrick's Day while refusing to receive Adams, the first time in 10 years this had happened. Adams was also denied the kind of visa that would have permitted him to raise funds in the US. More and more families of persons murdered by Catholic and Protestant paramilitaries are coming forward with their stories and standing up to the terrorists they once feared. Adams appealed to the IRA, which British and Irish intelligence officials no longer believe is a separate entity from Sinn Fein, to use words, not guns, to end British rule in Northern Ireland. But he faced a stark choice: remain linked to an increasingly discredited IRA or break with it and lead his followers into modern democratic politics without the backing of a murderous paramilitary force.

In July 2005 the IRA formally declared an end to its armed struggle against British rule and pledged to pursue its aims of uniting Ireland through "exclusively peaceful means." In September General John de Chastelain certified that the IRA weapons dumps had been destroyed. Some Protestants, especially Ian Paisley, claim that the IRA had not, in fact, disarmed. A half-year later, a report by the Independent Monitoring Commission (IMC) stated that the IRA is moving in the right direction but that some IRA members are still armed and involved in robbery, gasoline smuggling, and financial crime, perhaps without the knowledge of the leadership. The IRA admits that.

British intelligence reports also contend that the IRA kept some weapons, but Chastelain disagreed. Other reports say that the IRA's intelligence service, a formidable group, is still actively spying on public officials and providing information to organized crime networks. None of the reports contend that the IRA is still engaged in terrorist operations. However, there were suspicions of that in April 2006, when a senior official in Sinn Fein, Denis Donaldson, admitted to having been a British agent for 20 years and was soon thereafter shot dead after being tortured. The IRA denied responsibility. That Northern Ireland is more peaceful is beyond dispute. In 1972, 500 persons were killed; in 2005, the number was only 5.

A glimmer of hope was produced in May 2006, when the Stormont assembly met for a ceremonial hour. Sinn Fein proposed that the leader of the largest party, Ian Paisley, lead a power-sharing executive to revive the stalled peace effort. This was perhaps a ruse to portray itself as cooperative and Paisley as intransigent. In any case, Paisley, whose DUP had never accepted the 1998 peace agreement, declined, remarking that Sinn Fein had not done enough to disarm and distance itself from violence: "I am not saying I will never sit in Stormont with the IRA. I am saying I will not sit in Stormont until the IRA gives up its weapons. It's a conditional no, not a 'No, I'll never do it.'"

In the meantime, an impatient British government, which had funded the assembly and the members' $60,000 annual salaries for the previous three years, joined with the Irish government in setting a deadline of November 24, 2006, for the formation of a Northern Irish government that would take over from London such responsibilities as education, health care, and transport.

That got people's attention. The Royal Ulster Constabulary (RUC), which had once been 97% Protestant, was transformed into the Police Service of Northern Ireland, with one-fifth of the officers Catholic. In January 2007 Sinn Fein recognized that force. In March the voters went to the polls and confirmed that Paisley's DUP (with 30% of the votes) and Adams's Sinn Fein (with 26%) are the dominant groups. This enabled them both to claim a mandate to strike a deal, which they did. Both announced their willingness to share power.

On May 8, Paisley was sworn in as first minister, with Sinn Fein's Martin McGuinness as deputy first minister. The formerly recalcitrant Paisley said, "I believe Northern Ireland has come to a time of peace, when hate will no longer rule." After more than 3,700 deaths, this was a very welcome message. Of those, 1,800 were killed by the IRA, and about 1,000 by extremist Protestant groups. The British army killed about 300. IRA fighters killed 1,000 members of the security forces. Half were regular soldiers, and half, locally recruited police and soldiers.

Bertie Ahern hailed Tony Blair as the driving force behind the peace effort and declared that "we can, and are, shaping our future in a new and better way." A few days later, Ahern became the first Irish leader to address a joint session of the British Parliament, and he got a standing ovation. Blair noted at the power-sharing ceremony that "these islands have at last escaped the heavy chains of history." The settlement may well be his most illustrious legacy after a decade in power.

Prime Minister Teresa May

In the end, Blair had high praise for Paisley, whose "contribution to peace, after all the years of division and difference, was decisive and determinative." Both prime ministers convinced him that only a man of his stature could bring peace. Paisley succeeded in bringing most of his community onboard, but the die-hards in his unionist movement felt betrayed and could not forgive him. Their loathing was only increased by the jovial photos in the press of him and McGuinness enjoying each other's company. This ultimately forced him to shed his leadership positions. Rather than risking ouster as head of the Free Presbyterian Church of Ulster, which he had founded 56 years earlier, he stepped down in January 2008. In May he quit as first minister and as leader of the Democratic Unionists, which he had created 37 years earlier. He became Lord Bannside, but his passionate life came to an end in September 2014. Reflecting on his 88 years, he said, "No one can justify everything they've ever done. Things happen in the day when blood is flowing. It is a sad thing, but it is a fact. But we are rid of those days now."

His replacement for both was his longstanding number 2 in the party, Peter Robinson, a wealthy Belfast lawyer. Paisley remained only as an MP in London until May 2010 and member of the Stormont assembly. Power sharing continued.

Resistance to the agreement was softened by a generous hand extended by the central government. It amounted to a financial package of £50 billion ($75 billion) over 10 years to an area where one in three jobs and two-thirds of economic output come from the public sector. The central government spends over £2,000 more per capita than it does in Britain as a whole, and income is only about 80% of the British average. But this is important because getting the economy moving is not easy in a corner of Ireland where violence has discouraged both investors and local entrepreneurs. By 2008 more than $6 billion in foreign investments had poured into the north. One sign of the economic renaissance is the glittering, new Victoria Square in Belfast, an $800 million shopping center with a huge, glass dome hovering over the downtown skyline.

Securing the peace is the highest priority. Within days after the agreement, the oldest loyalist paramilitary group, the Ulster Volunteer Force (UVP), announced that it was going out of existence, although its weapons were merely put out of reach, not destroyed. Britain created a new Catholic-Protestant panel to oversee the police force, and for the first time, it includes Sinn Fein officials. However, policing remained a problem, even though crime by 2010 had gone down eight consecutive years, and overt sectarian violence became increasingly rare. The newly created Police Service of Northern Ireland (PSNI) is smaller and less experienced than the Royal Ulster Constabulary that it replaced. The British army officially ended Operation Banner, its longest continuous operation ever, in effect since 1969. But it left a garrison of 5,000 soldiers to offer support to the police. Few people are ready to remove the 50 "peace walls" that separate Catholic and Protestant housing, and a few more have been constructed.

More time is needed to build trust and complete the healing. That was demonstrated in March 2009, when two British soldiers, who had ordered a last pizza before deploying to Afghanistan, were gunned down when they stepped out of their Northern Irish base to take the delivery. Two days later a constable answering a call was shot in the head. These were the first murders of security forces since 1998, and four rejectionist groupings (the Real and Continuity IRAs, ONH, and the Irish National Liberation Army), who may number no more than a few hundred, claimed responsibility.

The remarkable thing was the political leaders' and citizens' response: Thousands joined in silent marches and vigils all over the province to condemn the killings. Sinn Fein deputy first minister Martin McGuinness called the dissidents "traitors to the island of Ireland" and "Neanderthals." Breaking with tradition, then–first minister Peter Robinson, a Protestant, attended a funeral mass for a Catholic constable murdered near Omagh in April 2011. The hard-line factions who reject the peace agreement seem to have no clearer strategy than to get Britain out of Northern Ireland by plunging the province back into bloody strife. Their chances of success are nil, given the fact that 90% of nationalists are reconciled to the peace settlement. But security forces worry that the dissident splinter groups have recruited former IRA veterans to join them and lend their expertise in booby traps and car bombs. Since the settlement has brought little economic improvement to the island, authorities fear that bored unemployed young people could be drawn into the small violent groups.

The year 2010 saw major progress in the power-sharing and reconciliation process. In February, after almost two weeks of marathon negotiations overseen by the British and Irish governments and supported by ex–US secretary of state Hillary Clinton and former president George W. Bush, a landmark agreement was reached giving the Northern Irish government direct responsibility for policing and justice. This includes responsibility for police, prisons, and the prosecution service. This "devolution of policing" was the last missing piece of the Good Friday agreement that established power sharing.

In March all the nationalist members and most of the unionists (except the UUP) voted for the historic measure in Stormont. In accepting it, Sinn Fein agreed for the first time to recognize and cooperate with the British state. Winning the DUP's unanimous support for the deal was a personal triumph for then first minister Peter Robinson and eliminated demands for his resignation. Despite a series of bomb attacks by deadly splinter groups attempting to undermine the agreement, it took effect on April 12. The same day, Northern Ireland's first justice minister in four decades was appointed, David Ford.

Power sharing has provided considerable political harmony and has ended most paramilitary violence, even though it has not eliminated the last die-hard bombers and gunmen. Nor are the Orange Order marches free of violence yet. Only three months after the handover of police powers, hundreds of rioters in Belfast battled the police with gasoline bombs, bricks, metal bars, planks, and concrete slabs, leaving 82 police officers injured. The violence, reminiscent of earlier times, erupted when the Orange Order rejected a new system for mediating the routes and timing of the marches. Nevertheless, power sharing has enormously improved life in Northern Ireland. In the May 5, 2011, regional elections, the DUP and Sinn Fein consolidated their positions, and their leaders remained in power.

A flag debate showed how much passion can be whipped up. The Belfast city council voted in late 2012 to stop flying the Union Jack every day at city hall; instead, it would be flown only for 18 days a year,

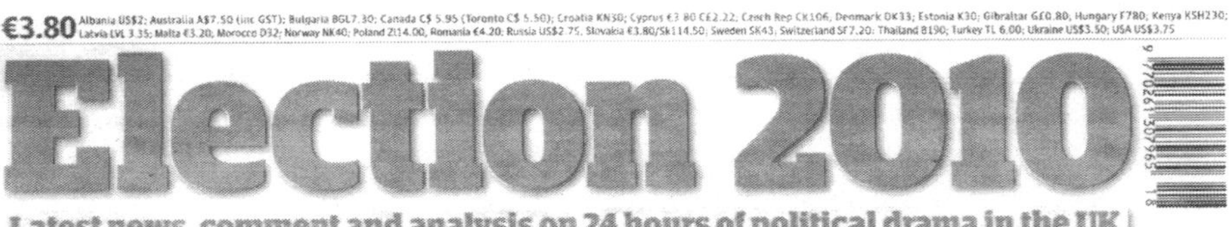
€3.80

Election 2010

Latest news, comment and analysis on 24 hours of political drama in the UK

International edition
Saturday 08.05.10
guardian.co.uk

the guardian
weekend edition

- Tory and Labour leaders make rival offers to Lib Dems
- Brown remains in Downing Street after inconclusive result
- Markets suffer most frenetic day since bank crisis began

Clegg: deal or no deal?

Patrick Wintour
Nicholas Watt
Allegra Stratton

David Cameron was last night trying to form the first Tory government since 1997 by offering a deal to the Liberal Democrats, including the possibility of cabinet seats and a cross-party committee of inquiry into electoral reform.

After being thwarted in his bid to secure an overall Commons majority, leaving Britain with its first hung parliament in 36 years, Cameron reached out to Nick Clegg with what he described as a "big, open and comprehensive" offer.

But it left senior Liberal Democrats divided on how to respond, with Gordon Brown also pitching to secure Clegg's support with a more concrete offer of reform of the electoral system – one of the Liberal Democrats' most cherished and totemic policies.

In an extraordinary day of political horsetrading, held against the background of volatile markets, Cameron said he was open either to a full coalition with the Liberal Democrats or a formal agreement whereby a minority Tory government was guaranteed more than the passage of its budget and the Queen's speech.

The carefully crafted proposal was designed to trump a rival earlier offer made to Clegg by Brown, who made a statement outside Downing Street in which he insisted he was getting on with government while the Conservatives and Lib Dems began negotiating. Brown made clear he would continue as prime minister until a deal was done. He said it was his "constitutional duty to seek to resolve the situation for the good of the country".

Cameron then took the initiative after an unexpectedly resilient Labour campaign left the Conservatives with 307 seats, a net rise of 98, but 17 seats short of an overall majority. Cameron's setback was greeted with relief by Labour, which finished with 258 MPs, down 91. The Lib Dems were surprisingly down five seats on 57, with other parties on 28. The Conservatives got a 36.1% share of the vote (up 3.8%), Labour 29.1% (down 6.2%) and the Lib Dems 23% (up 1%).

Facing fierce internal party criticism over his campaign's effectiveness, Cameron had to tread carefully in making his offer to Clegg in order not to spark a rebellion among his MPs, who are deeply worried electoral reform would leave them shut out of government for decades.

He admitted there were policy disagreements between the Tories and Lib Dems – including on the EU, immigration, spending cuts this year and defence. But he insisted there were also "many areas of common ground" such as a "pupil premium" in schools, a low-carbon economy, tax reform for the low paid and shared opposition to Labour's ID cards scheme. Crucially, he did not pledge a

Seats won
326 to win
306
258
57
28

Share of vote
Labour 29%
Conservative 36.5%
LibDem 23%
Other 11.5%

Key developments

- First hung parliament since 1974
- LibDems slump
- First Green MP
- First Muslim women MPs
- Legal challenges over ballots
- BNP routed
- Charles Clarke, Jacqui Smith among high-profile casualties

2-11»

Continued on page 2 »

including on the birthdays of the British royals. For weeks Loyalist protesters took to the streets to protest the decision.

The year 2010 witnessed an electrifying apology by newly elected prime minister David Cameron. On June 15, a 10-volume, 5,000-page final report was issued on the events of January 30, 1972, a fateful day known as "Bloody Sunday." British paratroopers opened fire upon unarmed demonstrators during a civil rights march in the Bogside area of Londonderry, leaving 14 men dead and 13 injured. It was a deeply held nationalist grievance, and relatives' requests for an investigation went unanswered. In 1998 then–prime minister Blair ordered what became the longest and most expensive public inquiry in British history to be conducted.

After 12 years, more than 900 witnesses and a cost of $288 million, Cameron stood up in the House of Commons to announce the conclusions: The soldiers had shown a "widespread loss of fire discipline. Some members of our armed forces acted wrongly." The demonstrators had not provoked the attacks. Even Martin McGuinness, who was present and probably armed with a submachine gun, did not "engage in any activity that provided any of the soldiers with any justification for opening fire. What happened should never, ever have happened." The shootings were "both unjustified and unjustifiable." And then the dramatic words: "On behalf of the government, I am deeply sorry."

In Londonderry, thousands gathered at the site of the shooting and cheered as the prime minister's speech was broadcast live on giant screens. The inquiry left some open questions. The main one is whether to prosecute any of the soldiers. However, few are in favor of such a move, especially given the fact that all IRA members accused and jailed for terrorist activities have been released as a part of the peace process.

The queen is also playing an important role in the reconciliation that is extending across the Irish Sea. In 2011 she went to Dublin. This was the first visit by a reigning British monarch to the Irish Republic. The following year she ended a visit to Northern Ireland by shaking hands with Martin McGuinness, who had belonged to the terrorist organization that murdered her cousin Lord Mountbatten in 1979. Elizabeth smiled but did not speak while McGuinness spoke to her in Irish, using words that translated to "goodbye and Godspeed." The brief meeting signified a new era. Prince Charles followed up in May 2015 by meeting with Gerry Adams in Galway. McGuinness died in 2017 without his dream of a united Ireland being fulfilled. He was replaced by Michelle O'Neill.

When clashes in the assembly and Belfast streets broke out in July 2013, former American diplomat Richard Haass was asked to help find a compromise on three issues: how violent crimes committed during the Troubles should be investigated, whether and when the union flag could fly from public buildings, and what rules should govern parades. Months of negotiations, seven position papers, and visits by both the British and Irish prime ministers failed to resolve the issues. But some progress was made in identifying areas of agreement and disagreement and on the issue of historical crimes.

The talks resumed. A gangland murder in Belfast with suspected IRA involvement in 2015 set off a political crisis that prompted Peter Robinson to step down as first minister. He was replaced in January 2016 by Arlene Foster, the first woman and also the youngest to occupy that post. When McGuinness resigned in January 2017 because of Foster's "arrogance" and "inflexibility," a snap election was called for March 2. The two unionist parties won only 38 seats in the assembly out of 90 (the new total number of seats). Foster stepped down as first minister but remained leader of the DUP. Sinn Fein surged. When Gerry Adams retired in 2018, he was replaced by Mary Lou McDonald, who sought to soften Sinn Fein's image. (See Ireland chapter that follows.)

TODAY'S POLITICAL PARTIES

Like any modern democracy, the British system could not function without parties. They recruit and select candidates, define issues that are important, educate voters about them, finance and fight electoral campaigns, put up governments that rule at all political levels, and provide well-organized opposition that continually remind the electorate of the government's shortcomings. For the government, the party is an essential tool for maintaining a parliamentary majority, and for the individual politician, it is the ladder to power. For the political activist, it is an important means for putting his ideas into practice. For the voter, it is an indispensable label for a set of politicians, policies, sympathies, or interests.

British parties bear some similarities to those of America, but there is a striking difference that stems from a fundamental difference in the two political systems: The real power in American parties is at the bottom of the hierarchy; a national party in America is nothing more than a loose coalition of state and local parties. By contrast, in Britain the real power within the party is at the top.

Basically, all British parties have a similar organization. At the lowest level are party units in the wards, which are grouped together into 650 constituency parties, each of which struggles for a seat in the House of Commons. These ward or constituency parties raise funds (part of which must be passed up to the national party), recruit members, campaign at election time, and select candidates.

National parties rarely try to overrule constituent parties' choice of candidates, although the national parties clearly influence the selection. The most obvious evidence is that about half of all MPs do not reside in their constituencies before their election to Parliament. Unlike the US, there is no legal requirement for this. The national party leaders search all over Britain for "safe seats" for important MPs. Constituency party leaders often decide that national party interests override their own local desires. All constituency parties are grouped into regional organizations, which, except in Wales and Scotland, have little importance.

At the national level, each party organizes an annual conference, to which each constituency sends representatives. This large conference debates and adopts the party's overall policy (which is never binding on the party if it is in power) and, in the case of Labour, elects the party's leadership. At the national level, two other party organizations also exist. The central bureaucracy assists the party at all levels. The parliamentary party consists of the MPs and members of the House of Lords belonging to it.

All British parties are coalitions of differing interests and ideologies. It is often assumed that British parties are class parties. While this, to a diminishing extent, is true of the Labour Party, the Conservative Party has always had an appeal which cuts across class lines. In terms of policy, the major parties have normally been far closer together than is often assumed. From 1945 until the early 1970s, there was a large measure of consensus among the major parties. All were agreed on a welfare state, the mixed public-private economy which permitted much state intervention in the economy, and employer-union-government collaboration (sometimes referred to as "corporatism").

Some observers even spoke of the "end of ideology" in Britain. That broad consensus collapsed in the 1970s, and both the Conservative and Labour Parties became more ideologically oriented. By the 1983 elections, the major parties had become more polarized than they had been in a half-century. Margaret Thatcher's embrace of market-oriented economics and rejection of state intervention, of "welfarism," and of "corporatism" was matched by revived class-warfare rhetoric in the Labour Party. Its moderate wing found itself placed on the defensive by the left wing, which demanded radical changes in Britain's social, economic, and political power structures. Sir Winston Churchill's observation was no longer correct that "four-fifths of the two major British parties agree about four-fifths of the things that need to be done." But four defeats in a row from 1979 to 1992 prompted Labour to move toward the political center. The payoff—three general election victories in a row—exceeded its wildest expectations.

The first-past-the-post electoral system is designed to favor the two large parties. However, the Conservative and Labour Parties have been steadily losing both seats and members. In 1951, 97% of all voters chose one or the other of these two parties; by 2015 that had declined to only 67.3%. This increases the likelihood of governing coalitions, not one-party majorities. The 19th century prime minister Benjamin Disraeli noted that England "does not love coalitions." Membership is also going down. In the 1950s, with a smaller British population, 4 million voters were card-carrying party members; by the 2010 elections, only 500,000 belonged to one of the three main parties, with the governing Conservatives counting only 200,000. Members who remain are less active than earlier.

The Conservative Party

The Conservative Party (also known as the Tory Party) is conscious of its heritage, which it traces back to the 17th century. Its pragmatic approach has always enabled it to appeal to British from all classes, even though its strongest appeal could be found among those who were well-off economically. At the heart of the Tory Party, as it was formerly known, is the unity of the whole nation. It has always preferred voluntary effort to public assistance, and this stems from its insistence on free enterprise in industry, advocacy of the profit motive, and indirect (sales) taxes rather than direct (income) taxes.

It has never argued that the state has no role in the economy, and it even nationalized industries under certain circumstances, such as the Central Electricity Board in 1926 and Rolls-Royce in 1971. Nor has it ever rejected the notion that the state should provide social welfare services sensibly. In her 1987 campaign, Margaret Thatcher said that all decent people want to help the ill, the unemployed, and the aged but that a healthy economy is needed to provide the level of services which the British want.

There has, of course, always been division within Tory ranks between proponents of more state intervention and those who favor less regulation and a much freer market economy. Some of the differences in political orientation within the party are reflected in well-established pressure groups: They include the Bow Group, which presses for policies which benefit all classes; the Monday Club (the old right); the Tory Reform Group (progressives); and the Charter Movement, who want to democratize the party.

It was publicly known in 1975, when Thatcher defeated Edward Heath for the party leadership, that the new leader represented a different Toryism than Heath. After she became prime minister in 1979, those persons in her cabinet who loyally supported her views were dubbed "dries." Those who had doubts about her medicine, especially about how it would affect millions of citizens and their families, were dubbed "wets." In a cabinet reshuffle after the 1983 and 1987 elections, she dismissed the "wets" in her cabinet.

Thatcher's stunning victory in the 1987 elections revealed that, although she was an unpopular and unloved leader, British voters respected her no-nonsense competence and will. They grudgingly accepted her bitter economic medicine of sound money, hard work, and standing on one's own two feet. She was the first prime minister to win a third consecutive term in modern British history and surpassed Winston Churchill and H. H. Asquith as Britain's longest-serving prime minister in the 20th century. Why did she win?

The first reason is that her opposition was severely divided. Second, the prime minister had won considerable stature and influence in the international arena. She could boast with justification that "we have put the Great back into Britain." The main reason for her victory was the undeniable economic success her government had achieved.

The United Kingdom

Post-Thatcher

The willingness of France and Germany to relinquish more sovereignty to Europe widened the chasm between the UK and its continental partners. Thatcher's cabinet had been rocked by high-level resignations stemming from disagreements over Europe. In 1986 Michael Heseltine stormed out because he wanted a European consortium, not one from the US, to purchase a British helicopter company. In 1989 Nigel Lawson left because he wanted to include the pound in the European Monetary System (EMS). The fatal resignation—and the catalyst for her downfall—was that of Sir Goeffrey Howe, the last surviving member of her original 1979 cabinet and an architect of "Thatcherism." He charged in Parliament that her obstruction in Europe carried "serious risks for our nation."

The devastating speech led to a successful challenge to her leadership in November 1990. After a historic 11-year rule, the longest prime-ministership since the Victorian era and the longest consecutive one since the Napoleonic age, Thatcher resigned. The events leading to her fall related to Europe, but the reason 45% of her parliamentary party colleagues voted against her was that she was guiding her party toward defeat in the next elections. For 18 months her party had trailed in the polls a Labour Party that had become more moderate, had overthrown its suicidal commitment to nuclear disarmament, and had embraced the EU. Her country was experiencing high inflation, a growing trade deficit, a slowdown in economic growth, and intense domestic opposition to her poll tax for local governments.

With her leaving, the UK entered a period under John Major, Britain's youngest prime minister in the last century, until Labour leader Tony Blair evicted him from Number 10 Downing Street. Major was a self-made man from a very humble background and with no university education. His father had been a circus performer and minor league baseball player in the US. Major was the Iron Lady's protégé and handpicked successor. Nevertheless, he backed away from strident Thatcherism, abolishing the hated poll tax in 1991. He buried the grudge Thatcher had borne against both the EU and Germany and became a more cooperative European. Like Thatcher, he benefited from an unexpected war, this time in the Gulf in 1991, which went very well for Britain and its allies.

He entered the 1992 elections with the highest popularity rating of any British prime minister in three decades, but nobody expected his stunning victory in the midst of Britain's worst recession in a half-century. He led his party to a 21-seat majority, based on 42% of the votes and 336 seats (down from 376).

The Tory Party was deeply divided, especially over Britain's role in the EU. Major's government was sometimes held hostage by several dozen vocal Euroskeptics in his own party, including Thatcher herself, who were determined to sabotage all moves to a closer European union. The government appeared to be at war with itself and was dogged by a succession of scandals and sleaze. Voters were tired of Tory rule after 18 years. Even the party's most significant achievement—a booming economy and unemployment half as high as when Major took office in 1992—played in the opposition's favor, since voters seemed to think they could afford the risk of voting Labour.

The 2001 elections brought the second devastating defeat in a row for the Conservative Party. It won only one constituency in Scotland and none in Wales. It has become a regional party confined to the southeastern English countryside. It failed to win a single seat in any major city outside London, where it captured only 13 out of 74. It was demoralized after its two worst election defeats since 1906. Party leader William Hague resigned immediately. His replacement, Iain Duncan Smith, was selected by a new kind of primary election: First, the parliamentary party voted on the contenders. The top two candidates then were submitted to a vote by all 250,000 registered party members in the UK (average age over 65).

The Tories were jolted in 2002 by stories of another sensational sex scandal, this time involving John Major. Miffed that he had not mentioned her in his autobiography and had not given her a cabinet post during his prime-ministership, former education minister Edwina Currie and later talk-show host revealed in her published diaries that she and Major had had a four-year affair from 1984 to 1988. She had indirectly alluded to this in her 1997 novel, *A Parliamentary Affair*. This lapse of judgment blemished both Major's reputation for honesty and the wisdom of his 1993 campaign, "back to the basics," calling for strict moral values.

Most Tories supported Prime Minister Blair's decision to participate in the war against Iraq in 2003, but this did not help the party in the polls. It remained internally divided, and Duncan Smith was a poor manager of people, a bad communicator and debater, and an uninspired strategist. In October 2003 he was deposed, becoming the first Tory leader to be dismissed without having the opportunity to fight an election. He confided to his colleagues that "only a lunatic would want to lead the Conservative Party."

He was replaced by Michael Howard, who was unopposed. The son of a Romanian-born father and Russian-born mother, Howard was the first professing Jew to lead a major British party. (Benjamin Disraeli was baptized as a child into the Church of England.) He led his party to defeat in the May 2005 parliamentary elections. It has won only about a third of the votes for three elections in a row. It gained some ground in the southeast and in prosperous London suburbs. But its continued division over Britain's place in Europe and campaign focus on the problem of immigration, demanding annual limits, turned many voters off.

Part of its problem is that Tony Blair's Labour Party adopted Margaret Thatcher's market reforms and notions of economic efficiency. By doing that, New Labour not only made itself electable, but it also made it very difficult for the Conservatives to define how they are different from Labour. In 1998 *The Economist* called Blair "the strangest Tory ever sold."

Howard announced immediately that he would step down. His surprise replacement in 2005 was his young (then 39) protégé, David Cameron, whose mantra was "change to win." Only in Parliament since 2001, Cameron was down-to-earth, pragmatic, flexible, decisive, unflappable, and cool under pressure. He quickly managed to make the Tories look human and approachable again. He was likable, quick-witted, informal, self-assured, and charming. He assembled around him a strong

British students celebrate the special relationship.

Daily Mail

PRINTED IN EUROPE FRIDAY

FRIDAY, MAY 8, 2015 www.dailymail.co.uk €2.70

Exit poll puts Tories on course for over 300 seats

Red Ed faces disaster with 'worst result for 30 years'

Clegg is 'humbled' – but SNP sweep the board

CAMERON 'HEADING BACK TO NUMBER 10'

Confident of victory: David Cameron

By James Chapman
Political Editor

DAVID Cameron appears to be heading back to Number 10 today after 'shy Tories' delivered an extraordinary late surge for his party.

Voters took to the polls in massive numbers yesterday and, although Britain was heading for a second hung parliament, the Conservatives were expected to pick up 316 seats, according to exit polls.

In a triumph for the Tories, they looked likely to be the first ruling party since 1983 to put on seats.

Labour leader Ed Miliband's career – and that of Deputy Prime Minister Nick Clegg – appeared to have been brought to a crashing end as both of [illegible].

Labour was on course for its worst result since Neil Kinnock's defeat in 1987, with a forecast of 239 seats. If TV exit polls are correct – and they were in 2010 – the Lib Dems face near wipeout and will be left with just ten seats.

The Scottish Nationalists appeared to have delivered an earthquake north of the border, winning all but one seat in Scotland. That leaves Nicola Sturgeon as the leader of what is easily the

Turn to Page 2

team of young modernizers who could give the party a new face by "detoxifying the brand." He sought to bring more women and minorities into the party and Parliament. The Tories' and his own image had to change if it wanted to rule. He went by "Dave," wore jeans and open-necked shirts, rode his bicycle to Parliament (sometimes his limo drove behind him with his briefcase), and supported environmental causesand LGBTQ rights. He made his party more socially liberal.

He was born in 1966 into wealth and privilege and is distantly related to the queen, being a descendent of a mistress of King William IV. At age seven, he was sent to an exclusive "public" school, Heatherdown. This prepared him for Eton, the traditional finishing school for the ruling classes, which had produced 18 prime ministers before him. He finished his education at Oxford.

The Tories entered the May 7, 2015, general elections head to head with Labour. However, voters, especially Scotsmen, were afraid of Labour rule. The Conservatives ended up winning 36.9% of the votes and 331 seats, a gain of 24 and an absolute majority. However, it remained practically invisible in Scotland, where it got only 1 seat out of 59, and in Wales.

Cameron, age 43 when he became PM (the age of John F. Kennedy when he won the presidency), was the youngest prime minister since the Second Earl of Liverpool two centuries earlier. In 2010 he was forced to enter the first coalition government in 65 years and the first-ever Conservative–Liberal Democrat government.

The Conservative Party remains ambivalent about Europe. The anti-EU UK Independence Party (UKIP), led by Nigel Farage, demands "we want our country back!" and Euroskeptics within his Conservative Party are nipping at his heels. In May 2015 UKIP captured 12.6% of the votes but only one seat.

Cameron wanted opt-outs from such things as the EU's social chapter, charter of fundamental rights, employment laws, environment, justice, security policy, and immigration. He and most of his party comrades wanted to remain in the EU, but they did not want the euro, and they wanted a new relationship that retains the trading advantages without the closer political union, the regulatory burdens, and the financial contributions.

Cameron said he would give "heart and soul" to win a vote to remain in the EU. If voters rejected it, the government would have to enter torturous negotiations for an exit from the EU. Surveys in 2015 had indicated that a majority wanted to stay in. The prime minister was caught between the strong anti-Europe faction in his Tory Party and powerful business groups who favored continuing close ties with Britain's most important trading partner. A referendum was held on June 23, 2016. The results were a disaster: 52% voted to leave.

Its relations with America are cordial for the most part, despite Cameron's statement that "we should be solid but not slavish in our friendship with America. I and my party are instinctive friends of America and passionate supporters of the Atlantic alliance." He is aware that "we are the junior partner." The first phone call from abroad to congratulate him after walking through the door at Number 10 Downing Street was from President Barack Obama. Both leaders rebranded their countries' ties as "the essential relationship."

Cameron created Britain's own National Security Council in 2010 with a staff of 200. It is a useful forum for senior politicians and meets with members of the American equivalent four times a year.

Cameron also announced that he would not run for a third term. However, events outpaced him after losing the Brexit vote in June 2016. He departed a few weeks later. He was replaced by Home Secretary Teresa May. She used her prerogative in 2017 to call new elections set for June 8. This decision backfired spectacularly: The Tories lost 43 seats and their majority and had to form a government with 10 demanding Northern Irish unionists.

The Labour Party

Although its roots extend far back into the 19th century, the Labour Party was officially founded in 1900. Under the influence of the small but well-connected Fabian Society, which sought to reform British society gradually from above rather than through violent revolution or labor union agitation from below, the party adopted in 1918 a new constitution which transformed it officially into a socialist party. It proclaimed that the goal of the party is to "secure for the producers by hand or by brain the full fruits of their industry and the most equitable distribution thereof that may be possible upon the basis of common ownership of the means of production and the best obtainable system of popular administration and control of each industry and service."

The United Kingdom

That purely Marxist objective helped prevent the Labour Party from sharing the fate of many socialist parties in Europe that split apart in the aftermath of the Russian Revolution. However, it became the source of continuous intraparty friction ever since. During most of its history, the party was in reality more moderate than its constitution might indicate. It sought to "democratize" the economy by nationalizing key industries and regulating others, to distribute wealth more equally, to expand social welfare services, and to eliminate class differences.

During the Thatcher government Labour took a leftward lurch and embarked upon an almost-suicidal political course. Grossly underestimating Britain's first woman prime minister and the public support for her economic austerity policies, the Labour Party committed itself to radical promises: unilateral nuclear disarmament, withdrawal from the EU, massive nationalization of industries, and huge increases in public spending.

This led to an electoral disaster, and in the 1983 elections, it suffered its worst defeat in 60 years. Its 27.6% was Labour's lowest popular vote since 1918 and was 20 percentage points lower than in 1966. Almost a quarter of those voters who had identified themselves consistently with the Labour Party abandoned it.

It failed to win a majority of the votes among the working class or among labor-union members. This was a severe setback for a party created by and organizationally linked to the unions; it seriously hollowed out the party's claim to be the party of the worker. Only the traditional working class remained more loyal: that segment who worked in nationalized or "smokestack" industries or who lived in council housing, Scotland, Wales, or the north of England. This represented the most significant basic shift in the social basis of British politics since World War II.

Within hours after the polls had closed, the move to replace the ineffective Labour leader Michael Foot began. The choice was Neil Kinnock. He began immediately to mend the gaping, intraparty split between the left and right, which had led to electoral disaster and the massive drop in party membership between 1979 and 1983, to a level comparable to that of 1945. He moderated his party's views on the EU, defense, and the status of capitalism. With a sharp eye on the social changes which have occurred in Britain, Kinnock announced that Labour must appeal to the "newly well-off" and should be a party which appeals to the haves, as well as the have-nots. Foot passed away in 2010.

Going into the 1987 elections, the party shied away from extremism. Its platform purged the earlier pledges to abolish the House of Lords (which has been critical of some of Thatcher's policies), to nationalize much more industry, and to control the country's banking system. It accepted the principle of selling public-owned houses, and it no longer opposed the UK's membership in the EU. An enormous electoral liability was Kinnock's decision to stand by his party's unilateral nuclear disarmament position. The electoral effect was suicide. The party suffered its second-worst defeat in more than a half-century, capturing only 32% of the votes and 229 seats.

In the 1992 elections, it faced important social changes which worked against it: Its traditional support base—trade-union members, manual laborers, and tenants of state-owned housing—is shrinking. Party leaders conducted a thorough rethinking of its positions. In order to be able to present a credible challenge to the Conservatives, Labour had to develop a moderate, nonsocialist program. It unveiled its new policy, which scrapped unilateral nuclear disarmament, as well as vote-losing calls for withdrawal from NATO, removal of US military bases in Britain, scuttling the Trident nuclear submarine program, and state ownership of industry. It reconciled itself to the market system.

The year 1992 seemed ideal for a Labour victory, but voters handed Labour its fourth consecutive defeat, even though it climbed to 35% of the votes and 271 seats. Voters continued to associate it with crippling strikes, chaos, and economic decline. Kinnock had begun to introduce the kinds of changes that would ultimately lead his party to victory in 1997, but he had failed at the time to persuade his countrymen that Labour's transformation and pragmatism were genuine and lasting.

In 1994 another leader who could bring the party victory was chosen: Tony Blair. The son of a lifelong Conservative, Blair was educated at a private boys' school and studied law at Oxford. He took no interest in student politics and spent his spare time singing in a rock band called Ugly Rumours. He entered Parliament in 1983 representing a traditional Labour constituency in the north. He bore no scars of Labour's dismal rule in the 1970s, and he was its first leader with no roots in the labor movement and with no grounding in traditional socialism.

This made it easier for him to complete the process of modernizing his party. He lessened its dependency upon and identification with unpopular unions. In the 1960s, union money made up 80% of the party's budget; by 1995 that figure was 50% and then 30% by 1998. That began rising again to 57% in 2005, 78% in 2006, nearly 90% in 2007, and more than 90% in 2010, as donations from wealthy entrepreneurs dried up. He remained silent during a 13-week railway strike in 1994, breaking a long tradition of unfailing party support for the unions' actions. He curbed the voting power of union leaders, who had controlled large blocks within the party. In 2014 the party further weakened its institutional links to the unions by changing the selection of its leader to a simple one-person-one-vote system. Their power was diluted by changes in the complicated rules governing party voting and policy making.

He persuaded the powerful NEC to accept his revision of clause 4 of the party constitution, setting aside the party's 1918 commitment to public ownership of key industries. This had been a major obstacle to its return to power. Blair confessed later that scrapping clause 4 had "shown me what I intuitively thought but wasn't sure of: that the party was actually behind change." Since it was a democratic process every step of the way, he was sure that most of the party's rank and file had changed and were behind the reform.

Campaign brochure for Charlotte Atkins

Through his patience, charm, and power of persuasion, he reversed the radicalism within the party and opened it up to fresh ideas. He led Labour toward the political center. He ceased regarding Labour as a tribal party focusing on the working class. By enhancing its appeal among the middle class in the heavily populated south of Britain, he aimed directly at the bedrock of the Tories' support. He was highly confident, disciplined, focused, energetic, and quick to master a brief. He was also sometimes accused of being brutally autocratic when it came to bringing his party in line with his reforms, a quality Margaret Thatcher is said to have admired in him. Unlike Thatcher, though, who relished battering her opponents into submission, Blair preferred logical argument and persuasion.

In the 1997 elections, he demonstrated what a skillful campaigner he was. He could orchestrate a tightly organized campaign, present himself convincingly in two television debates with his opponent (an innovation in British campaigns), "work a crowd" very effectively, and inspire voters without promising too much. His main challenge was to convince voters that his party had indeed shed the heavy baggage of the past. He stuck to a single message: that his party was now "New Labour." "The old ideologies are dead. New Labour is offering a new and different form of politics. . . . There has been a revolution inside the Labour Party. We have rejected the worst of our past and rediscovered the best. . . . We have made ourselves fit to face the future."

He distanced his party from the "outdated ideology" of high taxes financing expensive government programs, from powerful unions, and from unilateral nuclear disarmament. He established friendly relations with business leaders. He vowed neither to renationalize industries nor raise income taxes. Instead, he pledged to keep inflation low, to spend no more than the Tories had already budgeted but nevertheless to improve the struggling National Health Service and the school system, to introduce a minimum wage, to combat crime, and to reform the constitution.

Seeing too little difference between his program and that of the Tories, some observers dubbed him "Tony Blur." He responded by arguing, "I do not think everything that has happened in the last 18 years has been bad. My attitude is: keep what is working and change what is not." Clearly Britain's economy was already working well. This fact persuaded even more voters that there was little danger in voting for a Labour Party that promised not to tamper with one of Europe's most robust economies. Blair assured his countrymen within hours after his victory, "We ran as New Labour and will govern as New Labour."

The electoral payoff for Labour was historic: It won 418 of 659 seats on the basis of 43.1% of the votes. Its majority of 179 seats was its best performance ever. It wiped the Tories out of Scotland and Wales altogether and made deep inroads into Tory strongholds in southern England and London, capturing even Thatcher's north London Finchley constituency. In a stunning turnaround, women flocked to Labour, which won 53% of their votes (compared with 30% who voted Tory). The number of women with seats in the House of Commons shot up from 63 to 120, and 101 of them were from Labour. Most of the nine ethnic minorities, including a wealthy Muslim man, elected to Parliament ran on the Labour ticket. Blair's cabinet also contained many firsts: five women; an openly gay man (Chris Smith, secretary of state for culture, media, and sport, who later admitted that he is HIV positive); and a blind man, David Plunkett, as education and employment secretary. Plunkett resigned in 2004 because of his affair with a married woman and his attempts to speed up the visa process for her nanny.

In the June 2001 elections, which saw a startling 12% drop in turnout to 59%, the lowest since 1918, Labour slipped to 42% and lost six seats. Nevertheless, with 413 seats, it still commanded two-thirds of the seats in the House of Commons. This was the first time in its century of existence that it had succeeded in being reelected to a second full term.

Turnout rose slightly to 61% in the May 2005 elections. Labour's share of the votes fell by 4.5% to 35.2% of the total votes, the lowest percentage ever recorded by a winning party since 1832. Hurt by the growing unpopularity of the Iraq War, new tuition charges at universities, foundation hospitals, and damaged credibility from a wide range of other domestic policies (more than half the voters surveyed a few days before the elections said he could not be trusted), Labour also suffered a loss of over half its majority in the House of Commons, falling to a nevertheless comfortable 67. As in the two earlier elections, it benefited from the division of the opposition.

Blair became the first Labour prime minister in British history to win a third straight term. Turning 52 the day after the elections, he said that this would be his last election as prime minister. This was an unprecedented declaration for such a relatively young leader to make.

On June 27, 2007, he passed on the leadership to his chancellor of the exchequer, Gordon Brown, the intellectual son of a Presbyterian minister, an admirer of the United States, and excellent manager of the economy. He had entered Edinburgh University at the age of 16 and was elected its rector at 21. Hardworking and extremely smart, he held strong views about poverty and injustice.

Brown's three-year tenure as prime minister was troubled. He was reported to be mean to his staff ("grumpy Gordon"), and his declining poll figures and electoral prospects sparked within his party mutterings that he should go. He had to suppress two open rebellions. He failed to connect with the public. During the 2010 campaign, he committed one of the most damaging gaffes in recent British electoral history. In an arranged sidewalk meeting, a Labour voter asked him about immigration, a major issue in the election. Back in his limousine, Brown called the encounter "a disaster" and the woman "bigoted." But he had forgotten to turn off his lapel microphone, so his remarks were picked up by a TV station and broadcast. He never recovered.

Election day, May 6, 2010, was not a pleasant experience for the party that had ruled 13 years. It captured only 29% of the votes (down 6%) and 258 seats (a loss of 89). The only regions where it won big were Scotland (41 of 59 seats) and Wales (26 of 40). No party won a majority (this being the first "hung Parliament" since 1974).

The Liberal Democrats' price for a governing alliance with Labour was too high: that Brown step down as prime minister. According to Mandelson's memoir that appeared only two months after the election (*The Third Man: Life at the Heart of New Labour*), the embittered and exhausted leader moaned, "I have been humiliated enough."

The United Kingdom

Prime Minister David Cameron and Deputy Prime Minister Nick Clegg form the government, 2010.

Seeing his political future in ruins, Brown quickly resigned his leadership, and the jostling of contenders began. In the selection process, the unions have one-third of the votes, the Labour MPs another third, and rank-and-file Labour members also a third. Voters rank the candidates in order of preference. If no candidate garners 50% on the first round, the second choices of those who voted for the last-place finisher are distributed until one person has a majority.

The favorite was former foreign secretary David Miliband, a 44-year-old modernizer supported by the Blair wing in the party. He refused to repudiate New Labour's record and had the majority of support by the party's MPs and rank-and-file members. But his younger brother Ed Miliband (age 40) narrowly beat him 50.65% to 49.35% after four rounds of voting. "Red Ed" successfully tapped the unions, a segment of the party that had long been ignored. David gave up his parliamentary seat in 2013 and accepted a job as chief executive of the International Rescue Committee in New York.

A 2012 poll for the *Sun* showed that only 19% of respondents thought Miliband looked fit to be prime minister. In May 2015, the British marked their ballots accordingly. The results were a disaster, Labour's worst since 1987. It won 30.4% of the votes (up 1.5%). But it fell to 232 seats (a loss of 26). It collapsed in Scotland, winning only 1 seat, while the SNP captured 56 of 59. Miliband resigned as leader.

He was replaced by a man of the hard left, Jeremy Corbyn. He wants to take the party back to its roots in the working class. He is stridently anti-American, anti-NATO, antinuclear deterrent, and anti-Israel. He opposes an EU trade deal with the US. Being antimonarchy, he refused to sing "God Save the Queen" during a commemoration of World War II veterans. He has little support among Labour MPs, and moderates have left the party in droves. Labour entered the June 8, 2017, elections with its most leftist manifesto since 1983: renationalizing royal mail and some nail and energy companies, scrapping university tuition fees, and increasing spending on health and social services. It won 40% of the votes, a gain of 9.5%. Corbyn consolidated his position.

Tony Blair's Legacy

It became increasingly difficult for Blair to find a parliamentary majority. His party performed poorly in the May 2007 local and regional elections. Scandals involving questionable party donations, sexual misbehavior, and failure on the part of some of his ministers, along with the unpopularity of the Iraq War, beset Labour. These prompted irresistible calls for Blair to make way for his successor. An increasingly popular Tory Party with a dynamic new bike-riding green leader, David Cameron, was able to exploit this. On June 27, 2007, Blair handed the keys to the prime minister's office to Gordon Brown, his chancellor of the exchequer for a decade. What many analysts will discuss for years in the future is the legacy that this extraordinary politician and statesman will leave behind.

Leading his party to three straight electoral victories (something no Labour leader had ever done), Blair was Britain's most successful Labour prime minister ever. He moved his leftist party to the center, where elections can be won, and he eliminated Labour's reputation for incompetence in government. He made British politics competitive by making Labour electable again. He removed hereditary peers from the House of Lords and reformed that upper chamber irreversibly. He extended self-government to Scotland and Wales. He was also the driving force in achieving a power-sharing agreement in Northern Ireland, perhaps his greatest success.

He left Britain a better country. The average citizen is more prosperous, and Britain's openness to large numbers of immigrants boosted the economy without producing a serious backlash. The war in Iraq cost him his popularity. He persuaded a majority to allow universities to charge higher tuition fees, thereby beginning to solve higher education's chronic underfunding. Now 40% go to universities.

In his decade as prime minister, the challenges facing his country shifted from domestic to foreign policy, as he was forced to face terrorism, energy shortages, and climate change. He was Britain's most pro-EU leader ever. At the same time, he attempted to guard his country's traditionally close ties with the United States. More than any other leader, he built the coalition that ended genocide in Kosovo and terminated the murderous career of Serbian president Slobodan Milosevic. He was a key player in the successful war to end Taliban rule in Afghanistan. He brought peace to Sierra Leone, after murderous rebels kidnapped 500 UN peacekeepers and threatened to renew warfare.

Blair is still young and vigorous, and he remains an international star. The UN tapped his expertise on the Middle East by appointing him special Middle East envoy for the Quartet (UN, EU, US, Russia) the day he left Number 10. Among other jobs, he was appointed a senior adviser at JP Morgan Chase; a consultant on international politics for Zurich Financial Services, Switzerland's largest insurer; and senior green technology adviser at Khosla Ventures in Silicon Valley.

He agreed to teach a course at Yale University during the 2008–2009 academic year on faith and globalization and to work with the divinity and management faculties as a Howland Distinguished Fellow. He runs the Faith Foundation on reconciling religions. He employs about 150 people around the world to administer a variety of good causes, and he spends at least two-thirds of his time on unpaid work. He lectures for astronomical honoraria and signed a lucrative deal for his top-selling memoirs, *A Journey*. It is ironic that the two most important prime ministers since World War II who changed Britain the most—Blair and Margaret Thatcher—are far more popular in the United States than in their own country.

THE TIMES

Thursday November 6 2008 timesonline.co.uk No 69474 — 80p

Inside 24-page souvenir — Obama

Ben Macintyre, Maya Angelou, an extract from his autobiography Dreams From My Father and a new poem by Derek Walcott

Plus the victory speech in full

Obama gets to work

President-elect starts to form his administration

62.5%

The highest turnout since 1960

had sought medical treatment for a drinking problem. He was replaced by former Olympic sprinter Sir Menzies Campbell, who in December 2007 handed the leadership over to Nick Clegg (then age 40) after the party had been the big loser in the May local elections.

Unlike most British politicians, Clegg, a former EU trade negotiator and member of the European Parliament for five years, is a Europhile through and through who spent his formative political years in Brussels. He was born to a half-Russian banker father and a Dutch mother. He speaks five languages.

His privileged background parallels that of his partner in government, Prime Minister David Cameron. He was schooled at the elite private Westminster School and then at Cambridge University. He spent a year at the prestigious College of Europe in Bruges, Belgium, establishing friendships all over the continent. Like Cameron, he was 43 years old, the age of John F. Kennedy when he became president. Elected to Parliament in 2005, he is tall, handsome, self-assured, and well-spoken, as one would expect from a person with such an educated and cosmopolitan background.

Like Cameron, he reoriented his party toward the center to win elections. This was not easy, given the complicated na-

The queen and First Lady embrace

Source: *Maclean's*

The Liberal Democrats

In reaction to the Labour Party's earlier swing to the left, a group from the party bolted and in 1981 formed the Social Democratic Party (SDP). This new grouping sought to occupy the center ground of the British political spectrum, which had opened up because of the polarization between the two larger parties. Its strategy was to align with the older Liberal Party of the center.

The Liberals had been one of the two major parties during the 19th century, but it had not been in power since the Labour Party eclipsed it just after World War I. Their heaviest emphasis has been on individual freedom, and it speaks for decentralization of state power, for a greater focus of local political issues, and for workers' (not union) councils sharing control with management. Both the Liberals and the SDP strongly support European integration and reform of the electoral system in favor of proportional representation.

Just how important such a change would be for what is now named the Liberal Democratic Party (LDP or "Lib Dems," previously called the SDP-Liberal Alliance and the Social and Liberal Democrats) was demonstrated in the 2010 elections. It won 23% of the vote. Its even support across the entire class spectrum proved that it was not merely a fashionable "wine and cheese" grouping, as critics sometimes charge. But it won only 57 seats in the House of Commons, less than 9% of the total.

Many analysts had believed that the precursors to the LDP could supplant the Labour Party and that the former Social Democrats and the traditionally independent, undisciplined Liberals could forge a partnership that could "break the mold of British politics." But they had failed to establish themselves as an electable nonsocialist alternative. That made their merger unavoidable.

It was led for 11 years by Paddy Ashdown. He stepped down as leader in 1999, having rescued the party from the splits and name changes of the 1980s and having moved it close to the center of power. Former journalist Charles Kennedy, a good-humored Scotsman, replaced him and led the party in the 2001 elections, in which it captured an impressive 18.8% of the votes and 52 seats. The party's opposition to the 2003 war in Iraq paid political dividends as enthusiasm for the war wore off. In 2006 Kennedy stepped down as leader after being forced to admit that he

ture of the Liberal Democrat Party: On economic issues, many of its members are to the left of the Labour Party, but the wider public sees it as libertarian. For example, it wanted to end "the culture of spying on its citizens" by scrapping the nation-wide identity cards and the new biometric passports and by placing curbs on tens of thousands of closed-circuit cameras in public places.

His debating skills were demonstrated in Britain's first-ever televised election debates. He stamped himself as the candidate of change and touched off the campaign's biggest surprise: "Cleggmania." Before the debates, few Britons even knew what he looked like. Afterward he and his party appeared as a fresh departure from the agonizing parliamentary expenses scandal and the arrogance and abuse it symbolized. They tapped into the anger toward politics and politicians. Some observers called this the most "Americanized" election yet, with the candidates' wives traveling around, fulfilling their roles as potential first ladies.

Election day 2010 did not deliver the dramatic gains the Lib Dems had hoped for: They won 23% of the votes (up 1%) and 57 seats (a disappointing loss of 5). But because the Tories had fallen 20 votes short of a majority, they formed Britain's first governing coalition in 65 years with the LDP. Clegg became deputy prime minister, the most senior office any British Liberal has occupied since Lloyd George. Cameron and Clegg had not shown any previous liking to each other. Once asked what his favorite joke was, Cameron had answered, "Nick Clegg." But they were pragmatic partners determined to reform British politics in fundamental ways.

By entering the Tory-LDP coalition government in May 2010, the Liberal Democrats tasted power for the first time in almost a century. But "Cleggmania" disappeared, and the party suffered a frightful loss of popularity in the polls. Parties which choose to govern become more vulnerable to criticism; ridicule; and, in the case of the LDP, the sense that it is being marginalized. In the May 2011 elections and referendum on changing the electoral system, the LDP was doubly devastated. It had staked its future on electoral reform, but that was defeated in a referendum by 68% to 32%.

Liberal Democrats hoped they were not seeing a repeat of what happened to their party the last time it coalesced with the Conservatives in the 1930s: It split in two. The 2015 elections brought the party's worst nightmare. It lost half of its voters, plummeting from 15.2% to only 7.9%. Its 49 seats in 2010 shrank to only 8. Clegg won his seat, but he dutifully resigned as leader after this electoral catastrophe.

RECENT FOREIGN AND POSTCOLONIAL POLICY

Today the sun technically does not set on the British Empire. Fourteen islands, rocks, and scarcely inhabited strips of land on the map are still ruled by Britain: They include Pitcairn in the south Pacific Ocean; Bermuda, British Virgin Islands, Caymans, Leeward Islands, Turks and Caicos in the Caribbean area; the Falkland Islands, St. Helena in the south Atlantic Ocean; Gibraltar in the Mediterranean; and Diego Garcia (where the US leases a military base) in the Indian Ocean. Yet it must still deal with many problems that stem from its colonialist legacy. They have included both foreign policy problems and domestic political difficulties, such as how to control and treat millions of immigrants from the former colonies (see "Culture").

The Commonwealth of Nations is a loose, voluntary association of the former ruler and the ruled, and the head is the British monarch, even though some of its members are republics. In 1995 it opened its doors to such states as ex-Portuguese Mozambique, formerly French Cameroon, and ex-Belgian Rwanda (which formally entered in 2009). It holds its members to the Commonwealth's declared values. Zimbabwe was suspended, and then it quit in 2003. In 2005 and again in 2009, Fiji was suspended for failing to return to democracy. After Gambia was criticized in 2013 for human rights violations, it quit, calling the organization "neocolonial."

Member states, which numbered 53, represent a fifth of the earth's land area and encompass 2 billion people (half of them Indians). They regularly confer at Commonwealth gatherings. Sometimes Britain must assume additional, unwanted responsibilities under the aegis of the Commonwealth, such as in helping to arrange a transition to democracy in the tiny Caribbean island of Grenada after four years of totalitarian rule and an invasion by the United States and six other Caribbean island states. Few people seem to know much about the Commonwealth. Only a third of respondents in a 2009 poll in seven member states could name something it did, and only a third in Australia or Canada would be "sorry" or "appalled" if their country quit the organization.

Britain and its wealthy Commonwealth allies bear over two-thirds of the running costs, but decisions are made on the basis of consensus. Britain shares its embassy in Myanmar with Canada, and Canada returns the favor in Haiti. Britain also shares an embassy with Germany in Iceland. More such deals are being negotiated.

Britain also faces terribly complicated problems with the smaller enclaves it rules because local inhabitants there fear their larger neighbors and look to Britain for protection. It has declared that the principle of self-determination must not be violated and that a neighboring land can absorb subject peoples only by their consent. The principle is an admirable one, but it has a high cost. The 3,000 inhabitants of the Falklands, located 300 miles (480 km) off Argentina's southern tip, called upon Britain to defend them when Argentina occupied what it calls the "Malvinas" islands for 73 days in April 1982. These islands had first been discovered by an Englishman in 1690. After the French and Spaniards had claimed them, the British established a naval garrison there in 1833. Sovereignty has been disputed ever since. It has never been tested in an international court. In 1984 a House of Commons committee decided it was "unable to reach a categorical conclusion" on the validity of the UK's claim.

Britain's military victory in 1982, costing 258 British and 649 Argentine lives, did not convince Argentina to renounce its claims to the islands. Buenos Aires also has its eye on the Falklands' potential offshore oil reserves of perhaps 500,000 barrels a day. As a deterrent, London stations 1,200 troops, only 150 of whom are combat soldiers; 3 ships; and 4 Typhoon fighter bombers in the area. Prince William was sent to the islands on his first overseas military tour, flying helicopters out of the new Mount Pleasant Air Base, which doubles as an international airport.

Although Britain still refuses to discuss its sovereignty over the islands unless the largely British inhabitants request it, it established friendly relations with Argentina. The two countries set up a "sovereignty umbrella," under which they cooperate on practical issues while maintaining their separate claims to ownership. They collaborate on fishing licenses worth $40 million each year. A memorial to the 649 Argentine war dead was constructed on the islands. President Carlos Menem received a warm welcome in London in 1998, where he laid a wreath to the Britons who died in the war. Prince Charles visited Argentina the following year.

Nevertheless, Argentine politicians, including presidents, still cannot resist whipping up support at election time by verbally attacking "illegal" British rule over the "Malvinas." Four out of five Argentines believe the islands belong to them. In 2007, on the 25th anniversary of the war, Argentine president Néstor Kirchner called again for an end to the "illegitimate" occupation, cancelled charter flights to the islands, pulled out of a 1995 agreement on oil and gas exploration, and banned energy companies that did business with the Falklands. His successor and wife continues the increasingly belligerent approach to the islands.

The dispute flared up again in 2010, when Desire Petroleum, a British company, began exploratory drilling off the Falklands' coast. Argentina countered by requiring ships sailing in Argentine waters between it and the Falklands to have a permit. The US government sat on the fence and offended London by suggesting that it negotiate with Argentina over the islands. In part because of these economic ties, Falklanders have a per-capita GDP of $50,000, one of the world's highest. In response to the resurgence of Argentine nationalism, the islanders conducted a referendum in March 2013 on remaining British: With a turnout of 92%, only three voters marked "no."

The 32,000 inhabitants of Gibraltar cling to their rock and are largely self-ruling. But they rely on the protection of 5,000 British troops stationed there because they are afraid of becoming a part of Spain. In 1985 the border between Gibraltar and Spain was reopened, and discussions over its sovereignty and eventual disposition continue. [See Spain chapter]

Painstaking negotiations with the People's Republic of China (PRC) over Hong Kong resulted in an agreement that gave the PRC sovereignty over the colony in July 1997. But it committed China to guaranteeing Hong Kong's capitalist economy and lifestyle for 50 years.

Essential Relationship with the United States

Britain's foreign policy involves close cooperation with the United States and a primary focus on Europe. As separate sovereign states with their own interests, the Americans and British sometimes have different views on issues, ranging from the British-French invasion of Suez in 1956 to the American invasion of Grenada in 1983. But many people on both sides of the Atlantic still talk of a "special relationship" between the two countries stemming from their common language and heritage, as well as from their alliance during two world wars. They cooperate closely on defense, intelligence gathering and nuclear technology.

This relationship never excluded disagreement. Ex–foreign minister Geoffrey Howe spoke in 1983 of the "special intimacy and a special mutual confidence that we're able to talk with each other with the candor which one would normally expect only between one's own advisers." But some Europeans suspected that Britain is a sort of Trojan Horse for American objectives on the Continent. This, among other things, influenced former French president Charles de Gaulle to reject Britain's first attempt to join the European Community.

No country's leader seized the moment more decisively after the September 11, 2001, terrorist attacks against the US than did Tony Blair. They claimed 100 British lives and thereby became the worst terrorist strike against British citizens in history. He flew to America immediately after the disaster; visited Ground Zero, where the World Trade Center once stood; listened to President Bush's speech to the nation from the gallery of the House of Representatives; and offered stirring words to the Americans and his own people: The terrorists "have no moral inhibition on the slaughter of the innocent. If they could have murdered not 7,000 but 70,000, does anyone doubt they would have done so and rejoiced in it? There is no compromise possible with such people, no meeting of minds, no point of understanding with such terror. Just a choice: Defeat it or be defeated by it. And defeat it we must. To the Americans, we were with you at the first. We will stay with you to the last." The queen awarded former New York mayor Rudolph Giuliani an honorary knighthood for his leadership in the aftermath of the crisis.

Blair put his country's money where its mouth was. Within two months Britain had sent 4,200 troops to the war zone in and around Afghanistan. In the opening salvos against the Taliban regime, British submarines fired cruise missiles at key targets and put special operations forces and Royal Marines on the ground to assist the opposition's push to rout Taliban forces. In 2002 its commandos joined the Americans and other allies on search-and-destroy operations aimed at remnants of al Qaeda and Taliban forces. For a half-year, it commanded the international peacekeeping forces in Kabul trying to stabilize the traumatized country.

The UK took command of NATO peacekeeping forces in Afghanistan in May 2006, under Leutenant General Sir David Richards. In July it announced an increase in its troop strength amid debates at home over whether the mission has been underresourced, misrepresented, or misconceived. In 2010 it had almost 10,000 troops in Afghanistan, mainly in the dangerous south, to deal with fierce Taliban raids and tribal complexities by means of challenging counterinsurgency tactics. By July 2010, 315 of its soldiers had died, a third of them in Helmand Province alone.

Between them, the US and UK contributed more troops to NATO's effort in Afghanistan than all other allies put together. Britain withdrew its soldiers in the face of a rejection by three-fourths of Britons to a continued commitment in Afghanistan.

The American president and people benefited greatly from Blair's support, and the two leaders developed a close personal relationship. The prime minister was mocked in left-leaning British media as the "president's poodle." He was criticized at home for getting too little in return. However, his position was always that it is difficult or impossible to do much good in the world without a powerful and engaged American partner.

The March–April 2003 war in Iraq offered a further opportunity for Britain to act as a transatlantic bridge; it provided 45,000 well-trained troops, 15% of the total. With a sensitivity to growing European concerns about the US role in the world, Blair stood up for a disliked and distrusted American president and repeatedly condemned anti-Americanism, reminded his countrymen of past American contributions to their security, and warned that opposing the US would merely reinforce American tendencies toward unilateralism. He did this at considerable temporary damage to his popularity at home, and even 139 of his own Labour MPs voted against the war, one of the largest rebellions in parliamentary history. He tirelessly argued the case for military action against Saddam Hussein's dictatorship and withstood merciless heckling and a strange British form of disagreement toward speakers—slow hand clapping.

His eloquence and persuasiveness paid off; at the beginning of 2003, only 13% of Britons thought their country should go to war against Iraq, by the time war began, 56% were in favor, as was the majority of party leaders and MPs. He was able to demonstrate that America did not stand alone in the world and that the transatlantic divide ran down the middle of Europe rather than through the Atlantic. The result was a strengthening of the "special relationship" and an elevation of British influence in the world. One senior Bush official put it this way: "The special relationship had become a cliché which was being constantly trotted out, but all of a sudden it is very real. It is very deep and very operational." He continued: "This kind of partnership makes the United Kingdom a world player."

For his part, Blair reminded his party comrades at Labour's 2002 conference, "For all the resentment of America, remember one thing. The basic values of America are our values too. . . . My vision of Britain is not as the 51st state of anywhere, but I believe in this alliance, and I will fight long and hard to maintain it because alliance with America is in the interests of this country." Nevertheless, Blair was weakened politically by having led Britain into a war against Iraq that many British consider to have been unnecessary and for having gotten so little from the American president in return for his loyalty. "Bush's poodle" was a tag that hurt the prime minister.

The government was bruised by several inquiries into the political conduct of the Iraq War. In July 2004 the Butler Report argued that the government had oversold the case for war and that there had been intelligence failures. But it refrained from questioning Blair's "good faith," criticizing the prime minister individually, or saying that he or his government had distorted the evidence to build a case for war. "There was no deliberate attempt . . . to mislead."

Just days before the May 2005 elections, confidential documents from the attorney general's office at the time of the war seemed to indicate concerns about the legality of the war, even though the attorney general stated publicly that the war was legal, in his judgment. The documents did show some diplomatic discord between London and Washington. Both agreed that Saddam had weapons of mass destruction and had to be removed. But Blair wanted to work harder to "construct a coalition" and to "exhaust" efforts to deal with the problems within the UN. The British were also somewhat more concerned about what could go wrong once war began.

In November 2009 a fifth inquiry on Britain's role in the war opened. It was open to the public. Like the earlier inquiries, it provided no definitive proof that Blair had lied to start the war. The former prime minister gave a strong defense of his decision to send troops to Iraq.

Prince Harry, who had completed his officer's training, threatened to resign if he was prohibited from deploying to Iraq with his regiment. Military leaders decided against sending him on the grounds that his presence would make his unit an irresistible target for insurgents. However, in March 2008, he returned home from 10 weeks of combat duty in Afghanistan. His tour had to be cut short after American and other foreign news media reported his deployment, which British outlets had vowed to keep secret. He returned for a 20-week tour in 2013, flying an Apache attack helicopter. In 2015 he left full-time service with the armed forces.

Nothing tarnished the last stage of Blair's prime-ministership more than the bloody aftermath of the Iraq War. Gordon Brown's tricky task was to distance himself from Blair's Iraq commitment without being tagged as soft on defense. In April 2009 they relinquished the remainder of their command authority to the US, thereby ending a controversial six-year engagement that had cost 179 British lives. Winston Churchill's words in 1926 echoed in some British ears: "I hate Iraq. I wish we had never gone to the place." Staying there, he continued, was like "living on an ungrateful volcano."

Britain's most famous lieutenants: Princes William and Harry

Barack Obama enjoyed unprecedented popularity in Britain and elsewhere in Europe. Brown was the first to host Obama on the latter's maiden European tour as president. During that visit in April 2009, Queen Elizabeth departed from the usual protocol by wrapping her arm around Michelle Obama at the end of the first lady's courtesy call at Buckingham Palace. She almost never shows such affection in public.

As Britain reduces its military spending in an effort to reduce the budget deficit, some observers wonder if the special relationship with the US is over. The leaders of both countries deny it. Prime Minister Cameron said, "I and my party are instinctive friends of America and passionate supporters of the Atlantic alliance." His first foreign secretary, William Hague, affirmed in Washington three days after taking office that the US "is without doubt the most important ally" of Great Britain. Obama observed that "we see the world in a similar way."

Indeed the two countries' interests are aligned on the most pressing challenges they face: combatting violent terrorism, resolving the conflict in Afghanistan, dealing with a nuclear Iran, bringing the air war over Libya to a successful end, fighting the Islamic State in Iraq and Syria, and trying to persuade the Israelis and Palestinians to make peace. In any mix of core interests, Britain depends on close ties with America. Thus both countries can pursue their own interests in the context of a historic relationship. Both leaders agreed that the myths and emotion should be dropped, and the ties can be described as an "essential relationship."

In May 2011 the Obamas made a state visit to London, and the countries' leaders tried to give new meaning to the long-standing relationship. He became the first American invited to speak in Westminster Hall before a joint session of Parliament. He reminded his audience that his grandfather had been a cook in the Britsh army. When he finished, the dignitaries erupted in applause, and it took him a half-hour to leave the hall as they mobbed him for photos and handshakes. In January 2018 the US opened its gleaming new embassy, the most expensive ever built, in Nine Elms, a former industrial area along the south bank of the Thames.

Defense

For centuries Britain was a global power, whose interest in Europe was merely to prevent any one power or combination of powers from upsetting the military balance there and dominating the entire continent. After the Second World War, it shifted its primary focus to Europe. This is best seen in defense. It was a founding member of NATO, and until 1990 it organized its defense on the assumption that the chief threat was the Soviet Union. It therefore channeled the bulk of its resources into strengthening NATO rather than defending British outposts elsewhere. In 1971 it abandoned its defense commitments east of Suez.

The "NATO-first" policy necessitated fundamental changes in defense structure. Britain converted the once-mighty Royal Navy into a specialized force whose purpose was primarily to assist the American navy and to defend against submarines. In the 1970s it phased out its attack aircraft carriers. The Falkland Islands war in 1982 revealed how this change in force structure could affect Britain's commitments outside of Europe. It had to lease luxury liners and merchant vessels just to transport its troops and equipment to those faraway islands. The conflict prompted Britain to bolster its capabilities to project military power in the world by canceling the scheduled deactivation of an aircraft carrier and the Royal Navy's last two amphibious assault ships.

The heart of the British defense effort today is the army. It deploys a diminishing number of troops on the European continent, mainly in Germany. In 2010 it announced that, after 65 years of deployment on German soil, all of its 20,000 troops and the 23,000 dependents and British civilians working for the forces in that country would be withdrawn by 2020, a full 15 years earlier than expected. All 12 bases would be closed. The costs for this force are great, especially since Britain has a volunteer army. With the disappearance of the Soviet threat to Europe, NATO faces fundamental restructuring that affects the British military. In 1991 the allies decided to establish a sizable rapid-reaction force to confront unforeseen threats anywhere in Europe. This force is stationed mainly in Germany and is commanded by a British officer.

Within Britain itself, the most controversial aspect of British defense was its nuclear arsenal. Aside from France, the UK is the only European country to possess atomic weapons. The Thatcher government decided to replace the aging Polaris vessels (each carrying 16 missiles) with more modern submarines, capable of firing ultramodern, American-made Trident missiles, each of which could attack eight separate targets.

The Labour Party, which took power in May 1997, dropped its long-standing opposition to Britain's nuclear force. But that was reintroduced in 2015. In post–Cold War Europe, nuclear weapons have become largely irrelevant. The UK decided in 1998 to halve the number of its nuclear weapons at sea to under 200 on 4 Trident submarines. This is its total number of nuclear warheads, since the Royal Air Force scrapped its in the same year.

The government debated what do about its four Vanguard-class Trident submarines that reach the end of their lives in 2024. Stationed in Scotland, at least one is at sea on constant patrol. The Blair government decided in 2007 to devote £20 billion ($32 billion) to build a new generation of nuclear submarines to carry a reduced number (ca. 160) of American-supplied Trident missiles. This makes Britain's nuclear arsenal the smallest among the five permanent UN Security Council members and the only one of them whose warheads are based on a single platform. Since it relies on American Trident missiles, it keeps the cost of its nuclear arsenal at half the level of France's.

Although nuclear targeting is coordinated with the United States, only the British prime minister can order the use of Britain's nuclear weapons. The willingness of the British government since the 1950s to permit the deployment of American nuclear weapons on British soil, which are not under the direct command of the British prime minister, reflects NATO's importance in British defense planning. "Dual-key" safeguards were considered unnecessary because the UK had a firm agreement with the US (which has never been published) that no American nuclear weapons could ever be launched from Britain without the approval of the British government.

In 1991 Britain's participation in the war to drive Iraq out of Kuwait was solidly supported at home. The UK sent a powerful contingent of land, air, and naval forces serving under the overall command of American general Norman Schwarzkopf, whom the queen knighted after the successful campaign. In 1998 it dispatched an aircraft carrier back to the Persian Gulf to show its solidarity with the American and UN efforts to force Saddam Hussein to open his weapons facilities to international inspectors.

No sooner were the warriors home than the government began a steady reduction. In the two decades to 2010, it cut the army from 156,000 to 100,290; the navy from 63,000 to 35,650 and 6,840 Royal Marines; and the RAF from 89,000 to 39,750. Infantry battalions sank from 55 to 40, and front-line tanks, from 699 to 304. The British Army of the Rhine was halved to 20,000. However, Britain built up its special operations forces to 2,000–3,000. Its total active forces are 161,000, and its reserve forces, 199,280.

Navy to cut its fleet by half

■ Six destroyers and frigates to be mothballed ■ Retired First Sea Lord attacks 'outrageous' plans

The Royal Navy has responsibilities in the south Atlantic, off west Africa, in the Caribbean, and around the Middle East. It retains its three aircraft carriers (to be replaced by two new ones from 2016 to 2018) and four ballistic-missile submarines (Tridents). But its fleet of 28 attack submarines was cut to 12, and its 49 frigates and destroyers, to 25. The RAF lost 9 of its 30 front-line combat squadrons; its total front-line fighters and bombers sank from 630 to 500, some of which are flown by women. Its ships must often put to sea without their full crew or equipment. The air force took control of the navy's Harrier jump jets, and in 2007 its carriers sailed without planes four-fifths of the time. To keep up the crews' training, the navy allowed allied aircraft to land and fly off its ships.

Britain sent 35 combat aircraft, 8 ships, and 6,600 troops to participate in the air war over Yugoslavia in 1999. The UK has increasingly assumed peacekeeping responsibilities. In 2010 it had 900 deployed in Kosovo, 2,791 in Cyprus, 9,000 in Afghanistan, and 320 in Gibraltar. For training, it had 700 soldiers in the US and 557 in Canada.

Defense spending was cut by over a fifth from 1990 to 2015, to below 2% of GDP, the lowest since 1930. Despite the reductions, defense spending is still among the highest in Europe, the fourth highest in the world after the US, China, and Russia.

The government shows interest in a European defense capability. Blair gave his blessing to the European (now "Common") Security and Defence Policy (ESDP, now CSDP), which decided in 1999 to build a European rapid-reaction force that could act when NATO chooses not to do so. Britain's cooperation with France and Germany has tightened.

Faced with unmanageable defense costs, the British government signed a 50-year defense and security cooperation treaty with France in November 2010. The two countries account for half the defense spending in Europe and two-thirds of the military research and development. It was driven by the need to restrain their defense budgets while maintaining their willingness and capability to project power globally. The two countries had explored such defense cooperation before, most notably in the 1998 St. Malo Declaration following a meeting between French President Jacques Chirac and Tony Blair. But the Iraq War in 2003 prevented progress. This was one of the few times the two midsized nuclear powers found themselves on opposite sides in an international conflict.

The main items in the treaty are a joint expeditionary force, combined training, and maintenance for the new A400M transport airplane and shared A300 aerial tankers. France offered Britain access to its jet pilot school, and both will cooperate in developing armed drones and ways of combatting roadside bombs. They will jointly operate aircraft-carrier strike groups with the aim of ensuring a permanent carrier presence at sea. Perhaps most dramatically, they will cooperate on nuclear weapons while retaining their independent deterrents and means: Britain depends on American equipment, while France develops its own.

Immediately upon taking office in May 2010, the Cameron government ordered that a Strategic Defence and Security Review be made; its unveiling only five months later called for the largest defense cuts since the end of World War II: by 8% over four years. It described the forces as "overstretched, underequipped and ill-prepared" to meet the unconventional warfare challenges of the future. Military personnel were cut by 10% (7,000 from the army and 5,000 each from the navy and air force) and the army's artillery and tanks by 40%. The cuts left Britain with fewer readily deployable forces and reduced its ability to influence events. Its highly regarded special forces were left largely intact.

The aircraft carrier *Ark Royal* would immediately be scrapped, even though it is the only one in Britain's inventory that can launch fixed-wing jets; all 80 naval and air force Harrier jump jets would be taken out of service. Two new carriers are being built by 2020 at a cost of $9 billion, and one of them would be sold or mothballed three years after completion. The operational carrier would be equipped by a naval version of the F-35 Joint Strike Fighter. Replacement or modernization of the four Trident subs would be delayed by up to five years. As the Afghanistan war wound down, the government produced in 2012 another defense review that called for the largest overhaul of the armed forces since the 1950s. Regular troops would decline by 20% to 82,000, the lowest level since the Napoleonic Wars.

The Conservative-LDP government that took office in May 2010 relegated foreign affairs to the backburner, as it focused on saving the country's financial health. There would be no more "wars of choice" or "humanitarian intervention." Any focus abroad would be on the pursuit of the nation's economic and commercial interests. It also pledged significantly to increase spending on overseas aid. Its diplomatic footprint would be shrunk as the Foreign Office faced a reduction of a fourth of its budget. Its diminished military force would be used less for moral causes. The aim would be to bring the domestic economy in order, not to maintain or enhance Britain's influence abroad.

View of London from St. Paul's Cathedral

Like so many good intentions, these priorities did not survive the first contact with reality. When revolution broke out in the Arab world, Britain did not hesitate to intervene diplomatically and militarily. Cameron was the first foreign leader to visit Egypt after Hosni Mubarak was toppled. Along with France, it led the international effort to enforce a UN- and Arab League–mandated no-fly zone over Libya, using its submarine-launched Tomahawk cruise missiles, fighter jets, and attack helicopters. It struck at Islamic State targets in both Iraq and Syria. These were precisely the kinds of assets that are slated for severe cuts.

The prime minister argued that Britain need not choose between its interests and its values, between stability and freedom. There is serious concern that the UK will no longer be able "to punch above its weight" both diplomatically and militarily. Thanks to unpleasant experiences in Iraq and Afghanistan, much of the public is opposed to armed engagements. In August 2013 Parliament rejected the Cameron government's participation in an American-led air strike on Syria. That was reversed two years later.

ECONOMY

Britain for two centuries has been a highly industrialized and developed nation. It led the Industrial Revolution in the 18th and 19th centuries, but after World War II, it enjoyed less efficiency than some of its newer rivals. Only 20% of the present gross domestic product now comes from industry and manufacturing (employing 18.9%, still the world's sixth-largest manufacturer), while service industries provide 79% of GDP and 79% of jobs, and agriculture, 1% of GDP and 1.2% of employment. British farmers produce more than half of the country's food requirements. Two-thirds of Britain's agricultural land is used for grazing; the main field crops are wheat, barley, oats, potatoes, and sugar beets.

Because of the extraction of oil and natural gas from the North Sea, Britain became self-sufficient in these sources of energy in the 1980s. It remains one of the dozen or so largest oil producers in the world. But the North Sea supplies are gradually running out, and British drivers pay the highest gasoline prices in the world (about $10 per gallon in 2013). It already gets a third of its electricity from gas and does not want a greater reliance on this one source. The UK is no longer the biggest coal producer in western Europe, but its coal supplies could last for another 300 years if needed. EU environmental rules and halts in government subsidies caused many coal plants to shut down. Although it gets 20% of its electricity from coal, it will close all of its coal-fired power plants by 2025. Along with Sweden and Germany, Britain was the only country in Europe that was meeting its Kyoto greenhouse gas emissions target, so it does not resist such closures. Unlike Germany, which gets 28% of its electricity from renewable sources, Britain gets only 1%.

Having calculated that world energy demand will increase by 50% in 2030, especially given the increased needs of China and India, and worried about climate change, the government declared in 2008 that investment into a new generation of nuclear reactors is needed. In 1996 the government had privatized its nuclear-power arm British Energy, but the upfront capital costs of atomic plants make long delays inevitable. However, nuclear energy produces little carbon dioxide, the technology is well developed, and uranium can be bought from stable countries like Australia and Canada.

No reactors have been built since 1994, and its two oldest commercial nuclear stations were closed in 2007. Nuclear power provides about a fifth of Britain's electricity, but its 10 plants are aging, with only 1 to be left running in 2023. This sudden turnabout is controversial, but voters are generally receptive to the idea that nuclear power should continue to make up a part of the nuclear mix. Polls show that more British favor it than oppose it. Waste is stored temporarily at the Sellafield site, and plans call for a long-term underground facility to be built.

Temporary Decline in Economic Performance

Economic and social shifts in Britain helped to bring important changes in some fundamental assumptions. From 1945 to 1970, it had generally been assumed (and was broadly the case) that, despite temporary ups and downs, the economy would always continue to improve; that inflation was unimportant; that full employment was normal; and that, if the economy got a little out of kilter, it could be put back on course by reducing or raising demand through taxes and public spending (classic economic methods of the late British economist John Maynard Keynes). It was therefore widely accepted that governments should regulate the economy in order to maintain employment while expanding the welfare state out of ever-increasing national prosperity. By 1975, state spending amounted to more than 60% of national income.

The Keynsian assumptions, which more or less enjoyed an acceptance by both major parties, were torn asunder in the 1970s. At the beginning of the decade, inflation began to rise, reaching the stratospheric level of 25% annually in the mid-1970s and 22% in 1980. Unemployment began to rise steadily, and the old cure did not seem to work anymore.

As economic growth slowed to a standstill, governments were faced with an unpleasant dilemma: Demand for welfare services continued to grow, while the national income to pay for them did not. British economic discussions began to be preoccupied with "managing decline." The nationalized industries (most of which had passed to public control in the immediate postwar years) were performing poorly and were becoming an increasing drain on the nation's productivity, thereby discrediting the very idea of public ownership. Everywhere people began talking about the "English disease."

The Thatcher Revolution

Margaret Thatcher brought dramatic economic changes during her prime ministership from 1979 to 1990. Neither the Tory government of John Major nor Tony Blair's Labour government, which took office in 1997, moved to undo her reforms in any fundamental way. She denationalized more than a third of Britain's nationalized industries, including Rolls-Royce, British Airways, and the British Gas Corporation. The sale of these brought more than $40 billion into the state treasury, eliminated the need for taxpayers to subsidize them, and reaped handsome annual tax revenues. In 1987 the government began selling shares of British Petroleum. In 1988 plans were announced to privatize the electric industry in England and Wales. British Telecom was sold, and in 1996 its merger with the American MCI was made public. Thatcher's large-scale privatization program included two dozen major companies. Nevertheless, state spending still accounts for 39% of GDP (compared with 30% in the US), roughly the same percentage as when she took office.

Thatcher had argued that the state was overspending, and the shortfalls were being covered by public borrowing and expanding the money supply rather than by taxes. These expedients stimulated inflation and absorbed the capital that was desperately needed to finance industrial innovation. The cure, she argued, was to restrict the money supply and cut public expenditures, which would both reduce inflation and free investment capital. To create economic incentives, income taxes should be cut. Finally, trade-union power had to be curbed.

Her pride and her optimism were borne out by the facts: Since the country began pulling out of recession in 1981, productivity increased at an annual rate of 3.5%. The economy grew at an annual rate of 3%. Inflation was down from a high of 24.2% to 3.3% in 1995. Taxes had been reduced slightly, and the average voter's real pretax income had increased by 25% since 1979. From 1971 to 1994, real disposable income grew by almost 50%, and spending on social benefits increased by 168%. Britons live more prosperous lives. Nevertheless, the UK is the only EU country in which working hours have increased, to 43.4 hours.

Unemployment was higher when she left than the 4.3% when she took office. Nevertheless, 1 million new jobs had been created under her rule, in part because of incentives to small enterprises. Also, the jobs of those who were employed seemed far less threatened than in the early 1980s. Interest rates were falling, and the pound was much stronger. Its stock market was booming, and the UK had again become a leading creditor nation. Public borrowing had fallen to 1% of national income. Most important, she had restored morale and seemed to have ended decades of relative economic decline.

After her 1987 victory, London's *Sunday Times* pronounced that Thatcher had brought about Britain's "biggest transformation since the Industrial Revolution." Indeed, her economic performance profoundly changed her country. She created what she called a "property-owning democracy," in which "every earner shall be an owner." Two-thirds of Britons now own their homes, compared to 50% in 1979, and car ownership has risen from 54% to 66%. In 1979 four times as many Britons belonged to trade unions as owned shares in the stock market. But by 1989 the number of stockholders had tripled from 7% to 21%. As a result of a fall in union membership by one-fourth to 9 million, the number of union members and stockholders are now equal.

Thatcher enormously reduced the power of the once-mighty labor unions, which had been able to topple the governments of her two predecessors. She introduced laws that limit unions' legal immunities. They restrict picketing rights, ban secondary picketing and political strikes, make national unions financially responsible for the actions of their members, and require unions to have a secret balloting of members before declaring a strike. She rooted out one of the main causes of the "English disease" by taking on the bosses of the most powerful unions and crushing them: the steel workers in 1980, the coal miners in 1985, and the teachers in 1986. By 1987 strikes were at a 50-year low; workdays lost to union disputes declined from 29.5 million in 1979 to 1.9 million in 1986.

The reduction in the number and length of strikes was, in part, due to workers' and employees' fear of losing their jobs and to their realization that real earnings for those with work has risen almost 35% between 1980 and 1987. There has also been a change of attitudes: Many workers associate unions with strikes and therefore have increasingly turned their backs on the unions, whose membership has continued to decline. An important result for the overall economy is that the unions are no longer able to block the introduction of state-of-the-art technology in order to protect jobs. Thus, while from 1974–1980 output per worker in British manufacturing did not increase at all, from 1981 to 1987 it grew by 40%. So powerful had the unions been that many people wondered, "Who governs?" After she was finished, no one would suspect that it was the union bosses.

More and more workers became homeowners (43% by 1983 and one-third of even unskilled laborers by 1988), thanks in part to Margaret Thatcher's policy of selling many state-owned council houses to their occupants. By the time her party finally left power in 1997, 68% of all households owned their own homes. It is not surprising that the percentage of Britons who consider themselves to belong to the middle class increased from 30% of the population in 1979 to roughly 50% in 1987. Their lifestyles became more and more like those of the middle class; this was given added impetus by the education changes in the 1970s that largely did away with the several schooling tracks and brought most British schoolchildren together in one school. The massive occupational shifts and breakdown in elite structure in the educational system fostered increasing social mobility. It is no wonder that persons who lived in several classes in their own lifetime ceased to use class as a major political reference point. It is quite simply no longer accurate to speak of "two Britains," one a deprived working class and the other a traditional upper class.

Thatcher created a more prosperous and productive Britain that is still the basis for the country's exemplary economic performance. But her chief economic legacy was one of the mind. The pursuit of comfort and wealth had become marks of bad form. But she made prosperity an acceptable goal and free-market capitalism morally defensible. Tony Blair's Labour Party not only embraces both, but he also won the 1997 elections by promising that his government could manage Thatcher's economy even more competently. By the 1990s anybody working in Britain's offices and factories could see that they were much better and more productively run than was the case two decades earlier. Industrial relations have improved dramatically.

Labor Unions

Public sympathy and enthusiasm for labor unions gradually eroded in the 1970s and early 1980s. In order to gain wage restraint from the powerful unions, Labour governments made so many concessions to them that many persons began to blame the unions for high prices and many of the economic problems. Their revulsion at the excessive "unelected power" which union bosses wielded boiled to the surface in the 1978–1979 "winter of discontent," when coal and transportation strikes threatened to paralyze the entire nation.

Both the economic recession and the Conservatives' broadside attacks against the Labour Party in general and the unions in particular greatly weakened the latter. Between 1979 and 2007, their membership dropped from 12 million to 7.5 million. In 1979 more than half the workforce (55%) was unionized; 38% was in 1990, and 27%, in 2010. In 2011, 14.2% of private-sector employees and 56.3% of public-sector employees were unionized. Union-negotiated settlements cover more than 70% of those public-sector workers. By election time in 1983, almost three-fourths of all Britons favored stricter laws to regulate unions; an astonishing three-fifths of all trade unionists also favored legal curbs on union power. Union popularity declined further as the result of a protracted coal miners' strike in 1984–1985. Union leader Arthur Scargill fanned the flames of anti-unionism with public pledges to bring down Thatcher's government. He failed, and her ability to break trade-union power is her most lasting legacy.

In the 1990s strikes were at their lowest level in more than a half-century. In 1979, 29.5 man-days were lost to strikes; in 1995 that figure had fallen to 4.15. In the 21st century, the figures are even more dramatic: Only 158,000 working days were lost to strikes in 2005, compared with 12.9 million in the 1970s and 7.2 million in the 1980s. This is fewer than in the US and Canada and about half the rate for the EU and OECD countries. Perhaps because of affluence and higher homeownership, strikes also tend to be much shorter. One expert noted, "It's much more risky to strike now. If you don't do it right according to the law, you end up in court."

Unions affiliated with the TUC lost a third of their members after the Tories came to power in 1979. Even within the Labour Party the unions' influence has been reduced though not eliminated. The support of the trade unions for the party can still be helpful in a crunch. They provide more than half of its money.

The gap between the working and middle classes has also been narrowed by the changing composition of the labor unions. The increase in the number of civil-service employees, the growth of the service sector within the economy, and the rise of computer-related and other high-technology industries in the south of England and especially around London and Cambridge prompted the growth of so-called white-collar unionism. That is, union members were no longer exclusively manual workers in factories and mines, but they also could be teachers, engineers in a nationalized industry, secretaries in Whitehall, etc.

With rising inflation and talk of "paring down the public sector," these white-collar unions even became quite militant in pressing their demands. Thus, Britain began to experience a different breed of striker, from nurses and hospital personnel to civil servants. This militancy among the white-collar employees has helped even more to bridge the social gap between workers and employees and to break down class divisions.

There are still workers concentrated in large manufacturing or mining industries living in rented council housing in working-class sections and remaining in a largely isolated social environment. They confront employers and managers whose political attitudes are also traditional and are diametrically opposed to those of their workers. These groups are far more likely to retain a strong loyalty to either the Labour Party or the Conservative Party and a strong class-consciousness. However, these kinds of workers and managers are becoming a diminishing minority in Britain's more service-oriented economy. Union members in the service sectors work in an environment that brings them into contact with all other classes, a factor that reduces rather than sharpens class-consciousness. As a consequence, their voting behavior is far less class-bound. They can be attracted to parties that portray a new, nonclass image and seem capable of overcoming the old social divides.

Britain and Europe

In 1973 the UK entered the EU, a move that has had a dramatic impact on its economy. The EU now buys half of British exports, compared to a third in 1972. It provides half of its imports. Still, many British remain critical of their country's membership in the EU.

In practice, British governments have tended to put British interests ahead of European interests. They have been cool on a common EU energy policy, a directly elected European Parliament, and European Monetary Union (EMU). Britain traditionally showed little interest in deepening European integration, and it tends to be opposed to political and supranational integration. But it supports enlargement, perhaps to water down the union, as some critics contend.

Margaret Thatcher tried hard to reduce the British contribution to the EU budget. Declaring that "I want my money back," she insisted on a "British rebate" of two-thirds the difference between what Britain paid into the EU and what it got back out. The Blair government declared in 2005 that it would not give this up until significant changes were made in the union's Common Agriculture Policy (CAP), which gobbles up 40% of all EU spending; about a quarter of CAP spending goes to France. By 2005 Britain had become the fourth-largest net contributor as a percentage of national income and the second-largest in total cash contribution, two and one-half times more than France pays in.

Thatcher signed the Single European Act in 1986 because it was an economic, not political, step toward integration. In 1989–1990 she remained suspicious of "deepening" EU unity on the grounds that it would undermine national sovereignty and that it was no time to create new bureaucracies and weaken national parliaments just when eastern European nations were digging themselves out from underneath their bureaucracies and breathing new life into their legislatures. Not all British, not even all Tories, agreed with her foot dragging, and this contributed to her fall.

At the historic 1991 summit in Maastricht, Britain agreed to greater economic and political union on the condition that the UK could "opt out" of an eventual single European currency, which it chose to do when the euro was introduced in 12 EU countries. It also rejected moves to make an EU "social policy" mandatory for all members, and the Euroskeptic Tories threatened to stop observing it. There was much resistance in all parties, especially the Conservative Party, to the Maastricht Treaty. However, Parliament finally accepted it in 1993.

The Labour governments were more supportive of British membership in a more united Europe, although Prime Ministers Blair and Brown promised to put British interests first. With Nick Clegg and the LDP playing key roles in the Cameron government, the Tories' Euroskepticism was restrained. The UK would have to worry about meeting the criteria for the euro, even if wanted to join. Its budget in 2019 had a deficit of 1.3% of GDP, and overall public debt stood at less than half of GDP.

One of Labour's first acts in 1997 was to transfer the power to set interest rates from the chancellor of exchequer to an unelected panel of the Bank of England. Its greater independence was demonstrated in July 2013, when it appointed Canadian central bank chief Mark Carney as governor of the Bank of England. He is the first foreigner in 318 years to assume this post, which is arguably the most influential unelected job in Britain. Blair found it publicly expedient to announce in 2000 that "people don't want Europe interfering in every aspect of people's national lives."

Britain has always had two chief aims in Europe: slow down the drive for political union and prevent Franco-German domination of European politics. The temporary death of the EU constitution in 2005 accomplished both.

In the campaign the French government had heaped criticism on what it saw as the "Anglo-Saxon" economic model. In supposed contrast to France's and Germany's shorter work week, higher welfare benefits and restrictions on the influx of low-wage workers from central Europe, Britain is an economic free-for-all that lacks all these amenities. This is a caricature.

The failed EU constitutional treaty was doctored up by getting rid of the most unpopular provisions (about 10% of the original text). The revised version, which was not labeled a "constitution," was adopted by the member states in Lisbon in December 2007. The Lisbon Treaty was unpopular in Britain. Then Prime Minister Brown had the treaty ratified by parliament. Prime Minister Cameron announced in 2015 that a referendum on British membership in the EU would be conducted by June 2016 following tough negotiations on new terms for Britain. The result was a catastrophe: 52% voted to leave the EU, and Cameron lost his job.

Current Economic Situation

Spending for social welfare and health care has been greatly increased. Child and pensioner poverty rates have declined to near average EU levels. Income distribution has widened. All this is paid for by tax levels on par with most continental countries; government spending is 52% of GDP, but the Cameron coalition vowed to bring it down to 41%.

The Blair government introduced new market and financial discipline to the National Health Service (NHS). A 2006 study concluded that middle-aged English are "much healthier" than their American counterparts, even though the health-care system costs half as much ($5,635 versus $2,231) per capita than in the US Smoking and drinking rates are slightly higher in England, while there is greater obesity in the US Life expectancy is 79.4 for men and 83.1 for women. The NHS universally covers all citizens, while 16% of Americans under age 65 were without health insurance until the 2009 health reform, which seeks to lower that figure to 6%. The NHS therefore provides important psychological reassurance. Health-care costs, which have risen to 9% of GDP (faster than any other public service), or almost a fifth of government spending, were exempted from the budget cuts ordered by the Cameron government in 2010. The government tried to make the NHS more efficient, but the effort was chaotic, and a formidable array of critics called it "a mess." A pause to reflect on how to proceed was declared.

The British and French finally agreed to construct a twin-bore, 32-mile channel tunnel (dubbed "Chunnel") through which an auto-rail link between the two countries passes. Road vehicles are loaded on trains at terminals on both sides of the Channel and whisked at a speed of 100 miles per hour from one side to the other. The Channel became what Napoleon had described as "a ditch that will be leaped whenever one has the boldness to try." The two nations' leaders shared a bold vision of the future. In 1990 the burrowing French and British crews linked up under the channel, and the Chunnel opened in 1994.

It is mired in serious financial difficulties, having cost twice as much to build as projected. Repayment of the $11.2 billion debt had to be suspended while its finances were restructured, which was done in 2006 and 2007. The problem is that too few passengers are using this undersea link even to pay the interest on the construction costs. It was assumed that 10 million passengers would use the Chunnel each year, but in 2003 only 6.3 million did so. Also only 1.7 million tons of freight were shipped through in 2003, far short of the 5-million-ton estimate each year. The result was a severe cash crunch, although the tunnel operator, Groupe Eurotunnel, reported its first annual net profit in 2007. In 2013 the EU ruled that access charges were "excessive" and should be lowered.

In November 2007 Britain completed its $12 billion 109-kilometer (68-mile) high-speed railway linking the Channel Tunnel to the newly renovated terminal, St. Pancras Station. Its imposing ironwork train-shed had once been the world's largest enclosed space. The train journey to Paris now takes two and one-quarter hours going 186 mph, and passengers can also travel to Brussels. The Eurotunnel Group managed a small profit in 2009, despite a disastrous fire in September 2008 that disrupted traffic until February 2009. At Christmastime 2009 problems again struck when heavy snowstorms caused electrical outages inside the tunnel and interrupted service for about a week. Nearly 90,000 passengers were affected. A large illegal refugee camp on the Calais side of the Chunnel is the jumping-off point for thousands of men trying to make it to Britain through the tunnel. Their efforts are fraught with peril.

The United Kingdom has been heavily involved in overseas trade for many centuries, and the importance of that trade continues to grow. In the last 50 years, the export of goods and services has moved from being one-fifth of the gross domestic product to one-third. Of these exports, 9.1% go to the United States (which provides 5.8% of imports).

After the US, Britain is the world's largest investor abroad. After the U.S., it was also the favorite destination of foreign direct investment (FDI). Roughly a quarter of all foreign direct investment flowing into the western European EU nations goes to the UK. Many well-known "American" brands are now British: Brooks Brothers belongs to Marks and Spencer, and Diageo owns Burger King and Pillsbury. The Greyhound bus company is in British hands. The favorite candy in the UK, Cadbury, was acquired in 2010 by

The United Kingdom

The 600-foot long boring machine which led others in clawing through 7.5 million cubic meters of chalk-marl one mile beneath the sea which divides Britain and France

the American food giant Kraft. Foreigners own everything from London's water supply to its airports. Its steel industry has almost been entirely purchased.

In 1995 it surpassed Japan to become the largest source of foreign direct investment in the US. By 1999 the UK was directing 30% of its direct investment to America, while the US sends a fifth of its foreign direct investment to Britain. By 2003 the US had invested almost as much in the UK as it had in all of Asia, Latin America, the Middle East, and Africa. After the turn of the century, only the US and China attract more money from foreigners than does Britain. In part, this is due to the fact that Britain's labor costs are lower than in some major industrialized countries.

The City of London (a small area within greater metropolitan London) is of immense significance in international finance. It has the world's largest insurance market, the lengthiest listing of overseas securities, the highest proportion of the Eurodollar market, the biggest foreign exchange market, and the largest secondary market for Islamic bonds. It generates a fifth of all corporate-tax revenues in the UK. In 1986 a "big bang" occurred in the London financial world: The financial markets were largely deregulated, and foreign companies were permitted to trade in British financial markets for the first time. The overall effect was to make London the world's most important financial center, although it was hit hard by the 2008–2010 recession.

Each day, 600,000 people go to work in 580 banks; that is more than the total population of Frankfurt. Big American banks have their continental headquarters there, and London's traders have grown to control 30% of global foreign-exchange trading. Britain's financial institutions are fully competent in dealing with the euro, even though its political leaders are not yet ready for it. All this financial activity has helped make London the world's second-most-expensive city in the world for expatriate employers, after Moscow; New York was not even among the top 10.

Prime Minister Cameron inherited an economy in 2010 that was in a dire state. The recession had hurt it badly because of the country's overextended banks, the indebted private sector, and the excessively large public sector. Its growth rate was 2.7% per year from 1998 to 2006 and 1.5% in 2019. The earlier steady expansion pushed up per-capita GDP above that of Germany and France. Unemployment was 4.1% in 2019, while inflation was 2.1%. The budget deficit was down to 1.3% of GDP in 2019.

Given the seriousness of the public finance crisis, the Conservative-LDP government had no alternative to the most brutally austere budget since Thatcher's rule. It acted quickly so that it could pin the blame for the pain on the previous Labour government. As a beginning, the salaries of MPs and ministers were cut by 5%, and wider public sector pay decreases and layoffs would follow. The departments' budgets (except health and foreign aid) were cut an average of 25% over four years. The VAT was raised from 17.5% to 20%. It retained a 50% income tax rate on the wealthiest individuals.

In 2002, 400,000 rural Britons marched in London to dramatize what they called a "crisis in the countryside." It suffers from a depression in agriculture, made worse by the disastrous handling of the foot-and-mouth disease. Since the mid-1990s, farm incomes have halved, and weekenders and 100,000 Britons resettling in rural Britain each year have driven house prices so high (overall they trebled in the decade to 2007) that many locals can no longer afford to live where they grew up. The positive side of this real estate inflation is that the value of farmers' assets has risen by about 40% since 1992. Thus the average farmer possesses an net worth of £700,000 ($1.2 million).

In 2004 fox hunting that involves a pack of dogs sniffing out foxes and killing them was prohibited. Riding with hounds is still permitted, as is the shooting of foxes forced out of cover by a maximum of two dogs. Some judges have found the Hunting Act confusing and poorly written, and only a handful of hunters have been convicted of violating it. The Conservative-LDP government agreed in 2010 to allow a parliamentary vote whether to lift the ban. Since the abolishment went into effect, the 300 hunt clubs have seen their membership grow by about 45,000. However, most Labour and LDP MPs oppose lifting the ban; this includes Lib Dem leader Nick Clegg. A positive vote is therefore unlikely.

Britain is the fifth-most-popular tourist destination in the world, attracting 25 million foreign visitors annually; it is Americans' most popular destination. The 125,000 mostly small tourist businesses employ 1.75 million people, more than agriculture, food production, coal mining, steel, car and aircraft manufacturing, and textiles combined.

CULTURE

The impact and pervasiveness of British culture on the rest of the world has been out of all proportion to the size and population of the United Kingdom. While those who participated in the Beatlemania of the 1960s might disagree, two British gifts to world culture stand out as most important. First, the achievement of English writers in producing a magnificent body of literature has influenced the way people think around the world. Within English literature, certainly Shakespeare and the King James Bible have been most

Globe Theatre

important. One-third of the world's most translated authors come from the UK.

Second, the development of constitutional, parliamentary democracy set an example to all the world of how men and women may live in freedom and guide their own destinies. It also shows how compromise and civility rather than coercion are the best ways to pull together the social fabric. In a world in which the majority of human beings do not enjoy political or individual freedoms and other countries that attempt democracy are unable to achieve stability, the United Kingdom stands a worthy example of a free society living under laws.

The widespread knowledge of English as a first or second language throughout the world speaks for itself, be it the Americanized or British version. It has become the language of scientific expression almost worldwide. English is not spoken throughout England, Wales, Scotland, and Ireland in an identical fashion. Local expressions and local pronunciations vary widely. The urbanized lower classes of London traditionally speak Cockney English, which the average American can seldom understand. Language has traditionally been a key to identifying the social class of a British person. The reason lies partly in the educational system.

Education and Class in Britain

The traditional school system had been tracked in such a way that a child's educational program was more or less fixed at age 11. After the crucial "11-plus exam," some children went into trade or commercial schools. Others went into the more elite, state-supported grammar schools or the independent, privately endowed "public schools" (the most prestigious being Eton, Harrow, and Winchester). Technically only those schools that sent a delegate to a specific school conference in the 19th century have a right to call themselves "public schools." But the term is loosely used to refer to almost any private school. They were especially geared to preparing pupils for the few seats in universities, especially at Oxford and Cambridge (known collectively as "Oxbridge"), which held the keys to success in politics, industry, and scholarship. A 2007 study concluded that the top 10 universities in the world were either American or British: Cambridge and Oxford placed second and third; Imperial College London, fifth; and University College London, ninth.

In a 1992 study of the top 100 persons in Britain's elite, *The Economist* found that two-thirds had attended public schools, and more than half had studied at Oxford and Cambridge. Only a decade later, in 2002, those percentages had fallen noticeably to 46% public-school and 35% Oxbridge graduates. However, 15 out of 23 cabinet members in the Cameron government studied at an Oxbridge university. The number of women had climbed from 4% to a mere 5%.

The loosening hold of public-school and Oxbridge alumni reflects the growth of competition, especially in business, which has resulted from deregulation and globalization. Life in Britain's larger and more multinational companies is no longer as cozy as it used to be. Ambitious products of the country's expanded university system have claimed top positions once reserved for the well-born and those from famous schools.

Critics had long charged that the traditional educational system actually hardened and perpetuated class lines in British society. That is a major reason the old grammar and secondary modern schools were fused into "comprehensive" secondary schools, in which all pupils learn under one roof. State-sponsored schools can no longer select for ability, and state scholarships to the coveted private schools were eliminated. About 7% of all pupils attend the fee-paying "public schools" that provide a good education for average tuition fees of $21,000 per year; those costs can be as high as £30,000 ($46,000).

A reform proposed in the Blair years to provide more choice and competition among the state schools has taken flight under the Conservative–Liberal Democrat coalition: independent "academies." They are funded by the state but have more freedom in their operation. Between May 2010 and May 2011, their numbers jumped from 203 to 629. They include one in six English secondary schools.

Some say that these reforms actually lowered educational standards, and the gap between rich and poor people's education has in fact widened, as has income. However, to make the testing easier, less intimidating, and fairer, the old A-levels taken in the pupil's final year of secondary school, which were crucial for university admission, were changed. They now take "Advanced Supplementary," or AS-level, exams in their second-to-last year in school, and they are permitted to retake some of those tests to improve their grades. They then take the more difficult A2 exams at the end of their last year. Their final grades are based on the results of the two years combined.

British schools still reflect the social stratification of the country. A majority of pupils leave full-time education or training at age 16. As a result, less than half the workforce is classified as skilled, compared with 85% in Germany and 75% in France. According to an *Economist* survey in 2007, more than a third of adults left school with no formal qualifications. A sixth were judged functionally illiterate and a fifth innumerate. There is a strong feeling that British schools are not fully prepared for the challenges of the 21st century.

Two-fifths of university-age Britons (up from 5% in 1960 and one-eighth in 1980) study in 1 of the 87 universities or polytechnic schools. A funding boom for the universities occurred from 1997 to 2009, when their total income doubled, while student numbers increased by only 20%. Nevertheless, the dramatic increase in enrollment broke the budget and required that students contribute to the cost of their education.

Many of these students were distressed by the Labour government's decision to end tuition-free higher education and to levy in 2006 a flat-rate £3,000 ($4,500) yearly tuition charge. Adding the £5,000 ($7,500) the taxpayer provides, this falls well short of the $18,700 *The Economist* estimated it costs each year to educate a student at Oxford or Imperial College. This is on top of the more than $3,000 room and board costs, much of it borrowed or obtained through grants, including from local governments.

Although Britons with a university education earn 17% more over a lifetime, there is resentment over such tuition and over any talk of raising it to a level needed to cover the annual cost of a student. Oxford University chancellor Lord Chris Patten points out that universities charge half of what parents pay for a place at an average nursery.

Some enterprising British universities attract large numbers of non-EU foreign students and charge them American-level tuition. For example, Imperial College London charges overseas students £20,750 ($31,125) per year to study physics. Britain attracted 12% of the world's international students, second only to the US (20%). For instance, one-half of all undergraduate students at the London School of Economics (LSE) are non-EU foreigners. In 2005, some 9% of university students came from outside the EU; that is one-fourth more than in the preceding year. To improve its bottom line and be more able to compete with top American universities, Oxford announced its decision to raise its number of non-EU students from 8% to 15% over a decade, deemphasize undergraduate teaching, get away from its hallmark tiny tutorial groups, and have graduate students teach undergraduates.

Despite the emotional resistance to higher tuition, the Blair government succeeded in winning a House of Commons vote in 2004 by a whisker-thin five-vote majority authorizing a rise in tuition in English universities to £3,000 ($4,500) from 2006. Wales and Scotland are different; Scotland charges no tuition for Scottish students. Only the most affluent paid the full amount. Those from lower-income families paid less, and the lowest 30% paid nothing. Although low by American standards, this rise reflected an important shift in thinking that is very controversial in Britain.

The Cameron government's austerity policy called for a substantial reduction in direct grants to universities. To make up the difference, universities are permitted to charge between £6,000 ($9,600) and £9,000 ($14,400) in yearly tuition. Through a state-managed loan system, students can borrow interest-free what they cannot pay. In some cases they could borrow as much as £40,000 ($63,000) for a three-year education. They begin paying it back after graduation. When their income reaches £21,000 ($38,000) per year, they pay 9% of their earnings over that amount to settle the debt. After 30 years, any remainder is forgiven. This change drove many students and other protesters onto the streets, and a few of the demonstrations turned violent. Universities are also taking a page from America's book and are soliciting donations from alumni and other benefactors. For example, J. K. Rowling, who became richer than the queen from her Harry Potter books, gave £10 million ($16 million) to the University of Edinburgh, and Oxford University had raised £1 billion ($1.6 billion) by 2011.

A product of this educational system is Kazuo Ishiguro, the 2017 recipient of the Nobel Prize in literature. He studied English at the University of Kent in Canterbury and wrote *The Remains of the Day* and *Never Let Me Go.*

While there is considerable dissatisfaction with the educational system, there is little doubt that Britain's establishment and class system have changed dramatically in the last decades. Intelligent and ambitious individuals have always been able to succeed in Britain, whose society has long been less rigid than in many other countries. But in the UK today, status is largely earned, not inherited. BBC producer Nick Guthrie spoke of a revolution in the class system and argued, "it's not so much your family that matters; it's what you've achieved, and of course how much money you've got." Former prime minister Gordon Brown agreed, noting that on corporate boards "titles are out, for the most part. Today it's not who you are, but what you have done. . . . The old class system is not dead. But it is much weaker than ever before." It can even be a disadvantage to come from a privileged background. In 2010 David Cameron and Nick Clegg worked hard to master the common touch in order to increase their chances of electoral success.

An example of the new kind of establishment, based on money, athletic prowess, or celebrity, is the knighthood conferred in 2002 on Sir Michael Jagger. The musical superstar asked meekly, "does this mean I'm part of the establishment?" Considering his global reputation, massive wealth, and elegant country estate, the answer is yes.

Religion

Polls in 2012 revealed that only 59% call themselves Christian (down by 13 points in one decade). The Anglican Church of England (in Scotland the Presbyterian Church of Scotland) is the official state religion. The queen is its head, and Parliament approves its prayer book. Only in 2007 did the prime minister relinquish the right to select its bishops, 26 of whom have seats in the House of Lords, even though only 1 out of 6 Britons are Anglicans. The Archbishop of Canterbury, since 2013 former oil executive Justin Welby, is the spiritual leader of the world's 80 million Anglicans. It claims up to 30 million members on paper, but only a sixth of religiously active Britons belong. Church attendance has fallen dramatically in the Church of England. In 1960, 2.1 million attended on Easter Sunday, a figure that had fallen to 1.3 million by 1994. It is estimated that it lost about 1,000 church-goers every week during the 1990s. By 2012 around 3% attended an Anglican service at least once a month. In 2015 the Church of England consecrated its first female bishop, Libby Lane.

In 2005 only 3 in 10 Britons even belonged to a religion and attended services, down from nearly three-quarters in 1964. One study in 2007 showed that more people visit bingo clubs each week than go to church. The joke is that the C and E in the Church of England's abbreviation stand for "Christmas" and "Easter." Polls in 2002 indicated that barely 1 in 50 British families say grace regularly before meals, compared with close to half in the US.

Most worshipers are drawn to religions that are better able to satisfy the thirst for spirituality: immigrant religions (mainly Islam, Sikhism, and Hinduism); cults; Pentecostal or charismatic Christian churches, or new-age, nonmainstream faiths. In an attempt to lure worshipers back to the Church of England, its General Synod voted in 1992 to ordain women, a decision which had to be approved by Parliament and the queen in 1993. In protest, traditionalist Anglicans threaten to split away from the church, and some migrated to Catholicism. By 2012 a third of its clergy were women, some holding senior positions, such as canons and archdeacons. But until 2015 the church refused to appoint female bishops. The Anglican establishment is holding firm against ordaining LGBTQ people to the priesthood, as is practiced in some American dioceses. It also opposes same-sex marriages, although a bill allowing this sailed through the House of Commons, 400 to 175, in 2013. This issue has the potential of creating a schism in the church.

In 2008 then-archbishop Rowan Williams found himself in a furious tempest when he suggested that some aspects of the Muslim Sharia law, such as those regulating marriage, property, and inheritance, be recognized and formalized. He failed to anticipate the explosive effect of the very word "Sharia" in a public that has deep concerns about Islam in Britain.

He was condemned by all political parties and even some Muslim leaders, and the prime minister himself phoned him to request that he calm the storm. The besieged archbishop publicly apologized and explained that he was not advocating that Islamic law be granted equal status with British law.

One can no longer call Britain's 6 million Catholics embattled. Catholics have gotten one top job after another, including Chris Patton (chancellor of Oxford University), Michael Martin (earlier speaker of the House of Commons), and Mark Thompson (head of the BBC). Almost the only thing a Catholic, or even the spouse of a Catholic, cannot be by law is king or queen. Former pope Benedict feared that many of Catholics were falling away and that Britain was drifting from Christianity. He made the first papal state visit to Britain in September 2010 (his predecessor, John Paul II, had made a pastoral visit in 1982) to meet the queen and political leaders and to beatify Cardinal John Henry Newman. Some Anglicans are not pleased about the Vatican's creation of a new structure enabling traditionalist Anglicans uneasy about the ordination of women and gay priests to convert to Catholicism.

Thanks to the influx of as many as 500,000 central Europeans since the 2004 EU enlargement, about two-thirds of them Poles, many Catholic churches are experiencing a boom. One London church had fallen to 20 members when it introduced masses in Portuguese. Suddenly its attendance soared to about 1,400 each Sunday.

READ A BESTSELLER EVERY DAY

The Daily Telegraph

Wednesday, March 19, 2003

No. 45,960

'The weight of the events seems all the more awesome as the racket of the build-up dies away and the loudest noise in the desert air is the sound of birdsong'

Patrick Bishop on the Iraq border, Page 7

BRITAIN'S BEST-SELLING QUALITY DAILY

www.telegraph.co.uk

Blair: Back the war or I'll quit

Telegraph YouGov war poll

Tuesday March 18 2003

Britain's newspaper for Europe

guardian.co.uk

The Guardian EUROPE

Published in France, Germany and Spain

Diplomacy dies, now it's war

● Robin Cook quits cabinet and

● Support for attack jumps, but opposition still in the majority

● Bush throws down gauntlet to Saddam: Go into exile with your top men or face massive invasion

THE SUNDAY TIMES

MARCH 23, 2003

www.sunday-times.co.uk

■ Four US infantry scouts killed in grenade attack

■ Third wave of heavy allied bombing over Baghdad

■ Fears for ITN film crew after car ambushed

Price £1.40

Allies poised to take Basra

GULF WAR II

30 pages by award-winning correspondents on the first big conflict of the 21st century

SO WHO REALLY STARTED

The Media

Britain has nine countrywide newspapers with a circulation of over 200,000. London boasts both high-quality titles, such as the *Guardian*, the *Times*, and the *Financial Times*, as well as the more popular *Daily Mirror* and *Sun*, which launched a Sunday edition. After 168 years, the *News of the World* shut down on July 10, 2011, when evidence was discovered that it had hacked into voice-mail messages of celebrities, public figures, grieving families of dead soldiers, and a 13-year-old girl who was abducted and murdered. Two-thirds of the papers sold are conservative; in order of circulation, they are the *Sun*, *Daily Mail*, *Daily Express*, *Daily Telegraph*, *Daily Star*, and *Times*. Fewer than 10% are nonaligned: today the *Independent*, and *Financial Times*, which celebrated its 125th birthday in 2013. In 2005, the latter was judged the world's best newspaper by the Swiss-based consultant Internationale Medienhilfe. Only a fourth are left-leaning, chiefly the *Guardian* and the *Daily Mirror*.

The latter, with a circulation of about 2 million, was dealt a severe blow in 2004, when its editor was forced to resign after publishing shocking photos showing alleged British mistreatment of Iraqi prisoners that were proven to be fakes. The following year similar photos appeared in the press, which were regrettably not fakes.

Britain has among the world's most competitive and irreverent presses. However, most newspapers face financial problems, and they are losing readers to digital news. Since 1990 overall national readership has fallen by a fifth. Most troubling is that young people are not buying newspapers as their parents did and have not developed the habit of reading a daily at the breakfast table. Instead they are getting their news from TV, radio, or online.

Russian tycoons Alexander and Evgeny Lebedev acquired the *Independent*, which is the first new national paper since 1985 and which they sell for only 20 pence, a fifth the price of most quality dailies, and the *Evening Standard*, whose circulation doubled to 700,000 when it was distributed free. Evgeny is optimistic: "People are hailing the death of newspapers. But if you go into the Tube, you'll see almost everybody is reading one." The Cameron government introduced a new system of press regulation to deal with phone-hacking and bullying of celebrities and crime victims. It involves a tougher press regulator scrutinized by a committee.

Reuters, the news wire service with particularly good international coverage, is renowned for its meticulous accuracy and avoidance of editorializing. In spite of the fact that ownership of these London dailies is concentrated in a few hands, they keep a sharp eye on Downing Street, Westminster, and Whitehall. Bringing the important political news to all corners of the country, they do not stifle the lively regional press. They are also reinforced by widely read weekly news magazines, such as the *Economist* and the *Observer*.

The written media is supplemented by radio and television, which are controlled by two public bodies, the British Broadcasting Corporation (BBC), created in 1932 and whose directors are nominated by the government, and the Independent Broadcasting Authority (IBA), which permits private advertising. Both receive revenues (in the case of BBC, over £2.5 billion annually) from licenses which everyone who owns a TV must pay. Both are expected to remain politically impartial, and both vigorously resist being used by the government in power.

In 2004 the world-famous BBC (popularly dubbed "Auntie Beebs") found itself implicated in the worst crisis in its 82-year history. It had carried a story from a government weapons expert, who later committed suicide, that the Blair government had "sexed up" a dossier on weapons of mass destruction (WMD) in order to strengthen the case for war against Iraq. The government was furious. An independent judicial inquiry in 2004 issued the Hutton Report that cleared the prime minister and his aides of charges, reported without scrutiny by the BBC, that they had exaggerated or falsified intelligence reports to bolster the case for war against Iraq. It argued that the BBC had broadcast "unfounded" allegations against the prime minister and his aides and had failed to investigate its source's charges and the government's complaints properly.

BBC's two most senior officials resigned. But a majority of Britons did not believe the report's findings. Soon afterward, the government felt obligated to launch a formal inquiry into the reasons Britain's (and America's) intelligence services apparently failed in their prewar assessments of Saddam's weaponry. His government was again found innocent of wrongdoing, despite some exaggeration of the threat. Nagging questions about his use of intelligence information to justify going to war weakened Blair and cost his party some seats in the past election.

Although a 2004 poll revealed that the BBC was still trusted by three times as many Britons as was the Blair government, it has to deal with the erosion of its viewership over the years. In 2010, BBC provided only 46% of the TV viewing by skilled and professional workers aged 55 and over and only 23% of that by working- and lower-middle-class viewers between the ages of 16 and 34. It is more popular among the wealthy and elderly than it is among the poor and young. Since multi-channel TV came to Britain in 1990 and is now received by 88% of homes, BBC faces stiff competition, and a flood of American shows have appeared. However, BBC has a range of offerings, from radio to websites, and an estimated 98% of British adults use a BBC service each week, if only a few minutes of radio.

The BBC finds itself torn between its responsibility as a neutral public service news broadcaster and its desire to compete for its viewership by taking a more aggressive and controversial approach to the stories it covers. It got into trouble in 2007, when it manipulated bits of footage in its documentary *A Year with the Queen*, to make it look like she had stormed out of a photo shoot when she had not. In addition to "Crowngate," the BBC had to admit that it had faked the winners of phone-in competitions on several programs. Auntie Beebs found herself in hot water again in 2012, when it was revealed that a popular eccentric TV presenter, Jimmy Savile, had been a serial pedophile, with hundreds of victims, and that BBC might have concealed this information. The director-general of BBC resigned, and other top news officials followed him out the door. An official report pointed to a culture of deference to untouchable stars above the law and a climate of fear at the BBC that allowed predators to commit sexual assaults.

These scandals left the BBC's reputation with the public tarnished. It launched a 24-hour news service, News 24, to compete against Sky News and CNN. It continues to produce high-quality films, which Americans like to watch on public television. In 2005 BBC secured its future with another decade of generous public funding. It remains popular, even though its audience share is dropping. The BBC had to play its part in the Cameron government's austerity policy. In 2011 it faced a funding freeze, the shedding of a third of its staff, amounting to 650 jobs, and the closure of 5 of its 32 language services.

The British film industry is far too small to compete with Hollywood. But those who go to the cinema found 2007 a very good year, with the British films *The Last King of Scotland* and *The Queen* winning Oscars. In 2008 *Atonement* was nominated for best picture. *The King's Speech*, starring Colin Firth, won the Oscar for best picture in 2011. In 2012 Daniel Day-Lewis took the best actor Oscar for his portrayal of Abraham Lincoln.

Ethnic Changes in Britain

A basic change in British society is ethnic. It had for 900 years experienced almost no immigration, except from Ireland. By the second decade of the 21st century, it was in the midst of the largest immigration in British history. From 2000 to 2009, more than 5 million foreigners moved to the country for 12 months or more, and 13.2% of the labor force was foreign-born, an increase of two-thirds since 2002.

It is no longer a racially homogeneous society. As a consequence of decolonization, Asians and blacks poured into Britain from India, Pakistan, Africa, and the Caribbean. The population is 19% non-white (half of them Asians of Indian, Pakistani, and Bangladeshi descent), a percentage that is likely to grow because of the declining birth rate of white Britons. Only 45% of persons residing in London is white. In 2006 the Muslim population constituted an estimated 1.8% of the total. Of these, 45% were of Pakistani origin, 19% from India, and 13%–16% from Bangladesh. Muslims have the youngest profile of any religious group in Britain. About a third is under age 16. Their unemployment rate is triple the national average.

Britain is faced with the difficult problem of integrating large groups of non-white minorities, who tend to be concentrated in the decaying inner cities (half are in London), even though there is less residential segregation by race in Britain than in the US. Such concentration gives the impression that the minority presence in the UK is far greater than it actually is. A fifth to a third of London's population belongs to an ethnic minority. They often speak little or no English; 22% of Londoners and 42% of children in London do not speak English as their first language. More than a third of Londoners were born abroad (up from 18% in 1987). They worship religions that are quite unfamiliar to most British and groom themselves or dress in very different fashion from the rest of the population. Critics disparage the city as "Londonistan."

Foreigners continue to pour into London at a faster rate than at any time in its history, while Britons are moving out. Other cities' populations are declining. For example, Manchester's population shrank by 10%; Liverpool's, by 8%; Newcastle's, by 6%; and Birmingham's, by 3% in the 1990s, while London's grew by 4.8% over that period. The mix has also changed: In the 1970s newcomers came mostly from India, Pakistan, and Bangladesh.

Today two-thirds of new immigrants come from high-income countries. Among the wealthiest are Russians, whose numbers in London are over 200,000 and climbing. Faced with the prospect of a flood of immigrants from the eight former communist countries (as many as 600,000 came) that entered the EU in May 2004, Britain declared that they would be permitted to seek work in Britain, but those without jobs are not permitted to claim most welfare benefits for two years after arrival. An estimated half-million persons live illegally in Britain.

This central European influx has been good for the economy, and they pay more in taxes than they take out in benefits. Arrivals are now at the top and the bottom of the economic ladder. The foreign-born are more likely to have a university education than the native population (61% to 30%). More of their kids are less likely to drop out of school and more likely to finish university degrees. They are less likely to claim welfare benefits. Nevertheless, some Britons feel overwhelmed. Many feel that they push up house prices, pour into schools without knowing English, and hold down wages. But thanks to immigration, the UK is one of the few developed countries that have a growing population. Foreign-born women are helping to stabilize the birth rate at 1.84 children. Polish women bear more children in Britain than those from any other foreign country. If this continues, Britain's population would rise to roughly 71 million by 2032 and 77 million by 2050.

Ethnic minorities suffer the most from any economic downturn, especially unemployment. British blacks have not penetrated the top levels of business, the professions, the judiciary, or the cabinet as the American black elite has. Only 1% of soldiers are minorities (compared with 27% black in the US), 2% of the police (3.3% in London), and 5% of civil servants. This may change as a result of an increase in nonwhite enrollment at British universities; 12% of students are from ethnic minorities, double their representation in the overall population. In London 29% of nurses, 31% of doctors, and more than 20% of civil servants are already from ethnic minorities.

In an effort to improve their public image, the London Metropolitan Police and other police forces in the country have recruited more black policemen. This is the kind of policy enacted to prevent black-white racial conflict that has proved successful. Ethnic minorities no longer have to deal with the earlier combined hostility of the police, the local government, and public opinion. Only seldom are there clashes with whites or the police; more common today are clashes between ethnic minorities themselves.

In some ways Britain is a more integrated society than is the US, at least if one observes only the Afro-Caribbean population. There is more dating and intermarriage between white and black men and women. According to a 2014 survey, almost half of Afro-Caribbean men have a white partner; the figure for women was about a third. This is lower among British-born Indians, but the figures still show change: 20% for men and 10% for women. Pakistanis and Bangladeshis mix more slowly: About 8% of men and fewer women are in mixed marriages. In the US only 4% of black men and 2% of black women have a white spouse.

Since 1999, more immigrants are coming from outside the Commonwealth and the EU than both of those sources combined. This means that there are more black Africans with large families. They intermarry far less. Tolerance for interracial marriage is strong: 74% of respondents said in a 1997 poll that they would not object to one of their close relatives marrying a black percent, and 70% said the same about Asians.

A glowing example of integration is Trinidad-born V. S. Naipaul, who won the 2001 Nobel Prize for literature. He graduated from University College at Oxford in 1953 and remained in England. An eternal outsider, he is a prickly critic of religious extremism. The panel praised him for transforming "rage into precision" in such books as *Among the Believers*. Another foreign-born British novelist, 88-year-old Doris Lessing, won the Nobel Prize for literature in 2007. Born in Iran, she moved with her parents at age six to southern Rhodesia (now Zimbabwe), where she grew up. Her writing draws heavily from her experiences in Africa. A school dropout at age 14, she moved to Britain in 1949, where she joined the Communist Party and became a fierce critic of the South African regime. She explored the divide between whites and blacks in her autobiographical *The Grass Is Singing* and in her series of novels entitled *Children of Violence*. She died in 2013 at age 94.

A combination of tough anti-immigration policies, unusually detailed laws against racial discrimination, and the fact that legal immigrants have always been treated not as migrant workers but as permanent settlers with automatic rights to vote, to run for office, and to claim social security benefits had prevented the spread of the kind of anti-immigrant sentiment and support for racist parties seen on the Continent. But this has changed, as more than a half-million immigrants pour into the country each year. There are fewer asylum seekers than before; most are workers and people entering as spouses or relatives of Britons. The government unveiled plans in 2005 to apply an Australian-style point system, ranking applicant workers according to their skills and occupations. Those with little or nothing to contribute to the British economy or who risk becoming a burden to the welfare system would be weeded out.

Anti-immigrant feelings are rising: 64% of respondents indicated in a 2010 poll that the current level of immigration is making their country "a worse place to live"; 63% thought it made the National Health System worse, and 66% said it degraded the state education system. Polls in 2007 showed that race and immigration have become main concern in the UK. In a 2005 poll, 54% had agreed that "parts of the country don't feel like Britain anymore because of immigration." At the same time, 62% of the general public (and 87% of Muslims) had favorable views of multiculturalism, and 48% believed that "immigration is generally good for Britain." Only a quarter of Britons worry about racial balance in their country. They tend to regard ethnic minorities and immigrants as one and the same, whereas in America they have always been viewed as two different things. The fact that immigration has less to do with race in Britain makes it easier to criticize immigrants.

That gave hope to those whites who want to exploit the rising tensions at election time, such as the neo-Nazi British National Party (BNP), which favors repatriation of nonwhites, and the anti-EU UK Independence Party (UKIP), which promises "freedom from overcrowding" and an end to economic migration. As usual, these parties fell flat on their faces in the 2005 and 2010 parliamentary elections and failed to win a single seat.

Labour, which has always presented itself as the party of the underdog, receives the overwhelming majority of nonwhite votes. In the 1987 election, 27 nonwhites ran for office, and for the first time since 1922, nonwhites took seats in the House of Commons. In 2007, there were 15 members of Parliament from ethnic minorities, and there were even more in the House of Lords. The first Muslim women entered the House of Commons in 2010. Most black people in the UK are either British citizens or Commonwealth citizens who can vote in Britain. That is changing, though, as black Africans arrive in greater numbers.

It has been difficult to integrate black people and Asians into the political process, except in direct defense of their own interests. But there has been progress. Nonwhites in the UK have visible positive role models in sports, the arts, business- and the professions. There are grounds for optimism that the lauded English

The United Kingdom

Statue of Martin Luther King

tolerance and gradualism will lead more British to accept the immigrants and their children as nonwhite Britons. It is symbolic that in 1998 a statue of Martin Luther King was placed in the last remaining niche above the Great West Door of Westminster Abbey. In 2007 a nine-foot bronze statue of Nelson Mandela was unveiled outside Parliament to honor his campaign to end apartheid in South Africa. It joins statues of Abraham Lincoln and Winston Churchill in Parliament Square.

British Muslims and Terrorism

Just as the celebrations over winning the 2012 Olympic Games were dying down, during the morning rush hour of July 7, 2005, death struck 52 commuters in the heart of London. Four young British Muslims, three of Pakistani origin and one convert from Jamaica, killed themselves and as many as they could take with them in three Tube (subway) stations and one double-decker bus in al-Qaeda-linked attacks. Not surprisingly for a multicultural city like London, half the victims were foreign-born, and one was an American. They included victims from all major religions. Two weeks later similar attacks were botched without fatalities.

The bloody attacks on July 7 seemed to have been planned to coincide with the G8 summit meeting in Scotland, hosted by Tony Blair. He rushed back to London, vowing that "our determination to defend our values and our way of life is greater than their determination to cause death and destruction to innocent people in a desire to impose extremism on the world." In their usual way, British citizens and parties rallied around their leader in such a time of crisis and sorrow to show that they will not be intimidated. Then–opposition leader Michael Howard extolled "the calm resolute and statesmanlike way in which the government has responded." Former London mayor Ken Livingstone assured the terrorists, "Even after your cowardly attacks, you will see people from around the world coming to London to achieve their dreams." He continued to go to work every day by subway.

Such attacks had been long feared and expected. London's antiterrorism precautions are among the most elaborate and well practiced in the world. Intelligence services in London said that many such attacks had been thwarted in recent years. After much experience with aerial and terrorist bombing, Londoners are very resilient people. The very next day, they returned to their daily routines.

But life was not the same for Britain's 1.8 million Muslims, more than a million of whom are of Pakistani ancestry. A generously defined tradition of free speech had allowed extreme clerics to preach hatred and violence, to the frustration of the majority Muslim moderates. It is not clear what motivates homegrown terrorists. Most are not poor, and they are no more likely to live in heavily Muslim neighborhoods than in mixed or white ones. Three of the bombers had been born and raised in Britain; all four were British citizens. However, a 2006 Pew Global Attitudes poll of Muslims found that 81% of British Muslims considered themselves Muslims first and Britons second. That is stunningly high when compared to France, where only 42% considered themselves Muslim before French.

Britons are looking for answers to the question of why young men who had grown up in Britain and seemed to be at least partly assimilated could become so alienated that they would commit such treacherous acts against ordinary citizens in their adopted country. Three had spent some time in Pakistan, receiving some schooling and training. Al-Qaeda's leadership, based in Pakistan, has easy access to thousands of Britons of Pakistani origin who visit their ancestral country easily and frequently.

But it is a disturbing thought that Britain now has homegrown suicide bombers who are difficult to catch. Police and intelligence agencies must contend with diffuse and overlapping jihadi groups, who are willing to die in an effort to kill as many people as possible. A *Times* poll showed that 86% of British respondents supported giving the police new powers to arrest people suspected of planning terrorist attacks. Yet the surge in recruits and supporters of radical Islamic networks continues.

The UK is faced with the task of persuading moderate, law-abiding Muslims, who constitute the large majority, to rally around the Muslim Council of Britain (MCB) to try to root out extremism on the fringes of mosque life. The government would like to draw Muslims into the policing of their own communities. The Sunni Council in the Birmingham area responded by issuing an edict condemning "all forms of terrorism, be it state terrorism or otherwise." A 2005 poll indicated that 86% of British Muslims believed the use of violence for political ends is unacceptable, even though four out of five considered the "war on terrorism" to be a war against Islam. In 2007, 79% answered that suicide bombings are rarely or never justified, while 15% thought they were often or sometimes justified.

Polls a couple of weeks after the 2005 bombings indicated that two-thirds of Britons believed their country's involvement in the Iraq War had something to do with their being targeted. Britain's prominence as America's ally in both Iraq and Afghanistan no doubt feeds some persons' rage. In February 2008 a Muslim man in Birmingham was sentenced to life in prison for plotting to kidnap and behead a British Muslim soldier and to record it all on video "to cause panic and fear within the British armed forces and wider public." In secret recordings played in court, the man was heard instructing his five-year-old son on how to behead a person.

Blair took another position, arguing that such people as the bombers can always find an excuse to persuade themselves to take other people's blood. But one thing is incontrovertible, he said: Nothing justifies such slaughter of innocent people. The attacks reinforced his case for achieving the long-term task: help establish stable democracy in Iraq, promote peace between Israel and Palestine, and support democratic reform elsewhere in the Middle East.

On August 10, 2006, police thwarted a huge terrorist plot to blow up in midair 10 American planes departing from Heathrow Airport, causing what was described as "mass murder on an unimaginable scale." Authorities arrested two dozen young Muslims, most of them British citizens of Pakistani origin; accomplices were also detained in Pakistan. In three trials from 2008 to 2010, the final one the longest and costliest terrorism trial in British history, 10 men were charged, and all but 2 were convicted of plotting to commit murder. Three were given life sentences with no possibility of bail for 20 years.

Fueled by disenchantment at home, poor educational achievement, high unemployment, discrimination, and rage about fighting in Iraq, Afghanistan, and Lebanon that they see as part of a western "war against Islam," the ranks of violent Islamic extremists are growing in Britain. Many Britons are wondering whether their country has struck the right balance between encouraging cultural diversity and insisting on a shared national identity.

Immigration was an important campaign issue for all major parties, and it was a divisive issue in the Cameron-Clegg coalition government. Clegg and his LDP defend multiculturalism. But in a speech in Munich in February 2011, the prime minister said that, while Britain had benefited "immeasurably" from immigration, "state multiculturalism" had failed and had led many Britons to live segregated lives, without the desire to integrate. He said that somehow Britain must foster a stronger sense of national identity. The country's challenge is how such an open and liberal society that embraces diversity of all kinds can also create a sense of solidarity and belonging.

FUTURE

The Conservative government does not challenge the conventional wisdom of the foreign policy establishment that the alliance with the US is the UK's pivotal security relationship, despite the massive unpopularity of President Donald Trump. The UK does not so much as hint that Europe might be an alternative pillar of Britain's security. There is less talk about a "special relationship," now rechristened by both countries' leaders as an "essential relationship."

Prime Minister Cameron held a referendum on membership on June 23, 2016. The results stunned the world: 52% voted to leave the EU. Only Scotland (which threatened to leave the UK if this happened), Northern Ireland, Wales, and London voted to remain. The issues of immigration and "taking back control of the country" swung the vote to leave. Cameron was replaced by Home Secretary Teresa May. As a woman politician, she had much female company: One-third of MPs and three of the four leaders who run the countries that make up the UK are women.

Britain's two prime ministers

The first steps of separation required two years of difficult negotiations with Brussels and the 27 other EU member states until March 29, 2019. Not since World War II has Britain's future been so uncertain.

No one knows how this referendum result will affect Britain's and the EU's future. Only one out of four Tory members supported continued membership in the EU's single market, whereas 87% of Labour members did.

On January 15, 2019, May submitted her plan for separation to a divided Parliament; it was rejected by a vote of 432 to 202, the worst defeat in modern times. She barely survived a vote of no confidence the next day, but there is no consensus. Brexit has rewritten the rules of British politics.

Hoping to strengthen her hand in the negotiations with the EU, Prime Minister May called an early snap election for June 8, 2017. The results were a disaster for her Conservative government. It lost 13 seats and its parliamentary majority despite capturing 42.4% of the votes, an increase of 5.5% over 2015. Labour won 40%, an improvement of 9.5% over 2015, but it was still 64 seats short of a majority. This was Labour's third general election loss in a row. To scrape together a feeble majority, the Tories turned to the small hard-right Democratic Unionist Party in Northern Ireland, led by Arlene Foster.

Queen Elizabeth II, who turned 90 in April 2016, celebrated a rare event in June 2012: a Diamond Jubilee marking her 60th year as monarch. Not since 1897 had such a celebration taken place. In September 2015 Elizabeth surpassed Queen Victoria's length of reign. Her 95-year-old husband, Prince Philip, announced his retirement from public events in 2017.

The monarchy is still basking in the glow of a perfect wedding between William and Catherine, now the Duke and Duchess of Cambridge. Their first son, George Alexander Louis, was born July 22, 2013. Known as Prince George of Cambridge, he is third in the line of succession and will one day become King George VII. His little sister, born in May 2015, moved into fourth place in the line of succession. The "event of the year 2018" was the marriage of Prince Harry to American actress Meghan Markle in May. A biracial divorcée, her entry into the royal family reveals how much British society and the monarchy have changed. Since July 2019 Britain faces the future with a new prime minister: Brexit hardliner Boris Johnson.

The Republic of Ireland

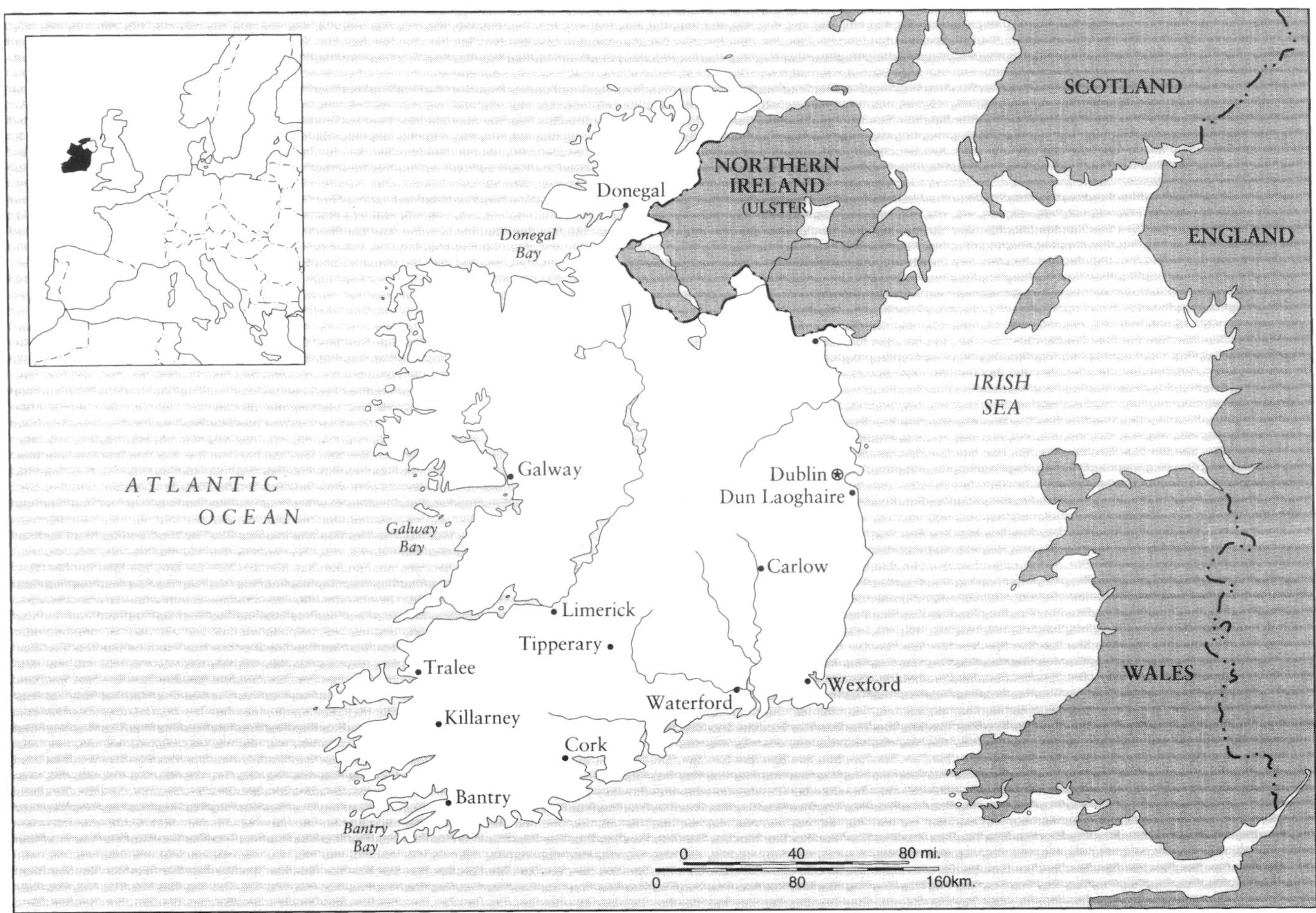

Area: 27,136 sq. mi. (70,262 sq. km, slightly larger than West Virginia).

Population: 4.7 million.

Capital City: Dublin (pop. 1 million, est.); a third live in or around Dublin.

Climate: Cool and damp (rarely above 65° or below 40° Fahrenheit).

Neighboring Countries: Great Britain lies a short distance eastward across the Irish Sea.

Official Languages: English, which is the first language of 98% of the population. Irish (Gaelic) is spoken as a native language by only 2% (ca. 70,000).

Ethnic Background: Celtic (some Norman and Norsemen).

Principal Religions: Roman Catholic 88.4%, Church of Ireland (Protestant) 5%, Presbyterian .4%, Muslims 19,000 and growing.

Main Exports and Imports: Machinery and transport equipment, chemicals, foodstuffs and tobacco, high-tech equipment, petroleum and other fuels.

Major Trading Partners: EU (57.7% of exports and 69.5% of imports), UK (15.6% of exports and 39.2% of imports), US (21.5% of exports and 12.8% of imports), Belgium (14.8% of exports), Germany (6.8% of exports and 7.7% of imports), France (5.5% of exports and 3.8% of imports), Netherlands (5.7% of imports), Switzerland (4% of exports), China (3.7% of imports).

Currency: Euro.

Former Colonial Status: "Given" to England in 1155 by the pope; turbulent English control until 1922; its own parliament, diminishing control until independence.

Dates of Independence: December 6, 1921 (dominion status); April 18, 1949 (independent republic).

Chief of State: Michael Higgins, President (since November 2011).

Head of Government: Leo Varadkar, Taoiseach (pronounced Tea-such), or Prime Minister (since June 2017).

National Flag: Three vertical stripes of green, white, and orange.

Green fields, white-washed thatched cottages, leprechauns, and men sitting in front of a peat fire spinning tales that are part fact and part fiction are images of Ireland that the first-time tourist seeks. This scene is also found on St. Patrick's Day cards, framed in green. While the tourist may miss much of what is new in Ireland, both the green fields and the confusion of fact and fantasy are still there for him to find. And both are largely the result of Ireland's location—it lies at the spot where the warm air and water of the Gulf Stream confront their cold rivals of the northern latitudes. This produces a climate in which temperature variations are rare; it is an unusual day when the temperature is more than slightly warm or cold.

The confrontation of warm and cold produces air that is frequently moist—thus the lushness of the green, and skies that are always changing—gray and sad one minute, brilliant and joyful the next. If the sky is not constant, why should reality be constant? And, perhaps it is the soft, moist air that blurs fact and fantasy. George Bernard Shaw wrote of Ireland to an English friend, "You've no such colors in the sky, no such lines in the distance, no such sadness in the evenings. Oh the dreaming! The dreaming!"

If one may generalize about the people of a nation, the Irish people reflect their climate. There is a gentleness about the Irish, an essential sadness punctuated by flashes of sparkling wit. And there is a willingness to let the line between reality and dream be as indistinct as that between the distant mountains and the evening sky.

Ireland

If its location has shaped the green beauty of Ireland and the character of its people, its location has been more responsible for shaping its history. Ireland is not merely an island; it is an island off the coast of another island. While its contact with the Continent has usually been indirect, its subjugation to England has been of paramount influence. Being one step removed from the mainland has kept continental armies and the cultural influences that they brought out of Ireland. Roman legions never tramped across its fields. Although Norsemen settled on the east coast and raided many other areas, Irish culture achieved a flowering of learning and artistic brilliance while the rest of Europe slipped into the Dark Ages.

As nation-states developed on the Continent, Ireland was involved in European dynastic wars only when England had a stake in the contest. The last continental troops to be in Ireland made an unsuccessful attempt to export the French Revolution. Ireland even managed to be one of the few European countries to be neutral during World War II. As the English, century after century, negotiated and fought rivals on the continent, they did not want to have to worry about the island on their other side. The English always felt a domination of Ireland was essential to their security. The Irish Sea, after all, varies in width from 120 miles to only 11 miles, thus the fates of England and Ireland have been intertwined for the past 800 years.

Ireland is like a small bowl floating in the Atlantic. Its mountains ring the coastal region; they seldom reach more than 3,000 feet (914 km) into the sky. But the steepness with which they meet the sea gives them the appearance of considerable height. The center of the island is relatively flat, with the Shannon River flowing from north to south like a fine crack in the bottom of the bowl. West of the Shannon, peat bogs provide much of Ireland's fuel. East of the Shannon, the plains are rich grasslands, superb for cattle or horses. In fact, the Curragh, the finest stable and racetrack in the land, has 5,000 acres of grass uninterrupted by either a tree or a fence. But even in the center of Ireland, one is never far removed from the sea, for the whole island is only 150 miles wide and 275 miles long.

Ireland is a beautiful and gentle land. Tragically, its history has not always been so.

HISTORY

The Early Period

The earliest remains of humans in Ireland date from about 7000 BC. These hunters and food gatherers lived along the coasts and near the rivers. By 3000 BC Neolithic settlers had introduced agriculture and pottery. Their most spectacular accomplishments, elaborate Megalithic burial chambers, can still be seen today. At Newgrange one may enter the massive chamber by crawling through a tunnel 62 feet long. It is so constructed that only at the summer solstice does sunlight come down the tunnel and illuminate the interior chamber.

About 300 BC the Gaelic Celts used their knowledge of iron weapons to gain control of the island. Celtic Ireland was divided into some 150 local kingdoms under the loose control of the kings of the five provinces. Meath later became part of Leinster, but the four provinces of Ulster in the north, Leinster in the southeast, Munster in the southwest, and Connacht in the west have retained fairly similar boundaries to this day.

Saint Patrick

One of the high kings who ruled at the Hill of Tara from 380 to 405 AD was Niall, an ancestor of the O'Neills, an important family in Ulster until the 17th century. Niall's troops attacked both Britain and Normandy. On one raid, a young Briton named Patrick was brought back as a slave. After several years in Ireland, Patrick escaped to the Continent, where he entered a monastery. In 432, after being consecrated as a bishop, Patrick returned to Ireland. He spent Lent in prayer at the top of Croagh Patrick, a mountain overlooking the Atlantic in County Mayo. Bound by age-long tradition, even now, more than 50,000 people a year make the strenuous 2,700-foot climb to the top. And it is typical that some do it as an adventurous outing and some do it as a religious penance. In fact, thousands climb over the rough stones with bare, and therefore bleeding, feet. The story is told that two young men were climbing and one of them saw some attractive girls up ahead. He said, "Let's hurry and catch up with those girls." The other one replied, "Oh, I wouldn't dare. It's for too much foolin' with the girls that I'm havin' to make the climb."

Certainly Patrick was one of the most successful missionaries of all time. Within a few years after his death, the whole island was Christian. Celtic Christianity developed in unusual patterns. Instead of the bishop and his diocese being the chief authority, the abbot and the monastery were the center of ecclesiastical life. The emphasis on monastic life had three major effects on cultural developments.

First, monks often practiced extremes of asceticism. To this day, Irish Christianity has maintained an emphasis on self-denial and penance that affects the Irish

The ruins of Rocktown Castle, County Limerick

character. Second, while the rest of Europe descended into darkness, Irish monasteries kept the light of western culture burning. Piety, painting, and learning were combined into one art form: the illuminated manuscript of the scriptures. Flights of imagination turned the letters of holy books into fantastic geometric shapes and celestial beings. The most famous illuminated manuscript, the Book of Kells, may be seen today in the library of Trinity College, Dublin.

Third, because monastic orders thought beyond the geographic boundaries of the diocese, Irish missionaries carried Celtic Christianity to Britain and the Continent. The Irish St. Colombo established a famous monastery at Iona off the coast of Scotland. But perhaps the most interesting missionary was St. Brendan—medieval manuscripts describe how he and a group of monks sailed in a leather boat from the coast of Kerry. They visited a land of sheep, then an island occupied by giant blacksmiths working at their forges, and later an area of great fog. Finally, they reached a new land of beauty and richness that was divided by a large river. Brendan returned to Ireland just before he died. The story has usually been dismissed as a fanciful legend. In 1977, however, a group of men built a leather boat and sailed from Brendan's creek in Kerry. They were blown to the outer Hebrides (where there are many sheep); wintered in Iceland (where volcanoes might be confused with giants' forges); were becalmed in the fog off the Grand Banks; and finally, in 1978, washed ashore in Canada. Perhaps Brendan, not Leif Ericson nor Christopher Columbus, was the first European to reach the New World.

Viking Raids and Norse Settlements

Unfortunately, the very success and more particularly the wealth of the monasteries brought trouble. Beginning in the 9th century, Viking raiders began to attack monastic and other settlements, plundering them for gold and valuables. Inevitably, the monks sought refuge in remote places.

The most spectacular of these is Skellig Michael, a tiny island off the coast of Kerry. Today, those who brave the four miles of rough seas in an open boat can climb the more than 600 steps cut into the stone face by monks over 1,000 years ago and visit the remains of the beehive huts perched 550 feet above the water. Tens of thousands of visitors come every year. But it remains shrouded in mystery. Its age is unknown, there are few references to it in written sources from the 8th century, and few artifacts have been found. UNESCO proclaimed it a World Heritage Site in 1996, and archaeologists are debating how best to preserve and study it.

Skellig Michael

By the 10th century, the Norsemen began to plan settlements. The Vikings established the first cities in Ireland near the mouth of important rivers. Dublin, Waterford, Cork, and Limerick all began that way.

At times the Celtic Irishmen intermarried with the Norse, and at times they tried to drive them into the sea. Brian Baru, after defeating the Norsemen in Munster, established himself as high king of all Ireland in 1002. Brian married the beautiful Gormflath, whose six feet of height was crowned with flaming red hair. Unfortunately, as so often happened in Irish history, treason destroyed a chance for national unity. Gormflath's half-Danish son by an earlier marriage plotted with his mother, his uncle, and other Danish chieftains to attack Brian. At the Battle of Clontarf in 1014, in which 20,000 men took part, Brian's forces were victorious and broke the Viking domination of Ireland. Tragically, at the end of the battle, a Danish soldier broke free and killed Brian in his own tent. It is even more tragic that neither Brian's brief unification of Ireland nor his freeing it of foreign domination proved lasting. No clear successor to him was able to establish control, and strife between local warlords continued as an Irish tradition. Because of these rivalries, new invaders arrived within 150 years.

The name Dermot MacMurrough has been a black one in Irish history for 800 years. It was he who invited British troops into Ireland. But it is easier to see the tragic consequences of his act in retrospect than it would have been in the 12th century. In fact, it was Adrian IV, the only Englishman ever to be pope, who set the stage. Wishing to bring the practices of Celtic Christianity into conformity with the rest of Roman Christianity, Adrian issued the papal bull *Laudabilitier* in 1155 that granted Henry II of England permission to control Ireland. For 20 years, Henry did not make a move across the Irish Sea. However, when Dermot MacMurrough lost control of the kingdom of Leinster, he asked for help from the Normans, who had then been ruling England and Wales for 100 years.

Norman-Anglo-Saxon Invasion and Control

Strongbow, Earl of Pembroke, led a group of Normans into Ireland in 1170. He married MacMurrough's daughter, and for a while it appeared that an independent Norman kingdom might be established. A year later, however, Henry II himself brought a large force of British Normans into Ireland. With the murder of Thomas Becket less than 12 months behind him (see the United Kingdom chapter), Henry may have thought it was a good time for some foreign travel. He not only established Normans loyal to himself as local rulers, but he also did away with the Celtic form of worship and brought Irish Christianity under the control of the Roman Catholic Church.

Two legacies of the Normans are still plentifully evident in Ireland. Many of the great names of Ireland came with the Normans: Joyce, Fitzgerald, Barry, and Burke. These names can still be seen on many store and pub fronts. A person driving through Ireland also still sees the remains of castles, the prototypes of which were built by the Normans. These are usually rectangular stone towers three or four stories high. Most are in ruins, but a few, such as Bunratty, Blarney, Dungory, Ca-hair, and Knappogue, have been restored and are open for visitors or popular medieval banquets. Over 300 castles still stand in Ireland.

As the Anglo-Normans became settled in Ireland, they adopted more and more of the Irish ways. The old saying is that "They became more Irish than the Irish themselves." Eventually, of course, such assimilation began to threaten the rule of the British Crown. The attitude of the English was shown in the statutes of Kilkenny in 1366. These provided a punishment of the loss of lands for any Englishman who spoke Irish, married Irish people, or adopted Irish customs.

English authority was strongest in the area around Dublin, known as "the Pale." Outside this region, local rulers paid only nominal homage to the British Crown and British ways. Thus the expression "beyond the Pale" as a term of derision expresses things from the English point of view. While they had only small loyalty to Britain, the Irish rulers could hardly be described as ardent nationalists. Ireland was so fragmented politically that the idea of allegiance to Ireland itself was not an effective alternative. Rather, each local lord simply looked after his own interests.

Religious Intolerance after the Reformation

It is interesting but futile to speculate what would have happened to relationships between Britain and Ireland if the Reformation had not come to England. Perhaps Ireland would have gone the way of Scotland and Wales and become part of the United Kingdom. But the Reformation drove an irreconcilable wedge of hatred and mistrust between the English and the Irish.

England vacillated between Roman Catholicism and Protestantism through several monarchs, but with the crowning of Elizabeth I, the English were ready to try to export the Reformation. For the next 400 years, religion and nationalism would be intertwined in Ireland. In 1579, armed rebellion arose in the southwest of the island. As a reprisal against the rebels and as a reward to her soldiers, Elizabeth confiscated vast areas of land from the Irish, and gave it to Englishmen. On one such parcel of land, Walter Raleigh planted the first Irish potato. It was a crop well suited for growing by the Irish and they soon became dependent on it, much to their regret during the potato famine 275 years later, one of the greatest tragedies in Irish history.

By 1588 Elizabeth's rule was strong enough that, as the ships of the Spanish Armada wrecked against the rocky shores of Ireland, the Irish obeyed her orders and slaughtered the would-be invaders. Only in Ulster in the north were the Spaniards spared. This was ironic; because Ulster held out against English rule, a sequence of events began that led in the 20th century to the north being the one area of Ireland loyal to the British Crown.

At the end of the 16th century, Hugh O'Neill led a rebellion in Ulster. He embarrassed Elizabeth's current favorite Essex but finally in 1601 was defeated at Kinsale by Mountjoy. In 1607 he and other Ulster chiefs fled to the Continent in "the flight of the earls." James I filled the vacuum by sending Scots Presbyterians to settle in Northern Ireland. These are the antecedents of today's Protestants in Northern Ireland loyal to the British. It is significant that the only Protestants in Ireland were imported.

Upheavals in the British monarchy brought violence to Ireland in the 17th century. Oliver Cromwell beheaded Charles I and in 1649 landed in Ireland. His purpose was to establish his brand of Puritanism in Ireland and end the possibility of rebellion. Tens of thousands of Irish were killed or driven into exile. Irish landlords in the fertile east were given the choice of death or migration to the rocky areas of the west. "Hell or Connacht" are still remembered as the only options open to them. By 1660, only one-quarter of the country was owned by Irish Catholics.

When James II, a Catholic, came to the throne of England, there was a chance of reconciliation. But there was an immediate rebellion of Protestants against James, who chose William of Orange, a Netherlands Protestant, as king of England; the decisive battle was fought in Ireland in 1690. Protestants in Ulster still celebrate the anniversary of the Battle of Boyne, fought on Irish territory, where William defeated the forces of James. This greatly irritates their Catholic neighbors.

As retribution for support of James, the English confiscated more areas of Irish land and imposed the Penal Laws. These forbade Catholics to vote, to hold office, to send their children to anything but a Protestant school, or to have wealth above a set limit.

The Georgian Era

Much of Dublin and many beautiful country homes were built by the Protestant aristocracy during the Georgian era of the 18th century. The vast majority of the population, Catholic peasants, subsisted on potatoes grown on tiny plots of land. The success of the American and French Revolutions inspired hope among the downtrodden people. The ideals of equality and fraternity were imported from the Continent. Theobald Wolfe Tone founded the United Irishmen, a group that sought to include those of different religions in the establishing of a republic. In 1798 a French force, with Tone in attendance-landed in Mayo on the west coast. The British commander Cornwallis was more successful than he had been at Yorktown, and the French Irish forces were soon defeated.

The English now tried to have Ireland conform to the pattern that Scotland and Wales had followed years earlier. The Act

The ancient mansion of Sir Walter Raleigh, Youghal

of Union, passed in 1800, abolished the Irish parliament and gave the Irish representation in the British Parliament at Westminster. Robert Emmet tried an unsuccessful revolution in 1803; his statue stands today in Washington, DC, but his words were engraved on the heart of every Irish revolutionary who came after him: "When my country takes her place among the nations of the earth, then and not till then let my epitaph be written."

Further Attempts at Freedom and the Potato Famine

Two names dominate Irish attempts for freedom in the 19th century: Daniel O'Connell and Charles Stewart Parnell. But their periods of influence were separated by the most terrible tragedy Ireland ever knew. In the first half of the century, Daniel O'Connell worked to improve the position of Catholics. He won election to the House of Commons in 1828 even though, as a Catholic, he could no,t take his seat. A year later, the Penal Laws that accomplished this were replaced. In the 1840s O'Connell developed a large following that demanded the repeal of the Act of Union. However, when he obeyed an order by the British government to cancel a mass meeting in Clontarf, his political support soon failed.

By the 1840s more than half the people of Ireland were dependent on potatoes as their principal source of food. In the wet summer of 1845, blight attacked the crop, and it appeared again in 1846 and 1847. Famine and death spread across the stricken land. The relief efforts of the British government were too little and too late. In a population of 8.5 million, 1 million starved and another 1 million fled their country. English-speaking countries around the world, particularly the United States, received a transfusion of Celtic, Catholic blood that would, in turn, help shape their destinies. Even as the famine subsided, immigration continued, and for the next 40 years, 1% of the population left each year. Many found their way to America, where in the 2000 census, 10.8% identified themselves as of Irish descent, more than five times as many as inhabit the whole island of Ireland. One hundred years after the great famine, the population was only one-half what it had been before the blight struck.

As Irish immigrants prospered abroad, many did not forget the cause of Irish independence. Money and occasionally arms or leaders flowed back into Ireland and supported various movements. The Fenians, a secret society favoring armed revolution and also known as the Irish Republican Brotherhood, was founded in 1856 in Ireland and the United States. In 1879, the Land League was founded by Michael Davitt and was supported by American money. It worked through parliament to achieve land reform. Charles Stewart Parnell became the leader of the Irish Parliamentary Party. He controlled enough seats in the British Parliament to tip the balance of power at various times. His Home Rule Bill passed the House of Commons but was defeated in the House of Lords. His next try for home rule might have been successful, but in 1890 a scandal broke when Parnell was the cause of a divorce between Kitty O'Shea and her husband. Although Parnell married Kitty, neither Victorian England nor Catholic Ireland would forgive him. How ironic it was that one man's illicit love of a woman delayed the possibility of home rule until it was too late to be effective.

In 1912, after severely limiting the power of the House of Lords, the House of Commons finally passed a Home Rule

The potato famine struck a severe blow to Ireland.

Bill, but by that time the Protestants in Ulster were afraid of being controlled by a Catholic majority. Sir Edward Casson organized the Ulster Volunteers, a military group armed with German guns, to oppose the move. The next year the Irish Republican Brotherhood and the Sinn Fein (pronounced "Shin Fane," meaning "Ourselves Alone") formed the Irish Volunteers to oppose the Ulster Volunteers.

But the outbreak of World War I caused Britain to postpone home rule for the duration of the war. With British attention focused on the Continent, the Irish Volunteers and the Irish Citizens Army staged an armed rebellion. On Easter Monday, 1916, rebels captured the center of Dublin. At the General Post Office, they proclaimed, "We declare the right of the people of Ireland to the ownership of Ireland and to the unfettered control of Irish destinies, to be sovereign and indefeasible. The long usurpation of that right by a foreign people and government has not extinguished the right, nor can it ever be extinguished except by the destruction of the Irish people. In every generation for centuries the Irish people had and have asserted their right to national freedom and sovereignty. Six times in the past 300 years they have asserted it in arms. Standing on that fundamental right and again asserting it in arms in the face of the world, we hereby proclaim the Irish Republic as a sovereign, independent state, and we pledge our lives and the lives of our comrades in arms to the cause of its freedom, of its welfare, and of its exultation among the nations."

Within a week the rebellion was crushed; because the British were at war, they reacted to the rebellion as treason and with great severity, executing most of the leaders. Eamon de Valera was spared because he had been born in the United States. Those executed instantly became heroes and martyrs to the Irish people, and hatred toward England became even deeper.

When World War I ended, the Sinn Fein again proclaimed an Irish Republic. De Valera was president, and Michael Collins led frequent terrorist raids on British installations. The British fought back with the Auxiliary Cadets (former officers) and the Black and Tans (former enlisted men). Both sides practiced atrocities, murders, burnings, and lootings. The Irish desire for freedom received worldwide publicity when Terrence McSwiney died in a British prison after a 74-day hunger strike. This strategy would later be used in the fight by India for its freedom from Britain and again in Ulster in the 1980s and 1990s.

Strife and Freedom

The three years of fighting are still known by the Irish as "the Troubles," though many years in Irish history could qualify for that title. Parliament passed the Government of Ireland Act in 1920 that allowed for two types of home rule, one for the six counties in the north and another for the rest of Ireland. In early 1922 the republican government led by Arthur Griffith and Michael Collins accepted a treaty that made 26 counties a free state within the British Commonwealth and left the 6 northern counties a province of the United Kingdom. De Valera refused to accept the treaty and for a year and a half led a civil war against his former friends. Collins was killed in a battle, and Griffith died, but de Valera was forced to give up his fight. William Cosgrave became head of the Irish free state; the boundary between the Free State and Northern Ireland was accepted in 1925.

Eamon de Valera returned to power in 1932 as head of the Fianna Fail ("Warriors of Destiny") Party that held a majority for 16 years. In 1937 a new constitution declared Ireland to be "a sovereign, independent, democratic state." Only formal ties with Britain remained.

Ireland was an important refueling stop for transatlantic military aircraft during World War II. It was officially neutral during the conflict, but tens of thousands of Irishmen served in the British armed forces. In 2013 the government pardoned 5,000 citizens who had fought on Britain's side. They had been branded as traitors after the war and barred from jobs in the civil service. Only about 100 were still alive.

In 1949, a coalition government led by John Costello took Ireland out of the Commonwealth and made it an independent republic. De Valera served as taoiseach, (pronounced "tea-such"), a prime minister,

Ireland

By the sea in County Cork

several times, but in 1959 he gave up leadership of the Fianna Fail and was elected president of the republic. During the 1950s, Ireland began a major push toward industrialization. Foreign capital was invited into the country and given tax incentives. By the mid-1960s, industrial output was growing at over 5% a year. Ireland joined the EC (now EU) in 1973, which gave a great boost to both its agricultural and industrial production. The improved economic situation brought about a rising standard of living. Automobiles and televisions became commonplace.

POLITICAL SYSTEM

A Written Constitution Derived from an Unwritten One

The Republic of Ireland (Eire) is Europe's newest independent state, having been founded in 1921 and having separated itself completely from Britain in 1949. It devotes much attention to strengthening a sense of Irish national identity, and the resentment resulting from recent British occupation is still very strong. Because of its long domination by Great Britain, it is hardly surprising that the Irish political system so closely resembles that of its former conqueror. Before Ireland gained its independence, many Irishmen had served in the British House of Commons. Therefore, they had not only gained their parliamentary experience in Britain but had also contributed to the very development of the British political system.

In some important ways, however, Irish democracy differs from the "Westminster model" of Great Britain. The Republic of Ireland has a written constitution that it adopted in 1937. Article 2 of that document mandated the eventual reunification of Ireland: "The national territory consists of the whole island of Ireland, its islands and the territorial seas." This article was removed in 1998 as a contribution to a daring Northern Ireland settlement.

The Catholic Church

The constitution also pledges to support the teachings of the Roman Catholic Church, and until 2018 it banned blasphemy. Legislation in effect since January 1, 2010, bans the publication of material that grossly insults any religion, and it provides for fines to back up the ban. Except for the Vatican itself, Ireland has traditionally been the least secular state in all of Europe. The Catholic Church maintains considerable influence in social affairs. It controls all but 462 of the 3,940 primary and secondary schools. In 2011 school authorities in Dublin announced plans to remove hundreds of schools from the Catholic Church's control to reflect the increasingly diverse population. Foreign-born residents now constitute 17% of the population, up from 6% in 1991.

Until 2018 non-Christian and nonbaptized children experienced difficulties securing a place in public schools; 85% of Irish favor ending all religious bias in the schools. Senator Donal Lydon once noted, "the Church has contacts at every level of society, in every corner. Its influence is everywhere. Any politician who ignores the views of the Church would need to be crazy." That is gradually changing as society is becoming increasingly secular.

In recent years, the church's political influence has declined significantly, as a younger generation is more reluctant to accept Catholic teachings, especially concerning sexual mores. This more liberal attitude was displayed in 2015 when it became the first country to legalize same-sex marriage by popular vote. Following a civil debate that lacked the emotional fights over divorce and abortion, three out of five voters approved. The Northern Irish assembly vetoed same-sex marriage. Three-fourths of respondents find the church's views on sex irrelevant. In the 21st century, 35% of the Catholics regularly attend Sunday mass, down from 87% in 1984 and 91% in 1974; in Dublin only 14% do so. Only 38% of Irish Catholics regularly take communion. Contraceptive devices have been legal since 1979. Ireland now has the world's largest percentage of married women under age 49 using them. Over 90% of girls age 18 to 24 use them. But that does not prevent 35% of all children from being born out of wedlock, up from 5% in the 1970s. The birth rate has fallen dramatically to two children on average, largely because more and more Irish women have entered the workforce: 54% in 2009, up from 7.5% in 1970. Nevertheless the birth rate is the highest in the OECD.

Following referenda in 1992 and 1995, Irish women were permitted to have abortions abroad; this was confirmed by a 2007 court ruling. By 2006 more than 4,000 women were going to Britain each year to have an abortion, up from 578 in 1971. This would be as if 500,000 American women had to go to Toronto each year to obtain an abortion. The abortion rate was over 10% by 2002. British abortion laws do not apply in the north, but a court ruled in 2015 that they should be available.

In December 2010 the European Court of Human Rights in Strasbourg ruled in favor of three Irish women plaintiffs that Ireland's laws and the constitutional protection for the "life of the unborn" violated their human rights. The court upheld Ireland's right to prohibit abortion in most cases. Only when there was a "real and substantial risk" to the mother's life could an abortion be performed.

In the face of furious opposition from the Catholic Church and antiabortion groups in 2013, parliament passed and the president signed a law allowing an abortion when the mother's life is at risk or there is a possibility of suicide. This law amend the constitutional ban on abortion and codifies a 1992 Supreme Court ruling that permitted abortion in certain circumstances.

Public disgust and a bitter national debate over abortion and the influence of

the church in Irish society were ignited in November 2012 when a practicing dentist from India, 17 weeks pregnant, died in a Galway hospital. The medical staff informed her that she was miscarrying. But despite her repeated pleas, they refused to perform an abortion as long as the baby's heart was still beating. She developed blood poisoning, which killed her. Her death emboldened the government to enact the legislation implementing the 1992 court decision. However, a strong anti-abortion lobby continued to exist.

In a May 2018 referendum, 66%of voters made abortion legal. In December this was ratified, 90 to 15, by parliament. Women can seek an abortion for any reason up to the 12th week of pregnancy and later in case of fatal fetal abnormality or risk to the mother's life or health. It remains illegal in Northern Ireland.

As a result of a close vote in 1995 (50.2%, with urban support outweighing rural opposition), couples are allowed to divorce after a four-year separation. The 60% yes vote in Dublin swung the result. All the parties and most of the media supported it. The campaign was bitterly fought: Opponents' posters read "Hello Divorce, Goodbye Daddy!" while proponents, irreverently referring to the spate of revelations about child-molesting and sexual transgressions by priests, waved signs reading "Let the bishops look after their own families!" These scandals involving clergy have shaken respect for ecclesiastical authority. The divorce rate has increased tenfold since 1996.

The government became involved in 2002 by ordering the police to set up a special team of detectives to investigate every case of sexual abuse involving priests ever reported. It also reached an agreement with 18 religious orders indemnifying them against abuse claims at state-financed schools they operated.

Critics charged that the government was slow to acknowledge the extent of the abuse and quick to exonerate the church. Taoiseach Bertie Ahern therefore ordered a retired judge to launch a new investigation. The report published in 2005 revealed one of the worst pedophile scandals ever in the southeastern diocese of Ferns. It identified 100 children who had complained of being sexually abused by priests. Some involved repeated rapes. It charged that the church and state had collaborated in covering up the abuse, and incriminated priests were transferred rather than punished. Compensation to victims could run into hundreds of millions of euros.

In 2014 the European Court of Human Rights overturned a series of Irish court decisions and ruled that an Irish woman was entitled to $157,000 in compensation because the government had not protected her from repeated sexual abuse in a publicly financed Catholic primary school in the 1970s. More claims are sure to follow.

A thorough inquiry nine years in the making was published in May 2009 that concluded that, over a half-century period from the 1930s through the 1970s, child and sexual abuse, as well as privation and a pervasive sense of fear and cruelty, was endemic in dozens of Catholic-operated institutions. It provided evidence that the government had colluded with the church to play down or cover up these transgressions. Many victims' groups were infuriated that no individual names were given for the hundreds of abusers, thereby preventing the explosive report from being used as the basic for prosecutions.

A second scathing 700-page report commissioned by the government and documenting the cover-ups and the widespread abuse in Catholic institutions appeared later in the year. It prompted the pope to act. He wrote an unprecedented pastoral letter on pedophilia in March 2010, apologizing to the victims and expressing his own "shame and remorse." This was seen as a vote of no confidence in the Irish bishops, and five resigned. Cardinal Sean Brady, the leader of the country's Catholics, apologized for not reporting abuses to the police. But he refused to step down after the deputy prime minister and three of the four parties in parliament called for his resignation.

In May 2010 the pope appointed a high profile team of prelates, including the archbishops of New York and Boston, to investigate Irish dioceses and seminaries with a view to contribute "to the desired spiritual and moral renewal" of the church. Bishop Liam MacDaid, who took office in July 2010, presented a dark picture: "Society has forced us in the Irish church to look into the mirror, and what we saw was weakness and failure, victims and abuse."

Undying public controversy caused relations between the Irish government and the church to descend to an all-time low. The Vatican responded to the prime minister's accusation that it had undermined the official inquiries into sexual abuses involving clerics by recalling its envoy to Dublin. Thereupon, the government closed Ireland's embassy to the Holy See.

Such unprecedented hostility affects young people's decisions to enter the priesthood. In 2009 more English youth were training for the priesthood (150) than Irish (99). In the 1980s over 150 new recruits

Ireland

Former president Mary McAleese

entered Irish seminaries each year; in 2010 only 16 did so. In 2011 six men were ordained, making the average age of a priest 64 years. The situation is worse for nuns. Just two took final vows in 2009.

Former president Mary Robinson spoke of the country's "new pluralism," which "means the movement of a predominantly Catholic country, where the Catholic moral code and doctrines had a very significant place, to a society still influenced by the role of the Church but having other voices and having a sense of space between legislators and the Catholic Church." In the spirit of the times, the 30-year censorship ban on *Playboy* magazine was lifted in 1996.

Whereas Protestants in Northern Ireland outnumber Catholics by about 58% to 42%, in the republic they constitute only about 5% of the population. Since independence their numbers have declined by two-thirds. Many younger Protestants left; of the 115,000 who remain, most are elderly. Nevertheless, they have played and continue to play a role out of proportion to their size. They were important in creating modern Irish nationalism, from Wolfe Tone and his United Irishmen at the end of the 18th century to Charles Stewart Parnell and the home rule movement in the 19th. The republic's first president, Douglas Hyde, was one, as were great Irish writers like W. B. Yeats, Samuel Beckett, and Oscar Wilde. They were products of the Dublin Protestant middle class. Ireland's premier university, Trinity in Dublin, was opened to Catholics only in recent years. Protestants created even such recognizable Irish products as Jameson whiskey and Guinness stout.

Two Languages

The constitution recognizes two official languages: English and Irish, the latter of which is a Celtic language, closely related to Scottish; Gaelic; and, more distantly, Welsh. It was spoken by a majority of Irishmen until the first half of the 19th century, when it rapidly lost ground to English. Irish is now "used frequently" by only about 5% of the people and is spoken as a native language by only about 2% (about 70,000 people) in seven small pockets along the western seaboard, an area known as the Gaeltacht. There are three dialects, and the speaker of one will not necessarily understand everything said in the other two.

Ireland is experiencing a resurgence of the Irish language. In 1996 polls, more than 1 million claimed "some proficiency" in it, and a half-million said they were "fluent" or intended to become so. Those numbers justified the creation of an Irish-language television station, called Teilifis na Gaeilge (literally "Irish TV"), which broadcasts homegrown soap operas and news and sports programs aimed primarily at educated and urbanized Irishmen. They also prompted the education ministry to create a dozen new all-Irish primary schools.

With state policy to promote the use of Irish, it is a required subject in the republic's schools. In Northern Ireland it is taught in Catholic schools, and 5,000 pupils attend Irish-language schools. Only recently did it become possible to receive a school-leaving certificate in the republic without passing an examination on the Irish language. Parliamentary documents are translated into it, and parliamentarians sometimes begin their speeches in the language. After a few sentences, though, they usually switch to English with the words "As I was saying . . ." Some persons wonder what good a sign does which reads "*Roinn na Plandeolaiochta. Aonad an Leicteron Mhiocrascóip'*," when the following words must be written underneath it to make it comprehensible: "Department of Plant Science. Electron Microscopy Unit."

Although Irish is still declining in the Gaeltacht areas, there is a trend among urban middle-class families to send their children to Irish-language schools. The state devotes €500 million ($685 million) to Irish instruction every year. When protesters confronted a government minister demanding that Irish be made an official EU language, he discovered when talking to them that they did not even speak the language. Nevertheless, in 2007 the EU gave Irish the official status as the 23rd official language so that it could be spoken in the European Parliament. When it joined the EU in 1973, it had chosen English as its working language.

In 2005 a law came into force forbidding the use of English names in road signs, government documents, or survey maps. Another law mandates that, outside the Gaeltacht, signs bear the Irish version of the place names along with the English. A further change in road signs was made in 2005: Speed limits are now posted in kilometers per hour, not miles per hour.

The Supreme Court

As in most countries, a written constitution also calls for the Supreme Court to uphold that fundamental document. The republic has one consisting of a chief justice and five others. It is empowered to decide on the constitutionality of laws if the president of the republic asks for an opinion. This provision, known in the United States as "judicial review," is not present in Great Britain because there is no written constitution. However, English legal concepts and common law did replace the ancient Irish law (known as the Brehon law) by the 17th century. Thus Irish justice does bear an unmistakable British stamp. One British usage that was done away with in 2006 was that Supreme Court and high court judges are now addressed as "judge," not "my lord." The Supreme Court demonstrated its power in 1993 by declaring hundreds of EU directives unconstitutional because they had bypassed the Irish Senate.

The President

The most notable divergence from the "Westminster model" is that the Republic of Ireland does not have a monarch, and all links with the British Crown were severed in 1949. Instead of a monarch, the republic has a president, elected by the whole people for a seven-year term. This term can be renewed only once. The office is chiefly ceremonial, but unlike the British king or queen, Irish presidents have been leading political figures who continue to exercise considerable influence within the system, even if their powers are restricted.

The first woman president in Irish history, Mary Robinson, was elected in 1990. For years she had opposed Catholic positions on contraception, divorce, and same-sex couples. Her election signaled an important change from traditional social attitudes. She became one of the most popular presidents in Irish history, enjoying a 93% approval rating in 1996. Not inclined to shy away from controversy, she unofficially met Sinn Fein leader Gerry Adams in 1993 and shook his hand in public in 1996, a political act that won her countrymen's praise. She became the first Irish chief of state to meet a British monarch. The fact that she is married to a Protestant manifests tolerance on this religiously torn island. In 1997 she became UN high commissioner for human rights.

Robinson's election as president in 1990 forced Ireland's leaders to take a fresh look at Irish society, which has proved to be more receptive to change than most had realized. She became Ireland's most respected politician and helped pave the

President Michael D. Higgins

way for many women to win seats in parliament.

Her successor was Mary McAleese, a Belfast lawyer and vice chancellor of Queen's University, who was the candidate of Fianna Fail. A resident of Northern Ireland, she was the first British subject to be elected president of Ireland. Under the Irish constitution, residents of the six "partitioned" counties of the north are considered citizens of the republic. She was a conservative Catholic who opposed the legalization of abortion and divorce, but she favored the ordination of women. She admited that she is an unabashed nationalist. She was not helped by the fact that she had a cousin serving a life prison term for an IRA murder. She disavowed any links with Sinn Fein and pledged to stand above politics, to "seek to heal the hurt of divided Ireland," and to "build bridges." In October 2004 she was reelected without opposition.

She was not able to run again in November 2011 because she had already served two terms. She was succeeded by Michael Higgins (known universally as "Michael D."), who captured 39.6% of the votes, defeating entrepreneur Sean Gallagher (28.5%) and Sinn Fein candidate Martin McGuinness (13.7%). In 2018 he was reelected to a second term with 56% of the first-preference vote. On the same day, voters repealed the never-used constitutional ban on blasphemy. In his 70s, Higgins is a poet, writer, and political science and sociology professor, who did graduate work at Indiana University and who has a long record in politics. A former culture minister and head of the Labour Party, his political views are well to the left of the mainstream, and he harbors a dislike for free-rein capitalism.

The Parliament

Despite the differences described, the Irish political system developed by using Britain as a model. Irish government is parliamentary. This means that there are no checks and balances among three equal branches of government as in the United States. The lower house of parliament is supreme because unless the government can find a majority in it to carry forth its policies, that government must resign. Parliamentary government in the Republic of Ireland has usually been stable and durable. Conflict in the republic now takes place almost entirely within the parliamentary traditions and standards of conduct left by the British.

The Irish parliament (called the Oireachtas—pronounced "or-rock-tas") is bicameral. The upper house is the Senate (Seanad) composed of 60 members, 11 of whom are named by the prime minister and 6 by the universities. The remaining 43 are selected from 5 panels of nominees representing the national language and culture, agriculture and fisheries, organized and unorganized labor, industry and commerce, public administration, and social services. The Senate has the power to delay legislation for up to 90 days in order to try to amend bills. However, the lower house can always outvote it.

One might ask why such a weak body should even exist. Upper houses usually have the greatest importance in federal states where regional interests must be represented within the national government. However, the four traditional Irish provinces (Ulster in the north, Connacht in the west, Munster in the south and Leinster in the east) are not political units. Further, the 115 local authorities are supervised by the National Department of Environment. Local budgets are financed partly by grants from the national government, since local property taxes (known as "rates") cannot possibly provide enough revenue.

The Republic of Ireland is a unitary state, and political authority rests largely with the central government. This centralized system exists even though local concerns are very important to Irish politicians. Thus, the Senate's purpose was never to represent provincial interests but instead to give some political power to certain groups, such as Protestants, which could not win it in free elections before the whole people.

Opposition to this weak Senate gained so much strength that the government decided to submit its abolition to a referendum in October 2013; the body survived by a close margin. One opponent, Peter Cunningham, described it as "the ultimate cosy club" that had "morphed into a salaried refuge for failed or retired politicians, party cronies and worthies whose activities have met with government approval." Many senators have other jobs and still receive a basic salary of €65,000 ($89,000) annually, plus up to €37,000 ($57,000) allowance for expenses.

Political power is centered in the lower house of parliament known as the Dáil (pronounced "Doyle"). This house is composed of 166 members known as Teachtái Dála, or TD for short, elected from 41 constituencies. Elections must be held at least every five years. The prime minister (called the Taoiseach—pronounced "teasuch") may choose to hold earlier elections if he desires to reestablish or widen his party's majority in the Dáil. The Taoiseach is by far the most important political figure in the republic. With his cabinet, which is composed of from 7 to 15 members, he establishes the country's policies and dominates his party in the Dáil in order to get his government's bills through parliament. He is also the best-paid head of government in the world. His salary is €310,000 ($450,000) per year, compared with the US president ($400,000) and the British prime minister ($387,700). In a gesture to share the pain with his fellow citizens, Taoiseach Enda Kenny reduced his pay in 2012 by €14,000 ($18,200).

Electoral System: Proportional Representation

In any democratic system, parties usually play a key role, presenting candidates and policy issues as alternatives from which to choose. They educate the voters; wage election campaigns; and, above all, rule or prepare to rule. Political parties are especially important in the Irish Republic because interest groups are far less tightly organized than in most other European countries. Thus, Irish parties are particularly important channels for interest groups expressing their concerns and wants at high policy levels.

Parties seek seats in the Dáil by means of a particularly complex electoral system—a form of proportional representation involving what is known as a single transferable vote in multimember constituencies. The voter marks his ballot by placing the numeral 1 opposite the name of the candidate of his first choice and may then place the numeral 2 opposite the name of his second choice, continuing on until he has numbered all the candidates. Thus the voter is able to say in effect, "I wish to vote for A, but if he does not need my vote or if he has no chance of being elected, transfer my vote to B. If B in turn does not need my vote, or he has no chance of election, transfer my vote to C," and so forth.

Thus, the system reflects more completely the voters' preferences for the three to five seats filled by each constituency.

This makes it easier for smaller parties and independents to win parliamentary representation. At the same time, it is designed to prevent fringe politicians and a high number of small parties from winning seats in the Dáil and thereby adversely affecting the stability of the parliamentary system. It is therefore one of the better proportional representation systems in Europe. However, this complicated system enormously slows down the tabulation of the votes, and it often takes several days to determine the final results of an Irish election.

The republic's electoral system affects Irish politics in several important ways. By permitting voters to discriminate among candidates of the same party (as does the American primary system), it pits members of the same party against each other. Thus, the individual candidate's appeal must veer from the policy of the national party and be far more closely tailored to local concerns. Politicians compete with each other to perform a variety of services for local constituents, and this strengthens an important characteristic of Irish politics: Personality and personal ties become far more significant than national policy issues.

Moreover, the local political clubs, not the national parties (which have very small staffs), recruit candidates and wage campaigns. Although it is not required by law, Dáil members almost always come from the constituency in which they are elected. Also, most TDs continue to hold local political office at the same time. All of these factors represent a strong decentralized tendency in Irish politics: Politicians show strong loyalties to their local constituencies, but at the same time, the national party leadership needs to maintain strong party discipline as it seeks a majority in the Dáil. Without such discipline, no government could possibly survive.

Political Parties

Irish political parties are noticeably different from British parties, whose bases were traditionally rooted in different social classes. The Republic of Ireland is a more homogeneous country, and it has historically been economically underdeveloped. It has no major national, regional, religious, or racial differences that could become the basis for different parties. There are, of course, social cleavages, but these do not have the overriding significance that they do in many other European countries. It is more likely that the dividing line between the two major parties is determined by the position one's father or grandfather took on the signing of the Anglo-Irish Treaty in 1921, which divided the island and created the Irish Free State. In 1932, after a bloody civil war followed by intense domestic political rivalry, the party that had accepted the treaty (now the Fine Gael, pronounced Finna Gwail, meaning "Family of Irish") suffered an election defeat and relinquished power to the Fianna Fail (pronounced "Fee-anna Foil"), which had originally opposed the treaty. The 1932 elections firmly established democratic government, which stands or falls on the parties' willingness to alternate power peacefully, in response to the wishes of the voters.

The "pro" or "anti" distinction between the two major parties does not mean very much today. But the importance of family ties in Irish politics inclines Irishmen to vote as their fathers and grandfathers did, and it encourages political activists to become leaders in those same parties. It is hardly surprising that parties that are not formed along class or religious lines are not very ideological in their orientation.

North Americans who observe the two major Irish parties have the same difficulties distinguishing between them that Europeans express about American parties. Perhaps the 1960s saying of George Wallace about the American mainline parties applies to their Irish counterparts: "There's not a dime's worth of difference between them." Both parties in the republic are catchall parties that attract voters from all social groups. Both are rather conservative, antisecular, nationalistic and predominantly male. Both are what one would call Christian Democratic parties elsewhere in Europe.

The Irish party system has developed into two more or less stable blocs. In the past three decades, the government has alternated between the Fianna Fail and a coalition combining Fine Gael and the Labour Party. Traditionally Fianna Fail did not enter coalitions, but it must often rely on support from small parties, making its governments more fragile. Fine Gael. Labour coalitions were made easier by the fact that there is very little ideological distance between them.

Fianna Fail governed most of the time since 1932. It is moderate to conservative on economic matters; it still has a slightly anti-British attitude, although it has eliminated many of the more militant elements in the aftermath of a party split in 1970 over the question of Irish unification. It attracts considerable support from businessmen and professional people, as well as parts of the urban working class. However, its greatest strength remains in the rural western regions. The native Irish speakers solidly support it because it has stamped itself as a party seeking restoration of the Irish language (at least nominally). It often sees itself as a grassroots party and demonstrates populist tendencies.

Hon. Enda Kenny, ex-Taoiseach of Ireland

Fianna Fail was able to stay in power after 1989 only by forming a historic coalition with its most bitter political enemies, the Progressive Democrats. This was the first time ever that Fianna Fail shared power while ruling. In 1992 Charles Haughey (who was given a state funeral in June 2006) was finally forced out after it had been revealed that he had been aware of police bugging of two journalists' phones. He was replaced as Taoiseach by Albert Reynolds, a self-made pet-food tycoon.

As party leader Bertie Ahern led the party to victory in the 1997 elections. As usual, it took weeks of haggling and deal making before the new prime minister could go to the elegant Phoenix Park residence of the president and ask for permission to form a government. He is a populist Dubliner from a lower-class background who is separated from his wife and lived openly with his girlfriend. Ahern vowed to "cut taxes, cut crime and work for peace in Northern Ireland." Although reputed to be "green" or pro-Catholic on the volatile subject of Northern Ireland, he pushed hard for progress in the peace talks.

Riding on a tide of popular contentment with the economy in 2002, Ahern's Fianna Fail became the first government in more than 30 years to be reelected. He did it again in May 2007, when his party captured 78 seats, making him the first Taoiseach since Eamon de Valera to win three elections in a row. With 11 years in office, he became the longest-serving Taoiseach in modern Irish history.

His reputation as the "Teflon Taoiseach" failed him in April 2008. He decided to resign on May 6 before being pushed out of office because of a financial investigation against him. Half the electorate indicated in a poll that it no longer trusted him to run the country. He had become an electoral liability. In 2012 an investigative tribunal he had established found that he had lied about the source of large deposits (totaling €200,000 or $260,000) into his bank account while he was in office. He resigned from Fianna Fail rather than being expelled. Ex-Taoiseach Albert Reynolds, who died in 2014, was also accused of abusing his power.

Ahern had gained stature as a statesman in May 2007, when he helped facilitate a dramatic Northern Ireland agreement and became the first Irish leader to address both houses of the British Parliament. His last hurrah was a speech before a joint session of the US Congress just a week before leaving office on May 6, 2008. Bill Clinton and Tony Blair gave him glowing testimonials for his effectiveness in the Northern Irish negotiations. He also had presided over Ireland's most successful economic boom, which reversed the traditional emigration.

Ahern was replaced as Taoiseach in May 2008 by Brian Cowen, who had been in politics since age 24, when he succeeded to his father's parliamentary seat. In his long career, he had occupied most top cabinet posts, including the Foreign and Finance Ministries, and shown competence in each. A severe property bubble burst, triggering a crisis in the public finances and bringing the banking system close to collapse. Unemployment grew to 13%. The government was forced to accept a humiliating €85 billion ($115 billion) bailout from the EU and IMF. One observer noted, "If this had happened in Michael Collins' day, there would be people hanging from the bridges." When the Green Party withdrew its six members from the governing coalition, Fianna Fail lost its majority, and new elections had to be held in February 2011.

The result for Fianna Fail was a humiliation and a disaster. It sank to 15.1% of the votes. Going all the way back to 1932, it had never gotten less than 39%. It lost three-fourths of its seats, dropping from 78 to 20, and became only the third-largest party in parliament. This was its worst defeat in 8 decades. Voters flocked back in the February 2016 elections. Led by Michéal Martin, it captured 24% of the votes and 44 seats.

Fine Gael is a traditional establishment party that draws a disproportionate share of its votes from the upper and middle classes and from farmers with large holdings. Its leaders also tend to be drawn from somewhat higher social strata. Although it tends to be moderate to conservative on economic matters, the party has moved slightly to the left to accommodate the Labour Party. Fine Gael is the most centralized and hierarchically organized in the republic.

In 1997 Irish voters continued a tradition maintained from 1969 to 2002: Never reelect a government, no matter how good its record. Despite the fact that the Fine Gael government presided over the strongest economy in the 75-year history of independent Ireland, with the fastest growth rate in the EU that won it the nickname "Celtic Tiger" and living standards that were near the EU average, it was thrown out of power. Its partner, the Labour Party, collapsed in the voting booths. The two parties were rudely reminded of an old saying in Irish politics: No good turn ever goes unpunished.

Its greatest triumph came in 2011, when it surged to 36.1% of the votes and 76 seats. Its leader, Enda Kenny, a former teacher and the longest-serving parliamentarian, became Taoiseach, presiding over a coalition with the Labour Party. Together they commanded two-thirds of the seats, the largest majority in Irish history. Both parties favor the abolition of the Senate, and Fine Gael seeks to reduce parliament by 20 seats. Kenny warned of hard times ahead, saying that Ireland was living its "darkest hour before the dawn." By 2014 it had become clear that Ireland was the first eurozone nation to emerge successfully from the EU bailout. Kenny's slogan in the inconclusive 2016 elections, "Let's keep the recovery going," did not resonate. The party won 25.5% of the votes, but it fell to 50 seats. Its coalition with Labour collapsed. After an unprecedented six-week deadlock, Kenny won parliamentary backing to continue as prime minister heading a minority government.

Unlike in Britain, the Labour Party in Ireland has never articulated socialist or Marxist ideologies. In fact, by western standards, it is hardly a party of the left although it does have a left-wing minority. It had been virtually excluded from urban politics in the eastern part of the country, and most of the working class voted for one of the two major parties, especially the Fianna Fail. Its main electoral support is found among rural, agrarian workers. Its importance in Irish politics was greatly enhanced by the fact that until 1997 it had been an essential part of any ruling coalition led by either Fine Gael or Fianna Fail.

Labour experienced disaster in 2016. It collapsed to 6.6% of the votes and a mere 7 seats.

Minor Parties

Despite the proportional representation electoral system, which usually permits many parties to enter parliament, small parties had almost entirely disappeared from Irish parliamentary politics. Nineteen minor party representatives and independents did win seats in the 2011 elections. These included the environmentalist Greens, who had entered a governing coalition with Fianna Fail in 2007. This was the first time it had been in government. It was their departure from the government in January 2011 that prompted the election the following month.

The Progressive Democrats (PD) broke away from Fianna Fail in 1985 in protest against its hard-line Northern Ireland policy. It temporarily displaced Labour as third-largest party, a position that Labour had occupied since 1922. The PD appeared to break the mold of Irish party politics; it temporarily supplanted Labour as Fine Gael's favorite coalition partner, although Fine Gael and PD compete for the same kinds of voters. It is approaching political irrelevance.

Polls long indicated that even though two-thirds of Eire's population believed ideally that Ireland should one day be a unified nation, the overwhelming majority abhorred the violent attempt to unify Ireland by bullets and bombs. It was precisely to overcome its isolation that the leader of Sinn Fein (the political arm of the Irish Republican Army—IRA), Gerard (Gerry) Adams, ended the party's boycott of the Irish (though not of the British) parliament. As he stated, "We've lost touch with the people for the simple reason that we have not been able to represent them in the only political forum they know. To break out into the broad stream of people's consciousness, we have to approach them at their own level." To many traditionalists, this approach smacked of betrayal. As one die hard remarked, "when you lie down with the dogs, you get up with the fleas."

Nevertheless, Sinn Fein is the only party with parliamentary seats in both parts of Ireland (and in London, although it refused to occupy its Westminster seats). Analysts concluded that the hard-left-leaning Sinn Fein's success was not primarily due to a rise of nationalist sentiment in the republic. Instead its young candidates exuded dynamism and concern in poorer areas on the island. It is Ireland's only truly leftist party. It appeals mainly to the urban poor. It is pro-same-sex marriage and favors liberalizing the abortion laws. All other parties were worried about it and gave a sigh of relief when it achieved minimal success in 2007 and 2011. It has become the main opposition party. It gained support by opposing the EU-mandated economic austerity policy. In 2016, it won 13.9% of the votes and 23 seats. Independent candidates captured 17.8% of the votes and 23 seats.

Foreign and Defense Policies

A central reality in the republic of Ireland's foreign and defense policy is that the Irish live on a politically divided island and are a politically and religiously divided people. Few foreign policy issues

THE IRISH TIMES

€1.27 (incl. VAT) £1.00 DUBLIN, TUESDAY, FEBRUARY 5, 2002 No. 46297

Pockets deep, mountain high

: Are school ski trips worth the cost?

How to succeed at work: do less!

>Or so says work guru, Rob Parsons: 13

Fianna Fáil should expel Noel O'Flynn

>Fintan O'Toole, Opinion: 14

…wlor set to begin …ngest jail term for a …in 60 years

…surance companies braced …major claims after floods

US not ruling out 'self-defence' combat

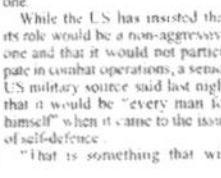

From Miriam Donohoe, in Zamboanga, Philippines

can be treated entirely separately from these facts. Most Irish citizens and politicians in the republic want to see these divisions overcome, and no Irish republican government has ever recognized the division of the island as permanent. Most people in the republic do not use the term "Republic of Ireland," which implies permanent division, but instead refer to their state almost exclusively as "Ireland." But the unification issue is no longer as important in Irish politics as it once was.

Younger leaders with no direct memories of the bloody struggle and with far greater interest in Ireland's economic development replaced the old revolutionary elite who fought for independence against Britain. A 2004 British Council poll of young Irish professionals revealed a dramatic transformation of Irish attitudes toward Britain: three-fourths have a broadly favorable view of Britain, and 81% described the relationship between the two countries as good to excellent. Irish unity remains important, but it is no longer as pressing as it once was. In fact, personal links with Britain are stronger than with Northern Ireland: Only half the respondents had ever visited the six northern counties, whereas 84% had been to London.

The Republic of Ireland lived for a long time in the shadow of Great Britain, although it has become a much more confidant nation and is no longer obsessed by its ancient hatred of the British. Because of Britain's part in Irish history and the continued presence of the British in Northern Ireland, the republic is inclined to remain neutral in conflicts where Britain is involved. It remained neutral in World War II. In fact, it even refused to observe blackouts in its cities at night. Thus German bombers were able to orient themselves by regrouping in the skies over Dublin and then flying in a direct line toward such British cities as Liverpool. In 1982, the republic also refused to go along with EU sanctions against Argentina when Britain, a fellow member, was engaged in an armed struggle for control of the Falkland Islands.

Ireland's policy of neutrality does not mean that the republic is ideologically neutral or politically indifferent. It shares the basic democratic, political, and economic values of other countries in Europe and North America. However, it is only one of four EU countries that have not joined NATO. This fact does cause disputes sometimes. For instance, when the Dáil debated the ratification of the EU's Single European Act (SEA), which calls for majority votes in the EU Council of Ministers and a completely free market, some members questioned how the republic could remain neutral and still take part in the security and foreign policy cooperation for which the act called.

The Supreme Court found that the SEA's political cooperation section was unconstitutional and therefore ruled that a referendum on amending the constitution was necessary. In the 1987 voting, 70% voted in favor of it, and 30%, against. This perennial question arose again in 2008, when the Irish debated whether the EU's Lisbon Treaty (a revision of the failed EU constitution) violated their treasured neutrality.

Ireland's long-established policy of military neutrality is increasingly irrelevant, since the country cooperates on European security matters, and Irish and British troops coordinate the fight against the IRA. In 1999 it decided to establish formal links with NATO through the Partnership for Peace (PfP). Following the September 11, 2001, terrorist attacks against the United States, Ireland offered its airspace and airfields to American military planes. In 2003 about 30,000 American soldiers passed through Shannon Airport during the military buildup around Iraq. However, Taoiseach Ahern declared, "Ireland cannot engage in support of military action because we work under the UN resolution."

It agreed in 2009 to accept two Uzbek detainees from Guantanamo Bay, Cuba, in order to help the US close the controversial prison. Ireland had served a two-year term on the UN Security council from 2001 to 2002. In 2010 it expelled an Israeli diplomat over the misuse of Irish passports by Mossad agents to assassinate a Hamas leader. The next year it expelled a Russian diplomat for using six stolen Irish identities to cover for spies operating in the US.

The republic is so enveloped by the military forces of the Atlantic alliance that it is able to keep its own defense forces very small. Internal security rests almost entirely with the unarmed police, the 10,000-strong Garda Siochana ("guardians of the peace"). External defense is the responsibility of the permanent defense forces that number 10,460, about 8,500 of whom are land forces. The navy has 1,110 personnel and 7 coastal and patrol vessels. The air force has 850 troops and is composed of fewer than 40 aircraft, including helicopters. Military service is voluntary, and there is also a reserve defense force of 14,875 that could be mobilized in time of crisis.

Ireland has contributed troops to UN peacekeeping units throughout the world, including in Kosovo (240 soldiers in 2010), Bosnia, Croatia, southern Lebanon, Cyprus, Western Sahara, Ethiopia/Eritrea, and East Timor. In 1991 the Irish government supported UN policy toward Iraq. Although Ireland played no direct role in the war, it did permit US military planes to refuel at Shannon Airport, thereby prompting many domestic critics to cry that its neutrality had been breached.

The European Union (EU)

Out of sheer economic necessity, Ireland joined the EU in 1973, at the same time that Britain entered. Ireland stood to benefit from EU regional aid and the Common Agricultural Program (CAP), which in 2002 accounted for 4% of its GDP, or $1.5 billion, and in no year exceeded 5% of its GDP. In three decades, such assistance has totaled over $32 billion. EU aid helps modernize Ireland's infrastructure. For a few years, CAP funds were a boon to Irish farmers, but their benefits were not lasting. Adjusting to CAP, western Ireland has been forced to change from its traditional dairy- and beef-farming economy to tourism and forestry. In 25 years its forestry industry is expected to be as important to the economy as its food industry is now. Its trade volume with Britain (to which

16% of its exports still go) remains important, especially since half its agricultural exports go to the UK. Brexit could devastate rural Ireland. The UK provides 39% of imports, but the EU provides 70.6% of imports and buys 57% of exports.

EU membership has served to shift Irish foreign trade and political attention away from Britain to a broader view of the rest of Europe. Brexit will adversely affect Ireland's foreign trade, direct investment, and the openness of its borders. Former president Robinson argued, "it lifts the burden of the relationship with our close neighbor. We are now partners with them in Europe. The history is still there, but it is less a tight connection and burden between us." For centuries Ireland had defined itself, in relation to Britain, as a victim. That is far less prominent now. Today it is more inclined to define itself in relation to Europe and the EU, in which it is recognized as an equal. It distinguishes itself from Britain and benefits from being the most pro-European anglophone country in the EU. This foreign policy reorientation has not altered the fact that hundreds of thousands of Irish still live and work in Britain, where they enjoy the same political, legal and social welfare rights as British citizens.

Some Irish worry that increasing integration with Europe may have negative effects on Irish culture. Arts Minister Síle de Valera, granddaughter of Eamon de Valera, said during a visit to Boston that EU regulations and directives "often seriously impinge on our identity, culture and traditions." Ahern's deputy prime minister, Mary Harney, also warned against a more centralized and bureaucratic Europe. She claimed that spiritually Ireland is "probably a lot closer to Boston than to Berlin."

In a June 8, 2001, referendum marked by massive abstention and indifference, a majority of Irish slapped the EU in the face by rejecting the Nice Treaty, which had laid out the process for enlarging the community. Many Irish were smarting from an earlier EU rebuke of the country's economic policy, were fearful of losing EU funding if a dozen poorer countries were admitted, and were uneasy that its neutrality was being threatened by Europe's acquisition of its own defense and security role.

A second referendum was held in October 2002, and this time the government spent 10 times more on the referendum campaign than it had the first time. Voters overwhelmingly endorsed the Treaty of Nice, 54% to 46%, with a turnout of 48.5%, giving the green light to EU institutional reform and enlargement and causing a sigh of relief throughout the community. Ireland is the only EU country whose constitution required that the new constitutional Lisbon Treaty be submitted to a referendum in June 2008. Voters rejected it. However, 60% of voters said yes in a referendum held in June 2012 to approve the EU fiscal treaty.

In 2002 Ireland gained more visibility in the EU when Pat Cox was elected president of the European Parliament. In the first half of 2004, Ireland assumed the EU presidency. It oversaw the entry of 10 new members and guided the discussions to salvage the new constitutional treaty on which the members could not agree. It assumed the rotating presidency again on January 1, 2013, celebrating 40 years of membership in the EU.

Leaders of the accession states were welcomed in a glittering ceremony in front of the presidential palace in Dublin on May 1, 2004. They looked to Ireland more than any other country as their model. Charles Grant of the Center for European Reform noted, "Ireland is a poor country dominated by a big neighbor, and all of the new countries except Poland are small countries dominated by big neighbors."

But it is poor no more, despite serious economic recession beginning in 2008. When it joined the EU in 1973, its per-capita income was a mere 62% of the EU average; by 2003 it had reached 136%. It slashed its top corporate tax rate from over 40% to 12.5% (6.25% of revenue from patents and intellectual property) and the state's share of GDP from 54% in the 1980s to only 33% in 2004. Foreign investment poured in. Unemployment fell from 17% in 1987 to 4.3% in 2006 and 5.3% in 2019. Cox stated the obvious: Membership "turned us from a stagnant, backward, failed part of the British regional economy into a modern and prosperous European country." This tiny land had become the third-richest country in the EU, and it is still one of Europe's richest nations. That was exactly what fascinates the new eastern partners and what they want for themselves. But this wealth had a significant consequence: Ireland became a net contributor to Brussels's coffers and therefore helped finance the assistance for the poorer new members.

There was nervousness throughout Europe over how unpredictable Irish voters would decide in a June 2008 referendum over the EU's constitutional revision, known as the Lisbon Treaty. Ireland was the only member state whose constitution required such a plebiscite.

Polls indicated that voters would say yes, but on voting day, they shocked the rest of Europe, just as they had done in June 2001, when they rejected the Nice Treaty. This time, in a convincing vote of 53.4% against and only 46.6% in favor, voters said no to the reform that was intended to enable the enlarging EU to make quicker and more coherent decisions in vital areas. The results dramatized the inability of EU leaders to persuade citizens that they can benefit from reforms described in a long, dense, complex 277-page legal document.

At a time when economic growth was slowing and the real estate market was collapsing, it was easy for opponents of the treaty to exploit the fears of anxious Irishmen. Many worried about immigration and the possibility that Brussels could usurp their power to levy their own taxes, determine their own family law, and decide when and how to use their own armed forces.

The Irish government negotiated a compromise with the EU in an effort to salvage the Lisbon Treaty. It agreed to hold another referendum on October 2, 2009, after the EU offered assurances that Irish neutrality would be respected, that there would be no interference in Irish taxation or abortion laws, and that all member states would continue to have at least one commissioner in the European Commission.

Irish voters are notoriously unpredictable, but the severe economic downturn made it clear to many of them just how much Ireland needed the EU and the euro to stabilize its economy. The "yes" campaign also played on the fear of falling under British influence. The Irish know that one of the main benefits of EU membership is to boost their self-confidence in relation to Britain. Armed with much more knowledge about the treaty than they had shown in the first referendum, voters accepted it, 67% to 33%. The May 2012 referendum over the EU's policy of austerity was also a cliff-hanger, but it passed, 60% to 40%.

Reunification

The vast majority of the citizens of the Irish Republic and virtually all of its political leaders share the goal of reunifying all 32 Irish counties. But they eventually wish to see this accomplished peacefully and with the consent of the Northern Irish. In Northern Ireland, about 1 million Irish Protestants outnumber the half-million Catholics, so Irish unity must take a form palatable to the Protestants. Violence spilled over from Northern Ireland to the south. The Irish government outlawed the provisional IRA; government raids and arrests provide frequent reminders that the IRA can expect no tolerance within the republic. In 1982 a Dublin court convicted an Irishman for possessing explosives, even though the crime was committed in Britain. This was the first application of a 1976 law that was part of an ongoing Irish-British cooperation against terrorism in both countries.

In 1981 a US court convicted the Irish Northern Aid (NORAID) committee for failing to list the IRA as its principal foreign agent. The Irish government ordered its diplomatic representatives in the United States to boycott the 1983 annual St. Patrick's Day parade in New York City because the organizers of the parade had chosen an IRA supporter as grand marshal. In explaining its decision, the Irish government noted that the IRA's actions, which include collecting money from unsuspecting Irish Americans to finance violent operations in Northern Ireland, "have deepened the wounds of our troubled history and continue to postpone the day of Irish unity and reconciliation." Dublin frequently appealed to Americans not to support violence in Ireland. Funds from NORAID declined, and the IRA sought to fill its coffers by means of extortion and racketeering in Northern Ireland.

Mr. David Trimble,
former leader, Ulster Unionist Party

The Irish government realizes that unification can be accomplished only in cooperation with Britain and Northern Ireland. This has brought the Irish and British prime ministers together for periodic high-level meetings to discuss the developments in the area. This was dangerous, as was shown by the attempt on Prime Minister Thatcher's life in the grisly 1984 IRA bombing of the hotel in Brighton where she was staying. She narrowly escaped death, and several Tory leaders were killed or wounded. The bombing inflamed anti-Irish sentiments to a height unequaled since the IRA murdered Lord Mountbatten in 1979, and it set back progress toward peace.

Nevertheless, consultation between representatives of Eire and the UK continues within the rubric of the 1985 Anglo-Irish Accord. For the first time, this permitted Dublin some say in Northern Ireland's affairs. The agreement enjoys majority support in the republic. In 1990 the pope appointed Bishop Cahal B. Daly, a fierce critic of IRA terrorism, as Ireland's primate. In 1993 optimism was ignited by a joint declaration by the British and Irish prime ministers offering Sinn Fein a seat at the bargaining table to discuss Northern Ireland's future if the IRA renounced violence. Prime Minister John Major promised that Britain would not stand in the way of a united Ireland if a majority of Northern Ireland residents supported such a step. Taoiseach Albert Reynolds pledged that there would be no change in the six counties' status without majority consent.

As a symbol of returning normalcy with Britain in 1995, Prince Charles became the first member of the royal family to make an official visit to the Irish Republic since 1922. Also in 1995, David Trimble, then leader of the Ulster Unionist Party, the main Protestant group, traveled to Dublin and met with Taoiseach Bruton. This was the first time since 1922 a unionist leader was received in Dublin. On November 26, 1998, Tony Blair became the first British prime minister since Ireland's independence to speak to the Irish parliament.

Talks involving eight Northern Ireland parties and the British and Irish governments continued despite sporadic outbreaks of violence. In 1998 a majority in Eire backed the deletion from their constitution of the mandate to unify the island. As a result of the 1998 Good Friday Peace Agreement, followed by dramatic "yes" referenda votes for the accord in both the republic (94.4%) and Northern Ireland (71.1%), Ireland reached the doorstep of peace. Trimble and his Catholic counterpart, John Hume, received the 1998 Nobel Peace Prize for their role in reaching a historic peace agreement in Northern Ireland that year. Despite continuing setbacks, there is optimism that "the Troubles" will end.

In February 2005 the Dublin government named Sinn Fein leaders Gerry Adams, Martin McGuinness, and Martin Ferris as members of the IRA's ruling army council. Joined by the British government, it dropped the polite fiction that the leaders and organizations of Sinn Fein and IRA are separate. Ahern declared an end to "creative ambiguity." They are both to be regarded as one and the same. Justice Minister Michael McDowell called the IRA a "colossal criminal operation" and launched a major campaign against IRA racketeering. For decades the IRA has operated a range of criminal enterprises to finance IRA operations, including robbing banks and armored cars, counterfeiting currency and goods, smuggling fuel and cigarettes, and trafficking in drugs.

In February 2005 the Irish government ordered the police to move in on IRA money-laundering operations, believed to center on hotels and pubs. Three million pounds in cash were seized at the home of a businessman. Five young men were convicted in a Dublin court after their vehicles were found filled with fake police uniforms, stun guns, balaclavas, lump hammers, and lots of Sinn Fein election posters. The Irish and British governments agreed to share cross-border policing duties.

At Easter 2006 the Dublin government revived the tradition of commemorating the failed 1916 rebellion against the British by marching 2,500 soldiers and veterans down the main boulevard, O'Connell Street, where most of the fighting had taken place. To showcase the current friendly relationship, the British ambassador joined the leaders of the six main political parties in attendance. The republic is divided over whether the 1916 rebels were heroic patriots or trouble makers, and there was lively debate over whether the parade was an appropriate way to remember the event.

In an attempt a month earlier to demonstrate fairness and tolerance of a unionist alternative tradition, the government had permitted a march down O'Connell Street, past the post office, by 300 loyalists, most of them relatives of IRA victims. However, they were blocked by republican dissidents. The result was the largest riot Dublin had seen for a quarter-century. Gangs of young and drunken thugs wrecked cars and looted stores. The damages were set at €10 million ($15 million). Tanaiste (Deputy Prime Minister) Mary Harney admitted that the riots had brought "shame on the city, shame on the country."

On May 8, 2007, a power-sharing agreement in Northern Ireland was celebrated after three decades of violence and five years of rule from London. The last step in this process was taken in 2010, a year that saw major progress in the power-sharing and reconciliation process. In February, after almost two weeks of marathon negotiations, a landmark agreement was reached giving the Northern Irish government direct responsibility for policing and justice. This includes responsibility for police, prisons, and the prosecution service. This "devolution of policing" was the last missing piece of the Good Friday Agreement that established power sharing.

In March 2010 all the nationalist members and most of the unionists (except the UUP) voted for the historic measure in Stormont. In accepting it, Sinn Fein agreed for the first time to recognize and cooperate with the British state. Despite a series of bomb attacks by deadly splinter groups attempting to undermine the agreement, it took effect on April 12. The same day Northern Ireland's first justice minister in four decades was appointed, David Ford. Power sharing has provided considerable political harmony and has ended most paramilitary violence, even though it has not eliminated the last diehard bombers and gunmen. In May 2011 the Northern Irish governing coalition of the Democratic Unionists and Sinn Fein strengthened their control of the Stormont assembly by winning reelection in regional elections. This was a clear rebuff to militants on both sides who try to keep ancient animosities alive.

The Orange Order marches free of violence yet. Only three months after the handover of police powers, hundreds of rioters in Belfast battled the police with gasoline bombs, bricks, metal bars, planks, and concrete slabs, leaving 82 police officers injured. The violence, reminiscent of earlier times, erupted when the Protestant Orange Order rejected a new system for mediating the routes and timing the marches. Nevertheless, power sharing has enormously improved life in Northern Ireland.

Irish village life

The year 2010 also witnessed an electrifying apology by newly elected British prime minister David Cameron. On June 15 a 10-volume, 5,000-page final report was issued on the events of January 30, 1972, a fateful day known as "Bloody Sunday." British paratroopers opened fire upon unarmed demonstrators during a civil rights march in the Bogside area of Londonderry, leaving 14 men dead and 13 injured. It was a deeply held nationalist grievance, and relatives' requests for an investigation went unanswered. In 1998 then–prime minister Blair ordered what became the longest and most expensive public inquiry in British history to be conducted.

After 12 years, more than 900 witnesses, and a cost of $288 million, Cameron stood up in the House of Commons to announce the conclusions: The soldiers had shown a "widespread loss of fire discipline. Some members of our armed forces acted wrongly." The demonstrators had not provoked the attacks. Even Martin McGuinness, who was present and probably armed with a submachine gun, did not "engage in any activity that provided any of the soldiers with any justification for opening fire. What happened should never, ever have happened." The shootings were "both unjustified and unjustifiable." And then the dramatic words: "On behalf of the government, I am deeply sorry." In Londonderry, thousands gathered at the site of the shooting and cheered as the prime minister's speech was broadcast live on giant screens.

London's Metropolitan Police released evidence in 2012 that agents working for the British army had worked with death squads in Northern Ireland. This included the 1989 murder of Belfast lawyer Patrick Finuncane, who had represented IRA terrorists. Two gunmen from the outlawed Ulster Defence Association broke into his home and shot him 14 times at point-blank range before the very eyes of his wife and three children. The report detailed how British intelligence was implicated in the murder. Then–prime minister Cameron immediately went to Parliament. There he condemned the murder as "an appalling crime" and apologized to the family. (See United Kingdom chapter.)

The normalization of the Irish-British relationship was cemented in May 2011 by the first royal visit to Ireland since George V went in 1911. It was the capstone for the Northern Irish peace process. Loaded with symbolism, the visit would have been unimaginable without the dramatically improved bilateral relations since the Good Friday Agreement. Queen Elizabeth II laid a wreath in the Garden of Remembrance in Parnell Square, which commemorates the Irish who died in the struggle for independence. She also laid one in the National War Memorial Gardens, which honor the 50,000 Irish who died fighting in the British armed forces during the First World War. She then went to Croke Park Gaelic soccer stadium, where British auxiliary police had killed 14 Irish civilians in 1920 in retaliation for the deaths of British authorities. These ceremonies sent a powerful message to most Irish.

The monarch acknowledged a "troubled past," but she assured that the two countries are now "firm friends and equal partners." Deputy Taoiseach Eamon Gilmore said, "This is about closing the door and moving on from the past. . . . It's about normalizing the relationship." The ties are very strong: An estimated 6 million British have an Irish parent or grandparent, and Ireland is the UK's fifth-largest export market.

In 2012 she ended a visit to Northern Ireland by shaking hands with Martin McGuinness, who had belonged to the terrorist organization that murdered her cousin Lord Mountbatten in 1979. Elizabeth smiled but did not speak while McGuinness spoke to her in Irish, using words that translated to "goodbye and Godspeed." The brief meeting signified a new era. Prince Charles followed up in May 2015 by meeting with Gerry Adams in Galway.

In reciprocation, President Michael Higgins made the first state visit to Britain by an Irish president in April 2014. He and his wife, Sabina, stayed as guests of the queen in Windsor Castle. This was a rare privilege. Martin McGuinness, who died in March 2017, also took part in the visit. As a further sign of the two nations' improved ties, the British government announced that two years later it would be represented at the centenary commemorations of the 1916 Easter Rising against British rule.

When clashes in the assembly and Belfast streets broke out in July 2013, former American diplomat Richard Haass was asked to help find a compromise on three issues: how violent crimes committed during the Troubles should be investigated, whether and when the union flag could fly from public buildings, and what rules should govern parades. Months of negotiations, seven position papers, and visits by the British and Irish prime ministers failed to resolve the issues. But some progress was made in identifying areas of agreement and disagreement and on the issue of historical crimes. (See preceding United Kingdom chapter.)

ECONOMY

In the last half-century, Ireland has undergone an economic revolution. Despite the worst economic recession in memory (and the worst in the eurozone) that plagued the country in 2009 and beyond, fundamentals for the resumption of a strong economy in the future remain in place: a small, open, low-tax economy; an educated, English-speaking, adaptable, and young workforce; and strong European and Atlantic links with an Irish diaspora ready to led a hand. The influx of foreign investment as a result of generous incentives and the increase in trade have added significantly to the prosperity of Ireland. More than 1,100 foreign firms employ half of all Irish workers involved in manufacturing. Foreign companies are also responsible for 80% of the country's nonfood exports. It has also acquired an impressive high-tech industry. By 1986 it had already achieved the highest ratio of high technology to total exports of any EU country.

What made Ireland so rich so quickly? There is a combination of factors: It cut spending, taxes, and borrowing, and it adopted the euro. It established a social partnership between trade unions and management that keeps wages down and respects the opinions of the unions. Labor markets were liberalized, making businesses relatively free to fire and hire. Also employer social security payments are lower. The EU poured in transfers equivalent to almost 5% of Ireland's GDP. The European single market was a boon to trade.

Roughly a fourth of all American investments in Europe go to Ireland; this is more than America invests in China. The US is Ireland's largest source of foreign investment. It is the biggest trade partner for services, the second-largest for trade in goods, and the second-largest market for tourism. Educational standards, including in business administration, engineering, and the sciences, are kept high, and English is spoken.

Although Ireland's birth rate is falling, it still has a relatively young population. Finally, more people are working. More women are in the workforce (54%), and labor-force participation for both sexes has risen from 60% in the 1980s to 70% today.

Outmigration had temporarily ended, and immigrants poured into the country, one-third to one-half of whom had Irish roots. By one estimate, a quarter-million people immigrated between 1995 and 2000. The Irish government estimated that 14,000 Irish returned from the US after 2001, more than half of them from New York. The US Census Bureau reported that by 2005 the Irish population in the US had shrunk by 28,500 to 128,000; the number of illegal Irish had dwindled to 25,000 to 50,000. One million Irish with active passports live outside the country.

The recession that began in 2008 and did continuing severe damage to the Irish economy reversed this inflow at least temporarily. The first to go were immigrants returning home to central Europe, but increasingly it was the Irish themselves, who left to look for greener pastures. In 2011–2012 they were leaving at the rate of 1,000 per week. Total emigration for those between 15 and 44 was 75,800 in 2012. Nearly 60% had university degrees. Almost half of Irish doctors were working abroad. One Irishman noted, "You don't go to parties any more. You go to going-away parties."

Like the UK, Ireland opened its doors to citizens of new EU member states after May 2004. There was an influx of 300,000 from those countries, mainly from Poland, who registered for work. This includes many students looking for temporary jobs while polishing up their English. Dublin's main afternoon newspaper, *The Evening Herald*, includes a Polish-language supplement, and there are other locally published newspapers and magazines available in Polish. Some Irish suspect uneasily that there are now more Polish speakers in the country than Gaelic speakers.

These newcomers were a key factor in the continued strong economic growth rate and for the construction boom. There is no evidence that they have displaced Irish workers, and they are still paid less than the Irish, although the gap is narrowing. But their presence sparked a debate over whether they are driving down wages. Trade unions pointed to Irish Ferries, which wanted to employ cheaper Latvian crews. Seven out of 10 newcomers are from Europe. There are tensions, but no anti-immigrant political movement has emerged.

Growth and prosperity in Ireland was dramatic. Less than 30% of all households are rented. The Irish entered the 1990s with a 50% gap between their living standards and those of the EU average. By 1998 income in Ireland had caught up with the European mean and surpassed Britain in per-capita GDP for the first time in history. Also, a variety of social welfare indicators in Ireland are as good or better than in Britain. Life expectancy for women is 83.5 years and for men 79.5. Ireland spends a higher percentage of its GDP on public education. Per capita consumption rose 10.5% from 1990 to 1996, twice the average rate of increase in the rest of Europe. Sustained economic growth, low inflation, a hard currency (the euro, to which some economists give credit that the recession

A new generation of Irish youth, Kinsale

was not even deeper), a healthy trade surplus, and relatively low unemployment (5.3% in 2019, a 10-year low) cohabited with a growing income gap between rich and poor.

It is an extremely productive, capital-intensive, and modern economy, only partly owned by foreigners, including companies like IBM, Intel, Fujitsu, Pfizer, Google, Facebook, and Motorola, as well as banks and financial institutions, like Citibank, Merrill Lynch, and Daiwa. Nine of the world's 10 top drug companies are there; one-third of all personal computers sold in Europe are manufactured in Ireland; it is the world's largest software exporter (ahead of the US). Dell's computer plant in Limerick was one of the company's most productive, but Dell shocked the country in 2009, when it left Ireland for a location in low-wage eastern Europe. HP Compaq is Galway's largest employer. The country is trying to invest more in research and development so that its own companies can grow to such status. Attracting foreign investment offers the island the best chance to recover economically and repay its debts. FDI pours in even after the recession, especially from America and particularly in the fields of pharmaceuticals, financial services, and information technology. By 2013 employment at foreign companies had returned to precrisis levels.

Agriculture has declined in importance in the last four decades—the percentage of the workforce employed in farming dropped from 43% to 4.7% in 2017; they produce only 2% of GDP. Industry's share in employment is 19%, producing 24% of GDP. Services account for 77% of employment and 74% of GDP. The agricultural life of Ireland benefited from EU membership, although income from the CAP helped fuel the rapid growth of welfare spending and thus contributed to the country's debt problem. Income in the farm sector has doubled in the past three decades, and today one-half of the value of agricultural production is exported. However, family farming remains relatively unsophisticated, and food processing has not developed as far as in some EU countries.

Two other sources of revenue are important to Ireland: tourists and pubs. By 2000 Ireland was the fastest-growing tourist destination in Europe, growing by 12% during the 1990s. Each year 5.5 million tourists (that is more than the number of Irishmen there are to receive them) visit the nation, despite the fact that Ireland is the only EU nation not directly linked to the Continent since the opening of the English Channel "Chunnel" in 1993. Americans account for 14% of the total, although they tend to spend more money than other visitors.

By 2019 the Irish drank in 8,400 pubs; the ratio of 1 pub for every 300 people was even more striking when one knows that half the population is under age 25, and thus the ratio of pubs to those old enough to drink was even higher. Annual alcoholic consumption per Irish adult jumped from 10.6 quarts of pure alcohol in 1985 to nearly 15.8 quarts in 2000, compared with the EU average of 9.5 quarts, despite high taxes on wine and spirits. This was the highest increase in the EU and brought with it more social problems, such as higher absenteeism on the job, auto accidents, and medical care costs.

With alcohol consumption up, both parts of Ireland moved to lower the legal driving blood alcohol content from .08% to .05%. This raised concern from an unexpected quarter—the Catholic Church. Since the number of priests is rapidly decreasing, more and more of them have to drive from church to church to say two or three masses per day. After each service, the priest must consume any communion wine left over since it is considered to be Christ's blood in the Eucharist; throwing it out would be blasphemous. The clergy must therefore sometimes drive impaired from parish to parish.

The air has been healthier since 2004, when smoking was banned throughout the republic in all pubs, restaurants, and workplaces (including company cars and trucks). Only prisons, police cells, psychiatric hospitals, and hotel rooms were exempted. In the decade since 2001, the smoking ban, changing drinking habits, and the economic recession reduced alcohol consumption by 21%. Such sobriety caused 833 pubs to close from 2007 to 2010.

The Irish economy is dependent on events outside of the country because of the important roles that trade and foreign sources of energy play in the life of the island. It is vulnerable to global recessions. It is a land that must import many essential raw materials. It does have a large quantity of zinc ore, as well as copper, sulphur, baryte, gypsum, and dolomite. Its only valuable energy source is peat, or turf bogs, which cover parts of the Central Plain and large areas along the south, west, and northwest coasts. It lacks sizable coal deposits, but it extracts natural gas near Kinsale Head.

Although recent discoveries on the ocean shelf may produce oil for Ireland, at this time the country has very little. Yet 70% of its energy needs are supplied by oil. Thus, the Irish economy was drastically affected by changes in oil prices while remaining dependent upon unstable world trade for its strength. It generates no nuclear power. Peat provides 6% of energy.

Saucy Irish youth

Almost 90% of Ireland's GDP is generated by trade. Manufactured goods account for well over half the value of exports. Since 15% of these go to the United Kingdom (and the percentage is steadily declining) and over half to the continental EU members (a percentage which has steadily risen since 1973), Ireland is vulnerable to economic ups and downs in those industrialized countries. In 2002 it joined 10 other EU nations in adopting the euro. Ireland again presents an image of financial stability that foreign investors like.

In 2015, total public debt stood at 100% of GDP (down from 131% in 1987 but up from 25% in 2007). Its 2004 budget deficit was only .4% of GDP, well below the 3% limit required to meet the EU's convergence criterion for the European currency. These statistics changed dramatically after the 2008 recession. By 2013 its budget deficit was 7.4% of GDP, one of the largest in the EU. Taxes are kept low for foreign firms in order to attract them to invest in Ireland, making it the EU's biggest tax haven. New investors receive tax breaks, and overall corporate tax rates are 12.5%, far below the EU average of more than 30%. Personal taxes also began to be reduced sharply. Ireland still has Europe's highest VAT at 21%.

FT WEEKEND

FINANCIAL TIMES | Saturday June 14 / Sunday June 15 2008 | USA

USA $1.85 Canada C$2.50

LIFE & ARTS COVER STORY
The golden age of tennis
How Wimbledon sells a vision of a bygone era

COMMENT PAGE 7
Dick Fuld
Can the embattled chief executive put Lehman's house in order?

LIFE & ARTS PAGE 3
Diane von Furstenberg
The fashion designer has Lunch with the FT

Newspaper of the year

Inside

Jancis Robinson tastes Chilean wines
Life & Arts Page 6

Irvine Welsh on Obama and the young Americans
Life & Arts Page 2

Anish Kapoor: an artist with a magician's toolkit
Life & Arts Page 16

Garden party Pope breaks with protocol for Bush visit to Vatican

Pope Benedict XVI yesterday broke with protocol by receiving George W. Bush in the Vatican Gardens, reviving a frenzy of speculation in Italian media that the US president might convert to Catholicism. 'Such an honour, such an honour,' Mr Bush said, as the pair entered the medieval St John's Tower for a private discussion **Report, Page 4** AP

Energy costs push up US inflation

By FT reporters

Fears of accelerating global inflation were further heightened yesterday when US consumer prices surged 0.6 per cent in May on the back of rising energy costs.

The jump in the US consumer price index was the largest since last November, as items such as air fares and petrol became much more expensive. However, core consumer prices – which strip out food and energy costs – were reasonably stable, rising only 0.2 per cent. The jump in US inflation came after it emerged that eurozone hourly labour costs rose 3.3 per cent – the fastest rate for five years. In Asia, India's inflation rate hit 8.75 per cent at the end of May – its highest level in seven years – prompting talk

The economic growth that Ireland enjoyed since the mid-1950s was impressive. After averaging 6% from 1993 to 1998, it slowed down. It stood at around 4.6% from 2004 to 2007. In 2009, however, it was deep in negative territory (–7%), and by 2013 the economy had shrunk by a total of 20%. In 2015 it grew by 7%, by far the fastest in the eurozone, and it grew by almost 8% in 2019. Before the recession the economy had speeded ahead so rapidly that Ireland had not had time to revamp its infrastructure. Roads are often clogged, hospitals are overcrowded, and housing is tight and expensive.

Average Dublin real estate prices quadrupled in the decade 1994–2004. Average Irish homes in 2006 cost $450,000 ($600,000 in Dublin), nearly 10 times the average level of industrial wages. This affected a lot of people, since almost a third of the Irish population generating close to 40% of GDP live in or around Dublin. Elsewhere, housing prices rose by 14% in 2003 alone. However, the housing bubble began bursting in 2007, falling almost 4% in that year alone and much more in the following years. In 2013 housing prices were nearly 50% below their peak in 2007; by 2019 they were 20% below. House prices in Dublin had risen by 10% in 2012 and continue to rise.

This severely hurt the economy, since a quarter of it was dependent on the property market, and construction accounted for 13% of economic output. With property values sliding, the banks, which held many bad mortgages, faced collapse, and bankrupt unfinished "ghost estates" became visible evidence of the disaster. The earlier Cowen government made the reckless decision in 2008 to guarantee the six largest banks' liabilities with public money, thereby devastating public finances and forcing Ireland to accept an €67.5 billion ($92.5 billion) bailout from the EU and IMF. Most of that money went to keep the banks afloat. It successfully exited its six-year bailout in December 2013.

Tax revenues plummeted, throwing the country's public finances into even further disarray and shooting the budget deficit upward. The government responded by charging public-sector workers a pension levy of 7.5% on average, which brought 100,000 of them into the streets of Dublin to protest. Taxes were raised, and salaries were cut up to 20% for public workers. As unemployment grew, even more mortgage loans fell into default, and the banks found themselves in an increasingly desperate position without sufficient capital to cover their crippling losses.

Inflation might be higher were it not for a "social partnership" created by government, labor, and business to slow wage-rate increases and secure labor peace. Its 5.3% unemployment in 2019 was below the EU average of 7.9% in 2019 (25% for youth). The earlier low joblessness was partly due to the annual investment by offshore companies, creating directly or indirectly more than 300,000 jobs.

In order to deal with the deep economic recession, the Cowen government introduced the harshest budget in memory in 2009. Taxes were raised, a property tax was introduced, and public expenditures were cut by 6%, including drastic reductions in health care, education, and child and welfare benefits. A hiring freeze was declared. Public employees had their pay cut by an average of 15%, and Cowen cut his own salary by 20% in order to set a good example. Despite a mass public-sector strike over pay cuts in 2009, the largest strike in three decades, the Irish accepted the austerity measures as necessary. There was a sense that all were together in having to accept the bitter medicine.

As the country which had the EU's highest sustained growth in population (more than 8% in four years to 2006, the EU's fastest) and labor force, the republic must provide jobs for those Irishmen who continue to move back to Ireland and from the agricultural into the manufacturing and service sectors. But it must continue to provide work for the growing number of young persons and women who are entering the labor market. The economic boom was also attracting other nationalities, including the British. Immigration to this once-poor island exceeded emigration. Net immigration by 2005 was running about 30,000 per year, but that was reversed by 2011. By 2015 emigrants were returning in droves. Foreign direct investment was flowing in. The government's strategy to create jobs for the EU's youngest labor force was through rapid industrial development, backed by a corporate tax rate of 12.5%.

In the past high unemployment set in motion a disappointing wave of emigration. Almost a fourth of Ireland's adults have lived abroad at some point in their lives. The impressive economic growth reversed the population flight, and skilled workers were returning to Ireland. Labor became scarce in such sectors as electronics, computers, information technology, and building. American firms advertised in American newspapers to fill vacancies in their Irish businesses. The state training agency (FAS) conducted worldwide recruitment, known as Jobs Ireland, to fill vacancies.

The republic's population had soared to 4.7 million in 2012, the highest since 1871 and up 1 million in only a generation. Its population was growing by 2.5% annually and was projected to reach 5 million by 2019. This is true despite the fact that its fertility rate has plummeted and is slightly below the level usually required for a stable population. The country remains underpopulated when one considers that the Irish island had more than 8 million inhabitants in 1841. Both parts of Ireland have only 6 million today. The overall Catholic population has fallen from 91.6% in 1991 to 84% in 2013. The number of Muslims has quadrupled to 19,000 in the same period and is the fastest-growing segment of the population.

The Irish know that they need workers, given their declining birth rate. They have to offer work permits to foreigners in order to meet its labor supply requirements. But the Irish have conflicted feelings about the climate of fear and uncertainty that the resulting diversity has created. Their country has become multicultural, with 17% of the population foreign-born, nearly as high a percentage as in the US. Such diversity has not provoked the kind of conflict found elsewhere in Europe. But there are undercurrents of racial unease, and regrettable racist incidents occur. This was made worse by an economic downturn. The government responded by denying automatic citizenship to immigrant children born in Ireland. This was overwhelmingly approved by almost 80% in a 2004 referendum.

U2 Credit: Anton Corbijn

Ireland grants to citizens of the eight former communist countries that entered the EU in May 2004 the right to enter the country to seek work. But like the UK, it sets a two-year waiting period for them to qualify for social benefits, although the attorney general indicated that such a waiting period might be illegal in the EU. No such limits apply to job seekers from Malta and Cyprus. Some returned home when the 2008–2009 recession struck.

The tradition of spirited trade-union activity has remained in Ireland. This is reflected in the 94 member unions of the Irish Congress of Trade Unions (ICTU), which have affiliates in Northern Ireland. About 60% of working Irishmen are members of unions, which were one among the strongest and most militant in the world. This is no longer true.

CULTURE

Ireland's culture, like its history, reflects the problem of a native people being dominated by a more powerful neighbor. For centuries the natives spoke Gaelic (usually called Irish); the Norman invaders spoke French; but as the English Anglicized them, they came to speak that language as it had evolved in the 14th century. As so many of the Irish-speaking people died or immigrated after the potato famine in the mid-19th century, English came to be the predominant language. Despite efforts to require schoolchildren to learn Gaelic, only 2% of the population (located primarily in the rural areas of the west) speak Irish as a first language. The fact that road signs and official government publications are still in Gaelic is quaint but hardly necessary. In fact, it is so difficult to find someone who speaks it that fluent speakers can wear a lapel pin called a *fainne* to invite others to address them in Irish.

Because of the poverty in which they lived for many centuries, the Irish developed worldwide recognition in only one art form; it required no capital investment—the use of words. The Irish have always prided themselves in their ability to talk and write. Celtic history is rich in legend and folklore, and more recently, a number of authors, poets, and dramatists have achieved international prominence. Whenever one thinks of masters of the English language, the names of Irishmen come to mind. Jonathan Swift, Thomas More, James Joyce, Oliver Goldsmith, John Millington Synge, Sean O'Casey, and Brendan Behan are influential in all of literature. And four Irishmen, William Butler Yeats, George Bernard Shaw, Samuel Becket, and in 1995 Seamus Heaney, won the Nobel Prize for literature. Born in Belfast the son of a potato farmer and cattle dealer, Heaney's poetry is stamped by the simplicity and nature images of his boyhood farm. With his characteristic modesty, he said that he is a mere "foothill of a mountain range" compared to Yeats and Becket. Beloved and popular on both sides of the Irish Sea, Heaney died in 2013, aged 74. Writers like Colm Toibin, Dermot Bolger, Mary O'Donnell, Evelyn Conlon, and Nuala Ni Dhomhnaill are widely read.

The Irish are indeed a musical people, but their music has most often taken the form of widespread participation rather than special expertise of outstanding composers or professional performers. The Celtic harp, along with the shamrock, is one of the most frequently used symbols of Ireland. Harp playing is heard wherever there are groups of expatriate Irish. Many American pioneer songs, bluegrass, and country music (but not western) have Irish roots. In rural Ireland, amateur nights where performers display a variety of talent are still popular. Even today, a visitor to a rural cottage may be told, "Now you mustn't leave until we have a little sing-song." Then all those present will sing together, usually unaccompanied by any musical instrument. The Cork jazz, Wexford opera, and Waterford light opera festivals attract thousands of visitors.

Among the famous Irish musicians is U2, a successful rock group and winner of two Grammy Awards in 1988. Although three out of four are Protestant, their unmistakable Irishness is revealed by the political content of some of their texts, which deal with fighting and dying on their island. The repertoire of the popular Irish American rock band Black 47 is also overtly political, as the title of its debut album, *Fire of Freedom,* indicates. Other musicians, such as Moving Hearts, Fleagh Cowboys, and Mary Coughlan, mix musical styles like rock and traditional and demonstrate that Ireland is still fertile ground for creative music. Ireland is also producing world-class films. A Dublin native, Glen Hansard, and his Czech partner, Marketa Irglova, won the 2008 Academy Award for best song, "Falling Slowly." It was the theme song for the Irish independent movie, *Once,* filmed in Dublin and funded by the Irish Film Board.

Celtic dancing (rhythmical patterns formed by four or eight dancers using rapid foot movements, with the arms usually held down at the sides) has spread around the world. Irish step dancing has burst out of the local parish hall and onto a world stage. The dance show-musicals Riverdance by Bill Whelan and Lord of the Dance starring Chicagoan Michael Flatley and Jean Butler are performing before packed audiences everywhere and are receiving global acclaim. After one performance, an observer claimed, "the speed and coordination took my breath away!" Another noted that Irish vernacular is being married to "American razzmatazz." These dance sensations were part of a larger cultural phenomenon in the 1990s. The Irish are becoming more urban, secular, experimental, self-confident, and less attached to nationalist certainties. Their once-rural-based arts are being transplanted to Dublin, where they find a new cosmopolitan expression and no longer serve a nationalist agenda.

Irish art in both Celtic and medieval times displayed a wild imagination with brightly colored swirls and fantastic figures best represented in the illustrated manuscripts. Until recently, Irish art has tended to copy work being done in England or on the Continent. But in the last quarter-century, there has been a revival of crafts that have used the old Gaelic and medieval symbols to create the beginnings of an indigenous modern art.

Until the 20th century, Ireland had only one university, Trinity College in Dublin, which was founded in 1591 by Queen Elizabeth I. Only recently was it opened to Catholics. In 1908 the National University of Ireland was founded. It has branches in Dublin, Cork, Galway, and Limerick. By 2015, two-thirds of 18-year-olds went on to higher education, compared with only 5% in 1960.

Education is free and compulsory for children through the age of 15. The system pays its teachers more in relation to average earnings than any other land in the OECD. It produces a well-educated workforce, especially at the upper end. This and the use of the English language are very appealing to foreign investors.

Both the postal and telephone services are operated by the government, which claims that 90% of all letters mailed reach their destination within one day. There are seven daily newspapers, five in Dublin and two in Cork. An autonomous public corporation operates radio and television broadcasting; licensing fees are charged, and advertisements also produce revenue.

Dublin, whose graceful Georgian buildings are now falling into the shadow of taller concrete and glass structures, continues to dominate the life of Ireland. A fifth of Eire's population lives within the city's boundaries, and over a quarter lives in greater Dublin. This reflects the fact that Ireland has become much more urban than it once was. It also means that some of Eire's poverty, which was largely confined to rural areas, is now more visible in the congested capital city. Dublin is the center of the nation's cultural, financial, and political life.

FUTURE

The Irish can be proud that Robert Emmet's vision has come true—his country has taken its place among the nations of the earth. They still aspire to unify with Ulster. But election battles are now fought on economic grounds and not over Northern Ireland. Ireland has reacquired the nickname "Celtic Tiger." Some prefer "Celtic Phoenix."

The economy has recovered, and a lot is going right. It has undeniable economic strengths, despite the deep recession that hit most industrialized countries. Economic recovery is steady and impressive. Unemployment is declining. Its exports are booming, but its reliance on foreign companies creates vulnerabilities to the ups and downs of the global economy. FDI is pouring in. Its flexible economy, with a 12.5% corporate tax rate, remains attractive to multinationals seeking a foothold in Europe. Its workforce is young, skilled, and adaptable, and the demographic outlook is favorable. Higher education has expanded dramatically. Almost a third of Irish students were the first in their family to attend university.

Its growing standard of living during the past half-century reached that of the EU, and for the first time in history, it overtook that of Britain. This wealth and success significantly increased the self-confidence and expectations of the Irish people and their demands on the government for continued prosperity.

The failure of any party or alliance to gain a majority in parliament and the frequent elections point to the difficulty any government will have in satisfying these aspirations. The February 2016 general elections were the most inconclusive in recent Irish history. Party leaders faced two months of tense negotiations to find a governing majority. With typical Irish wit, two-time Taoiseach Garret FitzGerald, who passed away in 2011, said before the 1982 election, "Whoever wins the election should have first choice on going into opposition." Enda Kenny emerged from the 2016 elections as head of a minority government.

In June 2017 Kenny stepped down. He was replaced as Taoiseach by Ireland's first openly gay and youngest (38) government leader, Leo Varadkar. The son of a Hindu doctor in Dublin, he was trained as a physician. He has a tenuous hold on power, since his Fine Gail minority government could be brought down at any moment.

By electing two female presidents in a row, including British subject from Northern Ireland Mary McAleese, and then the leftist Michael Higgins in 2011, voters signaled receptivity to reforms which enabled the country to enter the 21st century as a modern European nation. Sometimes the Irish say that their 1960s did not happen until the 1990s. In 1994 a bill was passed "without a ripple of controversy" legalizing same-sex relations. Public opinion loosened restrictions on abortion. Abortion and divorce are legal now. The diminished authority of the Catholic Church was visible in the May 2018 referendum to amend the constitution by giving women unrestricted access to abortions up to the 12th week of pregnancy. Two-thirds voted in favor. In May 2015 a majority of voters approved same-sex marriage in a constitutional referendum. A more liberal Ireland became the first country in the world to legalize same-sex marriage by popular vote. Being gay had been illegal until 1993. The traditional bastions of power and paternalism—state, church, and family business patriarchs—are under assault as never before.

Brexit threatens the current open 500-kilometer border between the two parts. Dublin wants to maintain the open invisible border without customs checkpoints. Northern Irish politics have been unpredictable. Sinn Fein's withdrawal from power sharing in the north caused Stormont's dissolution for over a year, well into 2018. Mary Lou McDonald replaced the retiring Gerry Adams as party leader and seeks to soften the party's image.

Ireland is justified in being optimistic about its own future. It took vigorous steps to deal with its financial crisis. Its society is stable. It no longer suffers from a lack of confidence, and it is no longer as sensitive about its relations with Britain. The queen's visits to Ireland in May 2011 and Northern Ireland in June 2012 turned a new page in the ties between the two countries, which she called "firm friends and equal partners." Nevertheless it commemorated the centenary of the Easter Rebellion in 2016.

At least one village watched the 2008 US presidential elections closely. Moneygall (population 300) in County Offaly unearthed records indicating that Barack Obama's great-great-great-grandfather, Fulmuth Kerney, grew up there before leaving for America at age 19. His line eventually produced Obama's mother, Ann Durham. A bemused Obama had to admit that "I've got pieces of everybody in me." His unpopular successor, Donald Trump, owns a golf resort on the west coast of Ireland.

When leaving for Paris in 1939, Irish dramatist Samuel Becket claimed that he preferred France at war to Ireland at peace. His country has changed dramatically. Frank McCourt, whose best-selling *Angela's Ashes* describes his youth in a poor and hide-bound Ireland before and during the Second World War, said about Ireland in the late 1990s, "When I go back I see it in a way the kids walk. The confidence. It's almost saucy. We have entered the age of Irish sauciness. God help us all."

THE IRISH TIMES WEEKEND

irishtimes.com

Pat's chat
Why he left RTÉ

MAGAZINE

Age-old rivalry
Can Kerry last the pace?

SPORTS WEEKEND

Seamus Heaney
1939-2013

Between my finger and my thumb
The squat pen rests.
I'll dig with it.

Michael Lynn's arrest
State makes its move

Comfort is best found in his poems

When

France

Area: 211,208 sq. mi. (547,026 km). This is the largest country in western Europe, four-fifths the size of Texas and four times the size of New York State.

Population: 67 million.

Capital City: Paris (pop. 2.4 million within city limits, 9.1 million within metropolitan Paris).

Climate: Pleasant, rather temperate, except in the south, where the weather resembles that of Florida.

Neighboring Countries: Belgium, Luxembourg, Germany (north and northeast); Switzerland (east); Italy and Monaco (southeast); Spain and Andorra (southwest).

Official Language: French.

Ethnic Background: Indo-European, of diverse origin.

Principal Religions: Roman Catholic (85%), Muslim (8.3%), Protestant (2%), Jewish (1%).

Main Exports and Imports: Capital equipment; consumer goods; automobiles and transport equipment, agricultural products, including wine and spirits; energy.

Major Trading Partners: EU (60.9% of exports and 67.3% of imports), Germany (16.8% of exports and 18.8% of imports), Italy (8.3% of exports and 7.6% of imports), Belgium (7.4% of exports and 11.1% of imports), Spain (7.5% of exports and 6.5% of imports), UK (6.7% of exports and 5.1% of imports), US (5.1% of exports), Netherlands (7.4% of imports), China (5% of imports).

Currency: Euro.

National Holiday: July 14, anniversary of the storming of the Bastille Prison in Paris in 1789, the spark that brought the French Revolution to an explosion.

Chief of State: Emmanuel Macron, President (since May 2017).

Head of Government: Edouard Philippe, Prime Minister (since May 2017). Unlike many nations where the presidency is merely ceremonial, France has a chief executive with broad powers. The prime minister concerns himself primarily with the daily workings of the government, and he also can wield great power if he is from a different party than that of the president.

National Flag: The tricolor—three broad vertical stripes, blue, white, red.

France is a land of visible contrasts. In many ways it appears divided. Within the past two and a quarter centuries, during which time the United States has had one continuous political system, France has experienced three monarchies, two empires, a half-dozen republics, and more than a dozen constitutions; its history is strewn with revolutions, counterrevolutions, and coups d'état, and its political party system is extremely fragmented. General de Gaulle, the founder of the present French Republic, once asked in exasperation how one could ever rule a land that has more than 300 different cheeses! Yet there is an underlying stability in contemporary France and a strong consensus concerning the importance of respecting individual rights and of maintaining a republican, democratic form of government. Indeed, France is one of a minority of stable democracies in the world and is therefore a haven for political refugees.

France also is highly centralized politically, economically, and culturally. The predominance of Paris is undeniable. No successful revolution ever began outside of Paris. King Henry IV's famous statement in 1593 justifying his conversion to Catholicism, that "Paris is worth a mass," was an early reminder that control over France must emanate from Paris and not from the provinces. The French capital often seems to be the place where French history is made and then merely presented to the provinces as the finished product. With a population as great as the entire continent of Australia (roughly one out of five Frenchmen lives in Paris or its suburbs), it is the residence of a fourth of France's civil servants and doctors, a third of its students and half of its university professors, two-thirds of its artisans and authors, a fifth of its factory workers and factories employing more than 25 persons, and two-thirds of its company and bank headquarters. Efforts since 1955 to decentralize the French economy have met with little success.

At the same time, France is a land of great diversity in terms of religion, landscape, language, customs, and styles of living. Such ethnic minorities as the Basques, the Alsatians, the Bretons, the West Indians, and the Corsicans preserve their own languages and cultures. Only in Corsica is there a serious movement for autonomy that enjoys any appreciable popular backing. There are other small and largely irrelevant movements in Brittany, the Basque region, and elsewhere. In general, ethnic diversity does not threaten the present French state to the degree that it does other European countries, such as Ireland, Belgium, and Spain.

France, it has often been said, is "weighed down by history." Frenchmen have a long memory for their own past, although they do not always agree about its high and low points. Yet, far from being a country exclusively living in the past, contemporary France is a highly dynamic and forward-looking nation. It is among the wealthiest, most technologically advanced, and most influential countries in the world. Clearly, France has a future, but Frenchmen would say that they have a *destiny*. From the time of the Crusades, the first of which was practically an entirely French affair, to the present day, Frenchmen have felt a sense of mission to civilize the world. In the 21st century, they still believe in "French exceptionalism," even as they grope for a clear French identity in the face of massive Arab and African immigration and de facto multiculturalism.

Perhaps no one expressed this mission better than the great realist de Gaulle, who opened his war memoirs with the following words: "All my life I have had a certain idea of France. This is inspired by sentiment as much as by reason. The emotional side of me tends to imagine France, like the princess in the fairy stories or the Madonna in the frescoes, as dedicated to an exalted and exceptional destiny. Instinctively I have the feeling that Providence has created her either for complete successes or for exemplary misfortunes. . . . But the positive side of my mind also assures me that France is not really herself unless in the front rank; that only vast enterprises are capable of counterbalancing the ferments of dispersal which are inherent in her people; that our country, as it is, surrounded by the others, as they are, must aim high and hold itself straight, on pain of mortal danger. In short, to my mind, France cannot be France without greatness."

The general, who once admitted that he preferred France to Frenchmen, disdained the petty squabbling of everyday politics. He denied that the essential France was to be found in the yawning provincial bureaucrat, the scandalous French president (Felix Faure) who died in the presidential palace while making love to his mistress, or the impetuous Parisian pamphleteer who plots to bring down the regime. He believed that one must inhale the heady air of the mountain peaks in order to see the true France: "Viewed from the heights, France is beautiful."

France is at the same time an Atlantic, continental, and Mediterranean country, and it is territorially the largest country in Europe west of Russia. The country is somewhat hexagonal in shape with rather regular contours. It stretches roughly 600 miles (960 km) from north to south and west to east. Through it flow five great rivers, the Seine, Loire, Garonne, Rhône, and Rhine, which originate in the central land mass (Massif Central) or in the mountains of the Alps and the Pyrenees. It faces three seas (the North Sea, the Atlantic Ocean and the Mediterranean) and has a coastline of more than 1,200 miles (1,930 km).

In the north, there are no natural barriers to separate France from northern Europe. Elsewhere, the Rhine River separates France from Germany, the Alps from

From atop Notre Dame Cathedral, a stone gargoyle stares vacantly over the Seine River and the rooftops of Paris to the distant Eiffel Tower. Courtesy: Jon Markham Morrow

Switzerland and Italy, and the Pyrenees from Spain. The geographical relief of France begins from the coastline to the valleys, and then rises to plateaus, highlands, and finally to mountains, the highest being Mont Blanc in the Alps (15,777 feet; 4,807 meters) and Mont Vignemale in the Pyrenees (10,804 feet; 3,293 meters).

Although France is large, it has the lowest population density in the European Union (EU). Its total population and economic riches are very unevenly distributed geographically. If one were to draw a line on the map of France from the northern port of Le Havre to Grenoble and then on to Marseilles (which school children learn as the *diagonale du vide*—"diagonal of emptiness"), one could see two halves of a country as different from one another as northern Italy is from southern Italy. The western half of France contains 56% of the territory, but only 37% of its people, and is steadily losing population. It tends to be less industrialized, and its agriculture is based on small farms and is therefore less efficient. East of the line are 80% of France's industrial production and three-fourths of the industrial employees. Economic development is particularly rapid in the northeast of France and recently in the Rhône-Alps and Marseilles regions. Farming tends to be more intensive and efficient, and a far smaller percentage of inhabitants live agriculturally.

Geographic and demographic statistics can hardly convey the beauty that for centuries has been called *la belle France*. The visitor invariably finds himself charmed by the smell of rich vines heavy with grapes; by the rolling green countryside studded with more castles than one finds in any other country; by the towering cathedrals whose bells resound throughout the countryside; by the warm beaches along the Riviera; and by the majestic, snow-capped peaks. As one begins to realize how this beauty blends with the Frenchman's proverbial joie de vivre ("joy of living"), one sees why the Germans have always described the good life as "living like God in France."

HISTORY

The Early Period

Although France has played a prominent role in European history for at least 1,500 years, it did not become a national entity or even approximately achieve its present shape until the 16th century AD. The legend of French unity goes back to Vercingetorix, the chief of a Gallic tribe called the Arverni, who led a coalition in an uprising against the Roman occupiers in 52 BC. Although he placed his foot soldiers in a hopeless strategic position and squandered his cavalry before the critical phase of the battle had begun, resulting in his troops' and his own capture, he is seen as the first patriot and resistance hero of French history.

The French profess a close kinship to the Gauls. But the latter were a people who left no literature, no language, and no laws; who worshipped many gods and practiced human sacrifice; and who, according to the Roman arch at Orange, fought naked, their hair buttered and in a long looped knot, with drooping mustaches and long narrow shields. It is doubtful that such a race had a profound impact on the French people and their civilization. Frenchmen today are amused by the caricature of the early Gaulois in the popular *Asterix* comic books.

They no doubt owe far more to the Romans, who occupied for centuries much of what is now France. The Romans built towns, roads, aqueducts, and theaters. They provided examples of centralization, efficient bureaucracy, written law, and a periodic census. They brought education and culture to France and gave the French an appreciation of abstractions. They also left a tradition of grandeur, spotting France with statues and monuments. Finally, their language—vulgarized by common usage—later developed into French.

Even before the fall of the Roman Empire in the 5th century, France had become an invasion ground for tribes from all over the known world: Visigoths, Burgundians, Alemans, and Franks (Germans who eventually gave the country its name). In the 8th and 9th centuries, Charlemagne, the warrior king who established himself as "emperor of the west," absorbed what is now France into a huge political unit encompassing much of present Europe, from Saxony to the island of Elba, including Bavaria and most of Lombardy in Italy. This great empire, however, did not survive his death in 814 AD, and France again became fragmented.

The Capets Claim Paris

Not until a century and a half later did conditions begin to develop which were favorable to unity. In 987 the Capet family, who owned large tracts of land around the region now called the Île-de-France, raised a claim of dynastic leadership over France. The Capetians chose as their capital a small town nearby, which had been established in 100 BC on a five-acre island in the middle of the river Seine by a curly-headed Celtic tribe of fishermen and navigators called Parisii. The Romans had named this city Lutetia and had built it up to a town of from 6,000 to 10,000 inhabitants. The city had also served as capital for the Frankish king Clovis, who had defeated the last remnants of the retreating Romans in 486.

The Capetians adopted Francien, a Latin-based dialect spoken around Paris, as their official language. Hugues Capet, born in 938, was the first Frankish king who could speak no German, and as a result of the Capetian example, German and Latin soon disappeared from the early French court. French became the language of the elite, both at the court and abroad (for example, Marco Polo wrote about his travels to China in French), and the political and military successes of the French dynasty gradually led to the language's adoption by all the people. This language became a powerful agent in the formation and expansion of the French nation and civilization. For that reason, few peoples in the world try so hard to preserve and spread their language as do the French.

Crusades

The First Crusade in the 11th century, sponsored by the French pope Urban II and organized by the French cleric Peter the Hermit, was conducted almost exclusively by the French knights. While building castles in Lebanon and establishing a Kingdom of Jerusalem (which endured at least in name until the 15th century), they showed a zealous sense of mission in extending French civilization, which they tended to see as embodying Christian values. This became a major rationale for most French military and colonial enterprises in the centuries to follow.

A crucial by-product of the Crusades was the weakening of the feudal bonds which tied serfs to their lords. French noblemen were often left penniless by the military expenses they bore, and many times they obtained needed money by freeing serfs and selling charters to cities. By the 13th century, serfdom had almost disappeared in France, and cities had sprung up everywhere, partly because of the trade the Crusades had created. Spices and textiles from the Orient were highly desired by the Europeans, and cities became the crossroads for such trade. France prospered.

Another indirect example of French expansionism occurred when William the Conqueror invaded England in 1066, conquering the Anglo-Saxons by 1070. Although French largely displaced Anglo-Saxon initially, at least at the court, the latter soon revived, and the two languages were combined, enriching each other. Court decisions and proceedings by the 12th century were written in a curious combination of English, French, and Latin. But William retained his holdings in Normandy, Maine, Touraine, and Anjou within what is now France; this later became a source of friction between the French and the English. William's great-grandson, the incompetent King John of

Crusaders and Saracens in battle (from a 12th-century stained-glass window)

England, lost many of the French territories in the early 13th century.

By the end of the 12th century, France, especially Paris (which by that time was the most populous city in Europe), was considered to be the world center of science and culture, having replaced Athens and Rome. In the 14th century, one-half of the people in the Christian world lived in what is now France.

Disorganization and Weak Monarchs

Despite the establishment of a unique language and a French dynasty, French history, until the 16th century, continued to be characterized most of the time by weak kings struggling against foreign rulers and by powerful, rebellious French noblemen, who often did not hesitate to ally with foreign powers against their king. Such division exposed France to the danger of absorption into a large kingdom dominated by England because of its control over much of France. But in the 13th and 14th centuries, three powerful French kings, Philippe Augustus, Louis IX (canonized in 1297 as Saint Louis), and Philippe IV (the Fair), succeeded in wresting control of some of the English domains in France. They began the slow process of patching France together, sometimes by legitimate feudal claims, often by intermarriage, and very often by war. However, England maintained its huge foothold in Aquitaine, acquired in 1154 and encompassing most of southwestern France below the Loire River; England was also allied with the Burgundians north of the Loire. In the 14th and 15th centuries, the French kings waged a Hundred Years' War to finally drive the English out of France.

Joan of Arc

In the midst of this struggle, a female savior emerged from the small village of Domremy in Lorraine. At the age of 16, Joan of Arc, the daughter of a French shepherd, claimed to have heard the voices of the Saints Michel and Catherine commanding her to free the besieged city of Orléans and to have the French king crowned in Reims. Having persuaded a French captain to give her a horse and an armed guard and flying a white flag, she set off to find the king. She told a distrustful Charles VII that she would drive the English out of France and be "the lieutenant of the king of heaven who is king of France."

Dressed in a man's armor and displaying remarkable skill in improving offensive military operations, she liberated Orléans, defeated the enemy forces at Patay and Troyes, and amid enthusiastic crowds proceeded to Reims to have the 26-year-old Charles VII crowned on July 17, 1429, in the way traditionally prescribed for French kings. Whenever she addressed the crowds as "Frenchmen," the response indicated that a new nationalism mingled with a divine mission was emerging.

Short-lived was the fortune of this girl. Dressed in men's clothing and violating the feudal law barring women from combat, she was distrusted by the clergy, the nobility, and even the newly crowned king. Mounted on a beautiful horse, she led her forces in a vain attempt to storm Paris and Compiègne, and though wounded by an arrow, she tried unsuccessfully to rally her troops. She was captured in May 1430 and delivered to the Duke of Burgundy, who was allied with the English and who sold her to them for a high fee. She was tried in Rouen by a French ecclesiastical court and, despite her own eloquent defense, was pronounced guilty of heresy. On May 30 she was burned at the stake in Rouen's marketplace, without the ungrateful king having made the slightest effort to save her.

Centuries later there is still no consensus in France concerning the legacy she had left. A monarchical France before 1789 had little use for saviors from the masses, and her mystical, religious aura made her out of place in an enlightened, revolutionary France. Nevertheless, Napoleon had a beautiful statue of her erected in Orléans in 1803, and the process to have her made a saint was initiated in 1869. Not until the humiliating defeat of France at the hands of the Prussians in 1870 was she embraced as a symbol of vengeance toward an outside power that had taken her native Lorraine. She was finally canonized in 1920.

Joan of Arc is to many Frenchmen the ideal symbol of patriotism: a pure lady warrior with a sense of mission who placed God solidly on the side of the French. She is undoubtedly the Madonna in de Gaulle's memoirs who incorporated France, since the great French leader also adopted the cross of Lorraine as his own symbol. His stubborn, righteous defense of France's destiny moved an exasperated Englishman, Sir Winston Churchill, to remark that "of all the crosses I have had to bear, the heaviest was the Cross of Lorraine."

Further Union Followed by Religious Wars

By 1453 the English had been driven from France, except for a tiny foothold in the northern port city of Calais. The Hundred Years' War had nevertheless been a cruel disaster for the French people. Within a century, the war and the plagues that had struck at roughly the same time had reduced the population by almost one-half. In the closing years of that century, Brittany, which had been independent, was integrated into France. Anne of Brittany, who in 1491 married the French king Charles VIII, sealed the union. She took her native Brittany as a dowry. Upon his death she married the next French king, Louis XII, in 1499 in order to preserve this union. Though France had made impressive strides toward territorial unity in the 15th century, the century to follow was not to be one of peace and unity.

In 1519 a minor German priest named Martin Luther courageously raised a challenge of faith to the powerful Catholic Church and began the Reformation that spread throughout the Christian world. A Frenchman, John Calvin, also developed a religious doctrine hostile to the church and was forced to flee to the Swiss city of Geneva, which he soon shaped into a Protestant "capital." He left behind a France seriously divided into two sects: the Huguenots (Protestant) and the Catholics. From 1559 until 1598, the Wars of Religion raged in France; this was a chaotic period dotted by eight distinct wars, assassinations, and massacres. These unfortunate events were related to the issue of the king's and other nobility's respective powers, as much as to theological matters.

The situation became particularly grave in 1572, when 4,000 Protestants gathered in Paris for the wedding of the 19-year-old King Henry of Navarre to Charles IX's sister. Henry, whose life was under threat, had announced his conversion to Catholicism, ostensibly to heal fanatical religious divisions in France. The Protestants were massacred on orders of the French king, and they promptly responded to this St. Bartholomew's Day Massacre by announcing that such a treacherous king was no longer to be obeyed. Henry quickly reassumed the Protestant faith, and the wars raged on. All involved finally realized in 1598 that the strife was without any redeeming value. Upon becoming king, Henry issued the Edict of Nantes, which promised Frenchmen religious freedom. Nevertheless, the religious issue continued to gnaw away at the unity of France for more than three centuries.

Joan of Arc triumphantly enters Reims.

The French Century

The 17th century became "the French century" in all of continental Europe. This was a period when forceful French kings and brilliant royal advisers succeeded in reducing much of the French nobility's powers and in establishing the present borders of France. The glitter of the royal court soon dazzled Europe.

When in 1624 Louis XIII chose an ambitious cardinal to be his chief adviser, he gained at his side a tireless servant of the French Crown and the French state. Cardinal Richelieu was not a man given to courtly debauchery, theological hair-splitting, or listening for voices from God. "Reason must be the standard for everything," he said, and "the public interest ought to be the sole objective of the prince and his counselors." Raison d'état ("reason of state"), the interests of the community, became for him the overriding concerns.

Since Richelieu was convinced that only absolute monarchical authority could elevate his country to the highest rank in the world, he proceeded to neutralize any powers that could challenge the central authority of the king. He had torn down all castles not belonging to the king that could be used to resist royal authority. In a swashbuckling era presented so vividly in Alexander Dumas's *The Three Musketeers*, Richelieu dared to ban dueling, a favorite pastime of the nobility, on the grounds that weapons should be drawn only against enemies of the state. While not attacking religious principles, he whittled away at the privileges granted in 1598 to Protestants, believing that a free, powerful Protestant party in France could easily undermine the centralized power of France.

At the same time, he sent money and troops to support the Protestants in the Thirty Years' War that ravaged Germany from 1618 to 1648. His reasons were simple: although Austria and Spain were fighting in the name of Catholicism, their victory in the struggle would have strengthened these great powers and thus presented a greater threat to France. Further, by sending French troops southward, eastward, and northward, France acquired territory along the way. France's borders thus moved outward. Clearly, the cardinal did not think religiously; he thought *French*. When he died in 1642 (followed in death a few months later by Louis XIII), he left behind an almost-unchallenged central authority, a powerful French army, a small but effective fleet, and a highly organized professional diplomatic service. He also established French as the new diplomatic language for the world, a position it enjoyed for more than 250 years. Above all, he left a tradition of total dedication to the power and glory of France.

Louis XIV, Cardinal Mazarin, and Anarchy

Louis XIV became king in 1643 at the age of five. This renowned monarch was able to build on the great works of Cardinal Richelieu and on the works of another cardinal who, though extremely unpopular, held France together against an angry and dangerous storm until the young king was ready to assume the reins of government. Cardinal Mazarin was a wealthy Italian, whose love of money did not prevent him from energetically serving the young king's mother and regent, Queen Anne, with whom he reportedly had more than just cordial relations.

Picking up where Richelieu had left off, Mazarin led France to victories over Austria. The Treaty of Westphalia in 1648 and subsequent victories over Spain left France the foremost power in Europe. Austria was seriously weakened, and Germany was fragmented, depopulated, and exhausted. French strength and German "weakness" through division remained a cornerstone of French politics until 1990. Indeed, many Frenchmen would have echoed the words spoken by the 1952 Nobel Prize for literature laureate and Gaullist political commentator François Mauriac after the Second World War: "I like Germany so much that I am glad there are two of them."

Having achieved a position of power in Europe, France became seriously weakened internally. From 1648 to 1653, it was rocked by a complicated series of civil disturbances which threatened the young king's hold on the throne and which in some ways anticipated the French Revolution that occurred a century and a half later. The parliament, the bourgeoisie (a class of persons who had risen socially above the level of peasants and manual laborers but who had no titles of nobility), and the Parisian mobs, all for their own reasons, created such an anarchical situation in Paris that the king and his mother were forced to flee to the palace of St. Germain, where they lived at Mazarin's personal expense.

Some French nobles invited the Spanish troops to reenter France, and Parisian mobs erected barricades and took law into their own hands. In the prolonged confusion, battles raged in the countryside and the streets of Paris, and finally Mazarin was forced to flee to Germany. However, after all order had disappeared, the key figures of this uprising, known as the *fronde* (named after the French word for "slingshot," used by rioters to smash windows in Paris), surprisingly lost their nerve, and this revolt against the centralized monarchy and the unpopular Mazarin gradually collapsed.

The 14-year-old Louis led his loyal troops in 1652 into a tired and shamed Paris. Louis never forgave the rebellious city and wasted little time in removing himself from the clutches of this beautiful but tempestuous and unfaithful mistress. The rupture between the king and Paris would later have disastrous consequences for the monarchy.

Louis Comes of Age

Immediately after Mazarin's death, the young king called a meeting of all the court's advisers and announced, "Now it is time that I rule!" No one questioned this. By then, the 23-year old monarch's imposing physical dignity and his polished manners, combined with an unhesitating decisiveness, rapidly brought him respect within France, which sometimes bordered on worship. France was weary of chaos and was ready to kiss the hand that ruled with firm authority. His prodigious lovemaking at the court, which has certainly lost nothing in the telling, greatly irritated his mother. But it did not prevent him from being a hardworking and effective king. Almost no state affairs escaped his attention; in 1661 he commanded his ministers not to sign or seal any order without his permission.

The entire kingdom increasingly felt the impact of the royal government. When the affairs of state became too great for one man to handle, he developed a bureaucracy and efficient procedures to enable his government to absorb the workload. All aspects of French foreign affairs, defense, finance, commerce, religion, and the royal household were channeled through the king's court. He appointed officials to secure royal control over all activities in the various regions in France. He supervised all major appointments in his bureaucracy and the army. Although there is no evidence that he ever really said "I am the state," there was no question that he would have readily agreed with such an assertion. He actually worked very hard to live up to his rather arrogant motto: *Nec pluribus impar* ("None his equal").

As a symbol of his magnificence, the "Sun King" ordered that a royal palace be built in Versailles, which would not only be at a safe distance from Paris but also would be unsurpassed in all of Europe for its beauty and dignity. For 20 years he had this gigantic structure, with its surrounding gardens, fountains, and smaller palaces, built and rebuilt. His finance minister, Colbert, was exasperated by the project, which almost emptied the royal treasury and which could only be financed by selling many of the state's treasures. However, once finished, this palace became the assembly point for much of France's ambitious nobility. There Louis could keep an eye on them and busy them with ritual duties, such as buttoning his coat or escorting the servants who brought his food to the royal table. Louis's preeminence was such that nobles competed for the honor of performing even the most menial functions at his court. For instance, the princess of Ursins, who later became the queen of Spain, was considered one of the luckiest persons at the court of Versailles because she performed the task of handing the king his dagger and night pot each evening as he retired to his private bedroom.

Under the conscientious guidance of Louis XIV, France achieved an incomparable political, military, and cultural ascendancy. The arts bloomed, and France was the richest and most populous country in

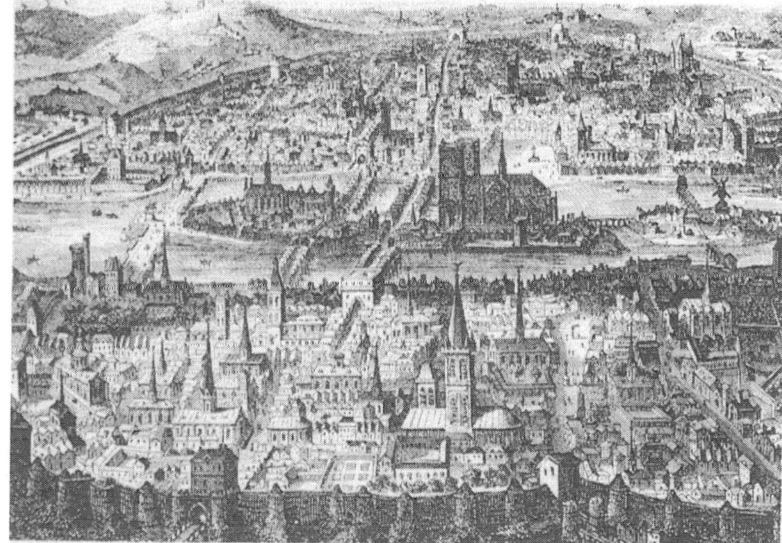

Paris in the 17th century

Europe. It also acquired the most powerful army on the Continent, and Louis was more than willing to use it. He conducted almost continuously destructive wars. He thereby was able to establish France's present borders, but he ultimately converted almost every country in Europe into an enemy of France. He ordered that the Palatinate in the western part of Germany be burned, resulting in the destruction of Heidelberg, Mannheim, Speyer, Worms, and hundreds of smaller towns. His soldiers ripped the bones of earlier Holy Roman emperors out of their graves in Speyer, a sacrilege that was not soon forgotten in Germany. The Treaty of Utrecht finally established an uneasy peace in 1713, two years before the king's death.

Even if France gradually exhausted itself financially and physically through almost-continuous warfare, it was certainly well administered. Louis's powers were broad, and he used them with great energy. However, he could by no means be called a dictator in the modern sense. He had to deal with a limited national treasury, an absence of a national police force, ineffective and slow means of communication, and regions that still jealously guarded their remaining powers. All in all, he gave Frenchmen an era which they still proudly call "the grand century."

Louis XIV, the "Sun King." Probably painted at about age 55+, it indicates he had lost his teeth, was overweight, and had bunions from wearing high heels and a double chin.

Stirrings of Discontent

The "Sun King" long outlived all of his children, and upon his death his five-year-old great-grandchild was crowned Louis XV. The new king ruled until 1774, when Louis XVI, a good man who never wanted to be king, succeeded to the throne. Both were rather weak and increasingly unpopular kings who were unable to guide their country's adjustment to the changes that occurred in French society during the 18th century. This was a formula for revolution. Greatly contributing to and benefiting from France's prosperity, the bourgeoisie resented its exclusion from political responsibility, which was almost entirely in the hands of the aristocracy. The rural peasantry, which comprised 80% of the population and owned 40% of the land, resented the aristocracy's rights to hunt on their land; its local police power; and its near-monopoly over rural mills, bake shops, and wine presses. The manorial lords appeared to live well without performing an obviously useful function.

The dissatisfaction with the aristocracy was fed by the enlightened ideas of the time. In the course of the 18th century, such thinkers as Montesquieu, Voltaire, and Diderot had brilliantly chipped away at the foundations of aristocratic society. An irreverent Frenchman named Jean-Jacques Rousseau had written in his bombshell book, *The Social Contract*, that "man was born free, but everywhere he is in chains," and he had proposed provocative ways of breaking these chains and creating a society of free and equal human beings. Rousseau was driven from France because of these ideas. He died in 1778.

Events in America that same year caused revolutionary ideas to pour in that brought the soup to a boil. A young revolutionary named Thomas Jefferson from Virginia had written, "all men are created equal and are endowed with unalienable rights." In rapid succession, the 13 colonies began to produce democratic constitutions, which were translated almost immediately into French and avidly read by intelligent persons grown weary of social hierarchy and inherited privilege. Benjamin Franklin, who was sent to France to persuade the government to help the American colonies in the struggle against the English, was lionized by France's high society. His rustic, egalitarian wisdom

The Mature Benjamin Franklin, 1777

Courtesy of Special Collections, University of Virginia Library was the talk of Paris. Most importantly, he persuaded France's leaders, who had lost their colonies in North America to the English in the Seven Years' War (1756–1763), to enter the struggle against the British. French assistance to the rebellious colonies was a very important contributing factor in the American victory; without the French army and navy, perhaps the ill-equipped and militarily untrained colonists would never have prevailed against their masters.

While the French government slapped its traditional enemy in the face, it had unknowingly allowed the bacillus of freedom to enter France through the back door. Some officers and many noncommissioned officers returned to France deeply moved by the events in America of which they had been a part, and they were very sympathetic and supportive of revolutionary movements in their own country. The world now had a concrete model of a large country ruling itself in a republican way.

Financial Woes Lead to Revolution

Another unforeseen consequence of France's aid to the Americans was that it brought France to the brink of bankruptcy; it doubled the national debt and consumed more than one half of the crown's income. It was not an extravagant court that caused France's desperate financial situation; only 5% of the public expenditures were devoted to the entire royal establishment. The French Revolution did not spring from a naïve, spendthrift Queen Marie Antoinette (called by the people "Madame Deficit") who was reported (incorrectly) to have asked why the peasants did not eat cake if they had no bread.

One-fourth of France's budget was devoted to war costs, and a whopping one-half was needed to service France's debts. Other countries, such as England, had similar expenditures, but France's financial crisis could not be solved because of its archaic and unequal tax system. The aristocracy and the wealthy bourgeoisie either evaded or won exemptions from taxation. The church also refused to pay taxes, so the tax collectors could turn only to the poorest French citizens. Thus, although the country was generally prosperous, the public treasury was empty.

Louis XVI, who like his predecessor had often opposed the aristocracy and sought strength from the bourgeoisie, well understood the problem, but he was so weak and unpopular that he could do nothing about it. In desperation, he convened an Estates General in May 1789, the first such meeting in a century and a half. However, the class antagonism in France was such that the three classes assembled (clergy, aristocracy, and bourgeoisie) simply could not work out reform in cooperation.

On June 17, 1789, the bourgeois element (the "Third Estate") decided to declare itself the National Assembly. When the king panicked and closed the hall in which the Third Estate met, the latter moved to a nearby indoor tennis court and proclaimed in the Oath of the Tennis Court that it was the true representative of the people and that it would not disband until it had produced a constitution for France. This was a revolutionary step, unleashing explosive events that an irresolute king could not control. It was the first act in the French Revolution, which went through many stages and lasted 10 years. Whether or not these events represented "the end of history," as the Prussian philosopher Friedrich Hegel maintained, neither France nor the world would thereafter be the same.

Revolution

The events at the Versailles meetings stirred up crowds in Paris, who began to look for weapons in arsenals and public buildings. On July 14, 1789, a crowd went to the Bastille, which, like the Tower of London, was a stronghold built during the Middle Ages to overawe the city and to provide a place of detention for influential prisoners. When the official in charge of the stronghold refused to distribute any weapons, the crowd successfully stormed the fortress. The mob, infuriated that almost 100 persons had been killed, slaughtered the guards who had surrendered. They then beheaded the commanding official with knives and paraded around Paris with the heads of their victims on spikes. This bloody skirmish and macabre display was a harbinger of ferocious acts to come. Nevertheless, Frenchmen celebrate July 14 today as their major holiday.

The unrest and violence spread to the countryside as manorial lords saw their properties sacked and burned by bitter peasants. The more fortunate escaped with their lives, but royal power vanished quickly. The Marquis de Lafayette, a revolutionary-minded aristocrat who had been a favorite on George Washington's staff during the American War of Independence, was given command over the guard in Paris. He designed a flag for the new France to replace the blue and white fleur-de-lis ("lily flower"). He combined the colors of the city of Paris, red and blue, with the white of the House of Bourbon. Thus, the tricolor, which is France's flag today, represented a fusion of the new and old regimes.

The sudden acts of violence had frightened the ruling group into granting important concessions. On August 4, 1789, the nobles relinquished their feudal rights, and on August 27 the National Assembly promptly proclaimed the Declaration of the Rights of Man. The US ambassador to France and author of the American Declaration of Independence, Thomas Jefferson, was asked to read and improve this French equivalent before its publication. He was also requested to sit in the National Assembly during the writing of the French constitution. He declined both requests for diplomatic reasons, although he was a passionate supporter in the young US of the French Revolution. This French declaration was one of history's most eloquent assertions of equality before the law; of the opening of public service to all classes; and

Lafayette and Washington in Harlem, New York

Thomas Jefferson

Courtesy of Special Collections, University of Virginia Library

France

Count de Mirabeau
Courtesy of Special Collections, University of Virginia Library

LA MARSEILLAISE.

of freedom as an unalienable individual right, limited only by the freedom of others. An enlightened constitutional monarchy was established. The king was forced to return to the Tuileries Palace in Paris. There he would be under the watchful eye of France's new, moderate regime, guided by Count de Mirabeau, who, like many aristocrats, had concluded that the future lay with the Third Estate.

Revolution Out of Control

It is always a great misfortune when moderate and democratic revolutionaries cannot control the beast of revolution once it has been uncaged. As in Russia a century and a quarter later, a more radical "second revolution" often overtakes the first one, wiping away many of the democratic gains in the process. This misfortune befell the French Revolution.

The first signal for such a change came on the night of June 21, 1791, when the king and his family attempted to escape to Germany. Caught at Varennes, close to the border, two days later, they were brought back to the Tuileries without glory and locked up in their palace. After this clumsy move, the king's commitment to the new order was no longer credible, and the people's loyalty to the king, which had already been eroded, disappeared entirely.

This new situation greatly angered the other monarchies of Europe, especially those of Prussia and Austria. The moderate Girondists, members of a revolutionary club whose name derived from the department (state) of Gironde and who had gained a majority in the National Assembly in 1792, responded to what they saw as a clear external threat to the revolution. They declared war on Austria. It went badly for France, but it quickly added a new element to the revolution. Seeing the "fatherland in danger," the citizens took up arms, and patriotism rose to fever pitch.

Nationalism and revolution joined hands as the French national anthem, the "Marseillaise," indicates. First sung in April 1792, the words and music had been written by an army officer, Claude Joseph Rouget de Lisle, who was stationed in Strasbourg. It got its name from the fact that a battalion from Marseille was the first to sing it in Paris. It was banned under Napoleon and for much of the 19th century. Not until 1879 was it permanently adopted. Because the bloody text is often deemed inappropriate for modern Europe, there are frequent calls to change the words.

The newly unleashed popular tide became extremely difficult to control. The Tuileries Palace was stormed by a mob who forced a humiliated king to wear a red hat of the revolution and to drink with them from a common bottle. The constitutional monarchy was overthrown, and in September 1792 suspected royalists were hunted down and massacred in prisons, monasteries, and elsewhere. In December the king was tried and convicted of conspiring with the enemy (a charge which was no doubt true), and he was beheaded one month later. Scarcely had the king's head fallen into the basket of the guillotine before France found itself at war with all the major monarchies of Europe.

Faced with a frenzied, imperiled nation, the moderates were pushed aside by the radical Jacobins, a revolutionary club who had met regularly since 1789 in the Jacobin Convent in the Rue Saint-Honoré and who was led by the fanatical Robespierre. A Committee of Public Safety was formed to cope with enemies abroad and at home. On October 10, 1793, the new revolutionary leadership declared that the government of France must remain "revolutionary until the peace." In clear text, this meant a "reign of terror," and political "trials" were begun at once.

On October 16 Queen Marie Antoinette was guillotined, followed by all the Girondists who could be arrested. For the next nine months, the guillotine would never cease from doing its grisly work. Until Robespierre and his followers' own execution in July 1794, France was subjected to a dictatorship in the hands of fanatically self-righteous people who asserted, "terror is nothing else than swift, severe, indomitable justice; it then flows from virtue."

Enlightened democrats make no claims to know absolute truth and therefore tolerate other men's views and weaknesses. By contrast, the ideologues who controlled

France in those bloody days had such an abstract conception of liberty that they lost sight of man. Out of love for humanity and the truth, they would have eradicated the human race.

The noted French author George Sand wrote that "during the terror, the men who spilled the most blood were those who had the strongest desire to lead their fellow men to the dreamed-of golden age, and who had the greatest sympathy for human misery. . . . the greater their thirst for universal happiness, the more relentless they became." Charles Dickens was no doubt correct when, in the opening sentence of his *A Tale of Two Cities*, he referred to the French Revolution, "It was the best of times, it was the worst of times, it was the age of wisdom, it was the age of foolishness." Perhaps at no other time could one see so clearly the worst and best in man.

Although Frenchmen today tend to remember mostly the noblest aspects of the revolution, the terror made it difficult then and now for persons outside of France to have a unified opinion of this first great European revolution. No doubt, many of the 17,000 victims of the terror were in fact enemies of the new republic. Only 15% of the executions took place in Paris, and more than half took place in western France, where the resistance to the new order was the greatest. Only 15% of the victims were aristocrats or clergymen. To some extent, then, the terror was a defensive measure. However, the number of innocent persons who were caught in the grinder was so great that the new republic disgusted highly respected friends abroad. Also, although France's foreign enemies were ultimately defeated, the French Revolution was knocked off its democratic path, and it was almost a century before France was able to return to relatively stable, republican government.

The French Revolution in Retrospect

The year 1989 marked the 200th anniversary of the French Revolution, and 5,000 events around the country commemorated this great convulsion. It created the opportunity for Frenchmen to look both back into their past and forward into their future. Not all Frenchmen cherish the spirit of 1789, as was shown by Catholic counterdemonstrations to remember martyrs in the Place de la Concorde on August 15, 1989, the production of a movie called *Vent de Galerne* that depicts the savage repression of peasant rebels in the Vendée; the tracing of descendants of the 3,000 persons executed in Lyons by the Jacobins; and the widespread apathy in many parts of the country.

There has been a fundamental rethinking of the causes and meaning of the revolution, and many simplistic explanations have been replaced by a much more complex picture. Some myths were corrected: Only seven prisoners were freed at the Bastille; execution by guillotine often took several "chops," and only 10% of those beheaded were nobles; most of the revolution's victims were shot, burned, or drowned rather than beheaded; and the statement attributed to Marie Antoinette, "Let them eat cake!" appeared in Rousseau's Confessions at least two years before Marie arrived in France in 1770.

Frenchmen have even become more ambiguous about their heroes and villains. Polls indicated that the era's most revered character is the Marquis de Lafayette, who broke with the Jacobins and fled France. He became a favorite on the staff of General George Washington at age 19, living in his house and riding at his side in parades and into battle. Biographer Douglas Southall Freeman wrote, "Never during the Revolution was there so speedy and complete a conquest of the heart of Washington." A televised reenactment of Louis XVI's trial with the ending left open so that viewers could decide his guilt or innocence also produced astounding conclusions: Only 27% of viewers favored beheading him versus 55% who voted to acquit him.

It is therefore not surprising that the government decided to focus as little as possible on the bloody elements of the past and almost exclusively on the idealistic achievements of the revolution that have undeniable relevance for France's future, such as the Declaration of the Rights of Man and the Citizen. This focus on human rights and the question of what it means to be a citizen in a free and modern republic relates directly to France's future as a multiracial, multicultural society. Some citizens are also beginning to ask whether France needs to have such a brutal national anthem, which calls on them to "drench our fields" with the enemy's "tainted blood." According to a July 14, 1992, poll, 40% of the French find the lyrics too bloodthirsty, but 75% are staunchly opposed to altering the hallowed verses.

The palace at Versailles

Napoleon

Robespierre was overthrown and beheaded on July 27, 1794. That date fell within the month of Thermador in the revolutionary calendar, which had been introduced on August 18, 1792, the date

France

Napoleon returns from Elba (Karl Stenben).

the constitutional monarchy began. The notables who assumed power moved rapidly to restrict suffrage and eliminate the masses from political influence in a tired, internally paralyzed France. In 1795 they created a directory, led by five directors, but this new form of government could not create order in France.

In the midst of such instability, a brilliant young general saw his great opportunity. Born into an Italian family from Corsica in 1769, Napoleon Bonaparte had been educated in French military schools and had gained notoriety by suppressing an uprising against the directory shortly after its founding. An ingenious innovator of lightning military tactics combined with effective use of field artillery, he understood how to win the unswerving devotion of his soldiers. He achieved great victories in Italy, and in 1799, while his troops were conducting a major campaign in Egypt, he returned to Paris and seized power at bayonet point.

For the next 15 years, France followed this man, who, though slight of stature (barely five feet tall), was a great leader in many ways. He clearly preferred order to liberty, and he quickly moved to establish order in France. Despite his authoritarian style of rule, he was an immensely popular leader who quickly showed that he was, at least to some extent, a child of the revolution. He introduced financial reforms and tightened the centralized administration of France. He promulgated a new constitution and a civil code which reflected the major accomplishments of the revolution: popular sovereignty, underscored by Napoleon's practice of submitting every constitutional change to a plebiscite; trial by jury and equality before the law; a citizens' army; office holding based on competence; abolition of feudal privileges; freedom of religion; and freedom of speech and press (at least in theory). Though they had often been ignored in practice during the 10 years since 1789, liberty and equality had within a decade become so embraced in principle that they have remained permanent elements of French public life.

Napoleon may appear today as a greater friend of monarchy than of the revolution. He signed a concordat with the Catholic Church in 1801, reintroduced slavery in French colonies in 1802, and allowed émigrés to return to France and reclaim their unsold properties. In 1804 he crowned himself emperor of the French, and during his reign he divorced his wife, Josephine, in order to marry an Austrian princess. He also placed his brothers, son, and marshals upon thrones throughout Europe as he proceeded from conquest to conquest. Nevertheless, in his own day, the other peoples of Europe saw him as a very embodiment of the revolution who carried its ideals to every part of Europe. These principles were always among his most effective weapons.

Napoleon remained a great military leader who sought both to secure France's "natural borders" and to pacify Europe under French leadership. This was essentially accomplished by 1802. However, his ambition was to be more than a peacemaker, and his lack of moderation not only sapped his own country's vigor, but it also ultimately doomed him to defeat. In May 1803 he began an endless series of wars aiming far beyond the mere protection of France's frontiers. Due to stunning victories, French domination by 1806 extended from Holland and the German North Sea coast to the Illyrian provinces along the east coast of the Adriatic Sea. Italy was completely under French control, and some territories (including Rome itself) were annexed to France. But his very successes helped to bring about his downfall.

His invasions stimulated nationalism outside France, and the other governments of Europe felt compelled to imitate France by making popular reforms and raising citizens' armies. Soon Napoleon discovered that he faced opposition, not just from hostile governments and ruling groups, but also from entire nations in Europe. He fought an unsuccessful guerrilla war in Spain, and in 1812 his Grand Army suffered a disastrous wintertime defeat in frigid Russia. The following year he was defeated at the Battle of the Nations in Leipzig that pitted France and its allies, chiefly the Rhineland Germans, against Prussia, Austria, Russia, Sweden, and England. His enemies pursued his disinte-

Napoleon's tomb in Les Invalides

At the court of Napoleon I

grating army into the heart of France, capturing Paris itself on March 31, 1814.

Napoleon was forced to flee to the island of Elba, where the victors erected a small kingdom for him, but in less than a year, he returned to France in order to regain his empire. Though exhausted from long, sustained warfare, the French succumbed once more to Napoleon's magic. In 100 days he prepared a new army, but his dreams were crushed by a united Europe on the Belgian battlefield of Waterloo on June 18, 1815. His wars had claimed the lives of almost 2 million soldiers. This time he was held as prisoner on the small British island of Saint-Helena in the South Atlantic, while the victorious European powers gathered at the Congress of Vienna to reconstitute Europe.

Napoleon died in lonely exile in 1821, but the "little corporal," as he was often called, still casts a giant shadow in the memories of Frenchmen. He brought France pride, and he rests in magnificent glory in the Invalides, a military hospital in Paris, where the mutilated from his Grand Army were cared for. To this day, the elite professional officers of the French army descend at midnight to their knees at the foot of Napoleon's giant illuminated statue to receive their commissions at St. Cyr, the military academy he had created.

The Monarchy Returns

In 1815, with 150,000 occupation troops on French soil, the Bourbons were again placed on the throne. Although one spoke of a restoration and although 70,000 returned from exile abroad, few believed that the clock was to be turned back before 1789. The royal family was compelled to live in Paris under the eyes of a population that had never made the kings' lives comfortable. The new king, Louis XVIII, the brother of the ill-fated Louis XVI, wanted no part of the revolutionary flag, the tricolor. He did accept a constitutional order which left things more or less as they were before 1815; feudal customs and special privileges of the nobility were not reintroduced, and France's law code, formalized under Napoleon; the tax system; personal freedoms; centralized administration, and the principle of equality before the law remained.

Louis's other brother, who was crowned Charles X in 1824, showed that he had learned little about France since 1789. He believed in the divine right of kings to rule, and he tried to restore the earlier authority of the Catholic Church. His men sought revenge against former Jacobins and Bonapartists, and the ultraroyalists demanded restitution of their properties. In 1830 he made his final mistake by suspending liberty of the press, dissolving the French legislature, and so restricting the electorate that practically only noblemen could vote. While the oblivious king was hunting in Rambouillet, dissidents publicly waved the tricolor and erected barricades in the streets of Paris, some of which reached a height of up to 80 feet. One nobleman, sensing danger, noted to his friend, "Things look bad. They are singing La Marseillaise!"

Three days of bitter street fighting (known as the *trois glorieuses*) convinced Charles that he could not master the situation, so he set sail immediately for Scotland. No Bourbon ever ruled France again; their last king had failed to notice that although the French population had grown tired of revolution and war, it nevertheless continued to take equality and liberty seriously. However, unlike the Americans, the French did not experience one successful 18th-century revolution which established a new democratic political order once and for all. The French Revolution had to be refought at intervals, and each revolution left France divided. It remained a country with a seed of civil war.

Another monarchy was established in 1830. The new king was the 57-year-old Duke of Orléans, Louis-Philippe, the son of the renowned Philippe Egalité ("equality"), who had voted for the beheading of Louis XVI and who soon thereafter was also beheaded in the name of the revolution. Louis-Philippe had fought for the revolution at Valmy and Jemmapes and then had gone into exile, visiting the United States at one time. Despite his romantic past, the new king was an uninspiring man. He was intelligent enough to disavow the divine right of kings and to proclaim himself the "citizen's king." He restored the revolutionary tricolor as the nation's flag, lifted censorship, and doubled the suffrage (although only about 200,000 in a nation of 32 million had the right to vote).

He was a moderate, business-oriented king who brought France more prosperity at home and peace abroad. But the fact that he was the target of more than 80 assassination attempts indicated that his rule was not universally acceptable to Frenchmen. He did not pursue glory, a fact the poet Lamartine lamented, "France is a bored nation." Although an admirer of the king, even Victor Hugo wrote in that great work of fiction about post-Napoleonic France, *Les Misérables*, that "his great fault was that he was modest in the name of France. . . . His monarchy displayed excessive timidity which is offensive to a nation that has July 14 in its civil traditions and Austerlitz in its military annals."

An economic crisis in 1846 made the voteless urban workers in Paris nervous, and the middle classes wanted an end to the narrow elite composed of a few thousand noblemen and upper bourgeoisie. The influence of the extremely unpopular premier, François Guizot, who was reputed (incorrectly) to have advised those in power to "enrich yourselves," helped fan the republican and democratic revival which was gaining momentum. On January 27, 1848, Alexis de Tocqueville, who had gained a great reputation for his perceptive study *Democracy in America,* told the French parliament, "I believe that at this moment we are sleeping on a volcano." The volcano erupted in Paris only a few days later. Wanting no bloodbath on his conscience, Louis-Philippe abdicated and departed for England.

The Second Republic, More Anarchy, and Another Napoleon

The Second Republic was declared, and a highly idealistic government under Lamartine's leadership proceeded to introduce universal male suffrage, to abolish slavery in the colonies again, and to guarantee every citizen a job by establishing national workshops at the state's expense. To the new leaders' surprise, their government suffered a crushing defeat in the first parliamentary elections in the spring of 1848. A new legislative majority eliminated the costly socialist experiments, most notably the national workshops. This action provoked desperate workers and idealists again to erect barricades in the streets of Paris and to resist the reaction that always follows each radically democratic experiment in France. In four bloody "June Days" of street fighting in Paris, General Cavaignac crushed the rebels, killing 1,500 and arresting 12,000 in the process; 3,000 persons were hunted down and executed later.

The frightful events in Paris set off rebellions in capitals all over Europe. French workers were left bitter and smoldering. Class hatred was hardened, feelings which remained a part of French life for the rest of the century and which, to a limited extent, continue to exist in France today.

After the June convulsion, there was a widespread desire for a return to order. A new constitution was written, calling for presidential elections by universal male suffrage. In elections held late in 1848, the winner by a landslide was a man who in the past had not displayed any political talent. He was not a dashing figure. He was short and rather paunchy, and his appearance was once described as that of a "depressed parrot." However, he enjoyed two immense advantages: His name was Louis Napoleon Bonaparte, and he was the nephew of the former emperor.

He had been raised in Germany and always spoke French with a slight German accent. He had served as a captain in the Swiss army and had participated in revolutionary events in Italy. In 1836 and 1840, he had made two almost-comic attempts to overthrow the dull regime of Louis-Philippe. In his trial in 1840, he had cried, "I represent before you a principle, a cause, a defeat. The principle is the sovereignty of the people; the cause is that of the Empire; the defeat is Waterloo!" Though he did not persuade the court,

The Café Concert **by Edward Manet**

he managed to associate his name in the minds of many Frenchmen with the Napoleonic legend, which had been experiencing a rise in popularity at the time. Streets in Paris had been named after Napoleonic victories, the Arch of Triumph that Napoleon I had ordered had been finally completed, and the "little corporal's" remains had been brought back to France and solemnly transported through the city before the wet eyes of thousands of nostalgic Frenchmen.

For his revolutionary activities in France, Louis Napoleon had been imprisoned for life in the fortress of Ham, where he spent his time in luxurious confinement, writing tracts on such topics as "The Extinction of Poverty." One morning early in 1846, Louis Napoleon slipped into workman's clothes and, with a pipe in his mouth and a board over his shoulder, walked out the front gate of the fortress. He was in England the next day, where he awaited his opportunity. In May 1848 his chance came, and he returned to France; by the end of the year, he had been elected France's president.

Louis Napoleon invoked the revolutionary principle of popular sovereignty, but he left little doubt that his would be an authoritarian regime. He once remarked, "I do not mind being baptized in the water of universal suffrage, but I do not intend to live with my feet in it." With his four-year term of office approaching its end, and with a hostile parliament that refused to change the constitution so he could succeed himself, he sent his troops to occupy Paris the night of December 1–2, 1851, and to arrest most of his opponents. When Parisians awoke the next morning, they learned that a coup d'état had just effectively put an end to the Second Republic.

In characteristic post-1789 style, Louis Napoleon asserted the sovereignty of the people as the first law of the land and promised a referendum on all constitutional changes. Also, in characteristic fashion, the Parisian population refused to accept this change without a fight. The barricades went up again; at one across the Boulevard de Montmartre near the Saint-Denis Gate, a military column panicked under the insults of the mob and opened indiscriminate fire on the fleeing citizens. Two hundred persons lay dead as a result of this unfortunate carnage. Although a terrified Parisian populace did not rise up again for 20 years, in 1871, Louis Napoleon's hope for a bloodless takeover was dashed; the December massacre was never forgotten or forgiven. Years later his wife, Eugénie, confided to a friend, "A coup d'état is like a convict's ball and chain. You drag it along and eventually it paralyzes your leg."

Observing the usual practice, Louis Napoleon proceeded rapidly to rewrite the constitution. He created a weak legislature and a strong president who could appeal directly to the people by means of plebiscites. After a year, he could no longer resist one last temptation: On the first anniversary of his coup d'état, he submitted a referendum to the people asking whether they favored "restoration of imperial dignity." Almost 8 million votes indicated yes against only a quarter-million who said no. On December 2, 1852 he was proclaimed Napoleon III, emperor of the French.

For all his talk of restoring France's glory, Napoleon III desired above all to establish order and to make it a prosperous, industrially advanced country. He expanded credit and stimulated new investment. Everywhere new industry and railroads sprang up. He liberalized trade, which boosted French commerce. Overall, French industrial production doubled under his rule; signs of dynamism were everywhere.

Perhaps the most lasting of his public works can be seen in the large cities, such as Marsailles and Paris. Napoleon III appointed Baron Haussmann to administer the department of the Seine, in which Paris is located. Haussmann completely transformed the city. He built the Paris Opera. He destroyed the narrow, medieval streets and laid wide boulevards and broad squares (such as the Place Étoile) with radiating avenues. It was noticed immediately that such wide boulevards would make barricade building, a periodic Parisian pastime, almost impossible and would facilitate military mobility inside the city. Nevertheless, these changes were badly needed to accommodate the capital's rapid growth and to make it a more modern, livable, and beautiful city. During the Second Empire, Paris was a prosperous, carefree, and culturally active

1900 Paris World Fair: Petit Palais

city that attracted admirers from all over the world.

In the first decade of his rule, Napoleon III restricted political parties and freedom of the press. He was a very popular ruler in France, however, and seeing that he had nothing to fear, he introduced greater political freedoms in the 1860s. He even took what at the time seemed to be a very radical step: He legalized trade unions and granted workers the right to strike. His regime certainly did not come to an end due to domestic resistance. Instead, he shared the fate of his uncle, falling victim to foreign policy entanglements. He conducted a very active colonial policy in Africa, the Near East, China, and Indochina, bringing the latter under French control in the 1860s.

In 1861 he decided to take advantage of the United States' preoccupation with its own Civil War by trying to establish a monarchy in Mexico dominated by France and ruled by Archduke Maximilian of Austria. In 1863 French troops entered Mexico City and placed the archduke on the newly created throne. But he never developed popular backing, and as soon as the American strife ended in 1865, the US invoked the Monroe Doctrine and demanded that France get out of Mexico. Napoleon III complied, and when by 1867 no French troops were left in Mexico, the naïve Maximilian, who had decided to remain with "his people," was executed by a firing squad. The Mexican adventure was a blunder that greatly diminished Napoleon III's prestige at home.

The fatal blow to the Second Empire was delivered in 1870, when the emperor tried to enforce France's long-standing policy of keeping Germany permanently divided. Provoked by the Prussian chancellor Otto von Bismarck, who sought to create a unified Germany under Prussian domination, the French government declared war against Prussia. Napoleon calculated that the southern German-speaking states would not support Bismarck and might even side with France, but he had made a grave miscalculation; southern Germans were swept up in the conflict.

War and Defeat

France entered the war extremely unprepared. Prussia had a far superior general staff, supply system, and strategy. Also, because of their faster mobilization, the German soldiers outnumbered the French, two to one. Smashing through Lorraine, the Prussian army cut Paris off from the two main French armies and delivered a devastating blow to the French at Sedan on the Belgian border. Napoleon III and more than 100,000 French soldiers were captured there, and the empire came crashing down. In Paris, a republic was declared, and the Parisians prepared for a long siege. The new government's 32-year-old leader, Léon Gambetta, escaped from the surrounded city of Paris by balloon and tried to raise a new army in the Loire area. However, the capture of the last trained French army in Metz in October 1870 demoralized the remaining untrained troops in France. In early 1871, after every last scrap of food in the capital had been consumed, including the rats in the sewers and the animals in the zoo, and after the trees in the Bois de Boulogne and the Champs Elysées had been chopped down for fuel, Paris and the troops in the provinces surrendered.

A humiliated France looked on as the German Empire was proclaimed in the Hall of Mirrors at the Versailles Palace. Germany then proceeded to set a very bad precedent by imposing a harsh peace on a prostrate France: Alsace and most of Lorraine, with their rich iron deposits and industry, were annexed by Germany. Further, France was required to pay the victor a very large reparations sum and to allow German occupation troops to remain in France until the sum was paid. For the next half-century, French policy would revolve around undoing these terrible losses. Referring to the lost provinces, Gambetta told his countrymen, "Never talk about them, always think about them."

France Drifts

While a new government under Adolphe Thiers saw no alternative to accepting this bitter peace, hundreds of thousands of Parisians saw the matter differently. They had suffered the most during the war and had been humiliated both by the Prussians' triumphant entry into Paris and by the transfer of the French capital to Versailles. Further, this traditional hotbed of republicanism resented the monarchist sentiment that dominated both the provinces and the newly elected National Assembly. Finally, Parisians greatly resented the new government's termination of the wartime moratorium on rents and debts and of all payments to the National Guardsmen, who had defended Paris and who, because of France's financial collapse, were now out of work and without subsistence. Again, Paris became a powder keg.

On March 18, 1871, the government sent cavalry troops commanded by two French generals to remove the guns from the promontory of Montmartre that overlooks the city. An angry mob attacked the cavalry and lynched the generals. Violence spread throughout the city, prompting the government's troops to withdraw hastily. Recalling the radical days of 1793, a new Commune of Paris, composed of radical republicans, socialists, and National Guardsmen, was formed. However, this strange mixture of idealists and rowdies spent more time debating socialist and political experiments than in preparing for their own defense. The government immediately besieged the city and, reinforced by French prisoners of war whom the Germans had released for just that purpose, prepared to storm the city.

The troops struck on May 21, and for one bloody week, the street battle raged. In the closing days of the struggle, the Communards, as the dissidents were called, shot their hostages, including the archbishop of Paris, and set fire to many public buildings, including the Tuileries Palace and the Palais Royal. Finally the remaining Communards were trapped in Père-Lachaise Cemetery, where they were executed against the Mur des Fédéré (now highly revered shrines for socialists and communists all over the world).

The government's vengeance was severe: Any person caught wearing a National Guard uniform or army boots was shot immediately without trial. In all, about 10,000 Communards, who were out numbered, more than eight to one, were killed in battle or executed without trial. Thousands more were imprisoned or driven into exile. Both sides, fired by hatred, had fought like animals. It had lasted 72 days.

Reflecting on the events, the French novelist Flaubert wrote, "What an immoral beast the mob is, and how discouraging it is to be a human being." Karl Marx, in his widely read pamphlet *The Civil War in France*, made a legend of the Commune, and these violent events widened the gap created in 1848 between the workers and the political left on the one hand and the rest of France on the other. A constant reminder of this gulf is the beautiful white Sacre Coeur (Sacred Heart) Church that overlooks Paris from the top of Montmartre. Built to commemorate the suppression of the Commune, it remains for the French left a prominent and hated symbol of a reactionary France.

Renoir's *The Luncheon of the Boating Party* (1881)

For a while a monarchist majority in the National Assembly pressed for the restoration of the monarchy, and Bourbon, Orléanist, and Bonapartist pretenders waited for the call. There were very good prospects for the aging Bourbon pretender, the Count de Chambord, who would rule as Henry V. But the count quickly showed how little he had learned about his own country. He insisted that the king have absolute authority, unrestrained by any constitution. He also insisted that the old fleur-de-lis flag of the former monarchy replace the revolutionary tricolor. Even the most die-hard royalists could see the folly of such demands.

Meanwhile the French people, who in the past 100 years had experienced about every conceivable regime and who were growing tired of provisional governments, pressed for a decision. In 1875 important constitutional laws were adopted calling for the establishment of a two-house parliament and a weak president. The wheel that always alternates in France between a strong parliament and a strong executive had again come full circle. The Third Republic lasted until 1940, longer than any French scheme of government since the revolution.

The capital was moved back to Paris from Versailles in 1880; July 14 was established as the national holiday, and "La Marseillaise" was made the national anthem. Paris began to bustle with artistic creativity. By the time the Eiffel Tower was unveiled at the World Exposition in 1889, Paris had assumed the place, in many foreigners' minds, as the intellectual and artistic capital of the world, of which it was often said, Every person in the world has two capitals—his own and Paris. Gertrude Stein put it this way: "America is my country, but Paris is my home." One can scarcely imagine contemporary culture without the creative contributions of artists, writers, and scholars in Third Republic France: impressionism in music and art (e.g., Renoir, Monet, Degas, Debussy) and the reaction to it (e.g., Bracque, Picasso, cubism, or fauvism); the positivism of Auguste Comte, the élan vital of Henri Bergson, and the discoveries of Louis Pasteur in medicine or Pierre and Marie Curie in physics.

Stung by its territorial losses in 1870, France, with Bismarck's encouragement, sought to reestablish a world empire such as the one it had lost a century earlier. It created French equatorial Africa and protectorates in Tunisia and Indochina (presently Vietnam, Cambodia, and Laos). Thus, by 1914 the tricolor flew in most of north, west, and equatorial Africa; in Madagascar, in several West Indian and South Pacific islands; and in small holdings elsewhere. Such a policy was not universally popular in France, but a colonial empire offered France the opportunity to resume expansion of its culture overseas. It also offered some economic benefits to France, which was experiencing a slower rate of population growth and economic progress than Germany and Britain.

Many French industries remained small, family-owned, and cautious, a situation which persisted in France until after World War II. At the same time, there was considerable worker unrest and violent strikes during the Third Republic. Legalized trade unions tended to remain dedicated to direct, sometimes-violent action rather than to pursue gains through the parliamentary political process. Such "syndicalist" tendencies (to which French trade unions are still attracted) reveal that the deep wounds of the Paris Commune never healed entirely.

At the beginning of the Third Republic, more than half of the population lived in rural areas, and that number had declined to only about one-third by 1940. While the visitor to France has always been struck by the amount of acreage that is cultivated, many farms remained small and relatively inefficient. In the 1870s plant lice threatened the wine industry with extinction. Only by importing American plant grafts was this precious jewel saved. Thus, in a certain sense, French wine is actually American wine.

Third Republic Politics

The Third Republic was seriously rocked by religious disputes, parliamentary instability, scandals, a world war, and economic depression. The new republic moved in traditional French revolutionary fashion to reduce the influence of the Catholic Church. Its anticlerical policies included the permission to divorce and the loosening of the church's grip on the school system. The result was a total separation of church and state in most of France by 1905.

The absence of party discipline and the distrust of any president who tried to play a guiding role in French politics (Third Republic presidents were said to be merely "old men who wore evening clothes in the afternoon!") produced a constant rotation of weak parliamentary coalitions. The resulting "parliamentary game" inclined French citizens to view politics with increasing cynicism and decreasing trust. Representatives rarely hesitated to vote themselves frequent and large salary increases. At the occasion of one such increase in 1905, a socialist member of parliament was heard to say "my indignation is matched only by my satisfaction."

Scandals further shook the confidence in France's political institutions. In the 1880s a dashing general named Boulanger was reputed to have wanted to put an end to the republic after gaining power legally. When he was summoned to the Senate in 1889 to answer to charges of conspiracy against the state, he lost his nerve and fled to Belgium, where he committed suicide two years later. Scarcely a year after his death, another scandal came to light. Since the 1870s a private French company had been attempting to build a canal across the isthmus of Panama. Unwise engineering and yellow fever bankrupted the company in 1889, but its directors bribed politicians and press in order to secure public subsidies for the project. The revelation of such bribery in 1892 helped convince many Frenchmen that all politicians were corrupt, an attitude which has by no means disappeared from France today. The French still tend to be far less shocked by political scandals than is the case in the United States.

A further scandal convinced many Frenchmen that it was not only politicians who could not be trusted but military leaders, as well. In 1894 Captain Alfred Dreyfus, the first Jewish officer to be assigned to the French general staff, was convicted of selling military secrets to the Germans and was sent to the infamous Devil's Island off the northern coast of South America. Later, probing journalists, aided by a skeptical army officer, discovered that the documents presented by the military had been forged and that Dreyfus had been framed. The army, seeing its honor at stake, refused to reopen the case, and many French conservatives and clergymen openly supported the army.

Dreyfus was later pardoned. He fought in the First World War and was promoted to lieutenant-colonel. He was awarded the Legion of Honor and died in 1935. But for more than a generation, this sordid affair, with its implications for anti-Semitism, the army, the church, and democracy in France, weakened the republic. Not until 101 years later, in 1995, did the French military formally and publicly acknowledge that the army had been wrong. On January 13, 1998, the 100th anniversary of Emile Zola's sensational headline article "J'accuse" ("I Accuse") in *L'Aurore* newspaper, Prime Minister Lionel Jospin laid a wreath on Zola's tomb in the Pantheon and called the Dreyfus affair "one of the founding events in the history of our country." In 2006 the French president and prime minister publicly honored Dreyfus on the 100th anniversary of his rehabilitation. Seven years later the entire secret military file used to convict Dreyfus was posted free online.

Until the 1890s Germany's chancellor, Bismarck managed to keep France diplomatically isolated in Europe. However, after the chancellor's fall from power in 1890, France was able to improve its relations with Italy and in 1894 to forge a military alliance with Russia. France's intense colonial activity led it into frequent conflicts with the greatest colonial power of the time, Britain. Nevertheless, after the turn of the century, France gradually settled its differences with England, and military and political cooperation between the two countries became much closer. The outlines of the Triple Entente alliance against Germany and Austria-Hungary before and during the First World War thereby emerged. Eventually, crises in Morocco and then in the Balkans brought about the devastating explosion which Bismarck had predicted shortly before his death in 1897: "One day the great European war will come out of some damned foolish thing in the Balkans." It did.

Courtesy of Edwin L. Dooley Jr.

World War I

The outbreak of World War I in August 1914 unleashed an outburst of patriotic sentiment in all major countries of Europe. Even workers rallied to the French cause, and trainloads of enthusiastic troops left their hometowns in railroad cars with words "*à Berlin*" written on the sides. Although not openly avowed, many French undoubtedly viewed the affair as an opportunity for revenge of the dismal defeat of 1870 and recovery of the "lost provinces." Never since that time did France experience such unity of purpose.

The British and French armies were able to stop the German advance within heavy artillery range of Paris. Thereafter, the armies faced each other during four weary and bloody years of trench warfare. This unimaginative method of fighting made it exceptionally difficult for either side to win. The enthusiasm faded quickly, as 300,000 French soldiers lost their lives in the first five months. Colonel de Grandmaison's axiom that "there is no such thing as an excessive offensive" produced untold carnage on such battlefields as Verdun, where a half-million soldiers were slaughtered in the spring of 1916. A young captain named Charles de Gaulle, who was wounded three times and sent to a German prisoner-of-war camp for the last 30 months, noted, "It appeared in the wink of an eye that all the virtue in the world could not prevail against superior firepower."

The defeatism and demoralization which such mindless frontal assaults produced led to large-scale mutinies on the French front from April to October 1917. Miraculously, the Germans never heard about them at the time. They also produced a frame of mind which the novel-

France

German troops enter Paris, 1940.

ist Jules Romains described in his book *Verdun*, which first appeared at an unfortunate time—1938: "Men in the mass are seen to be like a school of fish or cloud of locusts swarming to destruction. The individual man is less than nothing—certainly not worth worrying about. . . . My most haunting horror is not that I see men now willing to suffer and act as they do, but that having so seen them, I shall never again be able to believe in their good intentions."

Ultimately 1 million fresh American troops in France tipped the balance, and on November 11, 1918, the exhausted and starving Germans saw no alternative to capitulation. France had technically been victorious, but it was left breathless and demoralized; 1.3 million Frenchmen had been killed, and more than 1 million, crippled. Northeastern France, the country's most prosperous industrial and agricultural sector, was largely devastated. France's enormous human and material losses inclined French leaders to demand a heavy price from Germany in the Treaty of Versailles.

Germany and its allies were branded as solely responsible for the war, and Germany was therefore required to pay exorbitant reparations. France regained Alsace and Lorraine, established temporary control over the German Saar, stationed its troops in Germany west of the Rhine, and obtained mandates in the former German colonies of Togo and Cameroons and in Syria and Lebanon, as well. While France's demands were somewhat understandable, they played into the hands of a future German rabble-rouser named Adolf Hitler, who promised to undo the hated treaty. The settlement is a glaring example of the fact that policies that may be righteous are not always wise.

The Post–World War I Era

The French expected to rebuild their land with the reparations from Germany, but when it became apparent that an impoverished Germany could never pay the sums demanded, the French set about to do the work themselves. Displaying remarkable resilience, the French had, by the mid-1920s, cleared away the rubble; rebuilt homes, factories, and railroads; and achieved a measure of prosperity which exceeded even that of Britain. Unfortunately, many of the economic gains were wiped away by the Great Depression that spread to France by 1932. The last European country to be affected by Black Friday on Wall Street, France was so jolted that, when democracies all over Europe toppled, France tottered also.

The Nazi seizure of power in Germany in 1933 further destabilized France by pumping new life into right-wing and, in some cases, openly fascist groups in France. The best-known was the Action Française, which had emerged from the Dreyfus controversy and whose leader, Charles Maurras, powerfully and eloquently railed against Jews, Protestants, foreigners, and the French Republic generally. Offshoots and competitors of Action Française such as the Camelots du Roi or the Francistes, bullied people in the streets, dressed like Hitler's storm troopers, and ceaselessly pointed to the difference between the vigor and effectiveness of the dictatorships in Italy and Germany and the tired, ineffective parliamentary system in France. Royalist and fascist groups, supported by thousands of students and some communists, gathered on February 6, 1934, at the Place de la Concorde and stormed the National Assembly, located just across the Pont de la Concorde. The police stopped the assault, but 21 persons lay dead, and more than 1,600 were injured in this violent action against the feeble republic.

Storm Clouds and Paralysis

As storm clouds gathered over Europe, France had only short-lived, stop-gap governments that could not begin to cope with the mounting crises. In desperate economic straits, no French government could propose military increases to counter the dictators. Also, the memories of the First World War were so horrifying in the minds of many Frenchmen that they could not tolerate the thought of participating in another war, for whatever cause. *Surtout pas la guerre* ("Above all, no war!") was the slogan of Action Française. It was uttered with all the energy of "Hell no, I won't go!" in the America of the 1960s and 1970s.

Pacifism was widespread and was manifest in the writings of many of France's literary figures. In a letter to a friend, novelist Roger Martin du Gard wrote, "I am hard as steel for neutrality. My principle: anything, rather than war! Anything, anything! Even fascism in Spain . . . even fascism in France! . . . Anything: Hitler rather than war!" The highly respected writer, Jean Giono, dared to write, "I prefer to be a live German than a dead Frenchman!" even the minister of public works, Anatole de Monzie, said publicly, "I prefer to receive a kick in the behind than a bullet in the head." French patriotism after World War I had become tinged with the fear that the costs of war were simply too great.

A state of mind took shape that prepared France for defeat in the next war. As noble as it may seem sometimes, pacifism usually plays into the hands of the world's bullies, as France was soon to see.

With the fascist leagues active in the streets of France, the parties of the left began to speak of unified action for the first time. In 1935 the Socialists and Radicals

General Charles de Gaulle, London

formed a Popular Front that won a great victory in 1936 parliamentary elections. Under Léon Blum, the first Jew and first Socialist to serve as prime minister of France, the Popular Front, with the parliamentary support of the Communists, proposed a 40-hour workweek, paid vacations, collective bargaining, and the partial nationalization of the Bank of France. However, Blum was unable to find a solution to the problem of lagging production, and in 1938 his government fell.

France was the helpless observer of an aggressive German government, which in the mid- and late 1930s reoccupied the Rhineland, sent troops and squadrons to Spain to fight for Franco in its civil war, absorbed Austria, and occupied part of Czechoslovakia. After World War I, France had not only constructed the Maginot Line, but it also sought to protect itself by surrounding Germany with enemy powers. It forged military alliances with Belgium, Poland, Czechoslovakia, Romania, and Yugoslavia. Hitler merely pointed to this encirclement to justify his own aggressive policies.

In 1930, before Hitler came to power, just 12 years after the end of World War I, the French parliament voted funds to build an allegedly impregnable defensive line against invasion from Germany. The Maginot Line consisted of an elaborate system of underground bunkers, fortifications, and antitank devices and extended all the way along France's border with Germany. It was based on a conclusion drawn from the previous war that all advantages lie with the defense. Colonel Charles de Gaulle disagreed. He warned at the time in his controversial book *France and Its Army* that modern warfare requires great mobility with tanks and aircraft. Regrettably the book was read only by the German commanders, who reportedly carried it with them when they invaded France in 1940. Unfortunately the designers of the line neglected one of the basic principles of fortress building: Protect all sides. It was thought that the line could stop at the Belgian border since that state was supposed to remain neutral.

This shield mentality naturally meshed with the pacifist feelings in the French population and political circles. Léon Blum, who apparently believed in the power of a strong world conscience that hated war, opposed the extension of military service from one to two years and continued to speak of the need for France to take unilateral steps toward disarmament, as if such a French policy could incline Hitler to be more peaceful. As his government fell, France was frozen with fear. Political parties and alliances were such that the country was ungovernable.

French resistance leader Jean Moulin

Complicating the scene was journalism at its lowest. Most political parties and groups printed their own newspapers that propagated untruths daily about opposing parties, groups, and people. There were 39 regularly published in Paris alone.

World War II

Thus, when Germany invaded Poland on September 1, 1939, and when France reluctantly and finally felt compelled to

Allied invasion of Normandy, June 6, 1944

France

General de Gaulle inspecting Free French troops, London
Courtesy of Special Programs, University of Virginia Library

declare war three days later, it entered a disastrous conflict militarily and emotionally unprepared and half-consciously aspiring more to an armistice than to a victory. Germany and the Soviet Union quickly partitioned Poland, but Hitler delayed military action against France for three-quarters of a year. In France, one spoke of a "phony war," or a sitzkrieg, and precious little was done to prepare for a future onslaught. The German tank commander Heinz Guderian later wrote, "The relatively passive attitude of the French during the winter of 1939–40 incited us to conclude that the adversary had little inclination for war."

On May 10, 1940, Hitler unleashed his armies against France. Invading the Netherlands and Belgium (both neutral countries, thereby avoiding the face of the Maginot Line, which was unprotected from the rear), German forces used lightning warfare (blitzkrieg) tactics against a French army that was poorly and lethargically led and in some respects technologically outdated. French leaders refused to withdraw troops from the Maginot Line to confront actual German advances to the north, and their administrative confusion prevented badly needed French aircraft and artillery from being transferred to the actual front. This produced such disastrous reversals that the French government was forced to abandon Paris within one month. British prime minister Winston S. Churchill testified that French soldiers fought valiantly, but their political and military leaders were so quickly seized by defeatism that the French cabinet could not muster the tenacity or eagerness to persist after the shock of initial defeats.

Britain pleaded urgently that France both honor its earlier agreement not to seek a separate peace and even consider a political union of the two countries. The latter proposal was understandably unwelcome to a country that had spent centuries ridding itself of English domination and influence. A demoralized French cabinet, under the influence of the aging First World War hero, Marshal Pétain, chose instead to surrender on June 22, 1940, barely 40 days after the German attack.

The terms were very harsh. The northern half of France, including Paris, and the whole of the Atlantic coast to the Spanish border, were to be occupied by German troops at French expense. Alsace and the Moselle Department were annexed by Germany. The rest of France was to be ruled by a French government friendly to Germany. This government was to supply its conquerors with food and raw materials needed for the German war effort. The French army was to be disbanded and its navy placed in ports under the control of the Germans and the Italians.

The fate of the French navy especially distressed the British. They were unaware that the French naval commander-in-chief, Admiral Darlan, had secretly ordered his fleet commanders to scuttle his ships if the Germans or Italians tried to seize them. When the British tried to take control of the French squadron in Mersel-Kebir in Algeria, the French commander resisted. The British destroyed the squadron, an action that caused a wave of anti-British feeling in France. This sentiment played into the hands of the cunning Premier Pierre Laval and the 80-year-old Pétain, who had long opposed the Third Republic as a decadent, inefficient regime.

They quickly abolished the Third Republic and established a repressive Vichy Republic (named after the spa in France where the new government established its seat of power). Without prompting by the Germans, they denied Jews and Freemasons the protection of the law. In the July 1942 "Vélodrome d'hiver" roundup, 13,000 Paris Jews were arrested over two days and detained at that Paris sports stadium. A former police barracks outside Paris, called Drancy, served as a transit camp.

In all, 76,000 (including 11,000 children) of the 330,000 Jews in France at the beginning of the war were, with the help of the French police, deported during Vichy. Only 2,500 returned. In June 2006 a French court ruled that hundreds of Jewish families or their relatives are entitled to compensation paid by the French railway SNCF for its role in deporting them. In February 2009 France's highest court, the Council of State, formally recognized the nation's role in these deportations, but they effectively ruled out added reparations. In Jan-

General Leclerc and his troops preparing to capture Paris

uary 2011 SNCF buckled to pressure from the United States, which had threatened to stymie its bids for contracts to build high-speed rail lines from San Francisco to Los Angeles and from Orlando to Tampa. It offered its first formal public apology to Holocaust victims for transporting thousands of Jews to the German border, from where German trains took them to death camps. Restitution payments began in 2015. In 2019 payments of $402,000 were made to 49 Holocaust survivors and up to $100,500 to 32 spouses. Most lived in the United States. At the same time, some historians reminded the world that 1,647 French train drivers had been executed or deported and never came back.

Foreigners who had come to France to escape Hitler's persecution were penned up in French concentration camps and, unless they were able to escape, were later returned to Germany where an uncertain, usually fatal future awaited them. In fact, most Jews deported to Germany had been new arrivals in France who had fled Nazi persecution elsewhere. By the time Paris was liberated in 1944, about 60,000 Jews were left in the city, half of whom in hiding.

Some noted non-Jewish artists and intellectuals, such as Mondrian, Dali, and Chagall, fled to New York, while others, such as Sartre and Georges Pompidou, remained and coexisted with the occupiers. The Nazis decided that they would face fewer occupation problems if they permitted the French, especially Parisians, to be entertained. Despite censorship most French artists did just that. Singer Edith Piaf confessed, "My real job is to sing, to sing no matter what happened." Jean Cocteau expressed his astonishing opinion: "At no price should one let oneself be distracted from serious matters by the dramatic frivolity of war."

Many Frenchmen were relieved to have achieved a peace at any price; nevertheless, they felt a numbing feeling of humiliation and the awareness that this was a tragic debacle which had befallen the French nation. What followed was as much a French civil war as a war against the Germans. For the next four years, there were two Frances, one fighting against the Germans and one trying to ignore the conflict and to minimize damage to the French population. Any single Frenchman could find sound patriotic reasons for supporting either, and it was up to the individual to decide which France was his.

France still has not fully recovered psychologically from the terrible tension of the Vichy years. A poll in 1992 showed that 82% of Frenchmen considered the Vichy government to be guilty of "crimes against humanity," and 90% thought that their country should admit it. In a July 2004 ceremony to commemorate the "Vélodrome d'hiver" roundup, France's top public figures acknowledged the evils of anti-Semitism during the Vichy regime. This lamentable event was portrayed in vivid accuracy in the 2010 film *La Rafle*, a box-office success in France. Until Jacques Chirac assumed the presidency in 1995, the opinion of every president was that the Vichy state was not France. This is despite the fact that Vichy put some soldiers on trial for the defeat and executed Gestapo spies.

In 1994 the trial of Paul Touvier captivated France. Convicted of murdering Jewish hostages in 1944, he became the first Frenchman charged and convicted of a crime against humanity. This was also the first time a French court blamed Vichy for its role in the Nazis' Final Solution. In 1995 Jacques Chirac became the first president to accept the responsibility of the French state for the arrest and deportation of Jews during Vichy. In 1997 the bishop of St. Denis admitted for the first time the French Catholic Church's guilt in "acquiescing by its silence" in the persecution of the Jews: "We beg God's pardon and we ask the Jewish people to hear our words of repentance."

Maurice Papon was a police supervisor in Bordeaux from 1942 to 1944, who, according to documents first revealed by the satirical *Le Canard Enchainé*, was instrumental in the arrest and deportation of 1,690 Jews; very few returned. Still defiantly maintaining that he had only done what the Germans had made him do and that he had been a loyal member of the resistance, he became de Gaulle's postwar

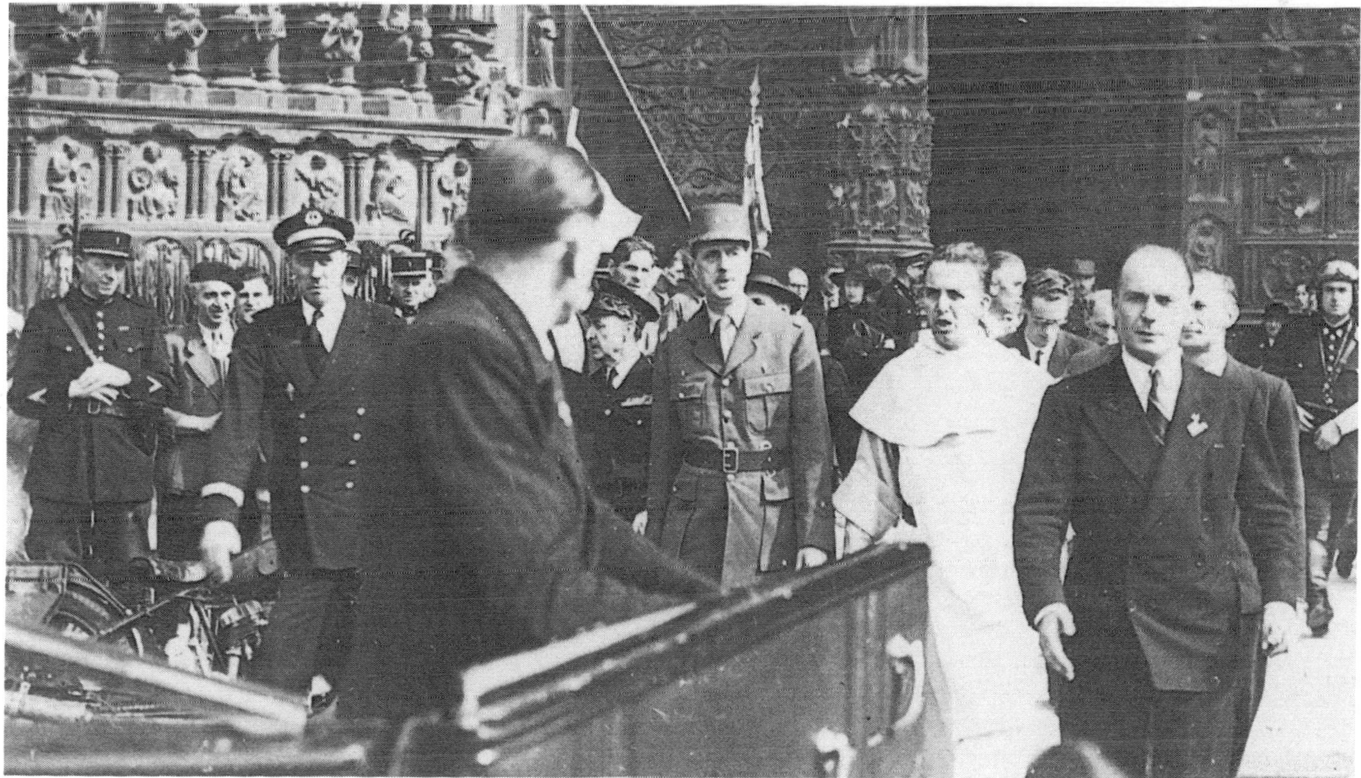

De Gaulle leaves Notre Dame Cathedral after the liberation of Paris. Courtesy: Central Audiovisual Library, European Commission

police chief in Paris, member of the National Assembly, Gaullist Party treasurer, and budget minister under President Giscard d'Estaing. He was found guilty in 1998 and sentenced to 10 years in prison, becoming the highest-ranking Frenchman ever convicted of complicity in crimes against humanity.

His trial had been the longest and most expensive in modern French history, and it forced the country to confront a part of its past that many still try to forget. After executing the Vichy leaders for treason, the policy was to keep France united, to avoid recriminations, and to draw a veil over the past. Vowing that he would "go into exile" rather than spend his last years behind bars, Papon fled to Switzerland. He was quickly apprehended. In 2000 President Chirac rejected his plea for release. Nevertheless, in September 2002, less than three years into his sentence, Papon was discharged under a law allowing early release for the ill and aging. He sparked anger when he walked unassisted from jail after the doctors had determined he was lacking in mobility. Controversy still surrounded him after his death in February 2007 at the age of 96. Many were shocked to learn that he had asked to be buried wearing his Legion of Honor medal he had received from de Gaulle's very hand.

During the war, France was the country from which the most art was looted; over a third of all privately owned art was stolen. Many of the most valuable treasures from state museums were rescued: *Winged Victory of Samothrace* was wheeled down a steep staircase, and the *Mona Lisa* was carried out of the Louvre on a stretcher and joined thousands of artworks hidden in southern France. The occupiers left what remained in the national museums untouched. It was a different story for Jewish collections. Thousands of treasures were seized and sent to the Jeu de Paume, which the Germans had set up as a kind of warehouse for stolen art. Hermann Goering visited it at least 20 times to help himself.

France has a respectable record in returning assets seized from Jews. A study in 2000 found that about the equivalent of $1.3 billion had been taken: 80,000 frozen bank accounts; 6,000 safe deposit boxes; 38,000 confiscated apartments; 50,000 "aryanization" cases to seize businesses and homes; and 100,000 works of art. About 90% of these were compensated in some form within a decade of war's end. Some were never reclaimed. France still has about $3 billion in unclaimed funds, earmarked for a National Foundation for Memory to keep alive the awareness of the Holocaust. In 2003 the government-appointed Commission for the Compensation of Victims of Spoliation recommended that the government and French banks pay Jews an additional $84 million.

One of hundreds of plaques honoring the fighters in the Battle for Paris

While working together with the Germans, the Vichy government introduced what it called a "National Revolution." Although this was, in some cases, fascist in inspiration, it sought among other things to strengthen the role of France's regions; to introduce economic planning at the highest political level; to concentrate small agricultural holdings into larger, more efficient farms; and to stimulate population growth through family allowances for children. Postwar France actually built on some of these Vichy innovations.

The Vichy government's powers were drastically reduced at the end of 1942, when the Germans, in response to Anglo-American military landings in North Africa, occupied all of France. Vichy's prestige declined rapidly, and when Frenchmen were sent to Germany involuntarily in order to work in German war industries, the ranks of the resistance began to grow. Nevertheless, more Frenchmen fought on the Axis (German) side than with the Allies. In fact, the last SS unit that defended Hitler in his final days in the Berlin bunker was French. There was also much "horizontal collaboration," and about 20,000 women had their heads shaved in shame. French women bore an estimated 200,000 children sired by German soldiers. Known as "*enfants de Boches,*" they suffered discrimination in France for a couple generations, and many were given to orphanages or put up for adoption. Ex–foreign minister Bernard Kouchner paid tribute to them in 2009, recognizing their misery.

By 1943 command over the entire French resistance movement had been gathered into the hands of General de Gaulle, who had fled to Britain in 1940 and who had organized there the Free French Movement. He reminded his countrymen by radio in a 3-minute, 400-word BBC address, "France has lost a battle, but not the war." Few French heard it since it was broadcast without prior announcement at 10 p.m. But by the time his 6′5″ (1.96 meters) frame had stood up, he had appointed himself as the embodiment of all that is noble about France. Nevertheless, it would be a couple years before more Frenchmen would believe that he, rather than Pétain, had steered the right course for their country.

His claims to be the legal French government-in-exile and the sole spokesman for France greatly irritated Churchill and Roosevelt, who for a time found it politically wise to maintain diplomatic recognition of the Vichy government. Speaking of Churchill, de Gaulle said, "we are angry at each other most of the time." Further, when Admiral Darlan was assassinated three weeks after he scuttled the French navy, Britain and the United States recognized another French general as "chief of state" in French North Africa. Roosevelt greeted him warmly in Washington, which infuriated de Gaulle. His wartime experiences with the British and Americans did not leave him with a strong admiration for the two countries, and his resentment was to disturb these two nations' relations with France even after 1958, when he became France's leader.

The French resistance fighters helped protect unfortunate Allied pilots and often provided useful military intelligence and other support to the Allies. There is no doubt that resistance against the Germans was very dangerous business. De Gaulle later estimated that 20,000 French resistance fighters had been executed and more than 50,000 deported from France before the Allied landings in Normandy. But German documents reveal that this movement had not constituted an effective military threat to the Germans, as had the resistance movements in the Soviet Union and Yugoslavia. Still, when the Allies landed on the Normandy beaches (which today are sobering and moving sites for visiting and reflecting), the French resistance played an important part in destroying bridges, assembling paratroops for action, and providing Allied units with useful information. Also, French military units that had been organized in London under de Gaulle's overall command fought side by side with the Americans, British, and Canadians.

Local resistance forces and delegates from de Gaulle's headquarters in London assumed political control in liberated France, arresting or executing Vichy officials. On August 19, 1944, resistance fighters rose up in Paris against the German occupiers. Six days later, Free French units commanded by General Philippe Leclerc took control of the city, which a disobedient German commander had saved from senseless destruction by refusing to burn and destroy as ordered by Hitler. De Gaulle arrived with the French troops, and the following day he led a triumphant march down the broad Champs-Elysées.

The Vichy government fled to Germany, and for the next year and a half, de Gaulle's provisional government exercised unchallenged authority in liberated France. The resistance movement had brought together persons from all backgrounds and political convictions, and de Gaulle hoped that this predominantly young, patriotic, idealistic, but at the same time practical core of Frenchmen would provide the spark for national revival and change. He announced during the war, "while the French people are uniting for victory they are assembling for a revolution."

His movement also encompassed French communists, although he was always suspicious that his desired revolution was not the same as theirs. Communists displayed undeniable courage and commitment after Germany had attacked the Soviet Union in 1941 "but never, as an army of revolution, losing sight of the objective, which was to establish their dictatorship by making use of the tragic situation of France. . . . I was quite as decided not to let them ever gain the upper hand or bypass me, or take the lead." He successfully blocked their efforts to gain a ministry controlling foreign affairs, defense, or the police. French Socialists and other groups also learned then and later what a mixed blessing cooperation with communists can be.

The End of Conflict and the Beginning of Bickering

De Gaulle engaged in feverish diplomacy in order to reestablish France's position in world affairs: He traveled to Moscow in November 1944, helped create the United Nations, fought successfully for a permanent French seat on the Security Council, and secured a French occupation zone in Germany as a victorious power. He also initiated a program of nationalizing the nation's coal mines, electrical production, natural gas, some banks, and other basic industries, such as the Renault auto company. Since many French business leaders had collaborated with the enemy during the Vichy years and since a national effort to rebuild the French economy was so obviously necessary, few people opposed such a policy.

Jean Monnet Courtesy: Central Audiovisual Library, European Commission

Frenchmen shared an almost-universal desire for the creation of a Fourth Republic, but they split on the perennial French dispute concerning the kind of republic that was appropriate for France. De Gaulle stood aloof from these controversies, although it was widely known that he preferred a strong executive and a weak parliament. "Deliberation is the work of many men. Action, of one alone!" Sensing that the old bickering party and parliamentary activity was about to reemerge, that his coalition was collapsing, and that his views on the future republic were not gaining support, he announced in January 1946 his resignation as temporary president. He apparently expected a wave of popular support to swell in his favor, allowing him to strengthen his hand in shaping the new republic, but such a movement failed to materialize. For seven years he tried to return to power, but in 1953 he withdrew completely from direct involvement and lived for the next five years in the political desert, awaiting a crisis that would direct his countrymen's eyes again on de Gaulle, the savior.

In 1946 that kind of political regime was created which de Gaulle had most feared: a parliamentary system with a weak president—practically a restoration of the Third Republic which, in his eyes, had so thoroughly discredited itself and France in 1940. In the plebiscite of late 1946, a bare majority voted in favor of the new constitution, an ominous sign for the new Fourth Republic. There was no clear majority, either in the parliament or the nation, so subsequent political instability was hardly surprising. There were 10 governments in the first 5 years, and by 1958 Frenchmen had witnessed no fewer than 25 governments. A coherent policy was

Captain (later General) C. E. Vidal shaking hands with his French troops in Koblenz, Germany, 1945
Courtesy: The late general C. E. Vidal

very difficult to achieve, and the "parliamentary game" appeared more and more to be divorced from the pressing needs of the public.

The governments of the Fourth Republic were faced with many crises in economic, foreign, and colonial policy, some of which they mastered and most of which weakened or destroyed them. Nevertheless, it is a great mistake to view France from 1946 until de Gaulle's return to power in 1958 as a hopelessly paralyzed country. France had a resilient population, a rather competent and dedicated bureaucracy, and a few leaders with sound judgment.

Economic Growth and European Cooperation

France set about very quickly to repair the destruction from the long war and to reestablish economic strength. The results, with massive assistance of the United States' Marshall Plan, were impressive. Between 1949 and 1957, its GNP increased by 40%, and from 1952 forward, its growth rate was more than 10% a year, consistently among the highest in Europe. Frenchmen poured into the urban areas from the countryside, thereby dramatically changing the face of French society. Fortunately, French industry was able to absorb them. At the same time, agricultural production increased by 24% from 1949 to 1957. Government financial subsidies for families with children, coupled with the people's increasingly optimistic view of the future, helped bring about one of Europe's highest birth rates, a welcome development for a country which for more than a century had experienced relatively low population growth.

France's rapid economic growth was greatly aided by economic planning, which, in contrast to planning in communist countries, was entirely noncompulsory. These periodic plans set targets and suggested investments to French industry, with a view to making the economy as efficient and modern as possible. Perhaps most important, such planning helped Frenchmen believe strongly in the possibility of progress. The Marshall Plan assistance which the United States gave to France and other western European countries encouraged such planning. It even had a further long-term benefit for Europe: A condition for aid was that European countries discuss and agree among themselves how such help should be used. These discussions opened possibilities of European cooperation that laid the foundations for the creation of NATO and the EU.

The fruits of this were not long in coming. In 1950, France's brilliant foreign minister Robert Schuman proposed an imaginative European Coal and Steel Community, which within two years provided a common market for these two critical commodities among West Germany, France, the BENELUX countries, and Italy, a step unthinkable five years earlier. Seven years later, Schuman and his countryman Jean Monnet, de Gaulle's wartime representative for economic negotiations with Washington and London and from 1946 to 1952 chief of France's General Planning Commission, were key figures in the creation of the EU by the same six powers. The French were not inclined to transfer any French sovereignty to the EU; indeed, de Gaulle later reiterated that this was to be a "Europe of Fatherlands," that is, of entirely sovereign nation-states. Yet they have clearly recognized that French interests are best served in a cooperative, democratic Europe, and they have strongly supported such a Europe.

At one time France sought to extend European cooperation into the military sphere, as well. When the Korean War began in 1950, there was fear in Europe that the Soviet Union might be considering an aggressive assault against western Europe. When the United States suggested that West Germany be permitted to rearm, the French became uneasy. Therefore, the government proposed a European Defense Community (EDC) that would integrate German soldiers into an overall European command. There would be no German general staff. However, Britain refused to join, and French public opinion also gradually turned against it. In 1954 the parliament, not wanting French troops to be under supranational control, rejected the proposal. After the vote the Gaullist and communist deputies stood up and sang the "Marseillaise." France, however, remained a member of NATO, which had been formed in 1949 and which West Germany also joined in 1955.

The Empire Crumbles

While France's economic recovery and contribution to a unified Europe, which included former enemy powers, were glittering successes of the French Fourth Republic, the government was brought to its knees by the painfully traumatic disintegration of the colonial empire. The two world wars had stimulated a desire in colonies all over the world for independence, but many Frenchmen believed it was impossible to restore French power, prestige, and prosperity without aid from the colonies.

The first disaster occurred in Indochina, which the Japanese had occupied during the war. When the French attempted to reestablish control after liberation, a powerful native communist resistance movement called the Viet Minh and led by Ho Chi Minh opposed them. Fighting broke out in December 1946, and all French political parties, including the communists, initially supported the war effort. However, eight inglorious years of fighting without victory created powerful domestic opposition to continuation of the conflict. The United States refused in principle to help the French in a colonial war, although it did provide about $1 billion in financial assistance. When in 1954 France sought relief for its embattled stronghold Dien Bien Phu and a quick solution to the war by asking that the US use atomic bombs against the Viet Minh, the request was turned down. After the Viet Minh captured that garrison in the same year, the French agreed to a temporary division of Vietnam and to a permanent withdrawal

M. RENÉ COTY S'ADRESSE AU PARLEMENT

EDITION DE 5 HEURES

LE FIGARO

Le Gaulois • 20 francs

132e ANNEE N° 4270 depuis la Libération

« Sans la liberté de blâmer, il n'est pas d'éloge flatteur. » BEAUMARCHAIS

VENDREDI 30 MAI 1958

150e JOUR DE L'ANNEE

REDACTION ET ADMINISTRATION : 14, Rd-Pt des Champs-Elysées, PARIS 8e ELY. 98-31

ABONNEMENTS - C.C.P. Paris 242-53

Belg. et Lux. 2 f. 50 - Suisse 0 f. 30 - Gde-Bret. 8 d. - Italie 50 lires

DIRECTEUR : Pierre BRISSON

Algérie, Tunisie, Maroc 25 f. - Espagne 2.75 pesetas

APRÈS UNE HEURE D'ENTRETIEN AVEC M. COTY

LE GÉNÉRAL DE GAULLE ACCEPTE

TOURBILLONS

Insoupçonnés du public, sous un ciel de printemps parisien, les tourbillons politiques du parlement ont failli prendre hier la violence d'un typhon. Hideux spectacle. Les communistes hurlant à la défense de la République l'égorgeaient allégrement au chant de la *Marseillaise*. Leurs complices et leurs dupes s'engouffraient derrière eux vers la guerre civile.

Dans cette monstrueuse cacophonie, quelques voix se sont élevées dont la résonance en s'amplifiant sembla peu à peu dominer le malheur.

Celle du président Coty dont l'avertissement, par sa noblesse et son courage, marquera une date dans la défense de nos institutions.

Dans un message au Parlement le Président de la République avait déclaré :

«Je demande au général de Gaulle de bien vouloir venir conférer avec le chef de l'État, et examiner avec lui ce qui, dans le cadre de la légalité républicaine, est nécessaire à un gouvernement de Salut National»

Aujourd'hui, M. René Coty consultera lui-même les chefs de groupe

Le général est reparti pour Colombey

Une réponse de l'ancien chef de la France libre à une lettre de M. Vincent Auriol

TUNIS : J.-F. CHAUVEL

Tension persistante en Tunisie

Incident près de Remada entre une patrouille française et une patrouille tunisienne

Hier soir à Matignon réunion d'urgence du gouvernement

PAGE 7 : L'ensemble de nos informations

LE PANTHÉON DE L'EUROPE

Remise des prix aux gagnants de notre référendum-concours

dans les salons du « FIGARO »

★

PAGE 16 : nos photographies

after free elections. For complicated reasons, such elections were never held.

Having had no time to recover from the shock of loss of Indochina, the French had to turn their attention immediately to a rebellion in Algeria that erupted in November 1954. Algeria was a much more complicated problem. Legally it was not a colony but an integral part of France, as Hawaii is part of the US. Located directly south of France, it (unlike Indochina) had an immediate strategic importance for the country. Further, there were more than 1 million French settlers living there, some of whose families had been in Algeria for more than three generations. Many were farmers, producing semitropical foodstuffs for France.

The Algerian rebellion shook France to the core. It unleashed conspiracies against the government, assassinations, and ill-fated military coups d'état. A half million troops were sent to Algeria to suppress it. It was a struggle that prompted the French military, which was left more or less to its own devices, to conduct unconventional warfare and atrocities against an enemy that often used terrorist methods and melted into the general population.

In response, French methods were sometimes unsavory. In 2001 a former French general in the secret service, Paul Aussaresses, wrote a book entitled *Special Services in Algeria 1955–1957*, in which he described in a matter-of-fact way how he and other French military routinely tortured and executed suspects, noting that as many as 3,000 suspects had simply "disappeared." He admitted having executed 24 suspected guerrillas himself and claimed to have only "followed orders." The book was a sensation in that he showed no remorse, and it reflected a "cold tone, lacking any hindsight and any humanity," in the words of the judge who fined him for "complicity in justifying war crimes." France has never officially apologized for its conduct during the war, which claimed the lives of 30,000 French men and women and at least a half-million Algerians.

The process by which Morocco and Tunisia gained their independence went much more smoothly. One of the most important and influential politicians to steer France through its crises in the 1950s was Pierre Mendes-France. Serving as premier from 1954 to 1955, he extricated France from Indochina, helped facilitate Tunisian independence in 1956, and began talks with Moroccan nationalists that would lead to France's withdrawal from the country. An ardent opponent of colonialism, he also favored concessions to Algerian nationalists.

The war brought an aging man out of retirement from the eastern village of Colombey-les-Deux-Églises: Charles de Gaulle. When the French military seized power in Algeria's capital city, Algiers, in May 1958 and soon thereafter on the island of Corsica, Napoleon's birthplace, many, especially French generals, believed that only de Gaulle could save Algeria or protect the country from civil war.

De Gaulle haughtily said that he would respond to the call of his fellow citizens only on his own terms: that he be granted unrestricted authority to cope with the crisis. In mid-1958, he was appointed prime minister, and he quickly went to Algeria and gave an enthusiastic French throng the highly ambiguous assurance "I have understood you!" He undoubtedly knew the situation was hopeless. In late 1958 an electoral college of notables elected him president of the republic. Parliament also approved his new constitution. This spelled the death knell of the Fourth Republic and the birth of the present Fifth Republic.

The de Gaulle Years in Power

Always a realist under his mantle of magnificence, de Gaulle was convinced that Algeria could no longer be held by force, but he proceeded very cautiously in seeking a settlement of the crisis. He did not want to provoke a military coup d'état in France itself. He shrewdly allowed all groups to think that he shared all of their own objectives. Sensing that the right time had come, he announced a referendum for early 1961 to decide whether Algeria should be granted self-determination. Fifteen million said yes; only 5 million said no. He thus had received a free hand to pursue negotiations with the Algerian National Liberation Front (FLN), and he directed Prime Minister Georges Pompidou to lead the negotiations.

This was an extremely unstable time in both France and Algeria, and de Gaulle felt compelled to assume sweeping emergency powers to master the situation. The cloud of a military takeover loomed over the country. Indeed, some French officers regarded the president's policy as "treachery" and formed the Secret Army Organization (OAS) with the aim of keeping Algeria French by any means possible, including terror, bombings, and assassinations. De Gaulle himself barely escaped three assassination attempts in 1962.

A breakthrough occurred in March 1962: France granted Algeria full sovereignty in return for the Algerian promise to respect the French settlers' lives and property, as well as French oil interests in the Sahara and military interests in a port city. Ninety percent of the people approved this settlement in a referendum. Three-quarters of a million French settlers from Algeria

". . . the whole room might tilt everyone into the garden."

(known in France as *pieds noirs*—"black feet") and some Algerians who had fought for France (known as *harkis*) left for mainland France. The promise regarding oil interests was not fully kept by the Algerians.

De Gaulle had already offered all the other French colonies the option of becoming independent while retaining cultural ties with France. By 1960 all had accepted this option, with the exception of Guinea, which rejected all ties with the French community that was to be established. Thus by 1962 the French Empire had practically ceased to exist.

It now possesses five overseas departments (Guadeloupe and Martinique in the Caribbean, French Guiana in South America, Réunion, and since March 2009 Mayotte in the Indian Ocean); five overseas territories (New Caledonia, French Polynesia, Wallis, and Futuna in the South Pacific and French Southern and Antarctic Territories, a smattering of islands in the southern part of the earth); and one special-status territory (Saint-Pierre and Miquelon in the Atlantic near Newfoundland). The inhabitants are French citizens with a right to vote and economic subsidies that enable them to enjoy a standard of living comparable to that of metropolitan France. Far from weakening France, the shedding of the colonial burden freed its hand for a more assertive foreign policy in Europe, the Middle East, and elsewhere, and it eliminated the searing domestic division that stemmed from unpopular colonial wars. In the years that followed, de Gaulle was able to show his countrymen that it was possible to have a measure of grandeur without a colonial empire.

Subway entrance, Paris. The Louvre is on the left. Photo by Susan L. Thompson

Prosperity and Social Benefits

While de Gaulle provided France with a constitution that could maintain a greater measure of political stability, he also sought to eliminate the bases of social conflict by introducing needed social reforms. The often enigmatic but always pragmatic general was a point of intersection between two seemingly contradictory forces. He was an agent of French modernization and also the guardian of the idea of French mission and grandeur. His task was to change France without discarding her glorious tradition. Among his followers were traditionalists, technocrats, social reformers, French nationalists, dreamers, and realists.

He continued work begun before 1958 to expand education opportunities, thus facilitating greater mobility, especially for workers and other formerly underprivileged groups. He stabilized France's currency and helped bring about a rise in real wages. He expanded the social security net that protects Frenchmen against ill health, unemployment, and old age. He also proposed that large firms distribute a portion of their shares to employees and include workers in the firms' decision-making practices, which some companies such as Renault, actually adopted.

In general, he furthered efforts to provide his countrymen with prosperity and higher common consumption standards shared by all. He could write with pride, "once upon a time there was an old country hemmed in by habits and circumspection. . . . Now this country, France, is back on her feet again."

Foreign Affairs—Estrangement from US Hegemony

With social peace and economic prosperity at home, de Gaulle could turn full attention to that which was undoubtedly his major interest: foreign affairs. He had been greatly displeased with France's position in the world when he came to power. Colonial wars had sapped almost all of France's attention and military strength. What was worse, the fate of Europe had been determined by the Soviet Union, the US, and Britain, and after the advent of the Cold War in 1946–1947, French security had fallen almost exclusively into the hands of NATO, with an American general in command. That is, France's security was basically in the hands of the US, a friendly but foreign country, which in his words, "brings to great affairs elementary feelings and a complicated policy."

De Gaulle and all his successors knew that the Soviet Union posed a threat to western Europe, which ultimately needed American protection. He also knew that the United States' tolerance level toward its European allies was high. He therefore decided that France needed and could achieve foreign policy independence. He unquestionably also had bitter memories of what he considered a personal snub by Churchill and Roosevelt during the struggles of World War II.

His first step was to develop French atomic weapons. When he was informed in 1960 of the successful French explosion in the Sahara, he exclaimed, "Hurray for France!" This nuclear capability, known in France as the force de frappe, has come to be supported by most of the French political parties, including the Communist Party.

Seeking to strengthen the center of western Europe, he signed a Treaty on German-French Cooperation in 1963. It basically called for regular consultation and semiannual state visits between the leaders of these two European powerhouses. A disappointed de Gaulle later referred to this treaty as a "faded rose" because it had failed to persuade the West Germans to loosen their own ties with the US, as he had hoped. Nevertheless, it was an important and imaginative policy observed by all his successors. For example, the first meeting President Mitterrand had with a foreign political leader after his election was with the West German chancellor. Further, Helmut Kohl's first foreign visit after becoming German chancellor in 1982 was to Paris. De Gaulle had provided an enormous boost for a development which few Europeans would have considered possible in 1945: For the first time in European history, the idea of a war between France and Germany had become unthinkable.

In 1967 he announced an "opening to the east" which amounted to direct French contact with the Soviet Union and actual participation in the era of détente. In 1967, when war broke out between Israel and its Arab neighbors, de Gaulle, unfettered by a colonial policy in North Africa, chose to adopt an openly pro-Arab position. Although many Frenchmen were displeased by his anti-Israel (and occasionally unconcealed anti Jewish) remarks, this policy was not reversed by his next two successors, who were only too well aware of France's dependence upon Arab oil. Mitterrand promised a more evenhanded policy toward Israel and the Arabs.

The US reluctantly honored de Gaulle's demand that American troops (whom he called "good-natured but bad mannered") be withdrawn from French soil, a move that greatly increased NATO's logistical problems. This was a logical step to follow his announcement a year earlier that France would withdraw from NATO's integrated command (although not from NATO itself). He did not oppose the presence of American troops elsewhere in Europe because he did not want to remove France from the NATO shield. It was always assumed that France would support NATO in the event of a Warsaw Pact attack against western Europe. This assumption was underscored by the fact that France continued to maintain 70,000 troops in West Germany and participates in many joint military exercises. De Gaulle was convinced that, in case of a ground war in Europe, Frenchmen would be more willing to make sacrifices to defend Europe because they would see this as primarily a French defense effort, not an American one. Thus, in his opinion, the western alliance would be strengthened, not weakened.

American leaders in 1967, bogged down in a hopeless Vietnam War, had little understanding for such logic. Many Americans remembered the many American soldiers buried in France as a result of World War II. However, after 1968, the White House had far more admiration for de Gaulle's character and policy. Kissinger noted in his memoirs that de Gaulle's policies, "so contrary to American postwar preconceptions, were those of an ancient country grown skeptical through many enthusiasms shattered and conscious that to be meaningful to others, France had first of all to mean something to herself."

The changes were by no means universally supported in France at the time, but by the early 1970s, they had been embraced by all political parties, including the communists. The basic Gaullist goal to create an independent Europe under French leadership and thereby to diminish US influence in Europe has not been accomplished. Nevertheless, his design to create an independent French foreign policy has been followed by his presidential successors, despite some changes in emphasis and style.

He gave France a role of which it could be proud, and he ultimately won the world's respect for his country. Kissinger recalled that the general "exuded authority" and told of de Gaulle's attendance at a reception given by former president Nixon on the occasion of General Eisenhower's funeral in Washington: "His presence . . . was so overwhelming that he was the center of attention wherever he stood. Other heads of government and many senators who usually proclaimed their antipathy to authoritarian generals crowded around him and treated him like some strange species. One had the sense that if he moved to a window, the center of gravity might shift and the whole room might tilt everyone into the garden."

The "Events of May" and de Gaulle's Exit

Under de Gaulle, France had not become a land of complete satisfaction and harmony. Many Frenchmen grew weary of his paternalism. His preoccupation with foreign affairs gradually slowed down the reformist impulse. While most Frenchmen shared in the increasing prosperity, income differences had actually widened during the Fifth Republic. Further, despite the educational reforms, only 1% of the children from the working-class families entered the universities. Class stratification was not breaking down as much as some would have liked. At the same time, some Frenchmen, especially the young and the educated, were becoming afraid that the new consumption-oriented society was not good for France; it became apparent that France's traditional schizophrenia about change and modernism had not been entirely erased.

Before departing for a state visit to Romania in May 1968, de Gaulle announced that France was an "island of calm" in a very troubled world. Scarcely had he arrived in Budapest when a furious storm erupted in France that brought the Fifth Republic to the brink of extinction. Student unrest at the new University of Nanterre, a slogan-besmeared concrete complex located at the edge of Paris, spilled over to the Sorbonne and to other universities in the country. Many small groups of anarchists and Trotskyite and Maoist students believed that the university was the ideal place to launch a revolution against the capitalist society. Trying to reestablish order, the police violated an old taboo by entering the university grounds. This tradition stemmed from the time when the universities actually exercised the privilege of ruling themselves, a privilege long since revoked by a highly centralized French regime.

With vivid pictures of the Paris Commune in their heads, students erected barricades in Paris, and night after night they battled police with bricks from the cobblestone streets for control of the Latin Quarter. For this reason, Parisian authorities later paved over all of the city's cobblestone streets, thereby eliminating this arsenal of projectiles. Miraculously, the chaos claimed only two dead.

De Gaulle's number 2 man, Prime Minister Georges Pompidou, was very conciliatory toward the students, but before he could restore order, French workers were on strike, and the French economy practically came to a standstill. The Paris Stock Exchange was burned, and the threat of civil war was in the air.

De Gaulle developed a bold plan of action. He quietly flew by helicopter to Baden Baden, the headquarters of the French forces in Germany, in order to assure himself that the French military no longer bore grudges against him and would help him in the crisis. Returning to Paris, he announced new parliamentary elections in a radio speech that reversed the entire situation.

The campaign that followed was one of the shortest (19 days) and crudest in France since 1945. De Gaulle presented the basic issue as a choice between himself or anarchy. He successfully raised the specter of a communist danger to France. He also freed the remaining OAS prisoners in order to placate the army and right-wing elements. Opposition collapsed when the communists decided that it was not yet time for a revolution in France and advocated a return to order. The elections held in June 1968 were a virtual landslide for the Gaullists. The left lost half its seats and found itself in utter shambles.

The "events of May" had so shaken de Gaulle's grip on power he decided that he needed to restore his authority. He announced a referendum for April 1969 and, as usual, warned that, if his recommendations were not accepted, he would resign. He combined a rather unpopular reform (a change in the election of senators) with a more popular measure designed

Honorable Valery Giscard d'Estaing

to strengthen the French regions. It was clear, however, that the chief issue was de Gaulle's popularity and his continued presidency, and on election day 53% voted against him. The general was thus handed the first referendum defeat in French history—a stinging rebuke.

Never tempted by dictatorship over his country, he resigned immediately and returned for the last time to his estate in Colombey-les-Deux-Églises in eastern France. Many Frenchmen asked whether this would be the end of the Fifth Republic, but they soon saw that he had not left a political void. He had left a sturdy constitution, in many ways well tailored to French needs. He had left a successor who easily won the presidential elections and whose greatest contribution to France was that he showed how the Fifth Republic could survive its creator.

In a 2005 television poll, de Gaulle was elected as the greatest Frenchman of all time. This was not merely a matter of popularity. The general remains as a kind of moral guarantor of today's French state, as well as of the Gaullist Party. He provides comfort and inspiration in the midst of uncertainty, decline, political stagnation, and a never-ending search for French identity. In 2008 a multimedia museum was dedicated to him at Les Invalides in Paris, and another opened in his home village of Colombey-les-Deux-Églises.

Georges Pompidou and Valery Giscard d'Estaing

The new president, Georges Pompidou, had been educated at one of France's elite Grandes écoles and had quietly taught French literature in a Paris lycée during World War II. He was characteristic of many successful French political leaders, including Mitterrand: highly literate and intelligent, with a humanistic education and a sharp, practical sense for the realities of modern and political economic life.

In foreign policy, Pompidou was only slightly less Gaullist than de Gaulle himself, although he was always more modest and less abrasive than the general had been. He did break with his predecessor's policy by allowing Britain to enter the EU. He stressed continued industrial growth and the protection of French economic interests in the world. He also sought to modernize Paris by constructing urban freeways and skyscrapers in the city. However, Frenchmen, who are always sensitive to any alterations of their capital, widely condemned this "Manhattanization" of Paris, and his successor therefore abandoned this face-lifting operation.

Pompidou died in 1974 and was succeeded by Valéry Giscard d'Estaing, who won a razor-thin victory over Socialist leader François Mitterrand. A product of the super-elite École Nationale d'Administration (ENA) and a former finance minister, Giscard, who possessed distinguished aristocratic looks and a logical and photographic mind, had emerged as leader of a cluster of parties in the center and moderate right of the French political spectrum which came to be known as the Union for French Democracy (UDF).

Giscard entered the presidency determined to establish a more relaxed style in the Elysées Palace. Calling himself a "conservative who loves change," he wore a business suit instead of formal wear to his inauguration and after the ceremony walked instead of motored down the Champs-Elysées. He allowed himself to be photographed in a V-neck sweater and took a ride on the Paris Metro. For a while, he even ate monthly dinners in the homes of ordinary Frenchmen, and once he invited a group of Parisian garbage men to breakfast in the presidential palace. But he, like US president Jimmy Carter, discovered that his people did not necessarily respect folksiness in their highest leaders. Soon he withdrew to the dignity of his office and eventually assumed such an aloof and aristocratic air that his political opponents were always able to score points with voters by attacking his "monarchical" style.

The only president to be elected under age 50, Giscard was a reform-minded leader. He brought question time to the National Assembly and gave the opposition the chance to challenge legislation in the constitutional court. He also introduced some social changes. During his term the minimum voting age was lowered from 21 to 18; divorce laws were liberalized; abortion was legalized; a minimum wage was made available to agricultural workers; and most of the emigrants housed in embarrassing shanty towns, known as "Bidonvilles," on the periphery of France's metropolitan areas, were resettled in newly built public housing. He also made the decision to permit immigrant families to rejoin their relatives in France, a policy that later became highly controversial.

Honorable Jacques Chirac,
ex-president of the French Republic

In foreign affairs he observed the basic Gaullist principles of French independence and active presence on the international scene. He modernized the force de frappe, sent warships to the Persian Gulf to underscore French interests in the area, and took an active hand in Zaire (Congo) and the former French West Africa. About 6,000 French troops, including Foreign Legionnaires, are stationed in Africa, where about 300,000 mainland French still live. The largest units are in Djibouti, Senegal, Ivory Coast, and Gabon.

He sent French troops in 1977–1978 to Shaba (formerly Katanga) Province in Zaire to halt an invasion of Angolan and rebel forces. While France continued to sell arms to Libya, Giscard approved French military operations against Libyan moves in Mauritania (1977 and 1979) and Tunisia (1980). He joined anti-Libyan efforts in Chad. He also approved the use of French soldiers in 1979 to help depose the butcherous leader of the Central African Republic, Jean Bédel-Bokassa, a man who figured in one of Giscard's most embarrassing and damaging scandals: While finance minister under Pompidou, he had accepted gifts of diamonds from Bokassa.

Giscard prided himself on his support of European cooperation. He increased France's role in NATO planning and exercises, although he never hinted at any willingness to lead France back into full participation. Sometimes, though, he chose to act alone, reaping condemnation not only from France's western allies but from many French, as well.

Giscard's main objectives were to reorder in a systematic and long-term way French industrial priorities. Industries such as textiles or steel, that could no longer compete in international markets were denied government subsidies and were therefore often forced to cut back on their operations. Future-oriented sectors, such as telecommunications, microelectronics, nuclear and aerospace technology, and seabed research, which could compete successfully, were granted support. To reduce French energy dependence on oil from over one-half of energy needs to less than a third, Giscard supported an atomic energy policy that made France Europe's largest producer of nuclear power.

On the whole, France was more prosperous and economically prepared for the future than when Giscard entered office. But his effort to strengthen the economy by making firms more competitive put many Frenchmen out of work. Combined with growing revulsion for Giscard's aloof and aristocratic manner and a scandal involving his acceptance of diamonds from an African dictator, a majority of the French voters in 1981 were convinced that it was time for change. Power passed to the Socialists under the leadership of François Mitterrand.

GOVERNMENT IN THE FIFTH REPUBLIC

In his famous Bayeux Manifesto of 1946, de Gaulle repeated the rhetorical question posed by the ancient Greek thinker Solon: "What is the best constitution?" He answered, "Tell me first for what people and during which period." De Gaulle suggested to his countrymen, "Let us take ourselves as we are." He asserted that French political parties, as indeed most individual Frenchmen, traditionally obscured the highest interests of the country and thereby created confusion in the state. He admitted that a parliament is necessary, but it could not be entrusted with the destiny of the French nation. Due to its very nature, France requires a powerful, popularly elected president who stands above the parties, focuses on the "national purpose," and wields the supreme power of the state.

The constitution of the Fifth Republic, adopted in 1958 and still in force, reflects these convictions. It contains a workable compromise between the need for national unity and the legitimate expression of many political ideas, social classes, and interests; between the need for a strong executive and a representative parliament; between lofty politics and common, day-to-day politics. It also incorporated the Napoleonic practice of involving the citizens directly in the political process. Beginning in 1962, they directly elected the president for a seven-year renewable term, lowered to five years in 2000; a reform in 2008 limits a president to two five-year terms. Through referenda, they are called upon occasionally to give opinions on major national policy issues.

Cafe life in Sarlat

Photo by Bill Remington

The Presidency

The French president's constitutional powers are immense, and the character of the presidents since 1958 expanded these powers far beyond the letter of the constitution. Unless his party lacks a parliamentary majority (a situation called "cohabitation" that did not exist before 1986), he appoints the prime minister and cabinet, chairs all cabinet meetings, and actively directs the work of the cabinet ministers. Within any one-year period, he may dismiss the National Assembly (lower house of the parliament) for whatever reason he chooses and call new elections. He may question the constitutionality of any law and require parliament to reexamine any piece of legislation. He may submit any issue to a referendum, including constitutional amendments.

These infrequently held referendums almost always demonstrated confidence in the president and therefore invariably strengthened him with respect to the parliament. He is commander-in-chief of the nation's military forces, and he negotiates and ratifies all treaties. He may not issue decrees. But if, in his opinion, the republic is in danger, he can assume emergency powers that enable him to wield full executive, legislative, and military authority. He is formally obliged to seek the advice of the Constitutional Council and is not permitted to dismiss parliament during this time. There is no provision for terminating such emergency powers. In effect, the French president determines domestic and foreign policy and has veto power over every imaginable aspect of policy, including constitutional amendments. Unlike his American counterpart, though, he cannot veto an act of parliament. He can be removed from office if he is convicted in a special tribunal (not by the parliament) of high treason. In 2007 parliament approved a constitutional amendment creating an American-style impeachment procedure to check the president's powers.

Nicolas Sarkozy won approval in 2008 for further reforms that affect presidential powers: He cannot issue collective pardons, and his right to pronounce decrees was limited. In a kind of war-powers act, he must inform parliament within three days of any military operation abroad and seek its approval if it lasts more than four months. He can address parliament in a "state of the union" speech, abolished since 1875. When confronting the need to

LE FIGARO

« Sans la liberté de blâmer, il n'est point d'éloge flatteur » Beaumarchais

Cannes
« Les Chansons d'amour », une comédie musicale de Christophe Honoré
Page 28

Sarkozy charge Fillon d'une « politique nouvelle »

Le nouveau premier ministre a été nommé hier.
La composition du gouvernement doit être annoncée ce matin.

Former prime minister François Fillon and former president Nicolas Sarkozy

ratify new membership to the EU, parliament, by a three-fifths vote, can authorize the president to seek such ratification either through a referendum or a parliamentary vote. Lacking such authorization, a referendum is required.

De Gaulle in 1964 described the presidency which he had created in breathtaking terms: "It must of course be understood that the indivisible authority of the State is confided in its entirety to the President by the people who have elected him, that no other authority exists, neither ministerial nor civil nor military nor judicial, which is not conferred and maintained by him."

Clearly this is hardly a presidency of the American type. The US president must deal with 50 powerful states and what has become the most powerful and assertive legislature in the world. One foreign minister complained that, in matters involving the United States, he had to deal with 535 secretaries of state. The French president traditionally appoints the prefects (governors) in the 101 departments (states, five of which are overseas) and until 1986 faced neither serious regional resistance nor a powerful legislature. In the 21st century, the power of prefects has been diminished by the requirement that they share responsibility with the departmental presidents and the 13 elected regional councils. Whereas the American president must deal with such nonconstitutional checks as an influential, independent, and often fiercely investigative press and electronic news media, the French president faced a meeker press for a long time. Until 1984, radio and television networks were controlled by the government and were hesitant to attack the president openly.

In contrast, the American president must operate in an environment in which the Freedom of Information Act and various "sunshine" laws have made more visible the working of government. The French traditional cult of secrecy and more impenetrable bureaucracy are a haven for the chief executive. The public appears to be more used to viewing the state as something that is walled off.

Some prefer to describe French presidentialism as elected monarchy, in which the incumbent's whims and favors are crucially important. The French satirical magazine *Le Canard Enchaîné* (*The Chained Duck*) once put it, "There's the President, and under him there's a vast void. And afterwards there is a nothing. And below that, nothing. But finally one stumbles over the government." Edouard Balladur asked with a degree of exaggeration, "In which other democracy is the president in charge of the executive and the legislature and the judiciary; in charge of the order of business in parliament, where by intimidation, force or a reverential majority he gets the votes he wants; in charge of the promotion of magistrates and of the public prosecution that sends them cases; in charge of a government that moves only at his whim?" Only de Gaulle could live up to the impossibly high expectations the French have for their president: monarchical in stature but able to connect with the people; extraordinary but "normal" at the same time; dignified at all times.

The powers of the presidency grew so much that President Mitterrand pledged to reduce them and to pass back to parliament some of the powers it had lost. He had always been a vocal critic of the Fifth Republic's constitution, as the title of his 1964 book indicated: *The Permanent Coup d'Etat*. In office, he did nothing to diminish presidential powers. Like all presidents, he succumbed to what political writer Denis Tillinac called the "Versailles syndrome."

Changes in the imperial presidency are underway. Growing public cynicism toward the political establishment emboldened journalists to break hallowed taboos against reporting on politicians' private lives. In 1994 the weekly *Paris Match* published a cover photo of Mitterrand in public with his daughter born from an extramarital affair two decades earlier. Mistress and daughter had been housed in government guesthouses and had traveled at taxpayers' expense. Although the magazine was sold out within hours, there was an outcry among public figures that it had crossed the line. Unlike in the US, this harmed neither Mitterrand, who made no attempt to conceal his daughter's paternity, nor his party. At his funeral in January 1996, his wife, Danielle, stood for the first time with his daughter out of wedlock, Mazarine Pingeot, and her mother, Anne Pingeot. In 2014, a young Swedish man announced that he is Mitterrand's son, the product of an affair the president had with a Swedish journalist.

Mitterrand died of prostate cancer. He had been informed of this condition several months after his election in 1981, but he ordered that it be kept secret. In 2005 a feature film on Mitterrand, *Le Promeneur du Champ de Mars* (*The Stroller in the Champ de Mars*, by Robert Guediguian), portrayed a cancer-weakened president in his final months in office with all his human frailties and missteps outside the view of the public.

In order to reduce the risk of seeing the same person occupy the presidency for 14 years, 73.5% of the voters in a 2000 referendum opted to reduce the term of office to 5 years, with no limit on the number of times to be reelected; parliament voted in 2008 to restrict the number of terms to two. All the major parties supported this reform. Even though only about one out of three eligible voters bothered to go to the polls to record their opinion, this change could alter the balance of power in the political system. Referring to such a significant shift by means of a referendum, political analyst Dominique Moïsi said this "ends Gaullism in a very Gaullist way."

The unusually long tenure of seven years had been designed to create a powerful chief of state who could provide France with the kind of stability that had been lacking in earlier republics. By the end of the century, France had achieved that stability, so an imperial presidency is no longer needed. The special aura of the magisterial presidential office declined. The reform reduced the periods of power sharing with parliament, known as "cohabitation." By making presidential and parliamentary elections coincide more frequently, France gains more coherent governments. However, critics argue that parliamentary elections only a month after presidential ones mean that the National Assembly has only a weak democratic mandate of its own, since it is filled with members who rode the president's coattails. The president still has the power to dissolve parliament once within a year's time.

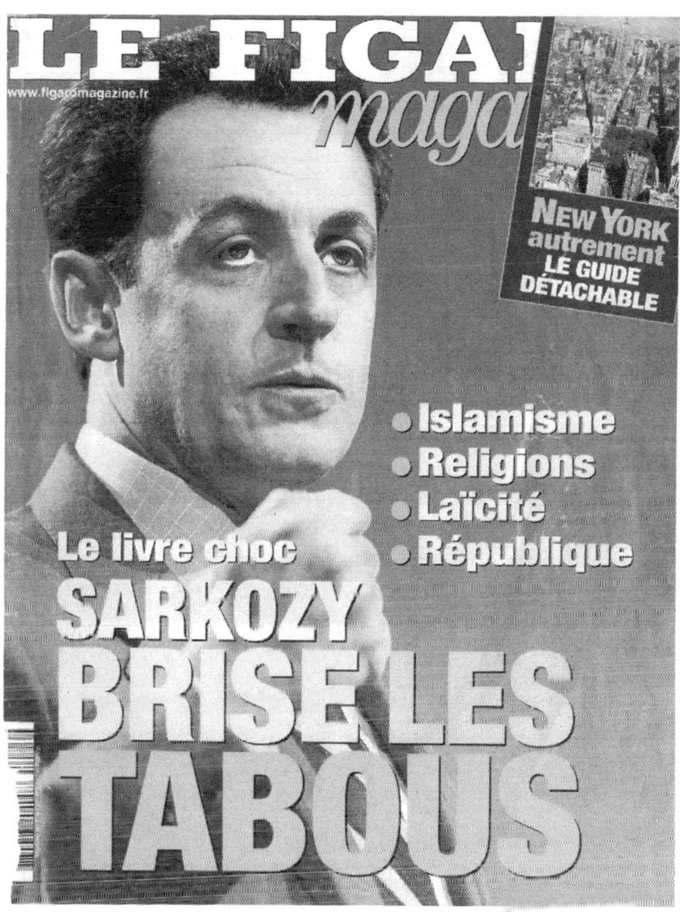

The Prime Minister and Cabinet

The prime minister and the cabinet ministers (the "government") have usually been drawn from all the parties in the president's majority coalition, although some have belonged to no political party. They are forbidden from having seats in the National Assembly. Ministers, including prime ministers, must give up their seats to substitutes, and if they later leave the government, they can reclaim their seats only by persuading the substitutes to stand down and by winning a by-election. If the prime minister and president are from the same party, the former is responsible for explaining and gaining support for the president's policies and for ensuring that the president's overall directives are carried out in practice.

The prime minister executes the laws. He supervises the drafting of the budget, which is submitted to the parliament for overall approval but which parliament rarely alters. Finally, he determines the agenda of parliament; government legislation always takes priority. He is the president's lightening rod and is dependent on him; from 1958 to 1991, only one prime minister resigned voluntarily. None survived a full five-year legislative term until Socialist Lionel Jospin managed to do that from 1997 to 2002. *The Economist* wrote that the prime minister must not upstage the president and must "let the president take the credit when things go well and to deal with the trouble when it all goes wrong." Of the 22 politicians who occupied the job from 1958 to 2018, only 2 (Pompidou and Chirac) went on to become president.

If the president's party does not have a parliamentary majority, then the president must select a prime minister whose party or coalition can get a majority of votes in the National Assembly. In this case, the prime minister is a very powerful political figure who establishes the main lines of French domestic and economic policy and shares with the president responsibility for foreign and defense policy. He appoints and instructs the top officials in the foreign ministry.

Parliament

The parliament has two houses: the Senate and the 576-seat National Assembly. Deputies to the National Assembly are elected for five years by universal suffrage. The president can call new elections before the end of the five-year term. The Senate has 330 members elected since 2003 for nine-year terms. One-third of them are renewed every three years by members of the National Assembly and elected officials at all levels down to municipal counselors.

Both houses of parliament have essentially the same powers with two exceptions: The National Assembly has the privilege of examining the government's budget first. Further, only the National Assembly can force the government to resign by assembling a majority against an important piece of government legislation. However, the Fifth Republic's constitution places severe limits on this latter practice, which in past republics had been abused and which therefore brought a merry-go-round of governments with extremely short life spans. Such a vote may be submitted only once during any legislative session, and all abstentions or blank ballots count automatically for the government. Also, if such a vote succeeds, the National Assembly is dissolved immediately, and new elections are called. This latter provision takes the fun out of the former "parliamentary game" of shooting down the government for the most trivial reasons and makes such a vote of censure a much more serious step for the parties and the individual deputies.

An additional limitation of the parliament's powers is that much of what is considered "legislation" in other democratic countries is defined in the French constitution as "rule making." The president signs decrees issued by the prime minister, thereby circumventing the parliament altogether for a limited period of time (ca. 18 months). There is a debate whether the president can refuse to sign a decree. Decrees authorized by parliament are called ordinances; an example was privatizations while Jacques Chirac was prime minister from 1986 to 1988.

Approaching the 50th anniversary of the Fifth Republic in 2008, which has provided a degree of political stability unknown in

France's past, President Nicolas Sarkozy commissioned his former mentor, ex–prime minister Edouard Balladur, to review the constitution. The latter submitted 77 reform proposals, some of them strengthening the presidency, such as allowing the president to address parliament (forbidden until 2008). Some would strengthen parliament's role: It would share the right to determine the daily agenda, which is now the government's prerogative; the government's right to pass laws by decree would be limited; parliament would get new powers over presidential nominations. Any changes in the constitution would have to be approved by a congress of both houses. One reform that must have pleased the president has already been enacted: his salary jumped from €101,000 to €240,000 ($310,000). This compares with the American president's salary of €343,000 ($450,000).

The number of parliamentary committees (which enable a parliament to develop the expertise to challenge the executive) is limited to six, and even these few committees are not permitted to amend a government bill before it comes to the floor. A party must have at least 15 deputies in order to form a parliamentary group. This brings committee assignments, subsidies, and other privileges. An increasingly weak parliament has been called "a device to provide majorities." There is little public interest in its debates, and people turn to their mayors rather than to their local deputies to pursue causes and grievances.

A final striking innovation in the constitution is the Constitutional Council, composed of nine members appointed by the president of the republic and of the presidents of the two houses of parliament for nine-year terms. Its purpose is to guard the constitution. De Gaulle did not originally design this body to protect individual rights but rather to protect executive power against parliament. It is ironic that today it emphasizes the protection of parliamentary and individual rights. In 1971 the Declaration of the Rights of Man became a reference used by the Constitutional Council.

Upon request of the three above-mentioned presidents or the prime minister or, since 1992, 60 members of either house of parliament, it can review the constitutionality of laws, treaties, elections, and referendums. The council cannot be compared to the far more prestigious United States Supreme Court, which possesses the power of unlimited judicial review. But in France a piece of legislation can be challenged in the Constitutional Council before it goes into effect; in the US, this can happen only after the law is in effect. For example, in 2012 the council ruled that the government's proposed 75% tax on incomes over €1 million ($1.3 million) was unconstitutional. Opponents of same-sex marriage also submitted the issue to the council in 2013 as soon as it was overwhelmingly passed in parliament.

From 1986 to 1988, when for the first time since 1958 the prime minister came from a different party than the president, the Constitutional Council was called upon to determine which powers and responsibilities belong to each office. It became the ultimate referee in the political system. A Council of State also exists to deal with administrative and public law. It provides recourse to individual citizens who have claims against the administration.

Decentralization

Since at least the 17th century, French national leaders consistently strengthened the powers of the central government at the expense of the regions and communes. In 1792 France was divided into 96 departments (plus 5 overseas departments by 2009), each headed by a prefect, a powerful and uniformed official appointed by and answerable to the national government. The prefect oversaw the work of locally elected mayors and councils in the 37,500 municipalities. For economic and administrative purposes, 22 regions, whose borders roughly approximate those of France's ancient provinces, each headed by a regional prefect, were created. They were later reduced to 13. The essential fact is that all important initiatives had either to originate or be approved in Paris. For example, the designs for school cafeterias, soccer fields, swimming pools, and other public facilities had to clear numerous bureaucratic and political hurdles in Paris.

This not only required personal connections and caused serious delays, but many Frenchmen feared that it also was creating excessive visual uniformity in a land admired for its rich diversity. Many observers also believed that centralization stifled individual civic action and stimulated suspicion toward the French state. Mitterrand took seriously his pledge to reduce the power the central government and the prefects had over subnational political units and to allow popularly elected regional and local assemblies and executives to handle their own affairs.

In the early 1980s, 10 devolution laws and 50 decrees designed to decentralize France were announced. Perhaps the most significant change was that the prefects, renamed "Commissioners of the Republic," were stripped of many of their administrative, financial, judicial, and technical powers. They must share responsibility with the elected presidents of the departments and the 13 regional councils, which were strengthened. Nevertheless, few French know or care much about their regional governments. Regional elections are mainly referenda on how popular the nation's governing party is. At the time of the 2010 regional elections, in which the Socialists won 21 out of 22 regions, voters were asked in a poll to name their regional president. Only 29% could do so.

During the 1980s local governments were granted more autonomy in spending, taxation, and borrowing. The result was more local activity to build new airports, wider streets, pedestrian zones, museums, concert halls, and stadiums. However, the shift of power from civil servants to local politicians also brought a higher level of local indebtedness and corruption.

Political Parties

It has always been difficult to rule France from the center, long referred to as the "swamp." Since the founding of the Fifth Republic, there has been a steady reduction in the number of parties with any hope for electoral success.

The Republicans

After numerous name changes, including the Rally for the Republic (RPR) and the Union for a Popular Movement (UMP), the Gaullist Party renamed itself the Republicans. It is a federation of parties that grew out of Jacques Chirac's successful electoral alliance in 2002, then called the Union for the Presidential Majority, with the same acronym. It merged several conservative and centrist groups.

Founded in 1976, the RPR and its successor seek to preserve the fundamental Gaullist values: foreign policy independence, caution toward a more united Europe, maintaining the institutions of the Fifth Republic, and economic and social expansion and progress. Even a third of a century after his death, de Gaulle basks in widespread approval. His predictions seem to have come true in the 1990s: the collapse of communism and the USSR; upheaval in eastern Europe; the unification of Germany, which Frenchmen accepted with only a little uneasiness; and the emergence of a Europe more independent of the superpowers. "Europe from the Atlantic to the Urals" was his concept before Mikhail Gorbachev picked up on it. In 1990, to celebrate his famous call for resistance on June 18, 1940, the obelisk at the Place de la Concorde was draped with a 35-meter-high radio model blaring popular songs of the time and coded messages from London to the Free French.

In May 1995 Jacques Chirac was elected president. But he was reduced almost to the status of a figurehead after the 1997 parliamentary elections, when the RPR crashed from being France's largest party, with 258 seats, to a minority, with only 134 seats. In 2000 the party picked the first female leader of a major French party,

Michele Alliot-Marie, a law lecturer and later defense, interior, justice and foreign minister. The RPR struggled to unify itself and to find a new identity more compatible with the rise of a global economy and the EU and the reduced French role in the world.

Chirac and his party faced the 2002 presidential elections in serious trouble. They were mired in scandals that came perilously close to Chirac himself. During the 18 years Chirac was mayor of Paris (1977–1995), fictitious jobs were created at the taxpayers' expense, and grateful public-works contractors made contributions to parties, especially the RPR.

Chirac won a massive reelection as president in 2002, thanks to voters' revulsion for his chief opponent, Jean Marie Le Pen. He organized a conservative grouping broader than his RPR to win the June 2002 parliamentary elections—the UMP. It decimated the left.

Until his defeat in May 2012, the party's leader was Nicolas Sarkozy. In 2004 he won the party presidency with 85% of the votes at an American-style party convention complete with French flags, music, and a giant video screen. A first-generation immigrant son of a Hungarian nobleman (real name: Sarkozy de Nagy-Bocsa) and of a French mother with Jewish roots, he had made it known to his school class mates that he would be president one day. Unlike most of the elite, however, he studied law instead of attending the National School of Administration (ENA).

He entered politics at age 20 and became a mayor at age 28. Chirac heard him speak at a rally and told him, "You are made for politics." Sarkozy was a gifted orator. He was catapulted into national fame in 1993, when, as mayor of Neuilly-sur-Seine, he personally negotiated with a hostage-taker who had stormed a local kindergarten, while the police sneaked into the school and shot the man dead.

France needed a new generation of leaders, and Sarkozy most represented that new France. He brought to the presidency fresh ideas. He spoke of the erosion of the work culture and the importance of self-reliance, achievement, and social mobility. As interior minister, he pursued a law-and-order policy to crack crime and drug rings in immigrant neighborhoods.

He had an uncomplicated approach to America and advocated closer relations. Sarkozy came to the presidency without the usual French anti-Americanism. He offered a fresh start for Franco-American relations. He urged French youngsters to embrace as a role model Martin Luther King Jr., and he said his favorite author was Ernest Hemingway. During a highly publicized (and, in France, criticized) visit to the US in September 2006, he argued that "friendship is respect, understanding, affection, but not submission. . . . I ask our American friends to let us be free, free to be their friends."

In the first paragraph of the English translation of his best-selling campaign book *Testimony: France in the Twenty-First Century*, he called America "the greatest democracy in the world." Later in the book, he wrote, "I don't see why my country doesn't take inspiration from its great ally," and, "I love the value Americans place on work and the desire for excellence that you find everywhere." On election night he assured America that France would "always be at its side when it needs her." However, the realities of French politics require that he be cautious to leave some light between his foreign policy views and those of Washington. He acquired the tag of *"Sarko l'Americain,"* and one of his Socialist opponents in the election called him "an American neocon with a French passport."

Sarkozy was a convinced Atlanticist, and in his first summer in office, "I came to visit the United States on holiday, like 900,000 French do every year. It's a great country." He paid an informal visit with both Presidents Bush at Kennebunkport, Maine, and was served his choice of hamburgers or hot dogs. Like the younger Bush, Sarkozy does not drink alcohol. He was granted the privilege in November 2007 of speaking to a joint session of Congress and was received with warmth and enthusiasm. Former undersecretary of state Nicholas Burns spoke for many Americans when he said, "we admire the way he has opened up to our country."

Confidential cables published by Wikileaks from American diplomats in Paris revealed a mixed view of the French president. On the one hand, he was "the most pro-American French president since World War II" and a "force multiplier" for American foreign policy interests. "Very much unlike nearly all other French political figures, Sarkozy is viscerally pro-American." He "identifies with America; he sees his own rise in the world as reflecting an American-like saga." He was especially fond of American movies and personally pinned the Legion of Honor on Clint Eastwood. During his tenure after 2007, the two countries had few foreign policy differences, and he changed the way many Americans view France. But he was high-maintenance and erratic. He had authoritarian tendencies and a tendency to decide policy on the fly. He was reported to be too impatient to consult with important allies before enacting his initiatives.

His willingness to reintegrate with NATO's command structure (on the condition that European defense capability is improved) is appreciated. His first foreign minister, Bernard Kouchner, made clear that France cannot pursue its interests through "permanent anti-Americanism." Both Frenchmen also have the hard-headed calculation that, if France's ties with the US are not strong, its weight in the world is diminished.

He persuaded the party to select its presidential candidate by means of primary elections involving all party members. He reached the presidency in May 2007, becoming the first French president born after World War II, the first Gaullist president never to have served under de Gaulle himself, the first Gaullist president since Georges Pompidou not to have graduated from ENA, and the first president whose father was not French. In the June 2007 parliamentary elections, his UMP became the first ruling party to be reelected since 1978.

Sarkozy and his party faced an uphill struggle to win again in 2012. His approval rating fell to only 22%, a record low for a president. In the first round of the 2012 presidential election, he placed second, with 27.2% of the votes, right behind François Hollande (with 28.6%) and ahead of Marine Le Pen (17.9%). He lost in the second round with 48.4% of the votes. He immediately announced he was leaving politics. The UMP was in a state of disarray.

The vacuum in the party, combined with his successor's disastrously low approval ratings, had prompted Sarkozy to announce that he would return to politics "out of duty and only because it is for France." Any plans were complicated by

Together, everything becomes possible.

his need to face formal charges of "abuse of frailty" for allegedly playing on the weakness of 90-year-old L'Oréal heiress Liliane Bettencourt to secure a donation to his presidential campaign fund in 2007. Sarkozy's comeback failed. The party's primary was won by his former prime minister, François Fillon, whose campaign was paralyzed by a scandal. He had paid his wife almost €1 million of public money for work she did not perform. Winning only 20% in the first round of the 2017 presidential election, he was eliminated.

The Union for French Democracy (UDF)

Former president Giscard d'Estaing had founded his own Independent Republican Party in 1966, renamed the Republican Party (PR) and then Liberal Democracy (DL), which joined the UMP in 2002. In order to enlarge his electoral and parliamentary base, he forged in 1978 a larger, loosely knit group of parties called the Union for French Democracy (UDF), which was more pro-Europe and free-market-oriented than the UMP.

In addition to diverse centrist political groups, the UDF included the Democratic Force (FD), formerly the Center of Social Democrats (CDS). Centrist, devolutionist, and strongly pro-European, this was the last remnant of the postwar reformist Popular Republican Movement (MRP), which had played such an important political role in the Fourth Republic. It also included the Radical Party, a pro-Europe social democratic product of 19th-century liberal tradition and one of France's oldest parties. During the Third Republic, it almost dominated French politics and led a particularly determined campaign against the power of the Catholic Church in politics and society. This always undisciplined party shrank in importance after World War II.

The UDF was never a sufficiently powerful political base for Giscard, although it was constructed around him. Conservatives were always plagued by divisions and bickering. In 1996 the former president retired from politics. To make it look fresher, the party's name was officially changed in 2000 to Nouvelle UDF (New UDF). But it was a difficult task to make this loose collection of disparate parties into a credible political force. It allies with the Rebublicans in national elections.

National Rally

The phenomenal rise of the right-wing National Front (FN), led until 2010 by the tough-talking former paratrooper Jean Marie Le Pen, was the 1986 election's biggest surprise. Foaming against France's 4.2 million immigrants, whom he accused of being responsible for high unemployment and crime, the party won 9.7% of the votes. It did particularly well along the Mediterranean coast, where there is much hostility to North African immigrants.

The timely abolition of proportional representation in 1988 practically eliminated the party from parliament. But its 14% showing in the 1988 presidential balloting and 15% in 1995 indicated that racist fears and resentments on which the party feeds are strong in French society. Its high vote (e.g., 28% in Marseilles) in regions, towns, and suburbs with large concentrations of immigrants, unemployed, and crime, as well as in some rural areas, was a warning to the government to eliminate the seeds of discontent that keep the National Front alive.

The other conservative parties refuse to deal with this overtly racist, xenophobic party, which opposes greater European unity and the euro. A populist, Jean-Marie Le Pen presented himself as a supporter of the "little guy" against a corrupt establishment. The party's supporters are predominantly young, urban, poor, and unemployed.

In the 2007 presidential elections, his support was undercut by Sarkozy, who also talked about law and order, restrictions on immigration, and the need to address the underlying issues which had fueled Le Pen's strength in the past: uncertainty and insecurity, unease over immigration and crime, disillusionment with the political class, and a faltering economy. After a Paris court acquitted him of racism in December 2010, Jean Marie Le Pen announced his retirement from politics.

Le Pen's youngest daughter, Marine, became his political heir. A twice-divorced, young (age 47 in 2016), working mother of three, she was elected party president in 2011 with more than two-thirds of the votes. Toning down her father's notoriously aggressive rhetoric, she seeks to soften and decontaminate the party's image and broaden its electoral base. She calls the Holocaust the "summit of human barbarism." She is media-friendly, responding to aggressive questions with easy grace. She appears on TV talk shows and is poised and courteous. She displays common sense. She avoids her father's provocative and xenophobic statements and once quit the party in exasperation after one of his outbursts. She has gotten rid of the phalanx of skinheads, who used to accompany her father at rallies. Her change of style appeals especially to women.

However, she shares many of her father's objectives: withdrawal from the euro and NATO (thereby avoiding "submission to America"); support for Russia, reintroducing the death penalty; rejecting bailouts and globalization, limiting immigration; reerecting border controls; overcoming the alienation of a depraved globalized elite and the common Frenchman; and "French first" in housing, welfare, and employment. She claims not to be against Islam but for France's traditional secularism (*laïcité*). Above all, she insists that the National Front is no longer merely a party of protest on the political sidelines but a potential governing party: "I am here to build the National Front's accession to power." Her father was an ideologue, while she is a politician who wants to win.

She compelled other candidates on the right to adopt her themes. A frightened Sarkozy tightened immigration and citizenship laws, banned the burka in public places, condemned multiculturalism, and closed Roma camps on the outskirts of

"Le Pen: The people," National Front campaign poster

Street musicians in southern France

Photo by Bill Remington

many cities. President Hollande continued the latter policy on the grounds that such settlements are unsanitary and dangerous. In addition to the up to 20,000 Roma in France, thousands have been deported or paid €300 ($370) to return home.

Marine's attempt to woo her voters legitimized the FN Party. In the 2012 presidential contest, she placed third in the first round, with an impressive 17.9% of the votes. While her father was strong in the south, she was effective in the north. A fourth of young voters, facing rising youth unemployment of 22.4%, voted for her. She picked up the discontented vote that used to go to the Communists. She refused to endorse either Sarkozy or Hollande in the second round, and Sarkozy won an estimated 58% of her voters. She failed to win a seat in the June 2012 parliamentary elections, but her niece Marion Maréchal-Le Pen, a 22-year-old law student, captured one of the party's two seats. She is the youngest legislator ever elected in the Fifth Republic. These are the party's first seats since 1997.

Le Pen is the most dynamic force in France. FN rattled the political elite by coming out first in the May 2014 European Parliament elections, winning a quarter of the votes, and second in the March 2015 departmental elections, ahead of the Socialists and at the top of the first round of the December 2015 regional elections. She placed second in the first round of the 2017 presidential elections, with 21.3% of the votes, before the other parties ganged up on her and her party in the second round. She won 34% of the votes, twice as many as her father had gotten in the 2002 election. Her anti-immigration rhetoric will continue to resonate. The former domination by two main parties has given way to a four-party system. To distance itself from its early history as a radical fringe group, the party renamed itself National Rally in 2018.

The Communists

The main reason the left had difficulty assuming power in France is that it has always been fragmented, with two parties particularly prominent: the French Communist Party (PCF) and the Socialist Party (PS). The PCF was founded in 1920 when delegates to the Socialist Party congress walked out to join the Comintern, the external arm of the Soviet's party. It converted the Socialist newspaper *L'Humanité* into an organ through which the new party consistently advocated a hard-line, class-conscious revolutionary policy, closely attuned to the aims of the Soviets. In 1936 the PCF refused to join the Popular Front because Socialists dominated the coalition, and it loyally supported Stalin's nonaggression pact with Hitler, which was the prelude to the devastating German attack on France in 1940. Once the Soviet Union was invaded by Germany, though, the PCF joined the resistance to Hitler's Germany and fought valiantly, thereby winning the admiration of such diverse persons as de Gaulle and Mitterrand.

When the Cold War poisoned relations between the west and the Soviet Union, the PCF did not hesitate to orient itself toward the latter. The Soviet suppression of uprisings in eastern Europe in 1953, 1956, and 1968 all ultimately won the PCF's approval. In the 1970s a thaw in the party began to occur. It officially disavowed the Marxist-Leninist concept of "dictatorship of the proletariat" and accepted in 1972 Mitterrand's offer of a common program of the left, including both Socialists and Communists. The course was an entirely new concept for western European socialists, who had seen clearly what happened in eastern Europe after socialist and communist parties had agreed to cooperate.

The PCF showed itself to be a difficult partner. Mitterrand's PS could count on only about 5% of the vote in 1972, whereas the PCF consistently received over a fifth of the vote in any election (and a third of all workers' votes). Therefore the PCF believed that it would soon be able to control its "junior" member. It was badly mistaken. The PS grew very rapidly in voter appeal and eventually overtook the PCF.

The PCF had second thoughts about its Eurocommunist course. It openly supported the Soviet invasion of Afghanistan and was returning to its pro-Soviet position. This was disastrous. To halt its stunning erosion, the PCF saw no alternative in 1981 to joining forces with the Socialist Party, but this alliance collapsed within three years. The PCF suffered a steady decline in votes and membership, especially among the young and intellectuals. The Socialists overtook the Communists in the traditional "red bastions" in the north. The PCF declined to where it stood a half-century ago.

The PCF shed such dogmas as the pledges to "abolish capitalism" and "nationalize the means of production." It entered the Socialist Party's governing coalition in 1997 and had four ministerial posts. It was staunchly opposed to the European constitution and helped defeat it in the May 29, 2005, referendum. One of its leaflets opened with the words "For years, one has been constructing Europe on the backs of the workers and against them."

The party is struggling to avoid disappearing completely and is trying to reinvent itself. If it modernizes its policies to adjust to a market-oriented new world not understood by Marx and participates in governments, it loses many of its core voters. If it does not do this, it becomes irrelevant and seals itself off from new voters. It got only a half-percent of the votes in the 2015 department elections. The PCF is fading from the electoral scene.

It loses many of its votes to other leftist groupings. They include such parties as the Workers' Struggle (Trotskyite, winning .6% of the presidency votes in 2012); the Revolutionary Communist Party; the Workers' Party (Trotskyite); and the Radical Party of the Left, led by Christiane Taubira, Guiana-born member of the European Parliament, the only candidate who was both black and female.

Although they are electorally insignificant, these far-left groups are still a strong political and social force in contemporary France. For example, the street demonstrations of 2008–2009 produced the New Anti-Capitalist Party, led by the telegenic Trotskyite Olivier Besancenot; it captured 1.2% of the votes for the presidency in 2012. A much more successful coalition of Communists and other far-left groups, the Front de Gauche (Left Front), led by firebrand Jean-Luc Mélenchon, attracted large, enthusiastic crowds during the presidential campaign and ended up with a surprising 19.6% of the first-round votes in the 2017 presidential election.

The Greens

The French public now focuses greater attention on environmental protection because of such highly publicized problems as the Chernobyl nuclear accident in the Ukraine, chemical factory accidents which polluted the Rhine and Loire Rivers, depletion of the ozone layer, global warming, and deforestation. They are also untainted by scandals, which have shaken other parties. French Greens (Les Verts) are on the left of the political spectrum, although they advocate protecting the high material standard of living rather than radically changing the structure of French society. They call for restraints on foreign capital in France and the preservation of small neighborhood stores, which are increasingly threatened by supermarkets.

Because of France's electoral system and because it lacks a tradition of pacifism, nuclear protest, or respect for the environment, the Greens do not have the political clout that their German counterparts do. Their standard-bearer is a German citizen, Daniel Cohn-Bendit. Known earlier as "Dany le rouge" (Dany the Red), he had been expelled from France for playing a leading role in the 1968 student rebellion. Known for his pugnacity, charisma, and rhetorical skills, he is an outspoken Europhile who already represented the German Greens in the European Parliament. He is the first foreigner to head an electoral campaign in France.

Led by Eva Joly, the "Europe Ecology, the Greens" captured a disappointing 2.3% of the votes in the 2012 presidential elections. They won 17 parliamentary seats in June, up from 4.

The Socialists

The ruling party since May 2012 is the Socialist Party (PS). It had become terribly divided over whether to support the EU constitution in the May 29, 2005, referendum. Although 59% of its members had voted to back it, deputy party leader and former prime minister Laurent Fabius defied the party line and opposed it. In June he and a dozen of his supporters who sided with the left and campaigned against it were ousted from their party positions.

The party entered the 2007 presidential elections with many ambitious contenders but one clear front-runner: Ségolène Royal. She is the daughter of an army colonel and graduate of the prestigious ENA, where she met her ex-common-law partner and father of her four children, then–Socialist chairman François Hollande. She was fresh, attractive, intelligent, and extremely media-savvy, with political experience as former minister for the environment and for family and education.

She experimented with a new style of participatory politics by engaging voters on her interactive website and posting her positions on a blog. Her entries were gathered into a book, since by tradition it is essential that serious French presidential candidates publish a book during their campaign. Because she lacked deep roots in the PS, she successfully attempted to shape public opinion before the 219,000 registered party members had a chance to elect the party's candidate in an open primary in November 2006. She won a landslide 60%, with 80% of party members participating.

Party leaders, including her then-partner, expressed outrage over her outspoken ideas, her populist methods, and her candidature in general. Former prime minister Laurent Fabius sneered, "Who will look after the children?" This remark would be a guaranteed vote-loser in many other democracies, also in France. At the end of a hard-fought election, she garnered a respectable 46.94% of the votes, and she led her party to a better-than-expected result in the parliamentary elections a month later, winning 205 seats, up from 140.

She had her eye on her party's leadership. That meant that her former partner, François Hollande, who had expected to be the party's candidate, had to step aside in more that one respect. In her book published six weeks after the presidential election, *Behind the Scenes of a Defeat*, she admitted that she had asked Hollande to leave her home after cheating on her. This was very unusual for French politicians to be so open about their private lives. But the French press has become more intrusive, and she preferred that "things be clarified for everyone."

There was a bitter struggle for control of a divided Socialist Party, which, by the time of its leadership election in November 2008, had not won a presidential election in 20 years, although it held a majority

Autumn in Paris . . . Susan and Wayne Thompson

Honorable François Mitterrand

of city hall and local posts. The bitter race left the party in full disarray and division.

The competition began to determine which Socialist would challenge Sarkozy in the 2012 presidential elections. Tops in the polls was Dominique Strauss-Kahn, a former professor and finance minister, who was managing director of the IMF, a job that gave him weight and credibility. He had already been tarnished by persistent rumors of serial womanizing and a 2008 sexual-harassment scandal. But by tradition the extramarital affairs of French politicians are tolerated and not reported in the press.

One of France's most popular politicians, he committed one of the most serious indiscretions in modern French political history. While staying in the exclusive French-owned Sofitel hotel in New York City, he is alleged to have forced a resisting chambermaid, who had entered his room unaware that he was naked in the bathroom, to perform a sexual act. She reported him, and police officers pulled him off an Air France plane within minutes of takeoff. He was charged with seven counts of attempted sexual assault and attempted rape and was kept in jail. After being granted bail, he was confined to house arrest in a $50,000-per-month luxury townhouse awaiting trial.

The criminal charges were later dropped, but the alleged victim also charged him in civil court in New York. That suit was settled, reportedly by a $6 million deal with the maid. Back in France, legal proceedings were initiated against him for alleged "aggravated procurement in an organized gang," legal language for "pimping." He was part of a group that is said to have procured prostitutes for sex parties in Lille, London, and Washington. That is a crime in France, while prostitution is not. His wife had enough and ordered him out of the house. To add further humiliation, a play about the scandal in New York, *Suite 2806*, made its debut at the Théatre Daunou in Paris. Critics called it "a modern-day Marquis de Sade." In June 2015 all charges against him were dropped.

He resigned his post at the IMF. He was replaced by France's finance minister Christine Laguarde, who learned her perfect English in America on an exchange scholarship and worked her way to the top of a leading American law firm, Baker & McKenzie.

François Hollande would have had no chance to win the nomination through an online party primary and ultimately to capture the presidency without Strauss-Kahn's stunning indiscretions.

With a turnout of over 80%, Hollande won the first round of the 2012 presidential elections with 28.6% of the votes, and the second, with 51.6%. He was inaugurated May 15, the first Socialist to become president since François Mitterrand in 1981. His party swept the June parliamentary elections, capturing an absolute majority, with 314 seats, up from 202. Turnout dropped to a record low of 57%. The 2017 presidential election was a disaster for the party. Hollande's popularity was so low (13%) that he did not seek reelection. The winner of the primary was Benoît Hamon, who captured only 6.4% of the first-round votes. Former prime minister Manuel Valls pronounced the party "dead."

Socialist Past

The PS was created in 1971 from the staunchly anticommunist French Section of the Workers' International (SFIO), François Mitterrand's own Convention of Republican Institutions, and various other socialist elements. Its rapid growth was partly due to the decline in some social groups which traditionally supported

Ex–prime minister Manuel Valls

Ex-president François Hollande

parties of the right: farmers, small shopkeepers, wealthy bourgeois families, and nonworking women. But the Socialist Party's success can be attributed mainly to the work of a man who was both farsighted and persistent but who, like de Gaulle, was also mysterious, elusive, and unknowable: François Mitterrand.

He was born into a piously Catholic bourgeois family in the Cognac region of France in 1916. His father was a railway stationmaster who inherited a thriving vinegar business. Brought up on Balzac's panoramic novels, Lamartine's romantic poetry, and Barrès's patriotic fiction, he acquired a love for literature, which remained his primary passion. He authored 10 books himself and certainly ranks with Léon Blum and de Gaulle as one of the most literary figures in French politics. His career did not always follow a consistently left-wing course. At age 18 he joined the youth group of the far-right Croix-de-Feu (Cross of Fire) and wrote for right-wing journals.

He studied law and political science at the Sorbonne in Paris. A sergeant in the army, he was wounded in the chest at Verdun in 1940 and was sent to a POW camp after his capture. After two unsuccessful attempts to flee, he finally succeeded. Asked many years later why he thought he could win the presidency after two unsuccessful attempts in 1965 and 1974, he noted that in 1941 he had succeeded in returning to France only on his third try. He became a civil servant and admirer of Marshal Pétain. He was awarded the highest honor given by the Vichy state, the Francisque in 1943, and from 1986 to 1992, he laid a wreath on Pétain's tomb every Armistice Day. He also maintained personal contact with a number of collab-

France

French National Assembly elections: 577 seats

The pendulum of French politics: left, right, left

1988

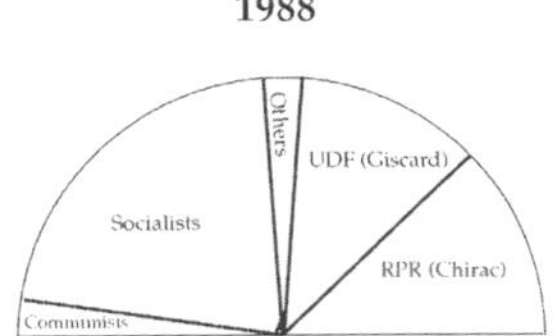

1993

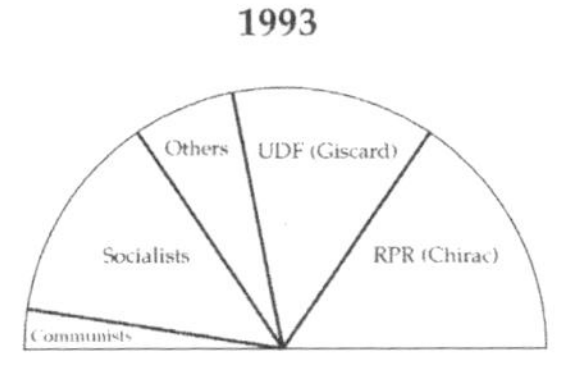

1997

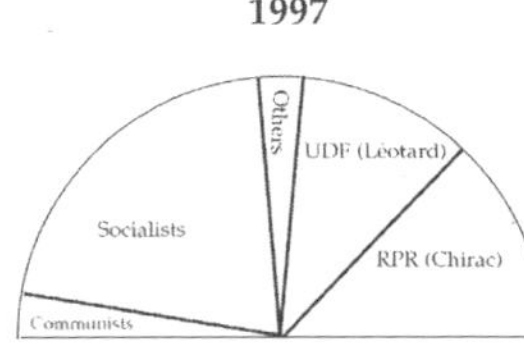

orators, such as René Bousquet, who had overseen the deportation of French Jews.

Mitterrand joined the resistance movement under the cover names of "Morland" and "Monier" in mid-1943. He changed his address at least weekly and narrowly escaped arrest and almost-certain execution by the Gestapo a few days before being flown to England on November 16. There he was interrogated by British intelligence and transported to de Gaulle's Free French headquarters in Algiers before returning to France in early 1944. During this time he gained respect for French Communists and a strong distaste for de Gaulle, who had demanded that he subordinate his activity to the general's leadership.

Mitterrand was hardly a new face in Fifth Republic politics, having occupied many ministerial seats during the Fourth Republic under diverse governments. His political views continued to be very changeable, leading to charges that he was a political opportunist. In the Fifth Republic, though, he was a consistent and ferocious opponent of Gaullism, in part because he wanted power himself. He was a man determined to unify the left in order to take control of France's destiny.

His first task was to establish a program acceptable to his own heterogeneous party. He set a clear leftist course for the 1981 elections. However, he never mentioned the word "Marxist" in the campaign, even though the party's program did contain some Marxist references and principles. In the campaign, Mitterrand hammered away at the many inequalities in French society and Giscard's unpopular style. He presented himself as the "tranquil force" which France needed. His countrymen listened.

Mitterrand's 1981 Election

Mitterrand's triumph was the first time that an entire generation of Frenchmen had experienced a transfer of presidential power from right to left. One of his first acts in office was to dissolve the National Assembly and to call new elections. This reveals a fundamental characteristic of the French political system. Despite the powerful office of the presidency, no incumbent had been able to rule long in the face of a determined, reasonably cohesive opposing majority in the National Assembly because of its budgetary and legislative approval powers. For the first time in the history of the Fifth Republic, a president faced a hostile parliamentary majority. The elections in June produced a landslide victory for the PS, which won an absolute majority with 288 out of 491 seats in the assembly.

The new government wasted little time in seeking legislation for the most far-reaching of its proposed reforms: the nationalization of certain industries and the decentralization of the French political system. The Socialists promised France in 1981 fundamental changes. After it was clear by 1983 that his socialist revolution had failed, the Mitterrand government pursued a more austere economic course and stressed modernization rather than socialization of France.

As an intellectual force, Marxism became far less popular than it once had been. Partly because of Mitterrand's maneuverings, the Communist Party became practically impotent and became locked in a steady decline. The trade unions, a traditional pillar of the PCF, became weaker than ever before in modern France.

Cohabitation—1986 to 1988

The 1986 electoral results created something entirely new since the beginning of the Fifth Republic in 1958: a president whose party was a minority in the National Assembly. The traditional conservative parties won a whisker-thin majority. Therefore, Mitterrand was compelled to appoint a conservative prime minister, Jacques Chirac.

SAMEDI 9 ET DIMANCHE 10 FEVRIER 2002

week-end **Les hypercinés** ou comment attirer les clients des hypers dans les complexes multisalles après leurs emplettes. /Désormais, la guerre se livrera de plus en plus sur un champ de bataille numérisé. /Avec notre reporter aux sélections de «Loft Story 2»... Pages 33 à 47

Libération

Prêts? Partez!

Jospin et Chirac ne sont pas candidats. Mais leurs équipes sont déjà organisées pour les mettre en orbite présidentielle. Page 2

Malaise dans l'échographie

Malgré un texte finalement favorable qui les décharge de leur responsabilité envers l'enfant en cas d'erreur de diagnostic prénatal, beaucoup de praticiens ont déjà arrêté leur activité d'échographie fœtale. Pages 10 et 11

Are you able to speak with the Queen?

Parler anglais et jurer fidélité à reine: selon un projet de loi, les candidats à la citoyenneté britannique devraient satisfaire à ces deux conditions lors d'un «examen de passage». Page 9

A Cargèse, chez Yvan Colonna

Quatre ans après l'assassinat du préfet de Corse Erignac, le tueur présumé reste introuvable. Le village comprend la fuite d'«Yvan», mais n'approuve pas l'assassinat. Reportage. Page 12

La faillite Enron panique les marchés

Depuis le scandale du septième plus grand groupe mondial par sa capitalisation boursière, les marchés sont pris d'une crise de foi. La chute de ce symbole du capitalisme moderne affole les investisseurs et les Bourses tombent dans le rouge. Pages 16 et 17

M 00135 - 209 - F: 1,20 € www.liberation.com 1,20 € (7,87 F) France métropolitaine

PREMIERE EDITION NUMERO 6451

Chirac had studied international relations at Harvard, paying his way by working as a waiter at Howard Johnson's. During the Algerian War, he served in the French Foreign Legion, after which he entered the prestigious Ecole Nationale d'Administration (ENA). His subsequent political rise was meteoric, working, as always, so energetically that Pompidou gave him the nickname "the Bulldozer." From 1974 to 1976, he had served as prime minister under Giscard. However, believing that he was given too little leeway to pursue his own policies, he became the only prime minister in the Fifth Republic to quit due to disagreements with the president.

Observers coined the word "cohabitation" to describe the relationship between a strong president and an equally strong prime minister who is not willing merely to execute the will of the president. This relationship changed the basic rules of the French political game from 1986 to 1988. It also showed that the institutions of the Fifth Republic are more adaptable and resilient in democratic politics than even de Gaulle had ever imagined.

The president's actual powers diminished somewhat, but they nevertheless remained formidable. "Cohabitation" was not a return to the parliamentary politics and "games" of the Third and Fourth Republics because the powers the president lost fell to a powerful prime minister, not to parliament. Nevertheless, it was a difficult relationship with which the French had almost no experience. Both the president and the prime minister had an interest in making this power sharing succeed. French politics has traditionally been characterized by polarization between the left and the right; the new experiment of cohabitation proved they could find common ground and cooperate with each other in the interest of the French nation. In fact, by election time in 1988, it had helped diminish the ideological gulf separating the major parties. Therefore, it actually strengthened French democracy. "Cohabitation" proved to be a workable alternative, and 70% of the French found it to be good.

Mitterrand could not stop a single policy the prime minister wanted to pursue. He was the first Fifth Republic president to have his wings clipped while still in office. He watched most of his power drain away from the Elysée to the Matignon Palace. However, by knowing how and when to assert his residual authority, he succeeded in halting the trend.

Having preserved his authority, President Mitterrand's popularity soared. By standing above the political fray and focusing on the nation's interests, he let Chirac, who was in the trenches doing day-to-day combat, acquire some serious political bruises. Mitterrand thereby enhanced his own prospects of reelection in 1988 and diminished Chirac's chances to win the presidency.

The End of the Mitterrand Era

The strength of de Gaulle's constitution had been demonstrated by the two-year "cohabitation" experiment, which coupled a Socialist president with a conservative prime minister. The 1988 elections led the country into yet another untested experiment: a minority government.

In presidential elections Chirac garnered only 46% of the votes to Mitterrand's 54%. In the subsequent parliamentary elections in June, the PS fell 14 votes short of a majority. Mitterrand appointed a popular and capable rival within his party, Michel Rocard, as prime minister with a cabinet containing some non-Socialists.

The minority government had to work with other parties to make the system work. But this is nothing unusual in Europe, where most major democracies have coalition or minority governments. The constitution had been designed in 1958 to enable a country with a fractious parliament to enjoy stable rule. No new elections can be called for 12 months, and governments cannot be brought down unless a majority unites against it. In other words, it is the opposition, not the government, which needs a majority. Rocard went far in introducing non-Socialist ideas on how an advanced economy should be run. He deserves much of the credit for transforming the PS from a party of doctrine to one of government.

In many ways Mitterrand had done more to transform French society and politics than de Gaulle. No one would have expected that he would be so able to convert the French to an acceptance of a market economy and the need for stable and rigorous economic management. In foreign policy he swept away some of the most important cornerstones of Gaullist foreign policy by nurturing a more trusting relationship with the United States and by championing greater European integration, including in the field of defense. In a 1992 referendum to accept the Maastricht Treaty, only a hair-thin 51% voted *oui*. The narrowness of that margin in one of the EU's founding nations was a stinging blow to France's political elite. It was in the context of greater European integration and closer Franco-German relations that Mitterrand sought to contain an enlarged, unified, and dynamic Germany within a Europe whose map is being redrawn.

He oversaw the most ambitious building program in Paris since Haussmann remade the capital more than a century earlier. I. M. Pei's glass pyramid in the court of the Louvre had shocked Parisians at first, but it gave new life to one of the world's finest museums. The Grand Arch at the heart of the suburb of La Défense, completed for the bicentennial in 1989, is a majestic, modern, 360-foot steel-and-glass version of Napoleon's Arc de Triomphe. The Bastille Opéra, opened in 1989, has been less successful in winning public admiration, but numerous other *Grands Travaux*, such as a new National Library, leave Mitterrand's stamp on Paris. In 2003 a street in central Paris was named after him: Quai François Mitterrand runs beside the Louvre along the Seine.

"The more just, the stronger France will be."

Mitterrand's party, which had been in power too long and had run short on vision, ideas, and energy, was swept from power in the most devastating defeat in modern French electoral history. It was a hard verdict, but it was not an ideological one, since the Socialist Party had already shed most of its socialist ideology. Before stepping down in May 1995, Mitterrand admitted that, with all the formal powers a French president has, he had "underestimated the ponderous nature of society, the slowness of its wheels, the weight of its traditions. You don't change society by an act of legislation."

Both of his families mourned at his funeral in 1996. During his 14-year presidency he lived officially with his wife, Danielle, but he spent most of his nights with his longtime mistress, Anne Pingeot, in a secret apartment. She and their daughter, Mazarine Pingeot, were sheltered in a variety of other houses paid for by the state.

France

The Chirac Era

Jacques Chirac's victory in the 1995 presidential election left the right in control of the presidency; with 80% of the seats in the National Assembly and two-thirds in the Senate, 20 of 22 regional councils, and four-fifths of the departmental councils; and in control of most of the big cities. Never in the history of the Fifth Republic had there been such a concentration of power.

Chirac promised a less monarchical presidency than that of his predecessor. He ordered that the fleet of military jets and helicopters at the disposal of the president and cabinet be disbanded and that ostentatious signs of power, such as motorcades with screaming sirens and motorcycles racing through the streets, be banned.

During his campaign, Chirac promised "profound change." As it became obvious that Chirac could not fulfill his campaign promises of lower taxes and bountiful jobs, his approval rating plummeted, and the worst strikes since 1968 broke out, involving millions of citizens, from civil servants and truck drivers to students, actors, and doctors. Demonstrators in 1968 had risen up against materialism and an allegedly soulless affluent society. Many French now revolted, not just because they refused to relinquish treasured welfare benefits and special privileges, but also because they had a feeling that life was getting worse and worse and that affluence and security might be slipping away from them. This is why strikers enjoy strong public support and why the government caves in to them so often.

President Chirac dissolved parliament and called new elections. In the June 1997 final round of elections, control of the National Assembly changed hands for the fifth straight parliamentary election in 16 years. Tired of Chirac's broken promises made only two years earlier, voters turned back to the Socialists, led by Lionel Jospin, a former diplomat, economics professor, and education minister.

Running in both 1997 and 2002 under a loose umbrella called the "pluralist left" (*la gauche plurielle*), the Socialists captured 253 seats (including 12 Radical Socialists) in the 576-seat assembly. Since that was short of an absolute majority, the government Jospin formed had to rule with the support of the Communist Party, which won 38 seats, and the Greens, which got 7. President Chirac, who had disastrously misread the mood of the French public, was obligated to accept cohabitation for the third time in 11 years. Jospin became the first prime minister in the Fifth Republic to serve a full five-year term.

2002 Elections

The 2002 presidential elections left France reeling. In the first round, Chirac won just under 20% of the votes, the lowest ever for an incumbent president. Socialist challenger Prime Minister Lionel Jospin fell to a disgraceful third place, with about 16% of the votes, behind Le Pen, who won almost 17%.

Le Pen and his National Front benefited from the sense of insecurity that gripped the country, especially in the aftermath of the September 11, 2001, terrorist strikes against the US, which fueled fears of Arab terrorists moving within France's large immigrant minority. This feeling of insecurity was exacerbated by the physical attacks by Arab immigrants on French Jews and synagogues. Le Pen said, "I want to reestablish security throughout the territory."

Le Pen was thus a symptom of a wider political malaise, including the fear of globalization, ugly xenophobia, and gloomy feeling of decline. He spoke of France as a country "in regression": in its economy, its public safety, and its morality. The endless series of corruption scandals surrounding the political class, including Chirac, sickened many French, especially the "little people" to whom Le Pen appealed.

The shock to the nation caused by Le Pen's success in the first round brought millions of Frenchmen of diverse political persuasions into the streets demanding a massive show of opposition to Le Pen in the second round two weeks later. These were anti–Le Pen rallies, not pro-Chirac ones. The most common slogan for the demonstrations was "Vote for the crook, not the fascist." The usually neutral French media broke with tradition and endorsed Chirac. *Le Figero* carried a banner headline, "For France."

This worked. In the second round, Chirac captured an unprecedented 82% of the votes with a turnout of 80%. He faced the anomaly of having been elected by the largest margin in French history, outdoing even his hero, Charles de Gaulle, but having very weak support from the public. A Harris poll revealed a day after the tally that only 13% of voters supported him because of his program; 75% gave as their main reason to shut out Le Pen.

Chirac's newly formed conservative Union for the Presidential Majority (UMP) dominated the parliamentary elections that followed on the heels of his presidential landslide. The right captured 399 of 577 seats, leaving only 140 for the humiliated Socialists. This victory not only left the right in control of the Senate and local government, but it also ended cohabitation of a conservative president and a Socialist government.

2007 Elections and the Chirac Legacy

An era came to an end in 2007: Jacques Chirac, the only remaining politician who served every Fifth Republic president since de Gaulle, left power after 12 years as president. He departed as the most unpopular president in the history of the Fifth Republic. He came into office in 1995 promising to "mend the social fracture," get people back to work, ease tensions in the explosive suburbs, cut taxes, and ensure prosperity. He accomplished none of these goals. Instead, he left a France that was frightened by high unemployment, growing debt, and a strong feeling of political and economic stagnation.

During his tenure, the French social system, while performing well in certain sectors, such as health care and public transportation, was in financial trouble. Yet he never stopped arguing that "our French model" must never be dismantled. His loss of the May 2005 referendum on the ill-fated EU constitutional treaty was a stinging personal rejection. He consistently backed down from pushing through unpopular reforms.

Nevertheless, he occasionally took some courageous stands: He spoke out against racism and anti-Semitism, and he admitted France's official culpability in deporting Jews to their deaths in concentration camps during the Second World War. He took the unpopular stand of advocating Turkey's membership in the EU. Although

Typical World War I monument seen in every French village

subsequent research revealed that he and his government wavered about whether to join the war against Saddam Hussein's Iraq in 2003, his ultimate decision not to participate was appreciated by a large percentage of his people. He enjoyed brief popularity, although France's diplomatic influence steadily declined after 2003.

He had more qualities to conquer power than to exercise it. A half-year before he left office, France 2 television aired a four-hour documentary on his presidency. This was the first time a sitting president had been assessed on prime-time public TV. One after another, political leaders told stories about his hunger for power, his opportunism, his betrayals and his nastiness. His tendency to change policies earned him the nickname, "The Weathervane."

It is no wonder that the three most promising candidates to succeed him—Nicolas Sarkozy (UMP), Ségolène Royal (Socialist), and François Bayrou (UDF)—all campaigned on anti-Chirac platforms in May 2007. In their varying ways, all ran against the current French system. This was especially remarkable for the winner, Sarkozy, who had occupied several posts in Chirac governments. Yet he and Royal were considered outsiders in their parties and were willing to challenge their conventional wisdom.

Twelve persons (down from 16 in 2002) competed for the presidency, but only the 3 of them had a realistic chance. Three of the others were Trotskyites, one was a Communist, and one was an alternative, antiglobalization, McDonald's-hating gadfly (José Bové). The high turnout in the presidential voting (84%, the highest since 1974) was not only a testament to the vibrancy of French democracy but also a signal of how important voters considered these elections to be for their future. They gave the three leaders three-fourths (76%) of their votes.

Sarkozy won 30.5% of the votes in the first round and 53.06% in the second round by sticking resolutely to his central message: France must change, the French must work more and be rewarded for their work, law and order must be restored, and immigration must be tightened. This was the highest result for a center-right candidate since 1974 and 10 points higher than Chirac ever got in the first round. Surprisingly since his chief opponent was an impressive woman, he captured 52% of the female vote, as well as a majority of voters aged 25 to 44 and over 60.

Royal, the Socialist candidate, captured an impressive 25.5% in the first round and 46.94% in the second. She failed to transform her leftist party into a modern social democratic one in the center of the political spectrum. When she tried to do this in the second round and called for an electoral alliance with Bayrou, who had presented himself as a bridge builder between left and right, she lost credibility. She won 11 of 20 Paris arrondissements, many ethnically mixed working-class suburbs, large parts of central and southwestern France, and voters under age 24. In polls asking voters which characteristics most apply to the two top candidates, the only category in which she beat Sarkozy was "friendliness" (57% to 29%).

Bayrou won 18.6% in the first round, but he failed to get into the top two. A collective sigh of relief was heard when Jean-Marie Le Pen, leader of the extreme right-wing National Front, received only 11% of the votes and a humiliating fourth-place finish. In the second round, 63% of his voters turned to Sarkozy and only 12% to Royal. Sarkozy had succeeded in absorbing Le Pen's voters and, it was hoped, defanging them.

Entering the parliamentary elections a month later, in June 2007, Sarkozy became the first president in two decades to intervene in his UMP's campaign. This marked a change in style from Chirac's aloof stance. But the new president had won a mandate to reform the country. He stated after his victory, "The French people have chosen change, and it is change that I will implement." For this he needed a strong parliamentary majority. The French gave him that but without the margin that he had hoped.

The UMP captured 39.5% of the votes in the first round and 47.79% in the second. This left them 324 of the 577 seats, plus 22 seats of its ally, the New Center. With 60% of the seats, Sarkozy had won a solid legislative base for his reforms. The Socialists did quite well, winning 28% in the first round and 45% in the second, securing an impressive 205 seats, up from 140 in 2002. Bayrou created a new Democratic Movement (MoDem) for these elections, but it captured only 7.6% in the first round, winning a mere four seats, including his own. The other big loser was Le Pen's National Front, which won only 4.3% of the votes and not a single seat. The Communists garnered 4.3% of the votes and 18 seats, while the Greens captured 3.3% of the votes and 4 seats.

Dubbed the "hyperpresident" in the press, the frenetic Sarkozy wasted no time in assembling the most diverse and inclusive cabinet in French history. He concentrated as much power in his Elysée Palace as possible, signaling his intention to be much more active in domestic politics than his predecessors. His prime minister was François Fillon, a lawyer and former education minister, who was a former enemy but later jogging buddy. His popularity ratings consistently remained above those of the president. This impertinence

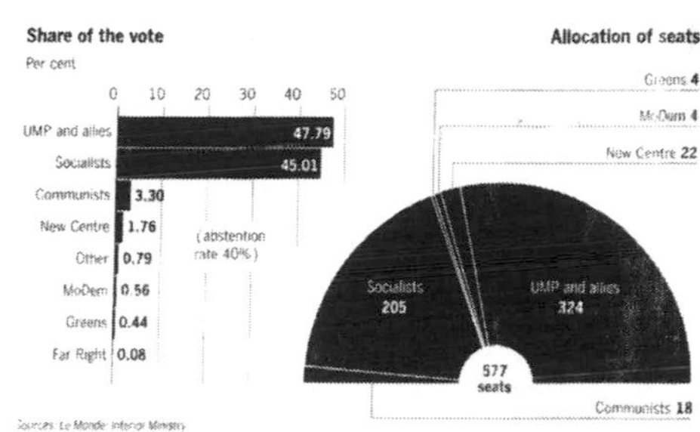

2007 parliamentary election
Source: *Financial Times*

was usually grounds for a prime minister's dismissal in the Fifth Republic.

Sarkozy appointed a sleek 16-person cabinet, half the size of previous ones. It contained Socialists and centrists. Only one member (Higher Education Minister Valérie Pécresse) had attended the elite ENA. It included seven women. Nine were lawyers, including Christine Lagarde, a former top attorney of a large American law firm with a perfect command of English, who was tapped to be the country's and G-8's first female finance minister. *Forbes* listed her in 2008 as 1 of the 15 most powerful women in the world. In June 2011 she was chosen to be managing director of the IMF. To reach out to Socialists, he appointed longtime TV celebrity Frédéric Mitterrand, the late Socialist president's nephew, as culture minister.

Perhaps the most surprising appointment was Socialist Bernard Kouchner, who is consistently rated in the polls as France's most popular politician. His Socialist party called him a traitor and kicked him out for joining a conservative president's government. Cofounder of Doctors without Borders and former UN head in Kosovo, he is one of very few French who supported the US decision to go to war in Iraq, although he later criticized its management. As foreign minister, he visited Baghdad for three days, the first such trip since 1988, in a gesture aimed at healing the wounds caused by the war.

Kouchner was a longtime critic of French anti-Americanism (once calling it "the motor of French foreign policy"). He joined the president in toning down the rhetoric in Franco-American relations. He also gave the new government a strong human rights stamp. To assist both of them was a new American-style national security adviser, Jean-David Levitte, an ex-ambassador to Washington. Together, they attempted to conduct a foreign policy that was less "arrogant"; more sympathetic to America, Britain, and Israel; less friendly to Russia; and more transparent on Africa.

France faced the spectacle of legal proceedings against two of its disgraced political leaders. Former president Jacques

Chirac was dogged by allegations of corruption from the time he was mayor of Paris, but he had immunity from prosecution as long as he was in office. With his immunity stripped from him in May 2007, he was called to court to testify on the charges stemming from his time as Paris mayor. He was charged with embezzlement of public funds relating to fake jobs. Putting an ex-president on trial is without precedent in modern French history; the last head of state to be tried was Philippe Pétain, who was convicted of treason. Chirac's lawyers argued that the constitution gave him immunity for acts done while president. Three-fourths (72%) of Frenchmen indicated that they favored treating Chirac as an ordinary citizen before the law, according to a 2007 poll.

Within a couple of years, they had lost their appetite to see him become the first former head of state to stand trial. In September 2010 the Paris City Hall dropped its charge against Chirac for embezzlement, and the UMP agreed to pay back €2.2 million ($3 million), the cost of the embezzled funds, interest, and legal fees.

He still faced charges for the 28 bogus jobs and misuse of public funds to further his own political career. He went on trial in December 2011. He did not attend due to "severe memory lapses." He was found guilty of breach of trust and misuse of public funds and given a two-year suspended sentence. Few political trials result in prison terms. His legal predicament did not diminish his standing in the eyes of his countrymen. In 2011 he was voted the most admired French politician. Sarkozy came in 32nd. In 2015 respondents rated him and his mentor, Charles de Gaulle, as the presidents who best embodied optimism.

In 2006 the Clearstream Affair helped paralyze the government, disgust the public, derail then–prime minister de Villepin's hopes to become president in 2007, and damage France's image in the world. It involved a baffling web of judicial and intelligence inquiries into secret investigations initiated by de Villepin alleging that Nicolas Sarkozy and other politicians had received kickbacks and bribes laundered through the Luxembourg clearinghouse Clearstream. French judges quickly determined that the accounts supposedly traced to Sarkozy were fabrications.

The scandal transcended the affair itself and revealed something about the power games played by the narrow political, industrial, and administrative elites. Even ENA's old-boy connections seemed to be at work in this scandal that was intended to undermine Sarkozy, who had not attended the powerful school.

On January 28, 2010, in the very courtroom in which Marie Antoinette was sentenced to the guillotine, the former prime minister was acquitted. Three of the other four persons on trial were found guilty.

2012 Elections

With a turnout of over 80%, Hollande won the first round of the 2012 presidential elections with 28.6% of the votes and the second with 51.6% to 48.4% for Sarkozy. Turnout was 81%. This was the first time since 1981 that a presidential incumbent had been defeated, and it ended 17 years of conservative rule. Hollande was inaugurated May 15, the first Socialist to become president since François Mitterrand in 1981. His party swept the June parliamentary elections, capturing an absolute majority with 314 seats, up from 202. Turnout dropped to a record low of 57%. Voters sent 108 women to the chamber, and 40% of all delegates were new. Seldom had a party been in such a commanding position. The Socialists already controlled the Senate, all but one of the regions, all major cities, and most communes. Sarkozy left politics altogether, refusing to lead the right in legislative elections a month later. He left his party in disarray.

Unlike Sarkozy, the 57-year-old Hollande, the son of a doctor and a social worker, is a graduate of the prestigious National Administration School (ENA) and has deep political roots in rural France (Corrèze in the south-central part). At age 26, he was an adviser to former president François Mitterrand, and he later headed the Socialist Party for 11 years. In 30 years of politics, he had never been a governmental minister.

Socialists, not Sarkozy, "down in the dumps"

He is known and liked for his easy humor. He is affable and funny and has a preference for consensus politics and a dislike for confrontation. He is described as "calm, sure of himself, at ease everywhere, likeable and impenetrable." Because of his image as a soft-centered politician, his nickname is "Flanby," a reference to caramel pudding. Perhaps his biggest appeal to voters was his promise to have a "normal presidency," one of "dignity but simplicity," in his words. There would be no more talk of "President Bling-bling." Leading up to the election, he stopped tooling around Paris in his three-wheeled scooter.

He fathered four children with his previous unmarried partner and 2007 Socialist Party presidential candidate, Ségolène Royal. His next partner was twice married and twice divorced, Valérie Trierweiler, a journalist for *Paris Match*. They were the first unmarried couple to occupy the Élysée Palace together; some referred to her as the "First Girlfriend." This created some protocol concerns. For example, she was noticeably missing when the president met the queen at Windsor Castle.

The press, which has become more intrusive into politicians' lives, reported that Trierweiler had a poisonous relationship with Ségolène Royal. During the June 2012 parliamentary election campaign, Trierweiler posted a tweet supporting Royal's opponent. Royal lost her seat in La Rochelle. Hollande had wanted to appoint her as president of the National Assembly. In April 2014 Royal was named environment minister in a major cabinet reshuffle. Trierweiler was severely criticized by her deeply embarrassed partner and his party for this "Tweetweiler affair." She publically admitted that she had made a regrettable mistake. Such publicly discussed domestic problems with a former and present partner undermine the president's self-styled image as a "normal president."

He was everything but that. Just when he had enough troubles with a weak economy and the lowest approval ratings of any postwar president, a celebrity gossip magazine, *Closer*, photographed him secretly meeting in an apartment right across the street from the Elysée Palace with film actress Julie Gayet. He came and went on the back of a motor scooter driven by a security guard. The president was wearing a helmet with the visor down but was recognizable by his black shoes. *Closer* published a seven-page spread complete with photos of him and Gayet; the copies flew off the shelves, and the public and media were riveted to the story.

Trierweiler learned of the affair from the tabloid, and suffering an "emotional breakdown," she checked into the hospital "in shock" for a week before moving out of the palace. Polls in 2014 indicated sympathy for the president; 77% of French respondents considered this a purely private matter and believed that a president should not be judged on the basis of the women in his life. The French are tired of talk of "First Ladies." Nevertheless, Trierweiler's tell-all book, *Thanks for This Moment*, became an overnight best-seller in 2014.

Hollande made good on his pledge to have gender balance in the cabinet; 17 of 34 governmental posts went to women. He passed over left-leaning party leader Martine Aubry for the post of prime minister and appointed Jean-Marc Ayrault. Like the president, he had never been a government minister. After one year in office, his approval rating had dropped even lower than the president's. The party had been demolished in the May 2014 European Parliament elections and 2015 department elections. The only bright note was the election of Spanish-born Anne Hidalgo as the first female mayor of Paris. She defeated another woman, Nathalie Kosciusko-Morizet of the Republicans.

In keeping with tradition, the president fires the prime minister when things go wrong. In April 2014 Ayrault was replaced by the popular Barcelona-born Manuel Valls. As interior minister, he had cultivated a tough-guy, law-and-order image, cracking down on illegal immigration and crime. A centrist and reformist, he had once even proposed ridding the party of the name "Socialist." Laurent Fabius, a former prime minister, remained as minister of foreign affairs; he subsequently was appointed to the prestigious Constitutional Council. This and other choices reflected Hollande's instinct for compromise, since Fabius and the new president were old enemies.

The president had wasted no time in attempting to create a new image for his new government. He imposed a 30% salary cut for himself, the prime minister, and all ministers. They had to use trains for any trip less than three hours and respect red lights when traveling in their ministerial cars; these requirements were quickly dispensed with. They were told to turn over any official gift worth more than €150.

He had campaigned on a promise of an "exemplary republic" and made ministers sign an unprecedented ministerial code of ethics, which did not prevent scandals in his government, especially involving himself. For example, his budget minister, Jérôme Cahuzac, who was charged with combating tax evasion, was discovered to have hidden a large amount of money in a secret Swiss bank account. Polls taken after this shock found 77% judging all politicians corrupt, including 63% of those who voted for Hollande. To combat the stench of corruption, the president felt compelled to require a publication of all his 38 cabinet members' estate holdings. This was an unprecedented moment of transparency in France, and two-thirds of the French favored it.

In terms of policy, he reiterated his campaign promises of a fairer society. His proposed 75% top tax rate for those earning over €1 million ($1.37 million) was ruled unconstitutional by the Constitutional Council. It was dropped. His "soak-the-rich" policy caused some well heeled French to leave the country. Its richest man, Bernard Arnault, took Belgian citizenship. Film icon Gérard Depardieu accepted Russian citizenship from President Vladimir Putin. The French star has long and deep connections with Russia, whose 13% flat income tax appears better than the French rates, which Depardieu claims took 85% of his earnings in 2012. He accused France of punishing "success, creation, talent."

He promised more than he could produce in a country slipping into recession. He expressed a strong antibusiness attitude and once said, "I hate the rich," and he declared war on the "world of finance." However, when the economy got worse, he had to make a U-turn in 2014: Discarding the left's doctrine, he promised cuts in public spending and taxes in order to revive growth and create jobs. This pivot deepened a left-right rift in the Socialist Party. Valls exclaimed, "I love business!"

2017 Elections

These were the most unpredictable elections in Fifth Republic history. The winner's rise defied all the rules of the Fifth Republic. It was the first time an incumbent president was so unpopular that he did not seek reelection. It was the first time the candidates of the two established parties for over a half-century—Gaullist and Socialist were both eliminated in the first round of presidential voting. For the first time, both had been selected by means of primaries. The victor, Emmanuel Macron, is the youngest president ever: 39 years. He is the first never before to have sought elective office. He had no party at the time he threw his hat into the ring. He quickly created a movement a year before the elections: En Marche, renamed Republique en Marsch! (Republic on the Move—LRM).

Born and raised in Amiens, he is the son of provincial doctors. A brilliant student of philosophy and an accomplished pianist, he studied at the prestigious École National d'Administration (ENA), during which time he had an internship in Nigeria. After graduation he earned a lot of money as an investment banker, then served as adviser to President Hollande and as minister of economy in his cabinet. He married his high school drama teacher, who is 24 years his senior. He speaks fluent English.

In his book *Revolution* and in his campaign, he argued for an open, tolerant, pro-European France. His platform called for support of private enterprise, looser labor rules, a more competitive France globally, and deeper ties with the EU.

In the first round, Macron led with 24% of the votes to Marine Le Pen's 21.3%. This was the first time that two outsiders reached the final voting in the second round. As expected, many voters cast their ballots against Le Pen, not for Macron. Nevertheless, Macron won with 66.1% of the votes, while Le Pen got 33.9%, her party's best-ever result.

Macron faces difficulties. Reform is always difficult in France. Street demonstrations and union opposition can always be anticipated. Indeed, a mass protest movement was ignited in November 2018, called

www.lemonde.fr

Le Monde

59ᵉ ANNÉE – Nº 18078 – 1,20 € – FRANCE MÉTROPOLITAINE — DIMANCHE 9 - LUNDI 10 MARS 2003 — FONDATEUR : HUBERT BEUVE-MÉRY – DIRECTEUR : JEAN-MARIE COLOMBANI

SUPPLÉMENT
La mode de l'été 2003, énergique, sophistiquée, c'est de l'athlétisme pure soie

CORSE
Polémique sur la prison de Borgo p. 8

SUPPLÉMENT
Le Monde ARGENT
Placement immobilier

La France dit non à l'ultimatum

LES ÉTATS-UNIS, le Royaume-Uni et l'Espagne ont déposé vendredi 7 mars à l'ONU une nouvelle version d'un projet de résolution qui constitue un ultimatum à l'Irak. Dans ce texte, Bagdad est en effet sommé de démontrer, d'ici au lundi 17 mars, *« une coopération entière, sans condition, immédiate et active »* sur son désarmement, sous peine d'une action militaire. L'ambassadeur américain auprès des Nations unies, John Negroponte, a déclaré que la date du vote serait déterminée lors des consultations entre les membres du Conseil, lundi. En fait, ce vote pourrait avoir lieu dès mardi.

Face à cette accélération des événements, le ministre français des affaires étrangères, Dominique de Villepin, a affirmé à l'ONU que Paris *« ne laisserait pas passer une résolution qui autoriserait le recours à la guerre »*. *« La France,* a-t-il ajouté, *dit non à la logique de guerre (...). Nous ne pouvons pas accepter un ultimatum dès lors que les inspecteurs font état de progrès ».* Le chef de la diplomatie française a proposé que les chefs d'État et de gouvernement se réunissent la semaine prochaine au Conseil de sécurité, à New York, à l'occasion du vote sur la nouvelle résolution. Les États-Unis ont rejeté cette offre.

En matière de désarmement, le chef des inspecteurs de l'ONU, Hans Blix, a salué dans son rapport *« une accélération des initiatives du côté irakien depuis la fin janvier ». « Vérifier le désarmement,* a-t-il conclu, *même avec la coopération active de l'Irak, ne prendra pas des semaines ou des années, mais des mois. »* Colin Powell a qualifié ce rapport de *« catalogue de non coopération ».*

► Nouveau projet de résolution : l'ONU sommée de constater avant le 17 mars que Bagdad n'a pas désarmé

► Le texte est déposé par Washington, Londres et Madrid

► Les inspecteurs font état de progrès et contestent les « preuves » américaines

► Villepin : « non à la logique de guerre »

Lire pages 2 à 4

"Yellow Vest," which severely threatened public order and his increasingly unpopular government. Perhaps the greatest challenge is developing an effective relationship with parliament, whose support every president needs. Half of his 577 candidates for the National Assembly had never run for any office. Without a parliamentary majority, presidents must settle for a coalition or minority government. Working this issue most intensely is his chosen prime minister, Édouard Philippe, a conservative and a fluent German speaker.

FOREIGN AND DEFENSE POLICIES

German unification in 1990 led many French to fear that their country would be overshadowed by Germany and would be driven to the margins of international politics. That has not happened completely, although the euro crisis has made it obvious that Germany is the most influential country in Europe and that France has become the junior partner. France plays an important role as a medium-sized power willing to use its force abroad. Until April 2009 it preserved its independence by not rejoining NATO's integrated command structure, although it had progressively intensified its contacts with the alliance. For example, in 1994 it began attending NATO defense minister meetings again. In 1995 it rejoined NATO's military committee, which brings the service chiefs together, and its officers began working more closely with SHAPE. It did not join the Defense Planning Committee.

Sarkozy rethought his country's relationship with NATO. This was part of a wider shift of French foreign policy: a rapprochement with the US, warmer relations with Israel and the Middle East, and a reappraisal of France's interests in Africa. "Our strategic thinking can't remain frozen when the world around us has completely changed." He recognized NATO's permanence and importance in Europe and the world and said that France must play "a full role." On a visit to Washington in November 2007, he indicated that he had already made his decision to rejoin the alliance's command structure on the condition that the US put aside its objections to expanding the EU's defense capabilities; Washington complied. In giving European defense a push, he stressed that this effort would not be in competition with the US and NATO but that it would complement them both. Nor would it be Europe's intention to duplicate the capabilities that NATO already has.

In March 2009 Sarkozy easily won a parliamentary vote of confidence, enabling France to rejoin the NATO integrated command structure. As a result, France was awarded one of NATO's top prizes: Allied Command Transformation in Norfolk, Virginia, which oversees changing NATO doctrine. It also took over NATO's regional command in Lisbon, the headquarters of the alliance's rapid reaction force, of which France had been a founding member. In 2004 it had offered several thousand troops and two generals in key command slots to NATO's new rapid reaction force. French generals also commanded NATO forces in Kosovo and Afghanistan.

Beyond these two important commands, France's entry has limited military significance because it was already playing an active role in the alliance: It sat in 36 committees and joined 2 more. Its military had long favored reentering the command structure, had been participating in NATO planning, had taken part in all of NATO's wars, and had begun in 2004 assuming posts in the military command. Many persons in France's political and diplomatic elite did not like the idea, but an opinion poll at the time of entry revealed that 52% of French respondents supported the resumption of a full role in NATO.

Prime Minister Édouard Philippe

Of its 10,000 soldiers deployed in missions abroad, one-third served under a NATO banner. In January 2007 it withdrew its 200 special forces troops working directly under US command in Afghanistan, but 50 remained to train Afghan commandos, and more returned. France also sent additional combat aircraft to Kandahar. By 2010 it had 3,750 soldiers in NATO's force in Afghanistan, including deployments in the dangerous southern part of the country. This was a risky move, considering polls at home showed that two-thirds opposed France's NATO commitment in Afghanistan. He turned down President Obama's request for more combat troops.

Chirac's meeting with British prime minister Tony Blair at St. Malo the end of 1998 agreed on a blueprint for such a new European defense. From 2003 on, British prime ministers met frequently with the French and German leaders to give impetus to a kind of European military force that would complement NATO. Within the EU, France and the UK provide over two-thirds of military research funds and half the money for equipment. They spend the most on defense and are the only ones with nuclear weapons and permanent seats at the UN Security Council.

The creation of combined joint task forces (CJTF) allows some of NATO's European assets to be used in military operations where the US has no interest in participating. The concept is meant to work within NATO and not against it. Also, an agreement between the EU and NATO called Berlin-Plus makes available to the EU a variety of NATO planning capabilities and equipment for operations without NATO participation. After all, 21 of the 28 NATO members also belong to the EU. There is some disagreement on how Berlin-Plus should work. The French do not accept that the EU can act only when NATO chooses not to.

The wars in the Persian Gulf and the former Yugoslavia convinced France that it could not do much in military operations without NATO assets and American help. It put some of its ships and aircraft under American control in the Balkans. Its troops that enforced the Bosnian peace settlement served in a NATO force, which in December 2004 was converted into an EU-commanded force. France dispatched the largest foreign contingent—4,000 troops—to Bosnia to play the leading role in the UN Protection Force, led initially by a French general. Its combat pilots helped enforce the no-fly zone over war-torn Bosnia. When NATO created a rapid-reaction force in 1995 to protect UN peacekeepers in Bosnia, France contributed 1,500 elite troops and assumed overall command. France was a major participant in the Implementation Force (IFOR) in Bosnia, assuming responsibility for maintaining peace in the most complicated spot imaginable: Sarajevo. Its troops remained after IFOR ended.

Many of the country's leading intellectuals embraced the cause of direct military intervention in the Balkans, fearing that ethnic cleansing could spread across Europe. This mood reflected a sharp break with the pacifist traditions of French intellectuals. That support continued in 1999, when France contributed 61 combat aircraft and 5 ships to conduct an air war against Yugoslavia in a NATO attempt to stop ethnic cleansing in Kosovo.

Ex-president Sarkozy and former foreign minister Kouchner had an Atlanticist view. Sarkozy stated that it is "unthinkable for Europe to forge its identity in opposition to the United States." After the US saw its influence and prestige in the world reduced by its Iraq policy, it no longer appeared as the "hyperpower" so many French had feared or distrusted. This made it easier for France to strengthen its ties with America.

Referendum on the EU Constitution

The strong Gaullist antipathy toward a more centralized Europe is gone. Nevertheless, France was the most nervous of all the 15 earlier EU members about the enlargement that came in May 2004: 55% opposed it, compared to 36% in the EU as a whole. Only 21% of French had ever traveled to any of the 10 new member states. The government fears its loss of leverage and leadership in an expanded EU, especially given the strong American influence in former communist countries.

Enlargement is painful for the French, who fear their voice is becoming diluted, their language threatened, and their jobs at risk. Europe once represented reassurance and comfort for them; now it seems to be a threat to their identity and prosperity. It used to be a means of spreading French values and influence outside France. Now the EU is seen as a way of imposing outside values and influences on France itself. Europe has been an instrument for preserving and multiplying French power. Now some perceive it as weakening France. France thought it could once dominate and control Europe; that is no longer possible with 27 members.

The country found itself in an unprecedented debate over Europe. This was manifested in the referendum on May 29, 2005, whether to ratify the EU constitution, drafted under the guidance of former president Giscard d'Estaing. Those who saw the wrong kind of Europe taking shape banded together to vote it down, 55% to 45%, with a turnout of 69%. What went wrong?

The entire French political establishment, elderly voters, the more affluent and better-educated, and two-thirds of voters in the 20 arrondissements of Paris supported the constitution. The unlikely coalition of opponents included renegade Socialists like former prime minister Laurent Fabius, the Communist Party, manual laborers (79% of whom voted no), Trotskyites, anti-globalization activists like José Bové, the anti-European right that advocates unfettered French sovereignty, the right-wing National Front, young voters, and baby boomers between ages 35 and 65.

The motives for rejecting it were multiple, but they mainly boiled down to one overriding concern: the specter of a bigger, more powerful Europe destroying the superior French social model and imposing upon the Continent the British economic model of reduced subsidies, longer working hours, more flexible labor markets, and greater competition. The majority associated Brussels with free-market reforms that would endanger workers' protections and accelerate the "delocalization" (a favorite slogan in the campaign, meaning outsourcing) of their jobs to low-cost eastern Europe or China.

A deep anxiety over globalization came to the surface. This fear was embodied by a mythical Polish plumber, whose kind would flood France, undercutting its wages and stealing its jobs. "British liberalism," "competition," and "profit" were dirty words in the campaign. The French have an especially ambivalent attitude toward Britain, which has a lower unemployment rate and income per capita that overtook France's in 1995. Nicolas Sarkozy, who supported the constitution, asserted, "The best social model is the one that gives work to everybody. It is not, therefore, our own." Turkish entry into the EU symbolized borders that are too open. It unnerved voters, even though the

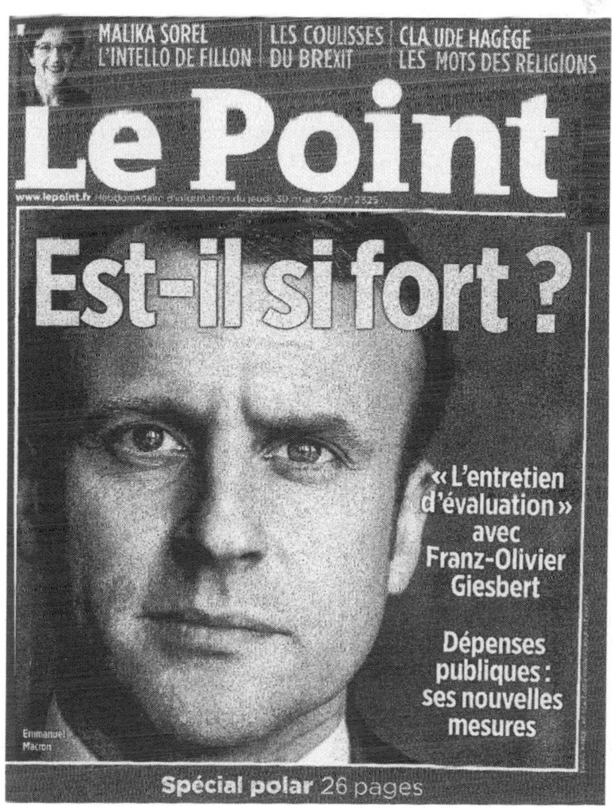

French recruitment poster

constitution said nothing about Turkey, and the government promised a later referendum on Turkish accession. In general, the no vote was a protest against a Europe the French no longer recognized and a project they no longer dominated.

Perhaps the main source of opposition was a deep revolt against the political elite that does not seem to understand the concerns of normal citizens. It commits the people to ever-closer union in Europe without being able to explain to voters why this would be better for them. Related to this was a protest against an increasingly unpopular Chirac government. The 2007 presidential election was on the mind of every citizen who voted.

Chirac did what French presidents always do when they make mistakes and things go wrong: sack the prime minister and appoint another. This time it was his protégé, Dominique de Villepin, even though he epitomized the very mandarin class against which the majority appeared to have rebelled. He demonstrated more denial than understanding of the kind of new world in which France finds itself. "The French know it and tell it to us with force: globalization is not an ideal, it cannot be our destiny." He vowed to stay "deeply attached to the French model."

President Sarkozy recognized this unease. Although stating that he favors globalization and free markets, he used his first appearance at an EU summit meeting in June 2007 to eliminate the wording "free and undistorted competition" from the EU's objectives. He returned to France hailing this change as opening the door to greater protectionism, an industrial strategy, and "European champions." "A country that abandons its factories is a country that has lost its identity." The economic recession that began in 2008 strengthened this rhetoric.

Nevertheless, Sarkozy guided his country back into the EU's good graces. He strongly supported the new treaty that was adopted in Lisbon the end of 2007 to replace the more ambitious constitution his countrymen had rejected two and one-half years earlier. This time he decided to have the parliament, not the people, vote on the Lisbon Treaty. This succeeded in February 2008 after then–foreign minister Kouchner reminded the deputies, "All of Europe is waiting for this signal from France." Perhaps this caution was unnecessary. At the time the treaty was signed in Lisbon, polls indicated that fully 68% of French voters would have accepted it in a referendum. The Lisbon Treaty called for an EU external-action service, a kind of supranational foreign ministry. The first head of it was Pierre Vimont, France's former ambassador to the United States.

Franco-German Cooperation

Another important departure is a dramatic increase in France's military cooperation with Germany. The two neighbors created an experimental joint brigade, whose command alternates between French and German officers. In 1991 they agreed to expand that unit to a corps size—35,000 troops. Actually most of the units are stationed in their home countries, while Eurocorps headquarters in Strasbourg is only a staff. In 2009 the two countries went a step further by agreeing to the first permanent basing since World War II of a battalion of German troops in eastern France as part of a Franco-German brigade. The French eased some of America's and NATO's fears by conceding that this Eurocorps, which also includes troops from Spain, Belgium, and Luxembourg, could operate under NATO for international peacekeeping and in time of war. In Afghanistan it commanded NATO's peacekeeping forces.

France has close links with the FRG. Bilateral ties, EU integration, and NATO tether Germany securely to the west. German unity made Germany, not France, the leader of a strengthened Europe, and France seeks to act with Germany's support in the name of "European interests."

In January 2003 the two neighbors celebrated the 40th anniversary of the Treaty on German-French Cooperation in grand style. Former president Chirac and ex-chancellor Schröder met at the Elysée Palace, and 603 German parliamentarians joined 577 counterparts in the Palace of Versailles. The next day, the two leaders met in Berlin. In their Elysée Declaration, they agreed to increase the frequency of their special meetings to every six weeks; to appoint in each other's capital a "secretary-general for Franco-German cooperation" who would coordinate, prepare, and follow up their common European policies; to dispatch the relevant minister to the other country's cabinet meetings when discussing a subject of interest to the other (as did Finance Minister Christine Laguard in 2010); and to propose common Franco-German legislation to each other's parliaments. In 2004 three Germans joined the French civil service. In 2019 the two neighbors renewed their vows of friendship in the city of Aix-la-Chapelle (Aachen). De Gaulle's words still rang true: "Never forget that for France there can be no other alternative but friendship with Germany."

It is uncertain how durable this special Franco-German partnership is. From the beginning it was a reconciliation of opposites, and the two partners have always had worldviews that were not totally compatible. Although the two countries' interests converged in the early 21st century, including their publics' aversion to war in Iraq in 2003, they both continue to pursue their own national interests, which are not always the same.

A prevailing opinion in Berlin is that Franco-German agreement is a "necessary, but not a sufficient condition for moving the EU forward." Agreement between the two countries is still necessary for any serious EU initiative to get off the ground; if they can agree, a measure has a good chance of being accepted in Brussels. But they can no longer dictate policy. The French hand in EU leadership is diminished and more controversial in an enlarged EU. France's worst fear is that a Europe of 28 will be an unworkable, uncontrollable mess. In such an EU, the Franco-German partnership might end up dividing Europe more than unifying it.

They hope that such integration at the top, along with partner relationships between cities (numbering 2,500) and combined military units, will help warm their citizens' hearts toward the other nation. A weakness in the relationship is that the two sides have to work so hard to maintain it. One French diplomat said, "It's the result of will and effort, not natural instinct." The reality is that the French and Germans are not particularly attracted to each other. One can see that in the choice of languages schoolchildren take. In 2006 only 800,583 French secondary-school pupils (15.7%) were learning German, and only 5% of German children were still learning French in their final year. But there is a reservoir of trust. A 2004 poll in *Libération* revealed that 84% of French respondents said they trust the Germans, but only 51% trust the British. In 2006 educators in both countries completed a common history book to be used in their schools.

Both countries faced a change of leadership, with Angela Merkel the German chancellor after the September 18, 2005, elections and Nicolas Sarkozy the French president after May 2007. They did not find a comfortable and trusting rapport with each other. She was not amused by Sarkozy's self-promoting tendency to steal the limelight and to announce initiatives without informing her. Sarkozy could be unpredictable and abrasive. But both leaders agreed that the German-French "engine" remains important, even though it is insufficient to drive the enlarged EU.

The well-practiced institutional machinery remains in place and works as usual with a new French president since May 2012. For all the talk of "Merkozy," Merkel and Sarkozy did not particularly like each other, but they learned to get along. Merkel's and Hollande's personalities are more alike, and they are both deliberative. There is a conviction in the Merkel government that the two nations are on different economic paths, with Germany far more positive toward the market economy, globalization, budgetary discipline, and penalties for those who do not obey the rules. France favors looser discipline, growth promotion, stimulus spending, and fiscal harmonization in the eurozone.

More serious is that the recession from 2008, and especially the euro crisis beginning in 2010, showed that the balance of power between the two countries had shifted in Germany's favor. The two partners are no longer equals; France appears to be the junior partner. Germany leads by default, not by choice. Thus, the euro crisis has changed the rules of European politics. The two still try to work out a common position ahead of important EU summits, so the shift in power is not obvious to everyone. However, until Germany's leaders agree on a measure, nothing happens, since Germany has become the European power that counts most.

Hollande announced during his campaign that "it is not for Germany to decide for the rest of Europe." That reveals major political change in Germany itself. It consults its own interests and no longer feels the need to please after the horrors of war. For example, Germany refused to follow France's lead and intervene militarily in Libya to enforce a UN no-fly zone in 2011.

A former French foreign minister lamented, "You can't call it the Franco-German couple any more because Germany has found its place as Europe's number one." France has difficulty adjusting to this new reality. The myth of an equal partnership is retained because it lends France an inflated diplomatic stature while it protects Germany from charges of unilateralism.

There is still a lot of symbolism in public view. On November 11, 2009, Merkel became the first German leader to commemorate on French soil Armistice Day ending World War I. She was invited to the Arc de Triomphe in Paris for a full military ceremony, where she publicly held hands with Sarkozy. She said in her speech, "When there is antagonism between us, everybody loses. When we are united, everybody wins." Hollande well understands that the special relationship between the two countries has traditionally multiplied French influence in Europe and the world. As has become traditional, Hollande's first foreign visit was to the German capital the day of his inauguration.

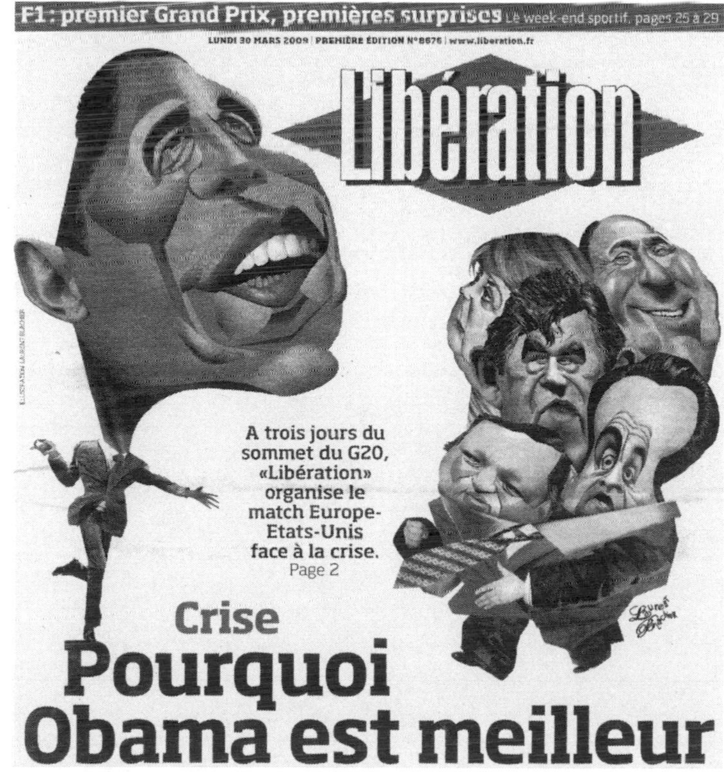

F1: premier Grand Prix, premières surprises Le week-end sportif, pages 25 à 29

Libération

A trois jours du sommet du G20, «Libération» organise le match Europe-Etats-Unis face à la crise.
Page 2

Crise
Pourquoi Obama est meilleur

The Crisis. Why Obama is better.

Military Forces

The end of superpower confrontation meant that France had to reexamine the three pillars of its defense policy—its nuclear forces, its draft army, and its operational independence from permanent alliances. Without a Soviet threat, it had problems defining a clear purpose for its atomic force de frappe. It became difficult to maintain its expensive triad of forces, which in 1991 consumed a fifth of total defense spending.

Its underground nuclear test series in 1995–1996 unleashed a violent world out-cry, especially in Asia and the Pacific, where they took place. Taken aback by the worldwide protest, Chirac swore that these tests were needed to perfect computer simulation programs that would make further testing unnecessary. In 1991 the French had finally signed the nuclear Non-Proliferation Treaty (NPT) to emphasize the need to stop the spread of atomic weapons. They signed an international treaty banning nuclear testing in 1996. Not until 2009 did they admit that many of the illnesses suffered in French Polynesia were linked to the nuclear tests, and they agreed to pay compensation.

France continues to maintain the largest and most diversified military capability on the European continent outside of Russia, as well as a credible nuclear force. Despite the changed security environment in Europe following the end of the Cold War, a consensus remained to maintain as the ultimate security guarantee a minimal nuclear force posture for the purpose of "dissuasion," the French version of deterrence. There is little public debate over this. A significant change is that these nuclear weapons are to be linked to European security, not just the defense of French territory and interests. The French are aware that there is little current interest in Europe for such a link and that the establishment of a European defense identity would be a precondition.

French nuclear strategy also changed in 2001, with a move away from an "anti-cities," "all or nothing" strategy to a wider, more discriminate range of options. This is made possible by advances in the weapons' precision. In 2006 former president Chirac spoke openly of one new option for French nuclear weapons beyond the vague defense of France's "vital interests": retaliation against a terrorist strike against France backed by a sovereign state. He did not mention any specific countries, but he was probably thinking of Iran.

The consequence of France's decision to maintain only a minimal dissuasion policy is that major reductions in its nuclear force posture and infrastructure became possible. In the course of the 1990s, France reduced its nuclear spending by more than 50%. It started eliminating its 18 land-based nuclear missiles on Plateau d'Albion (completed by 2005), reduced to 4 its planned new ballistic missile submarines, and closed its plants at Pierrelatte and Marcoule that produce fissile material for atomic weapons. Of the five nuclear submarines in use at the end of the century, four are always operational, with two at sea. One sub has 16 M4 missiles, each carrying 6 warheads. Four new strategic subs carrying upgraded missiles entered the force: *Le Triomphant* in 1996, *Le Téméraire* in 1999, *Le Vigilant* in 2002, and finally *Le Terrible* in 2008. This submarine force represents four-fifths of the total French nuclear arsenal of 350 warheads.

An airborne component remains: Three squadrons of Mirage 2000 N planes are equipped with ASMP missiles, and two fleets of Super Etendards, equipped with ASMPs, are stationed on aircraft carriers. France keeps secret the scale of its nuclear capability. A study by the Federation of American Scientists suggested in 2009 that it had 348 warheads, of which 288 are on submarines, 50 on air-launched cruise missiles, and 10 on bombers.

The aircraft carrier *Clemenceau* was decommissioned in 1997, and the following year it was announced that the aged *Foch* would also be withdrawn from service. In 2000 after a four-year delay the *Charles de Gaulle* came on line. This is the first French carrier constructed to be interoperable with US Nimitz-class carriers. It has compatible catapults and color-coded systems, can receive US aircraft, and carries US-built Hawkeye planes flown by US-trained pilots who control the airspace around the carrier and guide planes to their targets. All French navy pilots train in America for a year, and 10 American officers serve as exchange officers on the ship under French command. Plagued by troubles, including the loss of a propeller during a shakedown cruise, the *Charles de Gaulle* must spend four months a year in port for maintenance. A second carrier, the *Jeanne d'Arc*, has been ordered to accompany it. In the summer of 2005, the *Charles de Gaulle* stole the show in a naval review of allied ships sponsored by the British to commemorate the Battle of Trafalger. In 2011 it saw action in enforcing the UN no-fly zone over Libya. It was the first non-American ship to command the Islamic State task force against IS positions in Iraq and Syria.

In 2010 France offered Russia the first significant purchase of NATO weaponry since the end of communism. It signed a deal in 2010 to sell to the Russian navy two technologically sophisticated Mistral amphibious assault ships, built at the troubled Saint-Nazaire shipyard. They are capable of carrying tanks, other vehicles, helicopters, landing barges, and more than 400 soldiers. In the aftermath of Russia's 2008 invasion of Georgia, Crimea, and southeast Ukraine, France's NATO partners were not pleased with this sale, and France postponed delivery indefinitely. President Hollande also joined the German chancellor in negotiating a shaky cease-fire in Ukraine.

The 1991 Gulf War revealed that France's conventional forces were not equipped or structured to cope with faraway crises. Its draftees could not be sent out of France, and its equipment was found wanting. The war reinforced the case for a more professional army. Consequently, France began in 1996 to phase out its 10-month conscription and to create an all-volunteer army. By 2019 France had a total force of 209,000 troops, including 22,790 women. It also has 70,300 reservists. Over a five-year period, it disbanded 38 of its 180 regiments. This included 12 in Germany, where only 3,200 soldiers remained. In 2014 their last infantry regiment in Donaueschingen was disbanded, leaving no French soldiers permanently stationed in Germany. Army manpower was reduced from around 400,000 to 134,000, which includes 14,700 "marine infantry and artillery" and 13,490 women.

French troops in Kosovo Photo by Gerald Camier

It also includes 7,700 members of the Foreign Legion. In the past, most senior noncommissioned officers and a few officers were German. The majority of legionnaires killed in the Indochina War were Germans. But that has changed. Recruits for the five-year stints now come from 136 countries; 80% say they join for economic reasons, not for adventure. Their service is a fast track to French citizenship, and they are eligible for French pensions after 15 years. Each must give up his name and choose an assumed one. Only 18% are French-born, and they must relinquish their passports and be issued one from another French-speaking country. East Europeans make up 40% of its new recruits, and Asians and Latin Americans are among the fast-growing cadres. Only about 1% are Americans. There are no women, and the command language is French. They serve with regular French military forces wherever the latter are deployed, especially in Africa.

The Foreign Legion deployed with US military forces in Somalia in 1992 and later in Afghanistan. They were part of peacekeeping forces in Kosovo, Rwanda, and Cambodia. Recruits must demonstrate computer and technology skills. They are now as likely to work side by side with French police and army fighting terrorism in metropolitan France. They also participate in humanitarian relief missions, such as in South Asia after the 2004 tsunami.

France has trained 2,300 special operations forces, and these elite troops have fought with the Americans and other allies in Afghanistan. The navy has 43,995 sailors, including 1,700 naval marines, 6,800 naval air, and 3,000 women. Its air force consists of 57,600 troops, including 6,300 women. There were cuts in the land-based nuclear-deterrence force, military bases, schools and hospitals, and civilian defense contractors; 16 warships are being decommissioned. The professional officer corps remains at about 38,000.

France no longer spends more than most European countries on defense: 1.7% of GDP in 2007. The government embarked in 2002 on a costly defense modernization plan and shifted France's strategy toward creating a force that can be projected anywhere in the world. It ordered a second aircraft carrier, new spy satellites, reconnaissance drones, 50 new Airbus A400M heavy-lift transport planes, 34 helicopters, and 57 Rafale combat aircraft. By 2008 total armed forces, including the paramilitary gendarmerie, rose to 446,000.

The goal was to catch up with Britain's armed forces in terms of professionalism, equipment, and global reach. The most dramatic step in this direction was the 50-year defense and security cooperation treaty signed in November 2010. It was driven by the need to restrain their defense budgets while maintaining their willingness and capability to project power globally. The two countries had explored such defense cooperation before, most notably in the 1998 St. Malo declaration following a meeting between Chirac and former prime minister Tony Blair. But the Iraq War in 2003 prevented progress. This was one of the few times the two midsized nuclear powers found themselves on opposite sides in a recent international conflict.

The main items in the treaty were a joint expeditionary force, combined training, and maintenance for the new A400M transport airplane and shared A300 aerial tankers. France offered Britain access to its jet pilot school, and both will cooperate in developing armed drones and ways of combatting roadside bombs. They will jointly operate aircraft-carrier strike groups with the aim of ensuring a permanent carrier presence at sea. Perhaps most dramatically, they will cooperate on nuclear weapons while retaining their independent deterrents and means: Britain depends on American equipment, while France develops its own.

France aims to improve its interoperability with allies but, at the same time, to protect its ability to act alone "should it be necessary" and to "assume the role of lead nation" in any coalition. Its independent stance had been challenged by the reality of emerging European defense identity, which the French government advocates. More than any western country, France was rocked by the breakup of the old world order. It can no longer pose as an independent force between two superpowers; such a state of affairs has ceased to exist. France no longer hopes to put itself in a position of leadership in Europe with the future possibility of heading a counterweight to American predominance in a more multipolar world. But it insists on its independence and the right to disagree with its allies.

Response to Terrorism and War in Iraq

When terrorists hijacked four commercial airliners and flew three of them into the World Trade Center and the Pentagon in 2001, killing 3,000 persons, including many French, France did not hesitate to help. It shed its usual hesitation toward collaboration with the US. President Chirac was the first foreign leader to visit Washington after the attacks. He told the American president that France stood in total solidarity" with the United States and "our forces will take part. We will assume our role in a spirit of solidarity and responsibility." Ex–prime minister Lionel Jospin also declared, "the struggle against terrorism calls for solidarity and cooperation. Our solidarity is first with America, the ally to which we owe victory over Nazism, the friend with whom we jointly affirm the ideal of democracy."

French public opinion backed these stands. A charmed Chirac escaped an assassination attempt when an assailant fired at him while he was passing in the annual Bastille Day parade. The July 14, 2002, event was dedicated to Franco-American friendship and featured marching West Point cadets and 75 relatives of victims of the September 11 attacks on the World Trade Center.

As military action against Afghanistan began, it had a refueling ship and an Exocet-rocket launching frigate patrolling the waters close to the war zone with the American and British navies. It quickly put intelligence agents on the ground to work with the Afghan opposition and dispatched special forces who fought under US command. It deployed 2,000 on 3 naval vessels, as well as combat and reconnaissance aircraft. It stationed some of its fighter-bombers in neighboring Tajikistan and ordered six of them back to the war in Afghanistan. It also sent some of its AWACS airborne control aircraft to the Balkans to relieve NATO AWACS planes for use in protecting the US East Coast. French leaders regarded America's turning to its friends as inevitable. One advisor was correct when he said, "America's power in the world may be unrivalled in military, political and economic areas, but in the era of globalization even a superpower cannot disregard the need for allies."

According to a book published in France in October 2004, *Chirac Contra Bush: L'Autre Guerre* (*Chirac vs. Bush: The Other War*), written by two journalists for *Le Parisien*, Cantaloube and Henri Vernet, France was prepared in the fall of 2002 to provide from 10,000 to 15,000 troops for an invasion of Iraq. France agreed to Security Council resolution 1441 putting Saddam Hussein on notice to disarm. Chirac sent General Jean Patrick Gaviard to the Pentagon in December 2002 to discuss a French contribution. Reportedly they were especially interested because they believed that sitting the war out would have left French forces unprepared for future conflicts.

Another French author, Pierre Péan, in a best-selling book *L'Inconnu de L'Elysée* (*The Unknown of the Elysée*), wrote that France maneuvered for months while deliberating on whether to join an American-led invasion of Iraq. Research by former assistant secretary of state for public affairs under President Clinton James Rubin also showed France "scrambling to avoid a showdown with the United States." Rubin reported that the French government even advised at one point for "the Americans to bypass the Security Council altogether."

France

French intelligence agreed in part with the analysis that Iraq wanted to acquire a nuclear weapon, but it could not prove it. After weapons inspectors seemed to be having success in Iraq and public opinion in France became so hostile, the French president changed his mind. Relations soured between the French and American governments. The Chirac government later refused to admit that there had been any hesitation on his part.

In the end, the French government opposed military action against Saddam's Iraq, with which France had long enjoyed lucrative commercial ties. Chirac and his ex–foreign minister (later prime minister) Dominique de Villepin argued that UN arms inspectors needed more time to complete their work and that such a conflict would breed even more terrorism and easily spill over into France itself, especially given its large Arab immigrant population, which solidly supported Chirac on this question.

Chirac, who enjoyed overwhelming backing within his own country and majority support in public opinion elsewhere on the Continent, believed that the crisis offered him an ideal opportunity to enact his version of the earlier Gaullist doctrine: that Europe must act as a counterweight to a much-too-powerful United States and that France, with German backing, must be the directing force in Europe. Whereas British policy aimed to promote unity with Washington rather than trying to rein it in, French policy sought the recreation of a multipolar world in which Europe, led by France, could stand up to the sole superpower. The UN Security Council would be the sole source of legitimacy for countries going to war. With its veto power, it could stop or limit the use of American military force whenever it chose to do so. In the process, France's diplomatic weight and prestige would be greatly enhanced, and its interests, served.

This grand design ran into almost-immediate difficulties. Chirac's tactless remarks at an EU summit caused unexpected indignation throughout Europe that undermined any chances of placing France at the forefront of a united Europe. After 18 European governments, including most of those in central and eastern Europe, signed letters supporting US policy toward Iraq, he hinted in frustration that France might veto the application by former communist countries to join the EU. Chirac said that they "have not been very well behaved and have been rather reckless of the danger of aligning themselves too rapidly with the American position." Referring to Romania and Bulgaria, who were still waiting for an invitation to join, he stated, "if they wanted to diminish their chances of joining the EU, they could not have chosen a better way." The new partners in the east were furious.

Chirac's policy also poisoned France's relations with many of its other allies, including the US. When he declared on March 10 that he would veto "in all circumstances" any new resolution to bring about Iraqi disarmament, he unwittingly had called an end to all chances for a diplomatic settlement of the crisis. The US and Britain proceeded to defeat Saddam's regime in three weeks without France's support, even though the French government permitted coalition warplanes to use its airspace.

In France's own press and elsewhere, it began to sink in that France might have overreached its capacities. Chirac's condescending treatment of central European governments had split and weakened Europe rather than united it. The EU's nascent Common Foreign and Security Policy (CFSP) was left in shambles, thereby destroying any hope for a European pole dominated by France. France's dogged resistance to war had paralyzed the UN Security Council, thereby possibly weakening the only body in which France has equal standing with the US. France was temporarily left on the sidelines in a new post-Saddam Middle East, and it faced a difficult task in repairing its relations with the United States and Britain. Sarkozy, who almost never used words like "glory" and "grandeur" in his speeches, had also opposed the war in Iraq, but he saw a need to restore good relations with the US. He found a chastened America a more willing and cooperative partner.

In 2005 the US joined hands with France in a successful effort to order Syria to pull its troops and security forces out of Lebanon. The US and European allies asked France to take the lead in organizing a peacekeeping force in Lebanon after the military conflict between Hezbollah and Israel was over. Paris ultimately dispatched 2,000 troops despite its nervousness about getting involved in a country as lethal as Lebanon and doing anything that could cost it goodwill with Arabs at home.

It also came to light in 2005 that the French and American intelligence services had created in 2002 a top-secret center in Paris, code-named Alliance Base, to analyze terrorist suspects' transnational movements and to develop operations to catch or spy on them. Funded largely by the CIA's Counterterrorist Center, it is directed by a French general assigned to France's equivalent of the CIA—the General Directorate for External Security (DGSE). It also brings together case officers from Britain, Germany, Canada and Australia. To play down the American role, the working language is French. Osama bin Laden declared France a terror-

Guadeloupe

ist target after it banned the burqk killed in Pakistan by American commandos. But the government redoubled its counterterror efforts.

Chirac phoned President Bush after the short war was over, expressing his pleasure that Saddam's government had been demolished and offering to be "pragmatic" about postwar reconstruction. France refrained from telling Washington, "I told you so," and it pledged to forgive some of Iraq's foreign debt. Chrac ordered its navy to cooperate with the US Navy in securing the sea lanes in the Indian Ocean; sent troops to Haiti under American command in 2004 to help create order after the Haiti's president was forced to flee; invited President Bush (as well as the German chancellor for the first time) to attend the 60th anniversary of the D-Day invasion in June 2004, when 100 Americans were awarded the Légion d'Honneur; and publicly kissed the hand of Laura Bush when she visited Paris in 2003.

The French government seeks to reconcile its worst differences with the US. The United States remains France's largest trading partner outside the EU, with $50 billion in annual trade. Chirac dropped France's long-standing resistance to NATO's formal assumption of command over the international security force in Afghanistan. In 2005 France agreed to take part in NATO's effort to train 1,500 Iraqi security forces, albeit outside of Iraq.

After reelection in November 2004, President Bush made it one of his top priorities to restore good relations with Europe. In February 2005 he became the first American president to visit the European Union headquarters in Brussels, and he sent Secretary of State Condoleezza Rice to Paris a couple weeks later. The newspapers wrote of a "charm offensive." A former Stanford University professor, she gave a lecture to the political elite at Sciences Po and talked of a "new chapter" in Franco-American relations and of the need "to turn away from the disagreements of the past." This was desperately overdue. A German Marshall Fund poll in France had revealed at the time that 88% of French disapproved of Bush's foreign policy, and only 11% approved of his presidency. After Obama's election in 2009, that latter figure soared to 88% approval.

The French were receptive. Political analyst François Heisbourg concluded that it was not really rapprochement, but "we've both decided it's not in our interests to be at each other's throats." Americans appreciated this change: In May 2003 only 29% of them had a favorable opinion of France, but that figure rose to 62% by the end of 2009.

Americans shared the pain with the French on November 13, 2015, when France suffered the deadliest attacks on their soil since the battle of Paris in August 1944. Three teams of Islamic State terrorists killed 130 and injured 413. They made suicide attacks in a soccer stadium, shot 39 people in 3 restaurants, and gunned down 89 persons in Bataclan Theater during a rock concert. President Hollande declared that "France is at war" and announced a state of emergency that granted the police sweeping powers. His approval rating temporarily soared. The French were left with a sense of threat and shock.

Activism in Foreign Policy

France always tried to remain largely independent of other western industrialized nations in its dealing with the third world. No other country of comparable size maintains as big a military presence abroad. It had soldiers stationed in some three dozen countries and territories, including Germany (2,800), Kosovo (1,294), French Guiana on the northern coast of South America (1,435 army and an air unit), French West Indies (775 army, 450 navy and an air unit), and French Polynesia (640).

It maintains permanent military bases in three African ex-colonies: It has 1,690 army troops and an air unit on the east coast of Djibouti, 775 soldiers in Gabon, and 575 army troops and 230 sailors in Senegal. One thousand remained in Mali as part of a UN force. One of these bases will be closed in the future as France's relations with the continent are normalized. Like Sarkozy, President Hollande says that *Françafrique*, a pejorative term

Le Monde

www.lemonde.fr

59e ANNÉE – Nº 18072 – 1,20 € – FRANCE MÉTROPOLITAINE — DIMANCHE 2 - LUNDI 3 MARS 2003 — FONDATEUR : HUBERT BEUVE-MÉRY – DIRECTEUR : JEAN-MARIE COLOMBANI

SUPPLÉMENT
Le Monde ARGENT
Charmes et dangers de la « love money »
Marché de l'art

AUTRICHE
Schüssel reconduit la coalition avec l'extrême droite p. 3

RÉPUBLIQUE TCHÈQUE
Vaclav Klaus, nouveau président p. 3

THAÏLANDE
Guerre contre la drogue : plus de 1 000 morts en un mois p. 6

VERTS
Affaiblis et toujours divisés p. 7

DÉCENTRALISATION
Raffarin a présenté son projet p. 8

PARFUMERIES
Bataille entre Sephora et Marionnaud p. 10

LUTTE ANTI-DOPAGE
Réunion à Copenhague pour définir

France-Algérie, les retrouvailles

C'EST LA PREMIÈRE visite d'Etat d'un président de la République française depuis l'indépendance de l'Algérie. Du 2 au 4 mars, Jacques Chirac se rendra à Alger puis à Oran, et les autorités algériennes lui ont organisé un accueil exceptionnel. Pour Paris, il s'agit, après les dix années de guerre civile qui ont dévasté l'Algérie, de regarder désormais « vers l'avenir » et de « refonder » les relations entre les deux pays. Lundi, devant les parlementaires algériens, M. Chirac devait souligner la destinée commune de la France et de l'Algérie, plaider pour la démocratie et la relance de réformes économiques aujourd'hui en panne. Histoire et mémoire seront également présentes lors de ce voyage. M. Chirac se rendra au Monument des martyrs algériens de la guerre d'indépendance et dans un ancien cimetière français. Cette visite devrait également relancer les relations économiques entre les deux pays, la France étant le premier partenaire commercial de l'Algérie.

► La première visite d'Etat d'un président français depuis 1962

► Une déclaration solennelle signée par Jacques Chirac et Abdelaziz Bouteflika

► Dans un discours devant le Parlement, M. Chirac devrait faire l'éloge de la démocratie

► ONG et familles de disparus s'inquiètent

Lire pages 2 et 3 et l'éditorial page 11

Le Monde DOSSIER

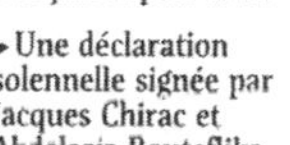

VIVRE À ALGER

Alger, la ville, le jour, la nuit

AVANT la visite de Jacques Chirac, une équipe de journalistes du *Monde* s'est promenée à Alger en toute liberté.

Lire notre dossier pages I à VIII

La guerre inéluctable de Washington

► Bagdad annonce la destruction de ses missiles

► Une « tromperie » selon les Américains

PATRIMOINE

Bartabas installe son Académie équestre dans les écuries du roi

referring to those "networks of a bygone era," is over. It has been replaced by human rights and bilateral links free of post-colonial paternalism. France has troops in other African countries in order to protect French interests and citizens, who number about 130,000 in sub-Saharan Africa. In 2008 there were 2,600 French soldiers on a peacekeeping mission in the Ivory Coast, but 1,100 of them were brought home in 2009, and 1,000 more were withdrawn from the EU's Darfur peacekeeping mission.

When rebels tried to topple the government of Chad in February 2008, France had 1,500 troops on the ground to rescue 500 foreigners and the American and German ambassadors. Although French troops did not enter the fighting, they were ready to evacuate President Idriss Déby, who had studied at the École Militaire in Paris, or prop up his corrupt government if necessary. Sarkozy declared "If France must do its duty, it will do so," despite earlier declarations that he intended to modernize France's Africa policy by refusing to defend dictators. It maintains 1,200 army troops and an aviation group in Chad.

France also sends two-thirds of its foreign aid to Africa, making it, the UK, and the US the continent's major patrons. Since 1990 it encourages the trend toward democracy in Africa by linking its aid to democratic reforms. It has lost to China its position as sub-Saharan Africa's top trading partner.

Although it convenes a Franco-African summit each year, it decided to trim its costs on that continent. Its military interventions have become rarer, although in 1992 it joined other allies to participate in the UN humanitarian relief operation in Somalia. It was the only European country to send troops to Rwanda in 1994. Its 2,500 soldiers managed to interrupt the first round of genocide and save thousands of lives.

Ex-president Chirac reiterated at a Franco-African summit in 1998, "The period of outside interference is over." That declaration had to be put aside in 2002, when French forces were rushed to the Ivory Coast, a former French colony that was once a model of stability in West Africa. A bloody and confusing uprising got out of control, endangering 20,000 French nationals and prompting the rescue by French soldiers of 191 American schoolchildren trapped in the crossfire. Paris tried to mediate a peace pact.

By 2004 there were 4,600 French troops, including Foreign Legion and elite reconnaissance forces, trying to protect the government and enforce the oft-violated ceasefires. This was France's biggest foreign military commitment. France called on the UN to become more involved, and 6,000 UN peacekeepers, mainly from West African countries, were sent.

The Ivory Coast's government forces broke a longtime cease-fire in 2004 and bombed a French peacekeepers' camp, killing nine French troops and an American aid worker. France hit back immediately, destroying the entire Ivorian air force. Demonstrators then turned on Abi-

France

French bread for euros

Courtesy: Central Audiovisual Library, European Commission

djan's sizeable French community, looting houses, burning businesses and schools, and forcing over 100 French nationals to flee in terror each day.

This festering crisis exposed the limits of France's new Africa policy of intervening less and resorting more to multilateral action. It maintains 1,000 soldiers in the Ivory Coast, but its base there had been downgraded to a temporary "overseas mission." It sent an additional 600 soldiers to the Ivory Coast in April 2011, when it answered a request of the UN to intervene militarily to save lives and to enable the winner of the presidential election, Alassane Ouattara, to assume the office that the loser, Laurent Gbagbo, refused to vacate. Although it supported the UN troops in the country, it retained its own command in Paris. The operation succeeded. The violence and killing were stopped, and the 12,000 French citizens were among the many who were protected.

In 2003 it attained EU and UN mandates to send its troops, accompanied by a small number of allied European soldiers including, for the first time, Swedes, to northeastern Congo to secure the airport around Bunia. This mission, called Artemis, was the first EU military deployment outside of Europe and was done with no coordination with NATO. President Sarkozy ordered more transparency in relations with Africa and downgraded a special presidential unit that once dealt with African heads of state.

France has long-standing interests in the Middle East. It sent a powerful 12,600-man air, naval, and ground contingent in 1991 to help drive Iraq out of Kuwait. This was a bold move, considering the large Arab population in France and the fact that Iraq had been France's best Middle Eastern customer and owed France $3 billion. In doing this it violated one of de Gaulle's most basic teachings: French troops should never be under US command. Former president Mitterrand answered critics, saying, "we are linked, we are allies, and we intend to do what we are committed to do." To renew French ties with Iraq, President Sarkozy visited Iraq in February 2009, thereby becoming the first leader of a European country that had opposed the 2003 US invasion to do so.

France demonstrated that it is ready to move outside its traditional area of operations and to match its military presence to its strategic interests rather than to its colonial links. In May 2009 France opened its first permanent base in the Persian Gulf: in Abu Dhabi in the United Arab Emirates (UAE). This is France's first permanent base outside of Africa, the first built outside of France since decolonization began in the 1960s, and the first in a country where it has no colonial ties. Its 500 naval, air, and ground troops there man a depot to support French maritime surveillance operations in the Gulf region. In March 2008 French forces took part in large-scale war games in the Gulf. In a separate deal, France also agreed to help the UAE build two nuclear energy reactors.

Other countries look to France to take the lead in deciding how to respond if Algeria, to which France annually provides $1 billion in aid, becomes a fundamentalist Islamic republic. France is torn between the desire to prevent Muslim extremists from coming to power and fear of making irreconcilable enemies out of potential rulers of Algeria. It supports the military junta in power, reinforced by its election, even though it has outlawed the popular Islamic Salvation Front (FIS). This policy creates problems within France itself.

France's nervousness is understandable. The threat of violence on French soil had become real. Out of a total of between 5 and 6 million Muslims in France in 2013, about 30%, or 1.5 million, are of Algerian origin. Authorities believe that fundamentalists wield influence over a small but growing minority of them.

In 2003 Chirac made the first-ever state visit to Algeria since independence four decades earlier, and he was welcomed with enthusiasm. The government in Algiers treated this high-profile visit as a momentous event in its postcolonial history. Its purpose was to redefine the tortured relationship with Algeria, gripped by a deadly civil war that had claimed at least 120,000 deaths. It was time for reconciliation.

Chirac, who had served there as a second lieutenant during the Algerian war, said that that conflict had been "a painful moment in our common history that we must not and cannot ignore, but it is time now to move forward." He signed a Declaration of Algiers, forerunner to a formal treaty underscoring a "special partnership" between the two nations. Everywhere he went, he was greeted with cries of "Visa, visa!" He promised to improve visa procedures, while his interior minister at home vowed to crack down on the large increase in visas issued.

France welcomes the euro

In December 2012 President Hollande paid a delicate visit to Algeria. He acknowledged the "profoundly unjust and brutal" nature of France's colonial rule. However, he did not make an apology for France's conduct, although Algeria has long pressed for such. France's pro-Arab foreign policy, driven in part by domestic considerations, put the country in conflict with the US's basically pro-Israel leaning.

When revolutions in many Arab counters were sparked in early 2011, first in Tunisia and then in Egypt, France was caught off guard, and it was slow to support the demonstrators who were demanding democracy and to condemn the brutal government crackdowns. Then–foreign minister Michèle Alliot-Marie vacationed with her parents in Tunisia when the protests were gaining momentum, flying in a private jet owned by a tycoon close to President Ben Ali. She stepped forward to offer French security expertise to contain the street riots. She was sacked. Prime Minister François Fillon and his family also enjoyed similar perks during a holiday in Egypt; hotel bills, flights, and boat rides were paid by the Egyptian government. Sarkozy demanded that the cabinet members take their vacations in France.

The most embarrassing criticism came from an anonymous group of former and current French diplomats writing an opinion piece in *Le Monde*, accusing the government of "amateurism, impulsiveness and a short-term preoccupation with the image in the media. France's voice in the world has disappeared, and its foreign policy is dictated by improvisation. Europe is powerless, Africa escapes us, the Mediterranean won't talk to us, China has kept us down and Washington is ignoring us!" As a result, the 16,000-strong diplomatic service felt ignored, dispirited, and marginalized.

Realizing that he had made serious mistakes, the quick-footed Sarkozy pushed France's allies to intervene militarily in Libya after both the UN and the Arab League requested outside help to prevent a massacre. Intense meetings were held in NATO, which Sarkozy had initially wanted to sidestep. France angered the US and UK by making its first air strikes to enforce a no-fly zone without fully informing its allies. Sarkozy recognized the rebels' governing council without consulting with his allies or with his own foreign minister, Alain Juppé. He ordered that weapons be dropped to rebels on the ground. His actions were very popular at home, despite the fact that French soldiers were also fighting in Afghanistan and the Ivory Coast. *Liberation* wrote that "France has pulled off a masterstroke." A poll indicated that 66% approved. Dominique Moisi claimed: "people are proud to be French again."

The same was true in January 2013, when President Hollande ordered fighter jets and attack helicopters stationed in Chad and France, along with 2,900 ground troops, to stop a jihadist offensive in Mali and to protect 6,000 French nationals in the region. France's EU and NATO allies, as well as the UN Security Council, supported the military action. The international legality of France's action was unquestioned. The US supplied drones and intelligence assets, along with transport and refueling planes. The operation succeeded in pushing the attackers back, at the cost of five French soldiers dead. Hollande was showered with gratitude when he visited Mali: "*Merci* Papa Hollande!" Two-thirds (63%) of the French at home approved. This rare example of presidential decisiveness lent authority to a man with no foreign policy experience and a reputation for indecision. France leads the struggle against jihadism in the Sahel region. It has 3,000 soldiers in Mali and Chad, with headquarters in the latter's capital, N'Djamena, and bases in Niger, Ivory Coast, and Burkina Faso.

The end of 2013 into 2014 the French sent 2,000 soldiers as head of a UN peacemaking operation in the Central African Republic (CAR). The mandate was to break a cycle of Christian-Muslim sectarian violence described as "pregenocidal." The soldiers had no early success in stopping the violence, fanning French concerns

Poster for the French census

that it could become a long and protracted fight.

President Hollande declared that "France wants to maintain its ability to react alone." It scrapped plans for a second aircraft carrier. The wars in Libya, Mali, and CAR pointed out deficiencies in intelligence gathering by drones, transport, and aerial refueling. These require help from its allies, especially the US and Britain. France joined the US-led air war in Iraq and Syria and became America's closest European ally in security policy.

Corsica

France also must deal with domestic terrorism from Corsica. Since the 1970s Corsicans suffered an average of 400 explosions a year by various and divided nationalist groups, who finance their operations by extorting "protection money" from local businesses. Supported by no more than 1 Corsican in 10, these groups do not agree among themselves about whether they are seeking independence or more autonomy. But in 1996 they took their struggle to the French mainland, bombing a courthouse in Aix-en-Provence and the Bordeaux office of the prime minister. The Corsican National Liberation Front (FNLC) claimed responsibility for the multiple explosions.

In 1998 the troubles escalated on "the impossible island." France's prefect, Claude Erignac, was murdered, and the assassins were never found. Bernard Bonnet replaced him and was given carte blanche to crack down on separatist terror, corruption, organized crime, and clan vendettas. He succeeded in reducing bomb attacks to 96 in 1998, armed robbery fell by two-thirds, and scores of separatist extremists were arrested. Dozens of local politicians and dignitaries were placed under investigation in some 80 corruption scandals.

In 2000 the French government sought to end the violence by recognizing the island's unique identity and history and by offering Corsica a limited form of self-government. The 330,000 islanders have more authority over culture, education, economic development, and the environment. The teaching of the Corsican language (closer to Italian than to French) is required in all nursery schools. In December 2000, a large majority in the island's legislature approved this plan for greater autonomy. By 2018 the French state had granted greater autonomy to Corsica than to any other region.

The separatist Corsica National Liberation Front announced an unconditional suspension of its military actions in 2003. In 2014 it emphasized that it had given up its 40-year war against the French state. In 2017 nationalist parties won 56.5% of the votes in the territorial elections. Their demands were reasonable rather than emotional: fair recognition with France.

ECONOMY

After World War II, France experienced an economic miracle no less impressive than that of West Germany. The US Marshall Plan, economic planning, membership in the EU, and decolonization were important factors in this success. From the end of World War II until the Sarkozy presidency in 2007, the French state supervised economic planning through an official "planning commission," now disbanded. Managers, union representatives, and government officials drew up "Le Plan," and parliament debated and approved it. It usually extended for a five-year period and set economic targets; investment priorities; statistical analyses of past, present, and future economic performance, and needs. The aim was to sustain balanced economic growth.

Traditionally, there were no coercive measures associated with the plan, but the state always offered industries many incentives to participate: It provided useful statistics and analyses, granted tax relief and tariff concessions, awarded government contracts, or provided loans for investment funds. Even though the formal commission no longer exists, the spirit of planning is still alive.

France possesses enough raw materials to supply about half of its overall needs, and it has a diversified and modern industrial base and a highly skilled labor force, 22% of which is employed in industry (producing 20% of GDP) and 75% in services (producing 78% of GDP). Most of the job creation in recent years has come from the dynamic services sector. Women constitute 43% of the workforce, compared with 36% in 1968.

With its cultural riches and geographic beauty, France employs many people in its tourist industry. With 78 million visitors every year, it is the world's most visited country, ahead of the US, Spain, and Italy. In 2009 Chinese visitors to France were the biggest spenders. One sees this in department stores, which have introduced signs in Chinese. It is Americans' second-favorite destination after Britain. A film commission survey in 2005 concluded that 62% of tourists chose to visit France after seeing it in a film. But the French do not reciprocate. With more second homes than any other nation, 90% of them stay in France for their holidays. In 2016 it was the fifth-richest country in the world, despite the fact that it has only 1% of the world's population.

At 1.6% in 2019, its inflation was falling. The economic recession did not hit France as badly as most other European countries and the US. Salaries had not been rising fast enough to match price increases. Unemployment fell to 8.9% in 2019, and it's over 23.7% for the young under 26 years and non-EU foreigners, 22% for the unskilled workers, and up to half for Algerian and Moroccan immigrants in some suburbs. One major reason for the problem is the high cost of French labor. Employers must pay a high minimum wage, plus an added 50% in benefits. A French employer must pay twice as much in social charges as his German counterpart. It is politically impossible to create new jobs by cutting the pay and benefits of those working.

Half the households in France pay no income tax. To strengthen incentives to invest and to produce, the government lowered the tax rates in 2000. The top personal rates dropped from 54% to 52.5% and corporate rates to 33.3%; President Hollande wanted to raise the top rate to 75%, but that was prevented by the Constitutional Council. Low-paid workers pay lower social security contributions, and the car license tax was abolished. Trumpeted by the government as the most dramatic tax cut in a half-century, the changes still leave the French with a higher tax bill than most of their competitors: 46% of GDP.

Government spending accounts for 57% of GDP, more than any other eurozone country and far above the OECD average of 38% and 37% in the US. In 2019 its budget deficit had decreased to 2.6% of GDP. But its public debt exceeds 90% of GDP and is rising fast. This was about seven times higher than in 1980 and exceeds EU guidelines for the euro.

The workweek was lowered to 35 hours for private companies and public workers. After fighting hard against the new law, employers discovered that, by averaging the hours over 52 weeks, they now had more flexibility to increase hours in busy periods and reduce them during slower times. They could respond better to seasonal demands. Thus workers found themselves doing shift work at awkward hours and six-day weeks. Also coffee breaks do not count in the 35 hours. Although wages were seldom cut, they were often being held down, and overtime was capped to the detriment of those wanting to earn more. The original law neither created new jobs nor boosted productivity. It is more difficult to judge whether a further aim of the reform—to balance work and life for the benefit of women—had succeeded.

The unintended results disappointed many employees, and some of them did what frustrated French workers always do: went on strike against the 35-hour week. More than 350,000 took to the streets in 2005 to defend it. While many private-sector employees concluded that the 35-hour week should be scuttled, the middle class in the public sector loved this latest entitlement, which permits French to work about 15%, or 300, fewer hours per year than Americans. A 2005 poll revealed that 77% of respondents liked their new lifestyles and did not want to work longer hours. However, it was blamed for 15,000 deaths in the 2003 summer heat wave, which depleted hospital and nursing home staffs.

In order to "increase the ability of workers to make their own choices," in the words of a government spokesman, legislation in 2005 scuttled the 35-hour workweek in all but name. It allowed employees to swap time off for money and to work as long as the 48 hours per week allowed by EU law. The state-imposed ceiling on overtime was progressively raised from 130 to 220 hours a year. Any time worked over 35 hours was made free of tax and social-insurance charges, and two-fifths of the companies employing more than 10 persons have taken advantage of this rule. In 2008 the 35-hour workweek was effectively ended by a new law that gave businesses the right to negotiate directly with employees to determine their working hours. The actual working hours in 2014 were 39.5.

The country has, in effect, a two-tier labor market: sheltered jobs for those lucky enough to have them and precariousness or joblessness for the rest, especially the young. It is a paradox, as the OECD confirmed in a 2005 study, that the French felt significantly less secure in their jobs than did Americans, Danes, Britons, or Canadians. That was a major reason for the "no" victory in the May 2005 referendum on the EU constitution. Without a more flexible labor market, unemployment will remain high.

The French labor code, which is longer than the Bible, has 30 pages detailing the procedures for dismissing an employee, beginning with warning letters and meetings with the person. Even after dismissal, an estimated 25% of cases end up in court, with the employee winning three out of four times. This nightmare makes employers reluctant to hire in the first place. The Hollande government and the unions agreed in 2013 to minor changes. Employers were given more flexibility to reduce working hours in times of economic difficulty, and the compensation courts can award to laid-off workers was lowered.

What unites the trade unions, civil servants, students, and the majority of the general public is a kind of conservatism: the wish to hang on to an idealized world of lifelong jobs and an economy insulated from the constraints of globalization, which has strongly negative connotations in France. Even free-market capitalism, which has made France the fifth-richest country in the world, is in disrepute: Only 31% agreed in 2012 that the free-market economy is the best system available. Leaders and media have convinced many French that they are victims of global markets. In his 2012 presidential campaign, President Hollande proclaimed that his "main opponent is the world of finance," a damaging statement from which he later backed away.

That antipathy was hardened by the 2008–2009 recession. The crisis was not as severe as in other countries: No large bank had to be rescued, and there was no wave of mortgage repossessions. Therefore, domestic support for the "French model" of active governmental intervention in the economy increased. Three-quarters of young French indicated in a 2006 poll that they would like to become civil servants, with ironclad job protection. Only a fourth of all jobs are in the public sector. "Jobs for life" are so protected and hard to get rid of that fewer and fewer employers produce them anymore. Two-thirds of young French who have a job a year after ending their schooling are on temporary contracts. By 2013, 8 out of 10 (82%) people hired were on temporary contracts, and half of those (four-fifths for the young) last less than a month. Without a permanent contract, one cannot rent an appartment or get a loan.

The government must avoid anything that smacks of what the French call "liberalism" (meaning a flexible labor market that responds to global challenges). Both unions and citizens fear the kind of global challenges that face all countries now, and they wish to build barriers against them.

It is a glaring contradiction that France, which is the world's seventh-largest exporter, has an economy that is, in fact,

10 questions for discovering McDonald's from the farm to the restaurant

more and more open and globalized. France fully exploits the open world economy and benefits enormously from it. It had steady trade surpluses until 2007. For example, Jacques Rupnik, a specialist on eastern Europe, estimated that France lost 6,500 jobs to companies moving operations to eastern Europe. But these were dwarfed by the 150,000 jobs in France created by its trade surplus with these countries.

Its private sector boasts world-class producers of cars, cosmetics, and insurance. A French company (Sodexho) feeds the US Army. In 2005 Cadarache in southern France was selected as the site for a €10 billion international nuclear-fusion reactor, the world's first.

At the same time, there is another French economy that coexists with the one that cowers before the threat of globalization. It is dynamic, highly trained, and comfortable in the private sector. French companies are brutally aggressive overseas. In the half-year to mid-2005, French companies bought $34 billion worth of foreign businesses, more than the $28 billion in all of 2004. French multinational corporations were the world's third-largest source of global cross-border takeovers. They are dynamically expansionist and are exploiting the globalized economy. Christine Lagarde, a former managing partner of a Chicago-based law firm and IMF boss as of 2011, rightly disagrees with many of her countrymen, asserting, "France has a lot to win out of globalization. We have incredible talents. We have great know-how. We have got a lot to offer."

France has usually had relatively peaceful labor relations. In part, this is because France's social security programs have taken much of the heat out of the issue of unequal income distribution. Only 8% of the workforce in the private sector belongs to labor unions (compared with 12% in the US and nearly 30% in Britain), and membership continues to decline. However, in the public sector, the share is about one-fourth (compared with 37% in America). This gives France the least unionized workforce of any industrialized country.

Nevertheless, its unions are socially and politically strong in spite of their numerical weakness. The reason is that they have an ensconced place in positions of power. They conduct all national collective bargaining agreements, which apply to all employees within an industry, whether they belong to the union or not. By law since 1945, every company with over 50 employees must have a works council (*comité d'entreprise*), financed by the companies. This body, dominated by unions, must be consulted on many major decisions that go far beyond working conditions.

The unions and employers are joint managers of the health, retirement, and social security organizations. Unions belong to every labor tribunal. They also maintain a conflictual culture in industrial relations, where dialogue with the government is often piped through a megaphone by striking workers. The timing for strikes can seriously harm the national interest. This happened in March 2005, when strikes in Paris were called on the very day the International Olympics Committee was in the city to evaluate it for the 2012 games. Not surprisingly, it lost its bid to London.

Unions representing public-sector workers are a mighty force, and they insist at a minimum on preserving what their members already have. Unions were once the vanguard of the leftists, but they are now the country's most conservative force. With their secure employment, public-sector employees are sheltered from the globalized competition that demands change and adaptation.

The Communists once dominated the largest union, the General Confederation of Labor (CGT), but that link has been severed. By 2006 the CGT had lost two-thirds of its members since the 1970s, with only 700,000 remaining. The French Democratic Confederation of Labor (CFDT) displays moderation, as does the leftist but anticommunist Workers Force (FO). The powerful National Education Federation (FEN) and the white-collar Confederation of Supervisory Grades (CGC and CFE-CGC) organize teachers and engineers and skilled technical personnel. Some nonunionized French, especially in the public sector, belong to so-called coordinations, ad hoc bodies that serve as liaisons between competing unions or spring up in protest at the unions' inattention.

A new union, Democratic Unitary Solidarity (SUD), emerged that belongs to the anarchist-syndicalist tradition and preaches class warfare. A wave of "bossnapping" occurred at factories. Though not a new tactic in France, bosses were locked in their offices overnight and sometimes roughed up in order to intimidate them and extract promises of job protection. While this would never be tolerated by the US public and politicians, the French government urged businesses not to press charges against the perpetrators out of fear that tensions would be heightened. In a 2009 poll, 45% of French respondents found such tactics acceptable, and two-thirds opposed any legal action against those who committed this form of coercion.

Although many signs of the old France remain, the economy is being modernized at an impressive rate. The Jospin Socialist government privatized far more of the country's industry than its center-right predecessors had done, leaving about 1,500 companies (compared with 3,500 in 1986) in which the state has a controlling share. It did all this without once using the word "privatize" in public.

One sign of the ascendancy of the "new economy" is the fact that half the graduates of the elite École Polytechnique now go into private business rather than into the civil service or large corporations. The result in the 21st century is an undeniable boom. Foreign investment plays a part in this. The US is France's largest source of foreign investment, and American companies employ 500,000 in France. Pfizer in France produces 80% of the Viagra consumed in America. Most of the shares in listed French companies are also owned by foreign investors, mainly American and British.

The Socialist government also quietly legalized practices that once raised ideological red flags: Stock options for young companies were legitimized in 1999, and private pension funds, heretofore illegal, appeared under the innocuous heading "workers' savings plans." Nevertheless, fewer than 13% of French own shares, compared to 23% of Britons.

Health care, costing 10% of GDP, remains among the best in the world, and the poor receive free treatment. In 2003 the government tackled an old health problem: cigarette smoking by a fifth of the adult population (50% of those aged 15 to 24). Taxes account for 80% of the cost of cigarettes, and three steep tax increases on tobacco raised the price of a package of cigarettes by 50% to €5.40 ($7), making France one of the most expensive places in Europe to smoke. For the first time, tobacconists responded by calling a nationwide strike, burning mountains of cigarettes in town squares. Although 90% joined in, the strike failed.

In 2006 lawmakers banned the sale of cigarettes to youth under 16 and cracked down on public smoking. Supported by an overwhelming majority of its population, France joined a European-wide movement by banning smoking in all public places. In 2008 this process was completed by including every commercial corner of "entertainment and conviviality," that is, bars, cafés, and restaurants. Some expressed amazement that this could happen in the country that gave the cigarette its name; has a Museum of Smoking in Paris; and even named a Parisian street after Jean Nicot, the 16th-century diplomat who took American tobacco to Catherine de Medici to treat her migraines and gave nicotine its name. The restriction on smoking contributes to the steady reduction of cafés in France from 200,000 in 1960 to 40,000 today.

A country where 82% of the women between the ages of 25 and 49 work, France is experiencing a rising birth rate of 2.1 children per woman, Europe's highest, even ahead of Ireland (1.99). This trend is encouraged by a number of government-funded programs, amounting to 5.1% of GDP, twice the EU average. They include free all-day nursery schooling at *écoles maternelles*. Mothers have four months of paid maternity leave and can chose not to work until the child is three and be guaranteed her full-time job when she returns. The state offers a monthly allowance of about $170 for two children, $400 for three, and $220 for every child thereafter. It is raised at age 11. Kids can go to subsidized summer camps. Families with three or more children are deemed *familles nombreuses* and are eligible for heavily subsidized rent and transportation, zero income tax, and state-funded parental leaves that can be extended for years.

Nevertheless, the French face a demographic time bomb: Whereas there are two workers today supporting one pensioner, by 2040 there might only be one. One thing the state cannot change is the expectation that women perform the lion's share of child care and domestic tasks at home: She spends an average of five hours per day on these, compared with only two hours for the man. She is also paid 26% less for her work than are men. In 2010 the World Economic Forum ranked France 46th in terms of gender equality, behind the US and most of Europe.

In accordance with its unsustainable traditional "pay-as-you-go" pension system, current workers are taxed to pay pensions of today's retired people. Public-sector workers could retire after 37.5 years with a full pension; the private-sector, after 40 years. This meant that many could retire at age 55 with a full pension. Railway, electricity, and gas workers and police could retire as young as 50 with full pensions, since the rules for such "special regimes" had been made in days past when such work was dangerous. Only 16% of French citizens aged 60 to 65 are still working. Given their high life expectancy, the average French man spends 24 years in retirement; a woman, 28. Ex–prime minister Raffarin noted, "Conceived more than 50 years ago, our retirement system no longer corresponds to the current and future demographic reality."

The government confronted the unions over this issue in 2003 and won. The reform brought public-sector workers in line with the private sector by 2008, requiring all persons to work 40 years (42 by 2020) in order to get a full pension. Government support for early retirement is being phased out, and the retirement age was to be raised from 60 to 62 in 2018. President Hollande pledged to lower it to 60 for those who began to work in their teens. Tax incentives are being introduced to persuade workers to invest in company-based savings programs like those in the US. Finally, a pension bonus is offered to those who work beyond 40 years. The public seems keenly aware of the growing pension deficit: Surveys in 2010 revealed that two-thirds believed the pension system was in danger of collapse, and 64% thought the retirement age will have to rise. When strikes against the pension reform gripped France in October 2010, up to 3.5 million took to the streets.

But railway and metro strikes had lost much of their potency because a new law requires a minimum service in schools and on public transport. Also workers are no longer paid when they walk out. However that requirement does not apply to ports and refineries. A majority of respondents sympathized with the strikers, but at the same time, 70% agreed that the changes were "reasonable." The massive street demonstrations and strike action that greeted this reform failed to stop it.

Agriculture

Three percent of Frenchmen are now employed full time in agriculture (compared with more than a third in 1945); they produce a mere 2% of GDP. De Gaulle had once said, "A country that cannot feed

***Trompe l'oeil*: false painted storefront in Lyon. Which are the real pedestrians?**

itself is not a great country." France is self-sufficient in all foodstuffs, and it gets tropical produce from the Antilles and la Réunion. It is the major agricultural country in the EU, producing 21% of the community's total output (before enlargement to 28 members in 2013) and possessing about a third of all agricultural land within the EU. It is the world's fourth-largest producer of cereals and meat. Only the US exports more food and drink products.

France remains one of the world's leading producers of wine (which accounts for 17% of agricultural output), although by 2002 its wine industry was unable to sell all it produces. The country's largest wine-producing region, Bordeaux, supplies two-thirds of the French market and has avoided the worst of the slump. But winegrowers in Beaujolais, Burgundy, and elsewhere face ever-stiffer competition from aggressive wine-exporting countries like Australia, New Zealand, South Africa, and Chile. In 1996 it exported three times as much wine as these countries combined; a decade later it exported 15% less than they did. France's share of the American wine market fell from 26% to 16% in 2004 and from 37% to 23% in Britain.

The main reason for declining wine revenues comes from a dramatic reduction in wine consumption in France itself. Sipping wine throughout the day has gone out of fashion. The average Frenchman today drinks 56 liters of wine a year, compared with 120 in the mid-1960s. By 2005 only 23% of French drink wine each day. By 2009 Americans had caught up with the French in total wine consumption.

Desperate winegrowers even resorted in 2002 to suing the government unsuccessfully over its campaign against drunk driving, claiming that it is illegal to discriminate between products, even those that make one intoxicated and those that do not. Speed cameras are everywhere now, and road accidents fell by 30% and traffic fatalities by 21% in the two years since 2002; during that same time wine consumption in restaurants declined by 20%. Regrettably more than twice as many people die in road accidents in France as in Britain.

As in other European countries, the farm lobby wields influence out of all proportion to its numbers. French farmers get around a sixth of the EU's farm subsidies through the Common Agricultural Policy (CAP), which consumes 40% of EU spending. This cornucopia means that Britain still pays two and a half times more into the EU budget than does France. EU subsidies account, on average, for 90% of a farmer's pretax income. Without it the average farmer would barely survive. But CAP funds are distributed very unevenly. A fifth of the largest and richest farmers,

"Will they dare elect him?"

Courtesy: Sonia Fernandez

especially the grain growers, receive 80% of the funds. The largest 30 farmers, including Prince Albert of Monaco, annually get an average of over €390,000 ($507,000). Some, such as wine producers, were traditionally able to compete well on the world market and therefore had no need for the assistance.

The importance of agriculture, not only for the French economy but also for the country's emotional rural roots in *la France profonde*, was demonstrated in the farmers' violent reaction to a compromise reached in 1992 between the EU and the US regarding GATT limits on agricultural subsidies. They took their tractors and manure to the streets of France, targeting not only the National Assembly and the European Parliament but also Coca-Cola plants and the 1,040 McDonald's restaurants, each of which serves 1,000 to 1,500 customers per day. France is the chain's second-most profitable national market after the US. All of them use only French farm products, and the head of McDonald's Europe, Denis Hennequin, is a Frenchman. McDonald's workforce of 50,000, many of them minority youth who can find employment nowhere else, make it France's largest private-sector employer. However, the facts that Coke had cornered half of the soft drink market by the mid-1990s and McDonald's continued to grow steadily gave them symbolic value.

The emotion and fury of their clashes with the police underscored their intense concern about the effects a slash in subsidies would have on rural France. Ex-president Chirac was able to persuade the German government to postpone full-scale reform of CAP until 2013, and he refused even to consider an EU budget compromise that would reduce any of its free money from Brussels. By contrast, Sarkozy recognized the need for CAP to be overhauled after 2013. This was a dramatic change of approach, compared with his predecessor. Because more CAP subsidies flow eastward to the new EU members, France has become a net contributor to the fund.

Farming is part of France's culture. Since they are rooted in the land, farmers cannot be transferred from one location to another like factories. The main issue is protection of France's farm interests, not of its consumers. Food constitutes only 16% of an EU family's budget, compared with over 50% when CAP started in 1968.

Already barely surviving economically, many farmers would be forced off the land and into crowded cities, leaving depopulated regions behind them. From 1993 to 2004, the number of farms declined by a third to fewer than 700,000. Only half of these are run by full-time farmers; 40,000 farms go out of business each year. Without the CAP subsidies, an estimated third to two-thirds of the farms would go under, with as few as 150,000 remaining. Farms grew in size by 40% between 1995 and 2005, but they still are less than a fourth as big as the average American farm.

Energy

France is concerned about its future energy sources. Its energy consumption doubled during the 1970s. It is heavily dependent upon the importation of fossil fuels. It imports 96%. It obtains roughly half its needs from Persian Gulf countries, one-fourth from Mediterranean countries, and one-eighth from Black Africa. It imports 90% of its natural gas. Some is produced in the southwestern region of Aquitaine, but these wells are rapidly being depleted.

By 2011 the high tax levied on fuel (75% of the price) helped drive gasoline prices to above $8 per gallon. In the past, such costs sparked severe demonstrations in strike-prone France. Truckers, joined by farmers, ambulance and taxi drivers, and Paris tour-boat operators, stopped work and blockaded oil refineries and fuel storage depots. Paris and other cities were partially brought to a standstill. The government stated that it would not give in, but then it reduced diesel fuel taxes after all. This capitulation helped spark similar outbursts elsewhere in Europe. The events underscored that, while the "new economy" has contributed much to France's economic boom, the old economy remains very much alive.

Nevertheless, France produces about half the total energy it needs. The reason is that it launched a full-scale program to develop nuclear power, especially fast-breeder reactors. Now Europe's largest producer of nuclear power, producing half the EU's nuclear energy, it is the world's fourth-richest country in uranium, with 10% of all known reserves. Its Eurodif enrichment plant at Tricastin represents a third of the western world's capacity and feeds a third of the world's nuclear reactors. By 2012, 78% of its electricity (compared with 19% in the US, 19% in Britain, 28% in Japan, and 33% in Europe as a whole) was generated by 58 nuclear power plants employing 100,000 people. This is the highest percentage in the world. It gets another 12% from hydraulic generators and the rest from oil, coal, natural gas, solar panels, and windmills.

The last plant was completed in 1999. In 1994 it fired up the world's only working fast-breeder reactor, which creates plutonium while generating electricity. Nuclear power provides the country with the EU's cheapest electricity, except in Denmark. France even has an overcapacity in electrical generation that allows it to export about 13% of its production. Its nuclear industry has also given it an edge in developing nuclear technology. It is the world leader in reactor design and construction, supply of nuclear fuel, and treatment of waste. French engineers developed a new reprocessing technique that produces less nuclear waste than in competitor countries. This enabled it to win the contract to build in Finland the first of a new generation of pressurized-water reactors and to land in 2005 the world's first international nuclear-fusion reactor, a €10 billion project in Cadarache in southern France. Since 2007 France has signed nuclear cooperation agreements with Morocco, Algeria, Libya, the United Arab Emirates, and China. In 2004 it closed its last coal mine.

There were always critics who argued that France had become overly dependent upon a single energy source and that such heavy use was unsafe. The volume of this criticism grew much louder when a nuclear disaster struck Japan in February 2011. It unleashed a broad public debate. The government ordered a safety audit of all nuclear power plants and the review of a past decision to keep plants older than 30 years running. The nuclear safety authority concluded that billions of euros must be spent to make the 58 plants conform to new safety standards since the Fukushima disaster. In his 2012 campaign, President Hollande promised to shut 24 of the plants by 2025. A 2015 law will reduce nuclear's share of electricity generation from 78% to 50% by 2025.

France is unlikely to abolish nuclear power altogether. Its reactors are among the safest in the world. Its decision to build a single standard reactor design not only reduces construction costs but also enables technical personnel to be used interchangeably in all the sites rather than being trained to work only in one site. Nuclear waste is stored on-site at reprocessing plants. Because of violent local opposition, it has still not succeeded in finding a deep-storage site for nuclear waste. In the meantime, low-level waste is stored aboveground, while high-level waste is stored in vitrified form in both steel canisters and concrete pits at La Hague and Marcoule.

CULTURE

The French have long fought what some critics see as a futile battle to preserve the purity of the French language. This struggle is waged particularly against the powerful onslaught of the English language. One author even wrote a book with the provocative title *Parlezvous Franglais?*, "franglais" being a combination of the words meaning "French" and "English."

The number of pupils learning English in school quadrupled in the 1980s, although a 2004 study found that French children speak English worse than all their neighbors. To combat this, the education ministry announced in 2008 that English instruction would be increased in the curriculum, with the goal that young French will be bilingual. "I've had enough of hearing that the French do not learn English. It's a big disadvantage for international competition," the minister said.

Lycée students take a break in Paris.

French scientists find it increasingly necessary to publish their works in English, and they often choose to deliver their lectures in English at international conferences held in France. English is the most frequently used language in the EU except at the European Court of Justice in Luxembourg. A 2007 survey of officials from the new EU member states revealed that 69% of them use English as their second language. To help them function in French, France offers them free crash courses at a castle near Avignon.

Jacques Chirac stormed out of an EU summit meeting in 2006, taking two ministers with him, when the French head of the EU's business organization, Ernest-Antoine Seillière, addressed the gathering in English. The former president (who speaks English) claimed to have been "profoundly shocked" that a French industrialist would speak English in an international meeting. Seillière explained later that he was speaking "the language of business."

Indeed he was. In many French companies, such as Danone and the oil giant Total, it is English that is spoken in the boardroom, in part because of the increased foreign presence there. Air France-KLM holds its meetings of "le strategy management committee" in English. Renault requires all of its management recruits to be fluent in that language. One French businessman recalled a meeting at the engineering group Alstom where English was spoken, even though every person in attendance was French. Business schools require much of their instruction and most of their readings to be in English. Commercial French is filled with anglicisms, including "le spin-off," "les road-shows," and "le cash-flow." At the same time, foreign companies must be careful. GE was fined €580,000 ($750,000) in 2006 for failing to translate English documents into French.

Sarkozy, who rejected the knee-jerk anti-Americanism that underpins much of the hostility toward English, no longer insisted that the French language be required at diplomatic events. However, in 2010 he appointed former prime minister Jean-Pierre Raffarin as his personal envoy to help French officials promote French in international institutions. The EU is becoming more and more an English-speaking organization.

Ordinary Frenchmen have adopted English words so quickly that in 1975 the parliament passed the Bas-Lauriol Law requiring that trade names, advertising material, product instructions, and receipts use only the French language. The text of the law even specified French replacements for such common expressions as "savoir-faire" (for "le know-how"), "boutique franche" (for "le duty-free shop"), "mini-marge" (for "le discount"), "aéroglisseur" (for "le hovercraft"), "credit-bail" (for "le leasing"), "matériel" (for "le hardware"), "gros porteur" (for "le jumbo jet"), "astronef" (for "le spacecraft"), "boteur" (for "le bulldozer"), "retrospectif" (for "le flashback"), "spectacle solo" (for "le one-man show"), "palmarès" (for "le hit parade"), "bala-deur" (for "le Walkman"), "mercatique" (for "le marketing"), and "zonage" (for "le zoning"). Some words escaped the sharp eyes of the language legislators: "le football," "le shopping," "le parking," "le living," and "le footing" (a word which is gradually being replaced in common usage by "le jogging").

Economic-Cultural Influences

Whether "le come-back" of pure French will succeed depends in part on "le marketing" of American investors in France. In 1983, the state's High Committee of the French Language stepped in to ban English words in the audiovisual field. Thus, "cameraman" and "close-up" became "cadreur" and "gros plan," and "drive-in theater" gave way to "ciné park." It also banned Anglo-Saxon terms in all government publications and speeches, legal contracts and schoolbooks. The counterattack has been generally successful in the computer field, such as "logiciel" ("software"), "la toile" ("the web"), "courrel" ("e-mail"), "arrosage" ("spam"), and "bogue" ("bug"), despite the persistence of a few terms, such as "un batch" of data or "un floppy disk."

In 1996 the High Committee sued the American sponsors of an English-only site on the World Wide Web because the material is not also available in French. It was thrown out of court in 1997 on a technicality. Former president Chirac argued, "the stakes are clear. If, in the new media, our language, our programs, our creations are not strongly present, the young generation of our country will be economically and culturally marginalized."

In 2005 he advocated setting up a French rival for Google's search engine, whose French-language version is used for 80% of Internet searches in France. Google was invented by two Stanford graduate students. In typical French fashion, this French version would be created by the government. In 2009 President Sarkozy promised $1.1 billion to scan French literary works, audiovisual archives, and historical documents. But when the prestigious National Library of France announced that it was negotiating with Google to digitize its collection, there was an outcry from the literary establishment that a company many regard with suspicion might be essential for the project.

The government has created a process to prevent English from dominating. Seven committees, including one in the Economy Ministry, suggest French replacements for English terms. These suggestions are sent to the Academie Française. If it and the Economy Ministry approve the changes, their use becomes mandatory for public bodies and law courts.

The French government wages a difficult battle. By 1995, 83% of high school pupils in EU countries were learning English (84% in France itself), compared with 32% learning French and 16% German. Only in Romania, whose Latin-based language is related to French, do more secondary school pupils learn French than English. In an editorial, the *Washington Post* spoofed the apparent obsession with enforcing language purity by imagining a bureau in Washington sending a disk jockey a letter like this: "It has come to our attention that you have repeatedly used the word 'taco' to describe the comestible for which the officially sanctioned word is 'corn meal crispette.' Please be advised that . . ." A *Dictionary of Official Terms* contains 3,500 new French words for advertising, broadcasting, public notices, and official documents and those dealing with goods, services, and conditions of work. All international conferences held in France must allow participants to speak in French if they want and must provide French translations of foreign-language speeches and documents.

French is the mother tongue of about 90 million people in the world and the occasional language of another 60 million. As such, it ranks only ninth in the world, behind English, Spanish, and Portuguese. The French insist that it remain one of the two official languages in most international bodies, but only a tenth of the documents produced by the UN Secretariat are in French. Already, about 85% of EU officials prefer to get information in English, which is their preferred second language. In an attempt to promote use of the language worldwide, France also foots the bulk of the bill for Francophonie, an assortment of 53 countries from Congo to Cambodia who enjoy "a shared use of the French language." Since French need not be the country's dominant or official language and since the membership includes such lands as Egypt and Moldova, it is doubtful that this organization is effective in achieving France's lingual goals.

France is the biggest domestic film market in Europe and the second-largest exporter of films after the US. It has the largest number of movie screens in the EU: more than 5,600. Fifty percent of the films French cinema fans went to see in 2002 were American, almost double the proportion a decade earlier but below the EU average of 70%. Of the tickets fans purchased in 2004, 47% were for American films, 38% for French, 4.9% for British, .8% for German, and a mere .2% for Italian. In 2011, French films accounted for 41% of all admissions in France. Four of the top five box-office films in 2004 were Hollywood blockbusters, as were two of the top three in 2006. The top film in 2005 was *Star Wars: Episode 3*, which did not quite reach the box-office champion of all time in France, *Titanic*. Steven Spielberg was invited to the presidential palace to receive the Legion of Honor award.

French cinema has made some impressive advances. In 2005, French films attracted larger audiences abroad than in France, increasing by 50% in only one year. Its films are appealing more and more to foreign general audiences rather than to the traditional art-house patrons; an example is Louis Leterrier's *Danny the Dog*. Three of its films were nominated for Oscars in 2005: *March of the Penquins, Joyeux Noël*, and *Darwin's Nightmare*. The first of these helped France have its best year ever in the US, where viewers tend not to like foreign-language films.

The French still make more films than do their European neighbors (200 features in 2005, compared with fewer than 40 in Britain). In the 21st century, the lead has been taken by a new wave of creative directors who are products of French film schools and criticism: Olivier Assayas, Catherine Breillat, Claire Denis, and Erick Zonca. The 2001 blockbusters *Le Fabuleux Destin d'Amélie Poulain* (*The Fabulous Destiny of Amelie Poulain*) and *Le Pacte des Loups* (*The Pact of the Wolves*) were smash hits in France and drew large crowds abroad. A decade later, *The Untouchables*, a feel-good French comedy, was the box-office smash. French films are making a comeback.

In 2008 a French performer, Marion Cotillard, won the Best Actress Oscar for her lead in *La Vie en Rose*, a depressing story of the life of singer Edith Piaf. A delightful animated story of a rat with a genius for smells who rescues a posh Parisian restaurant's kitchen walked away with several Oscars in 2008. Though an American film, *Ratatouille* was a hit in France and won praise from French chefs and the highbrow *Le Monde*, which called it "one of the greatest gastronomic films in the history of cinema." Not bad for a cute little rat with a golden nose! Jean Dujardin, who starred in the silent French film *The Artist*, became in 2012 the first French actor to win an Oscar as best actor. Although it was filmed entirely in Los Angeles, it received a subsidy from the French state.

Television has been influenced even more strongly by America. The most popular soap opera in 1992 was called *Santa Barbara*, and a French clone of the game show *Wheel of Fortune* topped the popularity charts. *Who Wants to Be a Millionaire* and *The Weakest Link* became the new hits. Reality TV made its debut in 2001 with *Loft Story*, which drew one of the largest TV audiences ever and divided France between millions of viewers who love such lowbrow entertainment and incensed critics who dismissed such trash television as the dumbing-down of French society. In 2004 the opening night of another reality-TV show, *La Ferme des Célébrités* (*Celebrities Farm*), attracted 46% of the TV audience. Viewers were fascinated by the celebrities' incompetence in dealing with farm life, something that has always had a special grip on the French imagination.

Ratings for American programs are as high as for French ones. About 70% of foreign TV shows purchased are from the US. Nevertheless, by law, 60% of TV programming had to be European (of which two-thirds French); 40% of songs on FM radio must be French, instead of less than 20% before the law was passed. Many of the teeth were extracted from this law in 1995, when the Constitutional Council ruled that it conflicted with freedom of expression. Nevertheless, in 2004 French music accounted for 63% of sales, up from 51% in 2000.

Anti-Americanism still exists on both the political left and right. De Gaulle's humiliation during World War II is no longer relevant, and thanks in part to the writings of Alexander Solzhenitsyn, Soviet communism fell from grace in French eyes. *Le Nouvel Observateur* even criticized anti-Americanism as "socialism for imbeciles." The dethroning of France as the world's cultural leader has hurt many Frenchmen. However, as ex-communist singer Yves Montand remarked, "if America has succeeded in invading us culturally, it is because we like it."

In the 21st century, what antipathy existed between the two countries, which have never fought a war against each other, had been fueled by the 85% disapproval rating in France of President George W. Bush's foreign policy. However, the French did not seem to generalize this dislike: In 2004, 72% had a favorable view of Americans, and 68% agreed that what unites the two nations was more important than what separates them.

The inauguration of Barack Obama in 2009 was officially greeted by elegant events all over France, the grandest being held in the reception rooms of the 16th-century Paris City Hall. The new American president's triumphant trip to Europe to participate in three summit meetings in April electrified Europeans and filled the newspapers. He acknowledged in France that it was America's "oldest ally, our first ally," and he wowed an audience of schoolchildren in Strasbourg when he held a "town meeting." A swooning

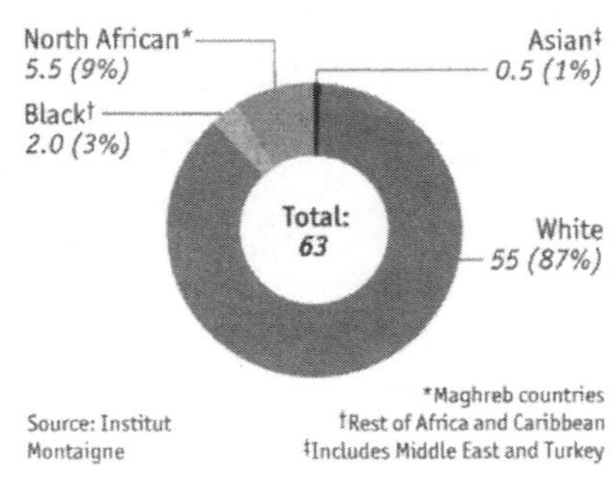

Source: *The Economist*

French commentator, Dominique Moïse, estimated that it would take a generation or two for France to produce a "French Obama." He called America a "source of hope" and concluded, "America, thanks to Mr. Obama, has returned to be the emotional center of gravity of the world." In 2009 the American president enjoyed an approval rating of 88% in France, compared with 57% in the US.

As France's economic and military influence declined, its independence from the US and its support from European allies seemed to be ways to enhance French power. Some French identify America with things they fear: globalization, capitalism, and the free market. The Socialist Party campaigned unsuccessfully for the new EU constitution under the banner "Strong in the face of the United States." Anti-Americanism is strongest at times of French uncertainty.

One earlier sign of America's acceptability was the hard-won contract negotiated by a Socialist government to build a $4 billion Disneyland 20 miles east of downtown Paris. It opened in 1992, promising to create 12,000 new jobs. The only saving grace for hard-line Americanophobes is that Disney himself is of French lineage; the family's name was not Disney at all, but D'Isigny.

In 1999–2000 the reaction against American popular culture was perhaps symbolized best by the antics of José Bové, a farmer who became something of a national hero for trashing one of McDonald's many new restaurants in the southern town of Millau. Using tractors, he literally brought down the roof. This act, along with protests at 40 other McDonald's establishments around France, was ostensibly in protest against the American decision to levy high tariffs on certain luxury foods imported from France, such as Roquefort cheese and pâté foie gras, in retaliation for the EU's and France's decision to ban American hormone-treated beef. By linking French culture with the protection of its food, Bové enormously widened his support within French society.

Chirac joined in by announcing that he "detests McDonald's food," and then prime minister Jospin also went on record that "I am personally not very pro-McDo," as the chain is called in France. How shocking it must have been when French nutritionists determined in 2004 that a Big Mac has a higher protein-to-fat ratio and is actually healthier than the French classic quiche lorraine. McDonald's cannot be blamed for the fact that 40% of French are considered overweight, according to a 2005 report by the French Senate.

The fact is that young French have always liked McDonald's since its first restaurant opened in the country in 1979. France is the chain's most profitable European country, the European manager is French, and the company is France's largest private-sector employer. KFC is expanding in its footsteps. A 2013 survey found that fast-food chains account for 54% of restaurant sales in France. In order not to turn Bové into a martyr, McDonald's decided not to take civil action against him. Instead it launched a publicity campaign stressing that its more than 1,040 franchises in 750 French cities are owned by French; employ thousands of French workers, especially minorities; and use French products almost exclusively (80%). Clearly more and more French love *malbouffe*, their word for "junk food." By 2009 the average French meal was wolfed down in 38 minutes, compared to 88 minutes a generation ago.

Bové's crusade tapped into far deeper issues gnawing at the French. They include fear of globalization and nostalgia for a bygone way of life, including long lunches. French voters on both the left and right instinctively mistrust globalization, which erodes French sovereignty and smacks of unrestrained free markets and American hegemony. The conventional wisdom is not that globalization should be prevented but that it should be regulated. President Hollande said in his 2012 campaign, "We're not just any country: we can change the situation."

The French government insists that the free-trade agreement that is being negotiated by the United States and European Union, which French businesses strongly favor, allow the right of "cultural exception." This permits the government to restrict foreign programs on TV and radio and to subsidize the French film industry. TV channels in France must ensure that 60% of their programing is European, including 40% French.

Academie Française

Since 1635 the Academie Française has striven, in the words of its first patron, Cardinal Richelieu, to "preserve the purity of the French language." The body itself selects individually 40 distinguished literary figures, known as "immortals." In 1932 they finally completed a French grammar book. They now meet every Thursday in order to compile a dictionary that is to serve as a criterion for good usage rather than as a list of all the words in the French language. After 60 years of work, the immortals reached the letter "R." Each word proposed for inclusion is first brought up before a special committee and then is voted on by the academy as a whole. In 1986 the academy added 912 new words; three-fourths of them were based on English or technical terms.

Such great French writers as Voltaire, Racine, and Victor Hugo were members, but no female writer, such as Madame de Staël or George Sand (pseudonym for Aurore Dupin, later Baroness Dudevant), ever managed to break the academy's all male tradition. Finally, in 1980 it chose Belgian born Marguerite Yourcenar, who at age 16 had begun to publish her string of poems, novels, and historical works, culminating in her monumental *Memoirs of Hadrian*. When World War II broke out, she decided to join the faculty of Sarah Lawrence College in New York, and she became an American citizen in 1947. After teaching 10 years, she moved to a wood-frame house on Mount Desert Island in Maine, where she could escape the literary circles and gossip of Paris and New York, which she detested. In 2015, the academy inducted its first non-French citizen: Dany Laferrière, a black writer from Quebec.

In December 2003 former president Valéry Giscard d'Estaing was elected into the academy with 19 out of 34 votes, despite vigorous criticism by some members, such as Maurice Druon, that "his works do not stand out in the history of French literature." His literary output consisted of four books on politics; two volumes of memoirs; and a steamy novel, *The Passage*, which *Le Monde* dismissed for its "total absence of originality." A year later he became the first former president to join. He was joined in 2010 by the sixth woman to become a member, Simone Veil. A Holocaust survivor who became a French minister, member of the Constitutional Council, and president of the European Parliament, she is one of France's most popular women.

All ambitious French politicians must write books as proof of seriousness, although campaign books seldom sell well. Excellent command of French is an essential prerequisite for the elite. Both top candidates for the presidency in 2007 came out with one or more during the campaign. Dominique de Villepin has eight to his credit, including two collections of poetry. François Mitterrand wrote over 20. In 2012 François Hollande published *The French Dream*. Jacques Chirac seems to have been the least productive, with five to his name, including his student thesis, "The Development of the Port of New Orleans."

In 1989 the French Academy found itself in the midst of a storm over a proposal to simplify French spelling by, for example, eliminating the circumflex accent in such words as *être*, replacing the "x" on the end of such plurals as *bureaux* with a simple "s," writing "f" instead of "ph" (thus *filosofes*), and doing away with unexpected double consonants in words like *traditionnel* when the noun is *tradition*. A government survey had revealed that about 20% of the adult population is functionally illiterate, twice the percentage in Britain. One poll of teachers revealed that 90% favor making French easier to write in order to combat both such illiteracy and to

Le Monde

www.lemonde.fr

58ᵉ ANNÉE – Nº 17749 – 1,20 € – FRANCE MÉTROPOLITAINE — DIMANCHE 17 - LUNDI 18 FÉVRIER 2002 — FONDATEUR : HUBERT BEUVE-MÉRY – DIRECTEUR : JEAN-MARIE COLOMBANI

SUPPLÉMENT
Le Monde ARGENT
Les fausses promesses des fonds garantis

PRÉSIDENTIELLE
Lionel Jospin pourrait se déclarer candidat dimanche 24 février p. 6

JUSTICE
Alègre face à sa seule victime survivante p. 7

SCIENCES
Hubert Reeves, conteur infatigable de l'histoire

Tension entre Paris et Washington

Divergences sur l'« axe du Mal » dénoncé par Bush, convocation de l'ambassadeur de France

AIGREUR, irritation, tension passagère ? Il ne se passe plus guère de jour depuis le discours du président George W. Bush sur l'état de l'Union, le 29 janvier, sans qu'Américains et Européens n'étalent publiquement certaines de leurs divergences d'appréciation. Le différend est multiple, mais porte essentiellement sur la manière dont le président républicain a présenté ce qui paraît devoir être la priorité de la politique étrangère et de défense américaine : la lutte contre un *« axe du Mal »* que composeraient trois pays développant des armes de destruction massive – l'Iran, l'Irak et la Corée du Nord – qui pourraient tomber dans les mains du terrorisme islamiste. Au service de cette priorité, M. Bush n'exclut pas de faire la guerre – contre l'Irak, notamment –, et de la faire seul si ses alliés européens manifestent une quelconque divergence avec Washington.

Démarche inhabituelle entre alliés, le département d'Etat a pris soin de faire savoir, vendredi 15 février, que l'ambassadeur de France aux Etats-Unis, François Bujon de l'Estang, avait été convoqué par une adjointe de Colin Powell pour discuter des positions de Paris. Le ministre des affaires étrangères, Hubert Védrine, avait qualifié de *« simpliste »* l'approche américaine de la lutte contre le terrorisme. Son collègue allemand, Joschka Fischer, a estimé que des *« alliés ne devaient pas être des satellites »*. Le commissaire européen chargé des affaires extérieures, le Britannique Christopher Patten, a, lui aussi, dénoncé l'unilatéralisme de Washington, estimant que de *« vrais amis ne sont pas des lèche-bottes »*. A Paris comme à Berlin, il n'est pas exclu que ce débat public avec les Etats-Unis reflète des considérations électorales. Il témoigne aussi de l'inquiétude des Européens devant une double évolution : la perspective d'une guerre avec l'Irak en pleine tension israélo-palestinienne.

Lire page 4 et notre éditorial page 19

HORIZONS
LES PRISONNIERS DU 11 SEPTEMBRE

▸ Guantanamo : la polémique entre Europe et Etats-Unis

▸ Enquêtes : retour à Mazar-e-Charif ; vies de prisonniers

▸ Droits de l'homme et terrorisme

Lire notre dossier pages 11 à 18

Ce que Didier Schuller a dit au juge

JEUX OLYMPIQUES D'HIVER

enable French to hold its own as a world language.

Proponents of simplification point out that French has in the past been changed by decree and that another change is long overdue, since the last one came in 1832, when King Louis-Philippe ordered all public servants to conform strictly to the French Academy's dictionary. As expected, the opposition to change is strong and furious. One teacher warned his colleagues acidly to "keep your filthy hands off our language." Therefore, the academy ruled in 1991 that changes should not be enforced but should instead be subject to the "test of time." They have been blithely ignored.

The language watchdogs were stirred again in 1998, when the Academie Française, whose members wear green medieval costumes and carry swords when they meet, stoutly resisted female government ministers having themselves referred to as "Madame la Ministre" (the word being masculine). The "immortals" cringed when the Education Ministry declared that all women's job titles should be linguistically feminized: a female member of parliament should be a "déput*ée*"; a lawyer, an "advocat*e*"; an inspector, an "inspect*rice*." In 2012 state administrators all over France received a memo banishing the word "mademoiselle" from official forms and registries, since it reveals a woman's "matrimonial situation," unlike "monsieur." Just how much the French admire their wordsmiths was revealed again on November 23, 1996, when André Malraux, a wartime hero, adventurer, and writer, was reinterred in the Panthéon. The ceremony was televised live on national TV, and his creative career was discussed exhaustively in the other media.

In 2013 American Supreme Court justice Stephen G. Breyer, who has worked hard to gain fluency in French, was inducted into a related prestigious French institution, the Academy of Moral and Political Sciences. This is one of five academies that belong to the Institute of France. It is limited to 50 French persons and 12 foreigners; Thomas Jefferson was a member.

Although all citizens of France can speak French, there are many tongues spoken by ethnic minorities, primarily on the periphery of the country. These languages include Provençal, Breton, Corsican, Italian, Catalan, Basque, and Alsacian. In 1993 the government faced protests because of its refusal to sign the European Charter on Minority Languages, adopted in 1988 by the European Parliament. In 1999 the Socialist government adopted only 39 of the charter's 98 clauses and again set off a wave of nationalist passion. The youngest member of the Academie Française, Jean-Marie Rouart, responded defensively, "At the very moment that our language is being bastardized by Anglo-Saxon expressions, it is to be undermined from within by having to compete with local dialects!"

Immigration and Ethnic Minorities

France's World Cup championship soccer team in 1998 demonstrated how multicultural France has become. Of 22 players, 8 were nonwhite (most of them born and bred in France), and another 4 of recent Armenian, Argentine, Kalmyk, or Spanish descent, not including the Bretons and Basques on the team. The same applied to its 2006 team, which came close to winning the World Cup, until the national emblem for minority accomplishment, Zinedine Zidane, intentionally head-butted an Italian player and was ejected from the game and from the sport in dishonor.

France has always been a magnet for foreigners, and today a third of all Frenchmen have at least one foreign grandparent. By 2010, 8% of residents were foreign-born. Six percent of the population had foreign passports in 1994. This was the same percentage as 25 years earlier, but then three-fourths were Europeans, compared with only 40% now; 39% of foreigners come from North Africa, and 6%, from sub-Saharan Africa. There is also a rapidly growing Chinese immigration.

Partly as a result of frightening unemployment, non-European immigrants face growing rejection and violence in communities where they live in large numbers. Except for music and sports, nonwhites are noticeably underrepresented in business, politics, media, and the professions. In parliament some nonwhites represent the 22 overseas French territories, but none has a seat from metropolitan France. In 2002, a black presidential candidate, Christiane Taubira, an economist from French Guiana, won 2.3% of the votes. A black journalist from Martinique, Harry Roselmack, was finally chosen in 2006 to anchor TF1's popular news program during the summer. Of the 555 deputies representing districts in continental France, none is of North African descent. Only 1 out of 36,560 mayors and none of the regional parliamentary members is nonwhite. Yet they are visible in the streets. Blacks officially number about 1.5 million, but the unofficial number is higher. Ex-President Sarkozy asked after a trip to the US in 2006, "Where is the French Condoleezza Rice or Colin Powell?" One would now add Barack Obama.

Mosques spring up next to empty churches, and exotic North African commercial establishments are everywhere. Some Muslim girls wear scarves to school, igniting an emotional debate about whether such headgear should be permitted in secular schools. The French ideal envisions a secularized, uniform French identity as the most effective guarantee of national unity. Citizens in France are regarded as belonging to the whole republic, not to separate communities, and by tradition state schools are to be protected from all forms of religious proselytizing.

The issue came to a boil in 2004, when a law, unlike any other in Europe, was enacted prohibiting ostentatious religious symbols like head-scarves in public schools. It does not apply to private day-care centers. The law was directed against Muslim fundamentalists; in Chirac's words, "fanaticism is gaining ground." Many French, 69% of whom favored the law, are uneasy about culturally assertive

I.M. Pei's glass pyramid at the Louvre Photo: Susan L. Thompson

Islam, and this fear is easily exploited by the far-right National Front. French feminists consider the headscarf a symbol of female oppression. To appear fairer, the law also banned the wearing of Jewish yarmulkes, Sikh turbans, and large Christian crosses.

Although 49% of North African immigrant women in France favored the ban (43% opposed it), thousands marched through the streets of Paris and other cities throughout the world to protest the action. Even the US State Department publicly questioned whether "it is really necessary to be outlawing their manifestation of their own faith" when people are "peacefully practicing their faith." In an attempt to defuse the tension, the government appointed the first North African immigrant prefect, Aïssa Dermouche (in Jura), whose car was bombed within days of his assignment. The ban was widely accepted when schools opened in the fall of 2004. The Education Ministry reported in March 2005 that only 48 pupils had been sent home for wearing religious symbols, including 3 Sikh boys.

In 2011 the government banned a very prominent symbol of Muslim faith: the niqab, or head-to-toe burka, ruling that its wear was "incompatible" with French values and nationality. Only an estimated 2,000 women wear such a garment in France. Most French Muslims come from North Africa, where women only cover their hair, not their faces. Nevertheless, the National Assembly voted in favor of banning the full-face veil in public. A single vote was cast against the law, although the Council of State said there was no legal basis for the ban.

There is a fine of about $215 for wearing it, or the offender can be forced to take an official course on citizenship. A fine of up to €30,000 ($43,000) and a year in jail can be levied against anyone forcing a woman to wear it. If the victim is a minor, that fine can be doubled. Polls indicate that voters overwhelmingly support the ban by 80%, but its enactment sparked protests in Paris. The majority accepted Sarkozy's argument that the full-face veil "is not welcome in France" because it "hurts the dignity of women and is unacceptable in French society." Switzerland, the Netherlands, and Belgium have similar laws. Another target is polygamy. Despite being forbidden in 1993, there are an estimated 16,000 to 20,000 polygamous families in France.

In April 2011 the governing party sponsored a controversial three-hour public debate on the nature of secularism and the challenges of Islam. Sarkozy's desire was that a westernized version of Islam, one that fits within the behavioral and cultural norms of the France, take shape.

Called *Beurs* (*Beurettes* for females), a term that North Africans do not consider derogatory, French-born Arabs sometimes face resistance from their own families when they try to integrate into French society. The animosity toward them has helped far-right parties, such as the National Front, to make significant electoral gains in those areas. In their defense, an antidiscrimination lobby, SOS-Racisme has emerged.

France has the largest Muslim population in Europe: from 5 to 6 million, or 8.3% of the total population. Their numbers are growing by 3.4% per year, 30% are from Algeria; 20%, from Morocco; and 10%, from Turkey. More than half the prison population is Muslim, and they are prime targets for proselytizing and terrorist recruitment. The percentage of population climbs in Marseilles to about 10% Arab and 17% Muslim. Half are French citizens. A third of French residents of North African descent live in about 750 suburban ghettos, where unemployment is three times higher than the nationwide rate.

Life is so desperate that, in one Paris park, Buttes Chaumont, radicals opened a training camp for Muslim boys in 2004 to prepare them for holy war in Iraq. Some were in their teens, and some spoke no Arabic. In 2014–2015, over 1,000 French Muslims were recruited to fight with jihadist forces in Iraq and Syria. The police, who pursue zero-tolerance policing, identified about 150 "no-go zones" in these dangerous suburbs (*banlieues*). Then–prime minister Valls called them "ghettos" for "apartheid."

In November 2005 they exploded with an intensity that stunned the entire country. Two boys in Paris were electrocuted in a high-voltage transformer. Rumors immediately raced through the city that they had sought refuge there from overzealous pursuing police. It turned out that there had been no pursuit, and the two officers present were later charged for failing to assist people in danger. But a wave of nightly clashes ensued. It spread to other cities throughout France. This was France's worst social turmoil since 1968. Mainly young Arabs clashed with police during three frightening weeks. More than 10,000 cars were burned; 255 schools, 233 public buildings, and 51 post offices were attacked or torched; 140 public-transport vehicles were stoned; and 4,770 people were arrested. One person died.

Using cell phone text messages, they coordinated their attacks and ambushed firefighters and police who arrived to restore order. The French government was shaken by its inability to contain the anger and violence. Finally it declared a controversial state of emergency based on a law not used since its enactment in 1955, during the Algerian War. This allowed local authorities to impose a curfew, restrict movement, and launch raids on residences 24 hours a day. The only sense of relief came from the gradual realization that there was no apparent Islamic inspiration to these riots.

In November 2007 even more ferocious violence erupted in another suburb (Villiers-le-Bel) north of Paris. As two years earlier, this was sparked by an incident in which two teenagers without helmets, riding a minimotorbike at 70 kilometers per hour, collided with a police car and were killed. For two bloody nights, scores of cars and buses were torched, and a police station, library, nursery school, local train station, car dealer, shops, and a McDonald's were destroyed. Of 82 police injured, 6 were victims of serious gunshot wounds. The fact that rioters were prepared with shotguns signaled a worrisome escalation.

It is not as if the government had done nothing since the last round of violence. There have been large injections of public money (€6 billion annually) to renovate housing projects, demolish tower blocks, and improve lighting. But with youth unemployment doggedly remaining at 40% in the suburbs, the danger of explosion is always present. Since the uprising, violent attacks rose by 37%, and arson and car burning continued.

The prolonged violence was a crushing blow to the country's self-image as a model of social equality and tolerance. Its roots lie in the economic and social alienation of the mainly North African population, who face bad housing, poor schools, social exclusion, discrimination, and mass unemployment. A study in 2005 revealed that job applicants with French-sounding names were 50 times more likely to be granted a job interview than those with African- or Arab-sounding names. Ex-president Chirac admitted that France confronts "an identity crisis."

The second- and third-generation immigrants often do not feel part of French society, even if they are French citizens and say they are French. Because France's notion of supposedly color-blind equality does not acknowledge racial or religious minorities, there are no programs or concepts in place to help groups who face discrimination or social inequality. Minorities are forced to integrate with the strictly secular society, but they are victimized by discrimination. Like many other European countries, France is experiencing dangerous disenchantment.

It is this feeling that a radical comedian, Dieudonné, feeds on. He is well known for his provocative statements about the Holocaust and Jews, and he has had seven convictions for anti-Semitic hate speech and condoning terrorism. He popularized a gesture known as the *quenelle*, which many French interpret as a kind of Nazi salute. It is made with one outstretched arm straight down and the other hand held to the opposite shoulder. He insists that it is merely an expression of opposition to the established order. He has political ties with the National Front, and the government has attempted to prohibit his public performances.

Fears that France will one day have a fanatic Muslim majority are unfounded. North African women living in France have an average of 2.57 children, barely above the French rate. Only a tiny minority wants to establish a caliphate in Europe. One almost never hears the muezzin's call to prayer. It is estimated that 15% to 20% of French Muslims do not practice Islam at all, and fewer than 5% attend mosque every Friday. About 70% fast during Ramadan.

France is vulnerable to a spillover of violence from the Middle East. This occurs when conditions of warfare and suicide bombings prevail in Israel and Palestine. Whereas incidents against Jews in the 1990s were mostly carried out by white supporters of Le Pen, most attacks are now committed by young North African men. This is a major reason ex-president Chirac was determined that France not become embroiled in the 2003 war in Iraq; French Arabs cheered the president for his decision to abstain.

France also has Europe's largest Jewish population (650,000, the fourth-largest after the US, Israel, and Russia). Like the vast majority of Muslims living in the country, two-thirds of Jews in France are of North African origin. They share many cultural characteristics, including cooking. They become a soft target for Arab radicals in times of tension. Despite government pleas that passions that flare up in the Middle East not spill over into France, they do. A synagogue was gutted by fire in Marseille over Passover, and attacks on Jewish sites dramatically increased. In 2003 vandals torched a new two-story wing of an Orthodox Jewish school in Paris. The next year, a Jewish community center in the center of Paris was set on fire. On the walls of the ruins, the words "Death to Jews" were written. An appalling desecration in 2015 of 250 gravestones in eastern France had an obvious anti-Semitic motive.

Violent hate crimes quadrupled in 2002 to the highest level in a decade, and in 2004 they doubled again, reaching the highest level since France began keeping statistics on them. The number of attacks against North Africans more than doubled in 2004. The majority was committed by supporters of the far right. However, two-thirds of attacks were aimed at Jews, mainly perpetrated by North Africans.

Parisian rabbis advise Jewish boys to wear baseball caps over their yarmulkes and girls to hide their Stars of David under their clothing to prevent attacks. The number of pupils in Jewish schools in greater Paris has doubled to 30,000 in a decade, with thousands more on the wait lists. The issue is the children's safety. More and more French Jews are also deciding to immigrate to Israel and the UK. The numbers climbed from 1,366 in 1999 to 8,000 in 2015.

Chirac declared that "an attack on a Jew is an attack against France," and Prime Minister Valls asserted in 2015 that "France without Jews is not France." The government ordered schools to show films like *Schindler's List*, *Sophie's Choice*, and *The Pianist* to combat the dramatic rise in racism. North African leaders in France condemn

the violence but cannot stop it. Complicating the problem is that European public opinion is broadly critical of Israeli policy toward Palestinians. These attacks fed the existing fear of rising crime and a feeling of vulnerability to global terrorism since September 11, 2001.

With its large North African population and colonial history there, France is a kind of bellwether in Europe for dealing with a Muslim population. The center-right government elected in 2002 sought to create a model Muslim citizenry, which would be French speaking and law abiding, would honor the 1905 French law establishing separation between church and state, would incline females not to wear veils at work or school, and above all to consider themselves French first and Muslim second. The government adopted a two-prong strategy to achieve this: Give them a "place at the table" while at the same time regulating their activities through, for example, French intelligence monitoring of Friday sermons in mosques and prayer centers and deporting radical imams (clerics) who do not have citizenship.

To help integrate Muslims into French society, the government created in 2003 a French Council of the Muslim Faith (CFCM), with members elected by representatives of the country's mosques and prayer groups. It is a platform for discussions with local and national governments about such things as building more mosques and Muslim cemeteries and wearing veils in schools, an issue that seriously split the council. Catholics, Protestants, and Jews have had such councils for decades.

Participation was high, with 992 of 1,200 (1,600 by 2007, only 50 of which are deemed "extreme") eligible mosques voting. The authorities were not entirely pleased with the outcome of the elections, since fundamentalist Muslims in the Union of Islamic Organizations of France (UOIF) came in second and won a strong voice alongside moderate groups. This prompted the government to warn that it would deport immigrant Muslim leaders if they espoused violence or anti-Semitism. In new elections in June 2005, power was tilted away from the UOIF, the most radical grouping.

There is widespread uneasiness over the presence of millions of immigrants, the majority of whom are Arabs and blacks. A 1998 poll revealed that almost 60% of respondents thought there were too many Arabs in France (down from 71% five years earlier), over a quarter believed there were too many blacks (down from almost a half), and 15% said there were too many Jews. Four out of 10 admitted to being "racist" or "fairly racist," almost twice as many as in Germany, Britain, or Italy. Other polls revealed that half no longer feel "at home" in France and want a "large number" of immigrants to leave. Half expressed a belief in the "inequality of the races." Although 10% of respondents in a 2004 poll admitted disliking Jews, 23% expressed prejudice against North Africans. Thus the latter face much deeper discrimination than do Jews. Over half agreed in a 2008 poll that "western and Muslim ways of life are irreconcilable."

Earlier immigrant groups are often among the opponents of the new arrivals. Portuguese- and Spanish-born workers in the Marseilles area are among the National Front's most fervent supporters. But the polls show that racist feeling goes far beyond the 25% who vote for the National Front. About 28% of those who say they are "racist" or "fairly racist" vote for leftist parties. The elder Le Pen's ranting against "invading Muslim hordes" who allegedly threaten Frenchmen with the same fate as America's "Red Indians—annihilated by immigration," prove so seductive that the leaders of more respectable parties borrowed from his xenophobic vocabulary. Chirac once criticized their "odor" and "noise." Giscard d'Estaing warned of an "invasion" and called for nationality laws based on blood to replace the statutes that grant French citizenship automatically to anyone born on French soil.

There is positive news, though. A Pew poll in 2006 showed that only 46% of French Muslims considered themselves to be more Muslim than French, compared with 81% of British Muslims. A 2007 survey showed that the French are the most immigrant-friendly population in Europe: 52% thought that the number of immigrants in their country was "about right," compared with 43% in the US, 32% in Germany, and 20% in Britain. They were also more likely to invite a member of an ethnic minority into their home for dinner. Six in 10 white Frenchmen said in 1998 that they would not try to stop their child or sibling from marrying a Muslim. In fact, half of boys and a quarter of girls of Algerian origin in France have their first steady relationship with a white. Fremainville, a tiny farming hamlet just outside Paris, even adopted a black Marianne, the potent bare-breasted symbol of French republican liberty springing from the French Revolution.

The government responded by declaring that France "can no longer be a land of immigration." It introduced policies to stop the influx of foreign workers, refugees, and their families, as well as to tighten citizenship rules, while speeding the integration of foreigners already there. The number of other foreign immigrants was cut by a third. However, once they arrive, most illegal immigrants are unlikely ever to leave. For instance, close to 44,000 foreigners were ordered to leave in 2000, but only 9,230 were expelled. From 400,000 to 1 million illegal aliens remain underground, despite a dramatic increase in forced deportations.

France was largely avoided in the 2015–2016 flood of refugees to Europe. High unemployment and bad publicity about the National Front were important reasons, as was the difficult asylum process. Only 30% of applicants succeed.

In an attempt to get the problem under control, the government announced a tougher immigration policy in May 2006. Under the prevailing system, three-fourths of legal entrants were family-related. The new law aims to raise the proportion of skilled immigrants, who are lured by three-year "talent" work permits. Newcomers are required to take lessons in civic education and the French language. To crack down on sham marriages, those bringing in a family must demonstrate the financial means to support them. The National Assembly passed a law in September 2007 authorizing the use of DNA testing to see if foreigners who apply for visas are really related to the family members they want to join in France. The automatic right for illegals to remain after 10 years in France was ended. As in the past, the effort to deport those without proper papers is fiercely resisted, especially if it involves schoolchildren.

France's law-and-order ex-president, Nicolas Sarkozy, carefully explained, "France needs immigrants, but France cannot and should not welcome all immigrants." Determined to crack down on illegal migrants and people-smuggling networks, the center-right government that took power in 2002 made a decisive move. Under pressure by Britain, it closed an overcrowded and uncontrollable refugee camp at Sangatte on the north coast set up by the Red Cross three years earlier. Located near the entrance to the "Chunnel," it had attracted thousands of immigrants who were trying to enter Britain illegally and who were willing to risk their lives to hop the fast-moving trains or follow the tracks through the darkness to the other end. After a new camp sprouted up in the dunes nearby, attracting 800 migrants, the government announced its closure by 2010. In 2014 a further camp was closed.

In 2010, as a part of its crackdown on crime and illegal immigration, the government closed 117 Roma squatter camps in central cities and deported 8,300 Roma back to their home countries, mainly to Romania and Bulgaria. They were given €300 ($420) and a one-way ticket home. Eight out of 10 voters applauded this, but it caused an outcry from the UN and the EU, which threatened an official reprimand. To try to stem the tide of immigrants pouring into France, the French and Italian governments agreed in April 2011 to restrict the Schengen rules for free movement across EU borders "in case of exceptional difficulties." France rounded up thousands of migrants, especially from Tunisia, near its borders and in trains and returned them to Italy. Any entrant who appeared to be a young North African is subject to questioning.

The French government cracked down on immigrants in other ways. It reduced the number of visas issued. It declared a zero-tolerance policy toward radical Muslims who incite violence, deporting imams (Muslim clergymen) who do. It used its newly merged (in 2008–2009) domestic intelligence service, the Direction Centrale du Renseignement Intérieur (Central Direction of Homeland Intelligence), to keep an eye on what goes on in mosques. Sarkozy wanted France to train imams; of the 1,200 or so in France, three-fourths are not French, and only a third speak French. The minimum age for girls to marry was raised from 15 to 18 in a bid to clamp down on forced marriages.

The judicial system pursues terrorists vigorously. For example, in May 2011 six men, some of them French citizens, were suspected of planning to go to Pakistan to train with Islamic militants and arrested. Since 2012 it is a crime to travel to militant training camps or fight in a jihadist war.

In March 2012 the police failed to prevent a 23-year-old Algerian French Muslim from Toulouse, Mohammed Merah, from killing seven persons in a shooting rampage. They could not explain how he had assembled a cache of firearms, including a Sten submachine gun. The gruesome crimes ignited a public discussion about the true identity of the young man: Was he French or something else? Some blamed al Qaeda, but the left-wing newspaper *Libération* pointed to the all-too-frequent isolation in France of persons of North African heritage. "Merah is certainly a monster, but he was a French monster. . . . It was not Al Qaeda that created Mohammed Merah. It was France."

A satirical magazine, *Charlie Hebdo*, became the focus of a protest in 2012 for publishing a 65-page cartoon strip mocking militant Islamists and portraying the life of Muhammad. It rejected requests by the government to reconsider dealing with such an incendiary subject in that way. The paper again published cartoons of Muhammad in January 2015, with tragic results. Two gunmen burst into its offices and shot dead 10 of its editors in a staff meeting. They also killed two policemen before being captured and killed. A companion seized a Jewish grocery store and killed four shoppers. The culprits were French citizens, born in Paris of Algerian origin. This was the worst terrorist attack on French soil in over a half-century. Four million French, joined by a dozen European leaders, marched in the streets to show their solidarity with the victims. They carried signs proclaiming, "*Je suis Charlie*" ("I am Charlie").

Ten months later, on November 13, 2015, Paris suffered its bloodiest day since the Nazis were driven out, as Islamic State gunmen killed 130 and wounded 413.

On Bastille Day 2016, bloody tragedy struck in Nice, when a terrorist driving a rented truck veered into a packed crowd and killed 84 persons, including 10 children. It is no wonder that many French have a sense of siege and frustration. Polls show that most crave a stronger crackdown.

Religion

Almost 9 out of 10 Frenchmen are baptized Roman Catholic, and two-thirds describe themselves as Catholic. The second-largest religion is Islam. Since 1905 churches in France have been separated from the state, except in Alsace, Lorraine, and the Moselle Department, which then belonged to Germany. In these areas, church-state relations are governed by the concordat, which Napoleon I signed with the Vatican in 1801. Protestants constitute barely 2% of the population, but their influence far outweighs their numbers in business, the civil service, and intelligentsia. Three former prime ministers, including Lionel Jospin, Michel Rocard, and Couve de Murville, were Protestants. In the French public mind, Protestantism is almost synonymous with austerity and moral rigor.

Only 6% French still goes to mass weekly, according to a 2013 survey (down from 35% in 1961). The number of Catholic priests had fallen from 40,000 in 1940 to only 9,000 today. A 1997 poll by the Catholic newspaper *La Croix* indicated that two-thirds of the youth believe that the church has little influence on their lives. While 90% of Americans indicated in 2006 that they believe in God, only 50% of French respondents said that. Because of the principle of "secularity," whereby the state must be strictly separated from religion, the government's involvement in the pope's visit to France in 1996 sparked months of controversy and hostility. Also, many French resent any attempt by the Catholic Church to interfere in their private lives. Contraception is widely practiced, and abortion is common.

By 2007 the number of weddings had fallen by more than 30% in a generation. Only half of those weddings took place in church, compared with almost all of them only a quarter-century earlier. France has the lowest marriage rate in Europe, after Belgium and Slovenia; it was 40% below American figures. Marriage is in decline in most of northern Europe. In 1998, one in seven couples lived together outside marriage, a number seven times higher than a couple decades earlier and double the proportion a decade ago; only 7% of French respondents considered such an arrangement as "living in sin." After all, President Hollande and his partner cohabited in the Élysées palace Without being married to each other. French family structures have not disintegrated because society has accepted this.

The government decided in 1999 that it was time to offer some legal recognition to the new kinds of unions, although it refused to call them "marriages." It introduced "civil solidarity pacts" (PACS) allowing couples, of the same sex or not, to enter into a union and be entitled to the same rights as married couples in such areas as income tax, inheritance, housing, and social welfare, though it does not grant same sex couples the right to adopt children. Any two people sharing a home can sign a contract before a court clerk, and any partner can revoke it by giving the other person three-months advanced written notice.

Charging that this law further undermines the family, the Catholic Church, half the country's mayors, and 200,000 irate marchers in the streets of Paris vigorously protested it. A poll taken in 2000, one year after the PACs were introduced, revealed that 70% of respondents favored them. The PACS had originally been intended primarily for same sex couples. By 2013, however, that situation had changed dramatically: The overwhelming majority of civil unions are between straight couples. More and more French are shunning traditional marriages, and PACS are almost twice as popular as marriages. They are easier to dissolve, but they confer fewer rights, especially regarding inheritance and pensions.

President Hollande and the Socialist government championed "marriage for all." In April 2013, after 136 hours of riotous parliamentary debate, same-sex marriage and adoption were made legal. The issue had been very divisive, prompting passionate, sometimes-violent homophobic street demonstrations. One attracted 1.4 million protesters. Catholic, Jewish, and Muslim clergy were unified in opposition, but 59% of French favored it, although only 40% supported adoption rights for married members of the LGBTQ community.

With the average French woman bearing only 1.8 children in the 1990s, there was fear that the country faced the prospect of a declining native population. But by 2011, the fertility rate had risen to 2.1%, the highest in Europe after Albania. More than 48% of all babies (59% of all first-born children) are now born out of wedlock, the highest rate in Europe outside the Nordic countries. This is mostly by choice, not by chance. Clearly illegitimacy no longer carries a stigma. Children born out of wedlock have the same inheritance rights as others, but unwed partners are not automatically entitled to inherit property after a companion's death. When then-president Chirac proudly announced in 1996 the birth of his first grandchild, no one seemed to care that his daughter Claude was not married to the child's father, an ex–judo champion turned television presenter.

Education

Control over the school system is concentrated in Paris. Education is free and compulsory between the ages of 6 and 16, and approximately 5 out of 6 children attend public schools. Mitterrand stirred up much controversy by promising to do away with private schools, which receive state subsidies, and to create a unified, secular school system. A half million persons protested in the streets against this policy, the largest public demonstration in French history. Such widespread protests prompted him to withdraw the contentious private school bill in 1984.

From ages 5 to 11, children attend elementary school, and then they spend 4 years in an intermediate school, called a college. After this, they proceed to a high school, called a lycée, which provides either vocational training or a baccalaureate degree leading to university study. It gives pupils a broad background that includes languages. In 1998, 75% were still in school pursuing the "bac," double the proportion only a decade earlier. In 2012, 90% passed it (compared with about 60% in the 1960s and 83% in 2007), a rate that diminishes its value, in the view of critics. Only 49% of immigrant boys and 58% of girls pass the bac. This gap contributes to their 40% unemployment rate. As the number receiving the bac grows, youth without it become sidelined in the job market. The examination for the baccalaureate is a traditional intellectual one.

France is one of the few countries that still include philosophy as one of its obligatory high school subjects. In a 30-page "letter to teachers," President Sarkozy complained about too much "theory and abstraction." That could be one reason 38% of pupils have to repeat a year by age 15. In 2008 the education minister revealed that his ministry was considering ending the preeminence of mathematics in the bac. In some lycées, history has been eliminated as a requirement for the bac.

Based on pupils' performance on the bac in 2005, all but 1 of the top 29 lycées in France are private. The exception is the famed Lycée Henri IV on Paris's left bank. This is why many parents choose private schools for their children: 14% of primary pupils and over 20% of lycée pupils go to private school, many of which are Catholic and some are Jewish. The state pays the teachers' salaries, and fees are normally under €3,000 ($4,100).

Any student with a bac is allowed to study at a university; universities are barred from rejecting students from entry. About 1.5 million students are enrolled in the 83 universities or special advanced schools, and about a third of these students are in the 17 universities in the Paris region. In 1968 a fourth of 18-year-olds and 4% of 20-year-olds were in a school or university; in 1990 the comparable figures stood at 55% and 22%. That latter percentage continues to grow. University fees are low.

The rapid growth of enrollment has brought severe overcrowding, and 40% drop out before completing their undergraduate degree. Universities are underfinanced, disorganized, and resistant to changes demanded by the outside world. Professor salaries are low by American standards. Graduates find that their degrees are now worth less and that there are too few jobs for them after graduation. The highest French university among the top 40 on Shanghai's Jiao Tong University's global ranking in 2011 was Université Paris-Sud, which placed 40th.

A group of eminent European scholars questions the methodology used in this ranking. Nevertheless, efforts are being made to improve French universities' world standing. For example, there is generous funding from a program called Idex to universities and grandes écoles that create clusters and pool their resources to compete with the world's top institutions. French business schools already enjoy better global visibility.

The unemployment line never threatens graduates of the 220 elitist grandes écoles, of varying specialties who are selected by highly competitive nationwide examinations (*concours*) following two further years of intensive preparation in the lycée (called *prépa*) after the bac. At the top of the pyramid is a handful of ultraprestigious schools. Because they are so hard to get into, families celebrate acceptance at these institutions more than graduation itself. Many students at the universities still suffer from a sort of second-class status, as they watch the best jobs being filled by graduates from the grandes écoles. These extremely selective institutions are prestigious and produce an elite in teaching, industry, government, and the armed forces. They educate only 6% of French students but absorb 30% of the state's budget for higher education. They are well organized, well equipped, and overwhelmingly white and upper middle class. They account for 30% of the master's degrees and a third of the PhDs awarded in France. Half of the top 200 business bosses had attended a grande école.

Following the military debacle of 1870, the École des sciences politiques (called "Sciences-Po"), which offers advanced training in political science and economics, was created to improve the quality of senior civil servants. President Hollande, his three predecessors in the presidency, and at least a dozen prime ministers studied there. Half of its budget is financed by the state. It led France in offering a three-year undergraduate degree, followed by *"un master."* In 2003–2004 the Education Ministry advocated such degrees for all universities. All Sciences-Po students spend a year abroad, learn two foreign languages, and take at least a third of their classes in a language other than French. Some take all their courses in English. Over 40% are foreigners, including many Americans. It has established exchanges with American universities. It accepts 3,500 students yearly, for a total student body of 12,000. Tuition is about $13,000 for undergraduates, and professors' pay is competitive. New subjects, including journalism, have been introduced.

Along with the elite School of Higher Commercial Studies, Sciences Po has been a pioneer in offering classes in English. In 2013 the education minister proposed a bill that would allow other French universities to teach more courses in English, despite a 1994 law requiring that classes be taught in French. The goal is to attract more foreign students, who already account for 13% of all university students. The proposal was greeted by rage and protests.

In 2001 Sciences-Po caused a stir by introducing a kind of affirmative action plan, later temporarily ruled unlawful by a Paris court, to create a special admission track for secondary school students in seven poor neighborhoods whose population contains large concentrations of Arab and African immigrants. Such pupils are exempt from the stiff competitive entrance exams other applicants must pass, but there is no fixed quota. By 2012, the school's working-class intake had risen from 3% to 12%.

No one disputes that the grandes écoles have always recruited almost exclusively from a limited sociological pool of white, well-connected, and wealthy families. There is a growing minority of students from farm and working-class families. But these schools reject affirmative action on the grounds that it would dilute their standards. It would seem to violate the meritocracy through education, which is blind to race, religion, and ethnicity and which is the cornerstone of the republican ideal.

France

The École nationale d'administration (ENA, whose graduates are called Énarques) accepts 120 students (a fourth to a third female) by examination from the other grandes écoles each year for the 27-month program. It was set up after the defeat in 1940 and the shame of Vichy to train elite administrators who would put the interests of the state above their own. It was in Paris until 1992, when ENA was moved to Strasbourg. Study at ENA is particularly important to those persons aspiring to top civil-service positions.

Currently about two-thirds of such offices are held by *Énarques*, who form a highly useful informal network of contacts for each other. Only about 6,000 of its graduates are alive today. Among them were all the major contenders for the presidency in 1995—Jacques Chirac, Lionel Jospin, and Edouard Balladur—as well as former president Valery Giscard d'Estaing. The 2007 election pitted Nicolas Sarkozy, who was not an ENA graduate, against Ségolène Royal, who was. It is perhaps not surprising that Sarkozy included only one *Énarque* in his cabinet but nine lawyers. Dominique de Villepin and six out of his nine preceding prime ministers were *Énarques*, as was President François Hollande.

The mayor of Montpellier spoke bitterly of the influential *Énarques*: "France is still run by civil servants. There is no difference between a socialist *Énarque* and a neo-Gaullist *Énarque*. They are intelligent, incorrupt and absolutely convinced they are right. The country is run by thousands of little Robespierres." One conservative politician, Alain Madelin, even said in 1997, "Ireland has the IRA, Spain has ETA, Italy the mafia, but France has ENA." One contemporary reason for the disdain toward the highly selected *Énarques* is that ENA produces technocrats wholly imbued with a theoretical, state-oriented way of thinking that is not well adapted to a world of global capitalism.

The glory of ENA is fading somewhat. Between 1995 and 1999, applications for its notoriously difficult entrance exams declined by 30%. Sciences-Po, which supplies 90% of the external exam's successful candidates, has a special program to prepare students for the entrance test, but aspirants enrolling in that program have dwindled from 1,000 per year a decade ago to 200. A major reason is that, in France's changed economic environment, it is the private sector, not the civil service, which beckons ambitious young people.

In addition, there are three Écoles normales supérieures, one in Paris—ENS Ulm (in the Rue d'Ulm), which concentrates on the sciences and humanities—and two in Lyon, one of which focuses on the sciences and the other on the humanities. Both institutions in Lyon want to merge and become identical to their counterpart in Paris. These elite schools train the top lycée and university professors, who must pass a rigorous final examination called the *agrégation*.

Finally, there are the Hautes Études Commerciales (HEC) and other business-oriented schools. They do well in international comparison: In 2006 the British *Financial Times* picked 7 French business schools as among Europe's top 10. There are also the École des mines and similarly specialized schools, such as the military academy at Saint-Cyr. In 1794 the military École polytechnique was established as a military school. Now it trains top public officials. Cadets begin with one year in the military to undergo officer training and then spend two years doing top-level engineering and scientific study.

In protest against underfunding, overcrowding, decrepit buildings, insufficient security at inner-city schools, and bleak employment prospects, especially in nontechnical fields, lycée and university students often take to the streets. Teachers sympathize because half their classes have over 30 pupils, and some have over 40. One result is that one in four teachers requests a transfer or job change every year.

There were renewed strikes in 2003–2004 by university students protesting American-style reform plans to make the universities more autonomous and to offer a three-year degree followed by a two-year master's degree. The education minister backed off in 2005 and agreed not to modify the *baccalauréat* exam. Scientists also took to the streets or resigned to demand more state support for research to stem the brain drain abroad and to protest plans to cut funding and 550 permanent scientific posts. The frightened government pledged to restore 120 of the jobs and invest €3 billion more in research by 2007.

Sarkozy had to backtrack on some of his plans for university reform out of fear that the renewed student protests in 2009, led by the far left, would turn violent. However, he shook up the centrally run universities. As of 2011, 51 out of 83 universities had accepted his offer of autonomy. They can recruit their own faculty, establish their salaries, and seek funds from the private sector. They cannot select their undergraduates nor charge tuition.

The American film *Dead Poets Society*, which portrayed a rebellion against a hidebound educational system, had a profound effect on debates in France concerning reform of the school system. The government proposed reforms to humanize the grueling bac, which on average requires 45 hours of work per week, including homework, and leaves time for only one of five secondary pupils to participate in school team sports. A major stumbling block for change has been the resistance of powerful teaching unions. In the meantime, many French ask why their once-excellent educational system is soaking up more and more resources and producing students with less knowledge and fewer job prospects.

The Press

Financial difficulties have steadily reduced the number of daily newspapers to fewer than 100. The most widely read is *Ouest France*, published in Rennes, a regional paper with a circulation of 762,450, twice as many copies as any of the national papers. The best-selling national newspaper is the lively daily tabloid *Le Parisien-Aujourd'hui*, with a circulation of about 400,000. The largest and most influential of the national papers is the moderately leftist and intellectual *Le Monde*, with a declining circulation of 399,000 and a readership of 2.1 million. To compare, in 2011 the eight main French national dailies together sold 1.2 million copies a day (down 10% from the previous year), the same number as the *Daily Mirror* in Britain sells every day at newsstands.

Azay-le-Rideau in the Loire Valley

The conservative *Le Figaro* (with receding circulation of 320,000) was purchased in 2004 by Serge Dassault of the airplane company of the same name. The left intellectual *Libération*, cofounded by Jean-Paul Sartre, also faces declining circulation, with 142,000. All three—*Le Monde, Le Figaro*, and *Libération*—have seen a large industrialist or banker take control or a significant share (Edouard de Rothschild in the case of *Libération*). All are from Paris. One of the few dailies with climbing sales is *L'Equipe*, an all-sports newspaper. As elsewhere, dailies face the challenge of the web.

In order to halt the growing concentration of the French press, the Socialist government approved in 1984 a law prohibiting publishers from owning both Parisian and regional newspapers and from controlling more than 15% of either Parisian or regional circulation. Many educated French read certain political and economic weeklies, such as *L'Express, Le Nouvel Observateur, Le Point*, and *L'Evenement du Jeudi*, which offer in-depth analysis and criticism.

The stock and trade of *Le Canard Enchainé* is satire, a weekly that is thriving, with sales of 450,000 to 500,000. It was founded in 1915 by two left-wing journalists to circumvent army censorship during the First World War. It is owned by its staff of about 40 journalists and cartoonists and is so fiercely independent that it carries no advertising. Its investigative reporting can drive cabinet ministers out of office, but it has a strict ban on writing about the private lives of public figures.

As elsewhere in the world, many French have turned increasingly to television, radio, and the Internet for news. Fewer than 5% of French between the ages of 15 and 25 believe newspapers will be their first source of information in 5 years. The trends that face French newspapers are familiar in other nations: aging readers, plus competition from free newspapers, TV, and the Internet. Most face the prospect of being bought by investors to stay alive. Newspaper readership has dropped over 3 million since 1970.

Even *Le Monde*, founded in 1944 at the instigation of General de Gaulle to replace the collaborationist *Le Temps* and to provide journalism untainted by Vichy, is losing money and circulation. It was owned and operated entirely by its employees. In the 1980s it temporarily improved its sales and financial condition by making its format more attractive and by selling and leasing back its headquarters building near the Opera.

In 2008 it faced another crisis. With losses and debts mounting, there was a drastic need for refinancing. But the staff associations resisted moves to improve efficiency and any solution that would eliminate their 60% controlling stake. Almost out of cash by July 2010, it was purchased by three businessmen for $139 million. They promised the staff full editorial independence and gave the journalists a blocking minority stake. But they attacked the unions head on, whose powers and featherbedding make it 40% more expensive to print newspapers in France than anywhere else in Europe. The papers must then charge higher cover prices, which drives down circulation even farther.

Renowned as rigorously intellectual and overwhelmingly serious, *Le Monde* received a black eye in 2003, when two journalists published a best-seller, *The Hidden Face of* Le Monde, accusing it of bias, conflicts of interest, hypocrisy, and business mismanagement. They argued that *Le Monde* twisted facts to cover up scandals, influenced French politics without declaring its interests, and hid the newspaper's financial weakness. The paper rejected the charges as an amalgam of "errors, lies, libels and calumnies." In 2003 it promptly fired Daniel Schneidermann, author of a follow-up book, *The Media Nightmare*, which attacks the French press generally and *Le Monde's* reaction to *The Hidden Face* in particular.

Until 1984 the state had a monopoly on television and radio. Radio programs are produced by Radio France, and French government holding companies partially own three independent radio stations (Radio Luxembourg, Europe No. 1, and Radio Monte Carlo), which broadcast from outside of France. Radio-France and the state-owned television companies were financed by annual license fees paid by those persons owning sets.

Critics charge that these companies, although nominally independent and responsible for their own programming, have been manipulated from the Elysées Palace. Mitterrand proposed reducing government influence over them by placing control into the hands of an independent board of directors that would include government officials, media specialists, and private citizens. In fact, little has changed in the management of the state-owned media.

The big changes in 1984 came with the legalization of private radio and television stations. So many private radio stations had cropped up that they could no longer be controlled. By legalizing them, the state broadcasting monopoly had been so irreparably punctured that it was only a matter of time until private television was permitted. More than 800 private radio stations exist already, providing a voice for all kinds of minority interests. Many local TV stations exist around the country. In 1987 the government took another momentous step by selling the largest of the old state networks (TF1) to the private sector. This was the first sell-off by any government of a state-owned TV network. The state kept two of the six channels.

To strengthen Franco-German familiarity with each other, the two countries started a joint satellite TV channel called Arte. However, its total audience had by 2003 stagnated to about 13 million viewers, 9 million of them in France. Many judge Arte as too highbrow and tend to associate it with Paris elites.

In 2006 France 24, the long-planned French rival to CNN and BBC World, went on the air with international news around the clock. It broadcasted in both French and English and was supposed to add an Arabic channel later. But the Sarkozy government produced a plan to strip it of its independence and to combine it with Radio France Internationale and TV5Monde to form France Monde. Broadcasting in English and Arabic was dropped.

The Arts

France continues to be a land rich and creative, and performing arts, although no longer occupying the indisputably primary position in the world, are topnotch. Its artists have also declined from their pinnacle, but their past greatness is preserved for the world to admire in such great French museums as the Louvre, the Musée d'Orsay, the Beaubourg, and the beautifully renovated Picasso Museum. Such concentration of priceless art presents many tempting targets for thieves, as one saw in 2010. In January a pastel by Edgar Degas was lifted from the Cantini Museum in Marseilles. A week later works by Pablo Picasso and Henri Rousseau were stolen from a private villa. Then in May a single burglar broke into the Paris Museum of Modern Art and stole five paintings by Picasso, Matisse, George Braque, Modigliani and Fernand Léger worth a minimum of $114 million.

Traditions date back hundreds of years in literature, art, music, and the theater. The writings of Voltaire and Rousseau are landmarks in rich French enlightenment. The music of father and son François Couperin were classic; that of Frederic Chopin, Jules Massenet, Camille Saint-Saens, and Claude Debussy, richly postromantic. During the Third Republic before World War I, Paris was enriched by impressionism in art (e.g., Renoir, Monet, Degas) and the reaction to it (Braque, Picasso, cubism, or fauvism). During the same period, there was the positivism of Auguste Comte, the élan vital of Henry Bergson, in medicine the discoveries of Louis Pasteur, and in physics the discoveries of Pierre and Marie Curie.

In 1988 Maurice Allais became the first Frenchman to win the Nobel Prize for

economics, for his study of markets and efficient utilization of resources. This feat was repeated in 2014, when the same prize was won by Jean Tirole of the Toulouse School of Economics. France also won its 15th Nobel Prize in literature in 2014, when Patrick Modiano was honored for his 29 books, plus screenplays, that focus primarily on collaboration and the German occupation of Paris.

The job of French minister of culture is one of great influence and patronage. Today, the arts in France, as almost everything else, receive state subsidies amounting to 1.5% of the national budget. They are highly concentrated in Paris. To try to spread French cultural activity into the provinces, de Gaulle's minister of culture, André Malraux, created cultural centers in 10 provincial cities, financed and operated jointly by the central government and the municipalities. He was a leading French writer and art critic who incurred the wrath of Parisian traditionalists by ordering that all public buildings in Paris be sandblasted to eliminate centuries of soot which had accumulated on them.

These centers are designed to promote artistic creativity and to bring the performing arts into the provinces. In May 2010 the first regional branch of the Pompidou Museum opened in Metz. It can select from among the 65,000 artworks, the largest contemporary collection in Europe, which the Paris Museum has in storage. The centers also serve as places for discussions on contemporary problems. Despite such attempts, many still speak with some justification of "Paris and the desert."

FUTURE

France is undergoing introspection over its place in an enlarged Europe and a world seemingly dominated by American and Anglo-Saxon culture and economic practice. By 2017 it had slid to 25th place in the global ranking of GDP per capita. It has been overtaken by the Netherlands in terms of total exports. The euro crisis beginning in 2010 demonstrated that Germany has become the leader in Europe and that France is now the junior partner in that important bilateral relationship.

President Macron's Republic on the Move (LRM) Party won a commanding victory in the June 2017 parliamentary elections. With a disappointing turnout of only 49%, it captured far more seats (62%) than the required 289 to win an absolute majority. The Republicans came in a distant second, and the Socialists placed last among the established parties. At first the nation rallied behind the new president, and there was a palpable sense that something dynamic was happening. That has changed. His approval rating has plummeted to 30%.

Macron faces serious challenges in enacting the reforms which he advocated. As expected, his attempt to loosen the rigid labor laws triggered strikes by rail, airline, energy, and refuse workers. To calm a nervous public fearful of terrorism, the president pledged to tighten rules on immigration and asylum. A key player is Prime Minister Édouard Philippe, a conservative and fluent German speaker.

In November 2018 a lengthy, sometimes-violent protest exploded. It was set off by a rise in fuel prices and grew to include protest of income insufficiency and inequality, high taxes, and Macron's perceived arrogance and elitism. Calling themselves "Yellow Vests," they tagged him as a "president of the rich." A majority of the French agree with parts of their criticism. In response, Macron launched a "great national debate" and promised to listen to the grievances.

Long stretches of the banks of the Seine in Paris and rivers in other French cities, such as Bordeaux, are being returned to pedestrian and bicycle traffic. The roads are giving way to parks and gardens or, in the words of the mayor of Paris, "places of life, beauty and culture." No people do that better than the French.

The Principality of Monaco

Aerial view of Monaco showing the Port of Monaco

Area: .575 sq. mi. (1.95 sq. km).
Population: 35,427 (2013).
Capital City: Monaco-Ville.
Climate: Mild Mediterranean.
Neighboring Country: France.
Official Language: French.
Other Principal Tongues: Italian and Monégasque (a mixture of French and Italian) are also spoken.
Ethnic Background: French (50%), Italian (15%), native Monégasques (about 7,100), and diverse other European peoples.
Principal Religion: Roman Catholicism is the state religion.
Main Industries: Banking; tourism; postage stamps; gambling; small industries, such as cosmetics, chemicals, food processing, precision instrument manufacture, glassmaking, and printing.
Major Trading Partners: France, Italy.
Currency: Euro.
Date of Independence: 1338.
National Holiday: November 19.
Chief of State: His Serene Highness Prince Albert II, Sovereign Prince of Monaco, Marquis of Baux (b. 1958), performed duties since July 13, 2005, enthroned November 19, 2005.
Heir Apparent: Prince Jacques Honoré Rainier.
Head of Government: Minister of State (in effect, prime minister) Michel Roger (since March 2010), appointed by the prince. There is also a government counselor for foreign affairs, in 2010 Jean Pastorelli.
National Flag: Red and white horizontal stripes.

The Principality of Monaco is one of the smallest sovereign countries in the world, smaller even than New York's Central Park. A densely populated, hilly city overlooking the Mediterranean Sea, Monaco is surrounded on three sides by the French Department of Alpes-Maritimes. The French city of Nice is nine miles (15 km) to the west of Monaco, and the Italian border is five miles (8 km) to the east. Three picturesque settlements are now unified into one city. Its older section, situated on top of a steep rock, has maintained its medieval flavor despite some characterless high-rise blocks on the skyline.

Overlooking crowded Riviera beaches and some of the most luxurious tourist resorts in the world is the 13th-century Genoese Palace, which was remodeled in the 16th century in Renaissance style. Here resides the prince of the House of Grimaldi, whose family has ruled Monaco, with periodic interruptions, since 1297. On January 8, 1997, the late Prince Rainier launched a year-long, $270 million celebration of his family's 700-year reign, the longest of any European dynasty.

Evidence of Stone Age settlements has been found within the present borders of Monaco. Founded much later by the Phoenicians, the city was known to the ancient Greeks and Carthaginians. Under the domination of the Romans (who called the city Herculis Moenaci Portus), Monaco was quite prosperous, and it was from Monaco that Julius Caesar set sail for his campaign against Pompeii. Its wealth was destroyed by the invading barbarians, who brought the once-mighty Roman Empire to its knees. In the 7th century, Monaco became a part of the Lombard Kingdom. Later it was absorbed into the Kingdom of Arles and was also subjected to a period of Muhammadan control. In 1191 the Genoese took control of Monaco, but they ceded domination in 1297 to the reining Grimaldi family.

As a minuscule land in a restless world, the independent principality of Monaco always needed the protection of a stronger power in order to survive. It allied itself first with France. In 1524 it accepted Spain's protection instead, but it returned to French safety in 1641. In 1793 the radicalized French National Convention dispossessed the wealthy and aristocratic Grimaldi rulers and annexed the entire Monacan domain to France. After Napoleon's fall from power, the Congress of Vienna awarded Monaco to the Kingdom of Sardinia as a protectorate in 1814. France repossessed the principality in 1848 and, after greatly reducing its territory, granted independence to the present tiny remainder in 1861.

France today continues to assume responsibility for Monaco's defense, and a 1918 treaty stipulates that Monaco's policies must conform to French political, military, naval, and economic interests. A further treaty of 1919 stipulates that Monaco would be incorporated into France if the reigning prince dies without an heir. This means that the city's self-rule depends entirely on the royal family. A former adviser to the prince explained, "The independence is given to the prince, not to the people and not to the country, and this is why the prince is so important." With the birth of twins to the royal family in December 2014, the succession is clear: although Princess Gabriella Thérèse Marie was born first, her brother, Jacques Honoré Rainier, will be the future ruler.

The Principality of Monaco

His Serene Highness Prince Albert II and the late Prince Rainier III

Prince Rainier III died April 6, 2005. He had been Europe's longest-reigning monarch. Rainier had been educated in Britain, Switzerland, and France and had volunteered for service in the French army in 1944. He married the late American actress Grace Kelly in 1956. She epitomized American affluence and Hollywood glamour and attracted the world's attention to the ruling Grimaldi family. She met an untimely death in an automobile accident on the hilly roads of Monaco in 1982. Their offspring ensure survival of the principality. Grace's magic is still alive, as shown by the popular 2014 film *Grace of Monaco*, starring Nicole Kidman.

Since 1865, an economic union with France governs customs, postal services, telecommunications, and banking. The principality even used the French franc until it adopted the euro when France did in 2002. Although it is not in the EU, it was permitted to mint its own euro coins with its own motif on the back.

Monaco refuses to tax its own citizens, who number only about 20% of the principality's residents. Most of the rest are French. These 7,600 Monégasques also receive preferential employment and housing subsidies. The latter are needed since land, at €24,900 per meter (compared with €14,522 in central London and €6,667 in Paris), is the most expensive in Europe. Housing costs are also the world's highest; in 2010 an apartment was sold for €240 million ($350 million), a world record. They are guaranteed government service jobs, and all companies must make their first job offers to them. Their only penalty was that they were banned from setting foot in the casinos until 2011. There are 35,427 residents (including about 25,000 rich foreigners), but 43,000 commute daily into the principality to work.

Most Monégasques have second homes in nearby Italy or France in order to escape the tourist crush. They also go to France for higher education, but thanks to the principality's healthy economy, they return.

More than half the residents are French, many of whom choose to reside and to locate their businesses in Monaco in order to avoid French taxation. French protests of this situation in 1962 unleashed a serious dispute. Nevertheless, a compromise was worked out in 1963; all French companies that do more than 25% of their business outside of the principality were brought under French financial control. French living in Monaco must pay French taxes. Other nationalities do not. In 2000 verbal warfare broke out again when France threatened to punish the principality unless it took effective measures against money laundering, tax evasion, and drug barons. It demanded that Monaco impose a wealth tax on French residents and disclose details of bank accounts. Compliance would make the principality less attractive.

In 2008 trouble erupted again in the wake of a tax-haven scandal involving tiny Liechtenstein. Attention focused on the other two blacklisted ministates which the OECD declared "uncooperative states" in terms of taxes: Monaco and Andorra. The principality faced the dilemma of how to maintain its banking secrecy while not being misused for tax evasion.

Prince Rainier was not pleased, calling the French attitude "incongruous" and demanding a renegotiation of its treaties with France "to give Monaco back to the Monégasques." The principality likes to portray itself as a secure haven for the well-behaved rich. In response to EU pressure, Monaco agreed in 2003 to collect taxes on foreign accounts and to return 75% of the levy to the country of residence without revealing account holders' names. In 2009 it signaled its readiness to be more transparent and to fight tax fraud in order to stay off the OECD's blacklist of secretive states. It signed 24 tax agreements that got it off the OECD list.

Monaco has undergone a remarkable economic transformation in recent decades. At the end of the 19th century, gambling and the belle époche casino accounted for 95% of the state's revenues. When Prince Rainier took the throne in 1949 at age 26, his realm was seen, in the words of Somerset Maugham, as "a sunny place for shady people." It was a glitzy but sleazy gambling center. The prince sought to upgrade its image in order to attract wealthy, respectable visitors, depositors, and residents and to provide long-term employment opportunities for native Monégasques. The principality derives half of its income from its 19.6% VAT, with another 13% coming from property sales. There are no income or inheritance taxes. Unemployment is official zero.

His main achievement was to stimulate the local economy by creating thriving banking and tourist industries. Benefiting from tax advantages, banks have doubled in number since the early 1980s to nearly 40. It is estimated that there is 1 cashier for every 400 residents. Tough laws permitting the seizure of profits from drug operations were introduced in 1993 in an effort to keep the banks' money clean. The principality now attracts over 7 million visitors each year. Many are day-trippers from Italy and France. More and more cruise passengers from giant liners are arriving every morning. The annual Grand Prix auto race attracts 150,000 alone. Tourist spending accounts for 25% of GDP. Monaco also has experienced a blooming of commerce and light industry.

In 1967 Prince Rainier won a long struggle with the Greek shipping magnate Aristotle Onassis over control of the famed casino of Monte-Carlo. Monaco's native citizens are not permitted to gamble in the casino, which is now owned by the Soci-

Monaco mourns the death of Prince Rainier III.

eté des Bains de Mer. Contrary to popular belief, less than 5% of the principality's revenues are now derived from its gambling royalties. Still, the social life of Monaco centers around the Place du Casino, with its lovely gardens. The Monte Carlo Philharmonic is one of the world's most recorded orchestras. The principality also boasts first-rate opera and ballet companies, as well as 55 galleries and 50 open-air sculptures.

The deceased prince also oversaw a major building program that changed both the look and the size of the city and won him the nickname "the Builder Prince." Few capitalist countries have such close ties between government and business. Since the town is hemmed in by its land borders, it could only expand outward into the sea. That is what happened. By filling land, he was able to expand Monaco's size by 23% at the expense of the Mediterranean. To win more space, a tunnel was built for the railway that used to dissect the principality. The old harbor was extended by constructing a pier to accommodate the largest cruise ships. Prince Albert II founded an ecology foundation and aims to make the environment his highest priority when developing the city.

Monaco's present constitution, which was promulgated December 17, 1962, reduced the prince's powers somewhat and increased parliamentary powers. Executive power is vested in the hereditary prince, who rules through his appointed minister of state. The latter official must be a French citizen and must be selected from a slate of three candidates put to the principality by the French president. Three state counselors (one of whom must be French) and palace personnel who are appointed by the prince assist the minister of state. France supplies senior civil servants, judges, policemen and firemen. The French judicial system applies in Monaco, and two Parisian judges form the Court of Appeal. Prisoners must serve their sentences outside the principality, usually in France, since its only jail can accommodate suspects awaiting trial but not convicted criminals. With 1 policeman for every 62 residents, this is one of the world's safest places.

Legislative power rests with an 18-member National Council elected by universal suffrage of native Monegasques for five-year terms. The prince shares the legislative powers in that he retains the right to initiate legislation. Although four political parties are now active in Monaco, one party, the National and Democratic Union (UND), dominated for four decades and controlled all 18 National Council seats. That ended with the 2003 elections, when the Union for Monaco coalition won an overwhelming majority.

The funeral of Prince Rainier III, attended by kings, queens and presidents, was held in the very cathedral where he had married Grace. On July 12, 2005, Prince Albert II, whose photo is displayed in every shop, assumed the duties of the throne to become the 31st descendant of Otto Canella, who had founded the house of Grimaldi. He was formally enthroned on November 19, 2005, with only one head of state (the Icelandic president) in attendance. He had graduated from Amherst College in Massachusetts and worked for a while on Wall Street and Moët and Chandon to learn finance and business.

He began early preparing for the transition to rule. He attended government meetings and assumed his father's duties during his frequent illnesses in the last years of his life. Albert was a member of Monaco's bobsled team in the 2002 Winter Olympics in Salt Lake City. He is also a passionate supporter of the AS Monaco soccer team. Non-French foreigners on the team do not have to pay income taxes. This enables the underfunded club to attract good players.

No sooner was his father laid to rest than a former Air France flight attendant from Togo announced that she had had an affair with Albert lasting several years and that her two-year-old son, Alexandre, had been fathered by him. She had been living in the prince's Paris apartment and had access to a villa on the French Riviera. After successfully suing the French weekly magazine *Paris Match* for €50,000 (about $65,000) for invading his privacy by publishing photos of him holding the child, Albert publicly recognized his paternity of the boy.

All Europe chatters about Albert's wife, Charlene, and his children.

The prince admitted in 2006 that he had also sired a daughter, Jazmin Grace, by a then-married California waitress on holiday along the Riviera, Tamara Jean Rotolo. Jazmin was born in 1992 and was a schoolgirl in Palm Desert, California. In 2011 he faced DNA testing for his third paternity. Given the fact that his sister Stephanie has three children out of wedlock and Caroline has two, this news did not shock the principality as one might have expected. Each child whose paternity he recognizes will have a share of his inheritance, estimated at over $1 billion. This will have no effect on the principality's dynastic succession, since only children born in wedlock are eligible.

On July 2, 2011, the 53-year-old monarch married Charlene Wittstock, a 33-year-old Zimbabwean-born South African national swimming champion, whom he met at a swim meet in Monaco in 2000. She is Monaco's first princess consort since Grace died in 1982, and her main duty is to have an heir. To qualify, she converted to Catholicism, the official religion, and took intensive French lessons. They live with their twins in the family's historic palace. To raise money for a needed renovation, the royal family sold 1,000 objects of Napoleon's memorabilia, including hats and stockings, raising €10 million.

France controls Monaco's foreign relations, and the principality is included in the EU through its customs union with France. Since 1993 it is a full member of the United Nations, and it serves on several UN specialized agencies. It also maintains 4 embassies (in Paris, Brussels, Bern, and Rome) and 110 consuls of its own, including ones in Washington and New York. In 1994 it signed a cultural convention under Council of Europe auspices. But because it is not considered to be either completely democratic or independent, it has never formally asked nor been invited to join the Council of Europe.

Monaco has no newspapers of its own, but there is a private radio station (Radio-Monte-Carlo) with programming in French, Italian, and Arabic. Also, Trans-World Radio has a seat in Monte-Carlo and broadcasts in four languages. One private television station (Tele Monte-Carlo) transmits programs in French and Italian.

FUTURE

Before his death in 2005, Prince Rainier III could look back on a half-century of successful rule in his ministate. With Prince Albert II and his 20-year-younger wife, Charlene; a succession to the throne; and an active program of home-based economic diversification, this minuscule 700-year-old principality can expect not only to exist but also to prosper in the coming years.

The BENELUX Nations

Belgium, the Netherlands, and Luxembourg are located at the crossroads of western Europe. Although they are collectively called BENELUX, a word derived from the first letters of each country's name, these small countries have developed differing traditions, national characters, and problems. Still, they have many things in common, and it is no accident that they cooperate with each other more closely than any other nations of the world. In fact, their example of international cooperation and their steady encouragement of tighter European integration have made them the core and motor for greater unity. The vast majority of the EU's institutions are located in Belgium and Luxembourg.

All three countries are very small and have no natural frontiers that could serve as barriers to unwanted intruders. They have therefore suffered recurrent invasions by all the great European powers. For a century and a half, they tried to keep themselves out of the grips of the major powers by declaring a policy of neutrality. But two disastrous world wars in the 20th century, which spared only the Netherlands from 1914 to 1918, left such a policy and the three countries in shambles. No one can easily forget the lines which the poet John McCrae wrote after visiting the Flemish battlefields: "In Flanders fields the poppies blow between the crosses, row by row."

Having paid a heavy price for their neutrality, all three countries became founding members of NATO in 1949. Its political headquarters are now located on the outskirts of Brussels, and its military headquarters, the Supreme Headquarters of the Allied Powers in Europe (SHAPE), are located outside of Mons, Belgium.

The Netherlands and Belgium have the highest population density of all Europe. All three have great numbers of foreign workers who bring both needed labor and social problems with them. These countries are not particularly rich in raw materials, but they have productive economies that have provided standards of living and social welfare systems for their populations that are almost unmatched in the world. Their central location and access to the sea made them prosperous trading nations, and the ports of Rotterdam and Antwerp are the largest and most active in Europe. With relatively small populations and high prosperity, these countries are heavily dependent upon trade and, therefore, upon economic and political conditions beyond their borders. Roughly half of these countries' GDP results from foreign trade. This heavy volume is an economic blessing, as well as a possible liability for the future.

To help secure their trade, they were pioneers in economic unions. In 1922 Belgium and Luxembourg formed the Belgium-Luxembourg Economic Union (BLEU), which made the two countries a unit for importing and exporting purposes. It also established a unified railway, customs area, and currency for the two countries. Luxembourg coined and printed money below 100 francs for local circulation, but Belgian currency remained dominant until the euro in 2002. The three countries' governments-in-exile in London in 1944 formed a customs union called BENELUX, which was later extended to include even noncustoms matters. Because of the striking difference in postwar recovery, BENELUX did not come into effect until January 1948.

In 1952 they were founding members with France, West Germany, and Italy of the European Coal and Steel Community (ECSC), with headquarters located in Luxembourg. Not only was it a farsighted idea to share these commodities, so crucial for heavy industry, rather than to risk fighting over them, but also the ECSC gave these nations the practice in economic cooperation needed to convince the six that a bold move to create a united Europe could succeed. The six signed the Treaty of Rome in 1957, and in 1958 the European Economic Community (Common Market) came into existence. Later the community grew, and its name was changed first to the European Community (EC) and then in 1993 to the European Union (EU) in order to emphasize that the union was someday to become a political one, as well as an economic one. None tried harder than the BENELUX countries to keep the idea of a united Europe alive in the 1960s, when the six were seriously split over the question of British entry.

All three countries are constitutional, parliamentary monarchies, whose monarchs are relatively popular, though not powerful. As modern constitutional monarchs, they "reign but do not rule." In contrast to the monarchy in Great Britain, which can be traced back more than 1,000 years, the BENELUX monarchies are young. The oldest, in the Netherlands, dates back to 1813. Throughout the centuries these small countries have been tossed back and forth among the great powers of Europe and have sometimes been forced together and sometimes split apart. A quick glance at their history shows why they have so much in common and are nevertheless different from each other.

Early History

The early history of these three countries is so intertwined that it is best considered by grouping them together.

About a half-century before Christ, after a long and destructive campaign, the Roman legions conquered the tenacious Celtic tribes, including the Belgeai and Treveri. In his commentary *The Gallic Wars*, Julius Caeser used the name "Belgium" to refer to all the territory we now call the BENELUX countries. This area, especially what is today Belgium and Luxembourg, was dominated for more than 300 years by the Romans, who built roads and villas and introduced agriculture, especially vineyards and fruit orchards. They also brought Christianity to the area, but it did not begin to flourish until the 6th and 7th centuries.

When Attila the Hun invaded what is now Germany, Germanic tribes were thrown into the Low Countries (the Netherlands) in about 300. Two centuries later another Germanic tribe, the Franks, invaded the area and established a linguistic frontier that exists today in the middle of what is now Belgium. North of the line, the Germanic tongues evolved into the Dutch language and into Flemish, a Dutch dialect spoken in northern Belgium. South of the line, vulgarized Latin, which developed into French, was spoken. Thus in Belgium the Latin and Germanic worlds met face to face and presented Belgium with a problem which, many centuries later, threatened to tear the country apart.

In the 8th and 9th centuries the entire territory that had been fragmented into many duchies, principalities, and other political units became a part of Charlemagne's empire. This was the time when the political center of gravity in Europe shifted from the Mediterranean to the northwestern regions. His great empire fell apart soon after his death, and for several centuries the BENELUX people saw their land converted into a constant battlefield between French and German contenders for control. During this time the Crusades opened up trade with the Orient, and especially Belgium experienced a flowering of trade and urban development. The beautiful canal city of Bruges became a wealthy city of trade and the arts. In the 15th century, the Dukes of Burgundy, who were among the most powerful in Europe, began to acquire control over what is now Belgium and Luxembourg by means of conquest, marriage, or land purchase.

Only the Netherlands was able to resist the Burgundian encroachment. As a country whose development had been retarded by its preoccupation with fighting back the sea, the Netherlands was not a very tempting target for Burgundian expansion anyway. At the end of the 15th century, the last descendent, Mary of Burgundy, married Maximilian of Austria, and the Burgundian holdings in the area passed into the Hapsburg family. Their son, Philip the Handsome, married the Spanish princess Juana of Castile; Spain and Spanish America also came under Hapsburg control.

A son born of this union in 1500 in the Flemish city of Ghent was destined to become one of Europe's greatest rulers. He became king of Spain in 1516 and the Holy Roman emperor in 1519. He was Charles V, and by 1543 he had unified all of what is now the BENELUX area, except the county of Liège, which led a separate existence until the 18th century. Charles ruled his far-flung empire from Brussels, a city established in 979 on the islands of the Senne River, which was then called "Bruocsella." His reign was a time of great economic prosperity and artistic and intellectual bloom for the "Seventeen Provinces," as the Luxembourg area was then called. This was the time of the great humanist Erasmus of Rotterdam; of Mercator, the

The Holy Roman emperor, Charles V

most widely known cartographer in the world; and of the painters van Eyck and Pieter Breugal.

The unity of the Seventeen Provinces might have survived if the Reformation which Martin Luther unleashed in 1519 had not divided Europe and with it the Low Countries. Charles V abdicated in 1555 in favor of his son Philip II, who had been raised in Spain; he decided to rule the empire from Madrid, leaving the administration of the Seventeen Provinces to governors. He was, however, determined to defend the Catholic faith, and he was cruel and inflexible in attempting to suppress the Protestant movement, which, in its Calvinist form, was particularly strong in the Netherlands. William of Orange-Nassau led Protestant resistance in the northern provinces. Because Spain was so severely weakened by its continuous struggles against England and France during the second half of the 16th century, the Netherlands was able to secure its independence in 1581.

Until Napoleon's conquests in the 1790s, the Dutch took control of their own destiny, while the Belgians and Luxembourgers continued to be dominated by other powers. In order to give the latter a sense of autonomy, Philip gave the southern provinces to his daughter, the Archduchess Isabella, and her husband, the Archduke Albert of Austria. It was a relatively happy time when the painter Peter Paul Rubens reached the height of his creativity. When Albert and Isabella died childless, the provinces reverted to Spain in 1621, and until 1713 the Hapsburgs fought over control of the area.

In one campaign in 1695, the French Marshal Villeroy, under orders of Louis XIV, bombarded the beautiful Grand Place in Brussels, with its majestic town hall, built around 1400; it survived only with its tower and its thickest walls. This disaster merely stiffened the courage and determination of the Brussels population, which began the very next day restoring the structure. The best artistic and architectural talent in the city joined in recreating one of man's greatest architectural treasures. Jan Van Ruysbroeck, the city's master mason, rebuilt the town hall. Wishing to retain the foundation and porch of the old bell tower while extending the new walls as far as possible, he placed the main portal of the town hall off-center with the central axis of the tower. Legend wrongly has it that he threw himself to his death when he discovered the error, but the "error" was in fact intentional. The Grand Place remains the vibrant heart of the city and has always been a favorite subject for painters and poets. It is a place for open-air markets, public meetings, political assemblies, royal receptions, and coronations. Earlier it was the favorite place for launching revolutions and for public executions. Each year, on a summer evening, the Grand Place is transformed into its medieval setting for a historical procession called the "Ommegang."

Both Luxembourg and Belgium passed into the hands of the Austrians, who renamed Belgium the "Austrian Netherlands" and who ruled over these provinces until 1794–1795, when French troops snatched them away. The Austrians had exercised a benevolent dictatorship, but some Luxembourgers, Flemings, and Walloons were infected by the fever of revolution emanating from France and welcomed the changes that came with the French republican troops. Belgium fell to the French in 1794, and the following year French revolutionary forces conquered Luxembourg and the Netherlands, which had been greatly weakened by its series of wars against England.

The French occupation brought fundamental changes to the Netherlands, which had been ruled by an enlightened oligarchy, with a high official called a Stadhouder (not a monarch) at the top. Although it was not a modern democracy, in that leaders who were exercising power had been elected by universal suffrage, the Dutch republic had nevertheless been one of the most democratic countries in Europe, with the possible exception of Switzerland. The old republic had been highly decentralized, with each province stressing its independent powers. The new regime that the French created and called The Batavian Republic, named after one of the tribes who had populated the country in the Roman period and who had revolted against Roman domination, was highly centralized in conformity with the French constitution.

The Napoleonic Code of laws and the selection of members of parliament on the basis of limited but free elections were also introduced. The Dutch grew restive under French control, especially after the Batavian Republic was abolished and Louis Napoleon, the brother of the French emperor, was made king of Holland in 1806. Quarrels with his brother forced Louis to abdicate in 1810, but only after he had tried unsuccessfully to have his son, who later became Napoleon III of France, crowned in his place. The Netherlands was annexed directly into the French Empire in 1810. Again, Napoleon's reversals gave the Dutch the chance to reassert their independence. In 1813, after Napoleon's defeat in the Battle of Leipzig, the son of the last Dutch Stadhouder, who had fled to England, landed at Scheveningen, not far from The Hague, and was proclaimed William I of the House of Orange-Nassau, king of the Netherlands. For the first time, the Netherlands became a monarchy with a Dutch monarch on the throne. Dutch troops took an active part in the final defeat of Napoleon.

In late 1794 French troops besieged the fortress of Luxembourg, which did not fall until mid-1795. It was annexed to France in the fall; French rule was very unpopular at first, but Napoleon was gradually able to smooth out many problems. When the French left the duchy in 1814, they left behind many positive and lasting gifts: the idea of equality, centralized and efficient administration, and the Napoleonic Code.

Gustav Wappers Episone of September Days 1830

The French were at first widely greeted in Belgium as liberators, and the introduction of the Napoleonic Code and an efficient, centralized administration was generally seen as an improvement over the old regime. Almost no one seemed to have realized at the time that decentralization would have helped Belgium's language groups to live together more harmoniously in a unified Belgian state. But the seemingly endless Napoleonic Wars soon sapped the Belgians' enthusiasm. After Napoleon began suffering disastrous reversals, especially in Russia in 1812, the Belgians joined the enemies of France. It was outside Brussels near a small town named Waterloo that the little dictator was defeated for the last time.

When the great powers of Europe met at the Congress of Vienna in 1814–1815, they combined the Netherlands, Belgium, and Luxembourg to form the Kingdom of the United Netherlands, with the monarch William I as king. European leaders, who suspected that they had supported the French too enthusiastically, distrusted the Belgians. They believed that the Belgians, therefore, needed to be controlled by the Dutch king. Further, the east Belgian cantons of Eupen, Malmedy, and Saint Vith were ceded to Prussia, whose borders had been moved as far west as possible in order to prevent any future eastward French expansion.

The union of the three countries did not last long. In 1830 the sparks of revolution flying from Paris landed in Brussels. The overwhelmingly Catholic Flemings and Walloons (Belgians who speak French) sensed religious discrimination by the predominantly Protestant Calvinist Dutch, despite the tradition of religious tolerance in the Netherlands.

Although it was the only thing that drew Flemings and Walloons together, Catholicism was enough to unify them against the Dutch. Such religious unity was later to prove the weakest of glue to hold the state of Belgium together. The use of Dutch in the south and in Brussels had been resented by the economically and culturally more influential French-speaking Walloons. The determination to elevate the French language above Dutch also was later to create extremely serious problems for this bilingual country. The eruption occurred in 1830, after an opera performance with a liberation theme. After a brief skirmish in Brussels, Dutch troops withdrew, and a provisional government proclaimed independence within three months. Seeing the utility of a buffer state on the European continent, the British announced that they would thenceforth guarantee Belgium's neutrality.

A liberal constitution, which is still in force, was proclaimed placing sovereignty in the people and providing for a constitutional monarchy. A German prince, Leopold I of Saxe-Coburg, who happened also to be a British citizen, became king in 1831. Since sovereignty was placed in the hands of the people, there was no doubt that the parliament, as the representative of the Belgian people, would be superior to the monarch. French was also declared to be the new country's official language.

The Dutch reacted to these events by attempting to invade Belgium, but the French and British announced their determination not to allow the Dutch to reassert their control. At a London Conference of 1831, a border between the Netherlands and Belgium was drawn, but this settlement pleased neither the Belgians, who claimed about half of Luxembourg, nor the Dutch, whose king wanted no settlement at all which would reduce the size of his kingdom. Finally, the Treaty of Twenty-Four Articles, signed in London in 1839, granted the Dutch a slice of northern Belgium. Belgium, in turn, was compensated through a grant of about half of Luxembourg's territory. Further, the great European powers guaranteed the neutrality of Belgium and Luxembourg. This settlement finally satisfied all but the Luxembourgers, who saw their already-tiny state reduced to about one-fourth of its pre-1815 size.

The Congress of Vienna had made Luxembourg (which means "Little Castle") an autonomous duchy, with the Dutch king as the grand duke, but Luxembourg lost all its territory east of the Moselle, Sure, and Our Rivers. The congress also made Luxembourg a member of the German Confederation and granted the Prussians the right to man the fortress in the capital city in order to be able to keep a closer eye on the recently defeated French. This arrangement meant that Luxembourg was wide open to Dutch royal ideas, Prussian military demands, and Belgium's liberal cravings.

At first the Dutch king ruled in a rather authoritarian way, and when the Belgians rebelled against Dutch rule in 1830, most Luxembourgers outside the capital city also arose. Although they were unable to establish their independence, Luxembourgers were gradually able to create separate institutions and administrations. Political autonomy was granted in 1839, and in 1848 the country received a liberal constitution similar to that of Belgium. The Dutch became more benevolent rulers and cooperated in Luxembourg's movement toward democracy and independence. Finally, in 1867 the Treaty of London, drawn up in an attempt to reconcile differences between Bismarck of Germany and Napoleon III of France, proclaimed Luxembourg an independent and neutral country. Only a year later, Luxembourg adopted a constitution that in revised form remains in force. Upon the insistence of Napoleon III, the Prussians withdrew from the duchy, and the fortress was razed.

The only disappointment for the Luxembourgers was that the Dutch king remained the grand duke. However, when in 1890 there were no male heirs to the Dutch throne, Adolf of Nassau, whose family was related to the Dutch ruling family, became the grand duke of Luxembourg and chose to reside in Luxembourg City. Nevertheless, the close historical ties with the Netherlands continue to be symbolized by the fact that the two countries have almost exactly the same flag.

From 1890 on, all three BENELUX countries have been fully independent and sovereign states. Proximity, economic interests, and political values continue to bind these three democracies very closely together.

The Monnaie Theater, Brussels, where the torch of liberation was lit

The Kingdom of the Netherlands

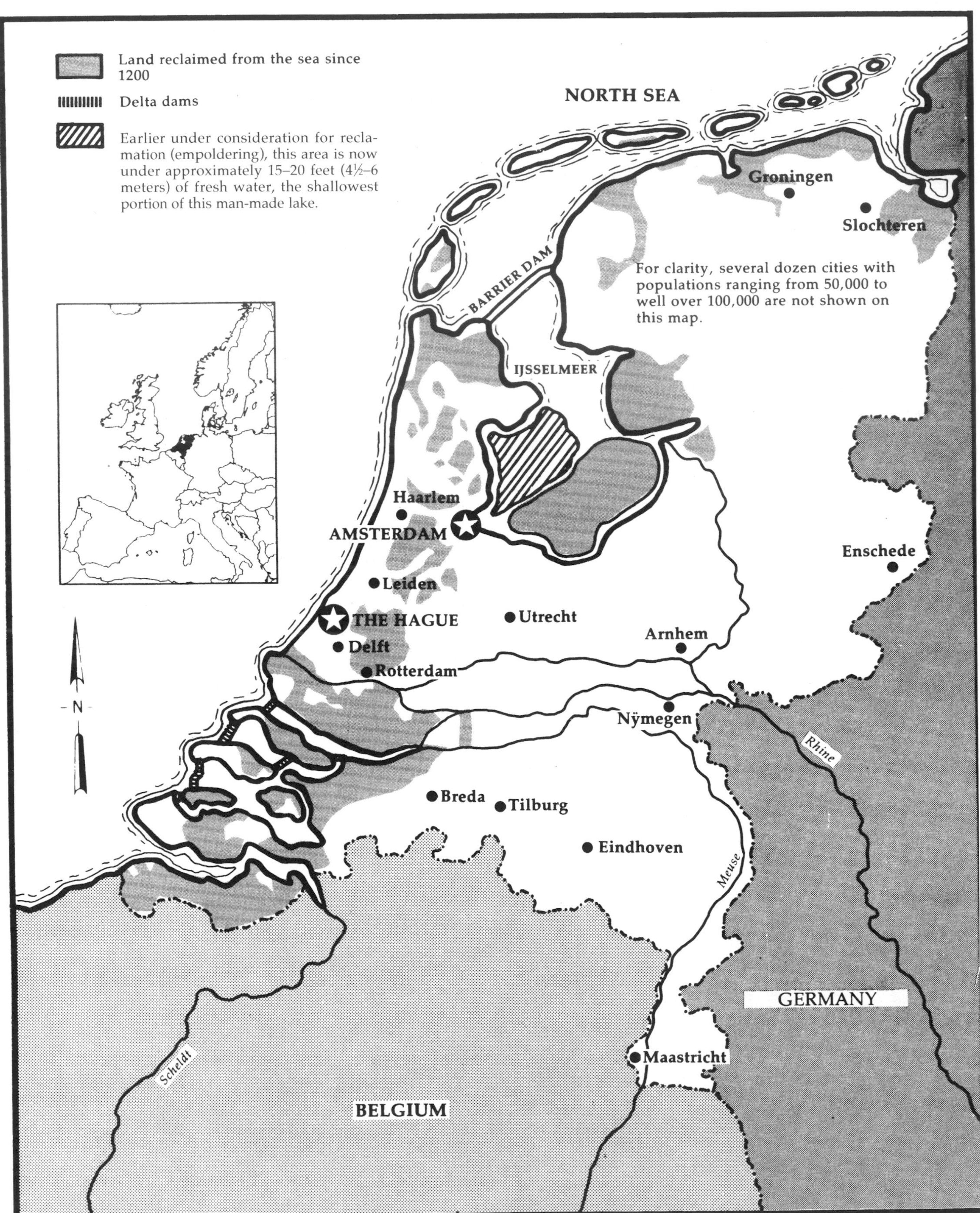